The Cambridge Companion to Music in Digital Culture

The impact of digital technologies on music has been overwhelming: since the commercialisation of these technologies in the early 1980s, both the practice of music and thinking about it have changed almost out of all recognition. From the rise of digital music-making to digital dissemination, these changes have attracted considerable academic attention across disciplines, within but also beyond established areas of academic musical research. Through chapters by scholars at the forefront of research and shorter 'personal takes' from knowledgeable practitioners in the field, this *Companion* brings the relationship between digital technology and musical culture alive by considering both theory and practice. It provides a comprehensive and balanced introduction to the place of music within digital culture as a whole, with recurring themes and topics that include music and the Internet, social networking and participatory culture, music recommendation systems, virtuality, posthumanism, surveillance, copyright, and new business models for music production.

NICHOLAS COOK is Emeritus Professor at the University of Cambridge. He is the author of *Music: A Very Short Introduction* (1998) and *Music as Creative Practice* (2018), and won the SMT's Wallace Berry Award for *The Schenker Project* (2007).

MONIQUE M. INGALLS is Assistant Professor of Music at Baylor University, Texas. Author of *Singing the Congregation* (2018), she is series editor for Routledge's Congregational Music Studies series and co-organiser of the biennial international conference 'Christian Congregational Music: Local and Global Perspectives'.

DAVID TRIPPETT is Senior Lecturer in the Faculty of Music, University of Cambridge. Author of *Wagner's Melodies* (Cambridge, 2013), his wide-ranging research has received the Einstein and Lockwood Prizes (American Musicological Society), the Nettl Prize (Society for Ethnomusicology), and an American Society of Composers, Authors, and Publishers (ASCAP) Deems Taylor award.

Cambridge Companions to Music

Topics

The Cambridge Companion to Ballet
Edited by Marion Kant

The Cambridge Companion to Blues and Gospel Music
Edited by Allan Moore

The Cambridge Companion to Choral Music
Edited by André de Quadros

The Cambridge Companion to the Concerto
Edited by Simon P. Keefe

The Cambridge Companion to Conducting
Edited by José Antonio Bowen

The Cambridge Companion to Eighteenth-Century Music
Edited by Anthony R. DelDonna and Pierpaolo Polzonetti

The Cambridge Companion to Electronic Music
Edited by Nick Collins and Julio D'Escriván

The Cambridge Companion to Film Music
Edited by Mervyn Cooke and Fiona Ford

The Cambridge Companion to French Music
Edited by Simon Trezise

The Cambridge Companion to Grand Opera
Edited by David Charlton

The Cambridge Companion to Hip-Hop
Edited by Justin A. Williams

The Cambridge Companion to Jazz
Edited by Mervyn Cooke and David Horn

The Cambridge Companion to Jewish Music
Edited by Joshua S. Walden

The Cambridge Companion to the Lied
Edited by James Parsons

The Cambridge Companion to Medieval Music
Edited by Mark Everist

The Cambridge Companion to Music in Digital Culture
Edited by Nicholas Cook, Monique M. Ingalls and David Trippett

The Cambridge Companion to the Musical, third edition
Edited by William Everett and Paul Laird

The Cambridge Companion to Opera Studies
Edited by Nicholas Till

The Cambridge Companion to the Orchestra
Edited by Colin Lawson

The Cambridge Companion to Pop and Rock
Edited by Simon Frith, Will Straw and John Street

The Cambridge Companion to Recorded Music
Edited by Eric Clarke, Nicholas Cook, Daniel Leech-Wilkinson and John Rink

The Cambridge Companion to the Singer-Songwriter
Edited by Katherine Williams and Justin A. Williams

The Cambridge Companion to the String Quartet
Edited by Robin Stowell

The Cambridge Companion to Twentieth-Century Opera
Edited by Mervyn Cooke

Composers

The Cambridge Companion to Bach
Edited by John Butt

The Cambridge Companion to Bartók
Edited by Amanda Bayley

The Cambridge Companion to the Beatles
Edited by Kenneth Womack

The Cambridge Companion to Beethoven
Edited by Glenn Stanley

The Cambridge Companion to Berg
Edited by Anthony Pople

The Cambridge Companion to Berlioz
Edited by Peter Bloom

The Cambridge Companion to Brahms
Edited by Michael Musgrave

The Cambridge Companion to Benjamin Britten
Edited by Mervyn Cooke

The Cambridge Companion to Bruckner
Edited by John Williamson

The Cambridge Companion to John Cage
Edited by David Nicholls

The Cambridge Companion to Chopin
Edited by Jim Samson

The Cambridge Companion to Debussy
Edited by Simon Trezise

The Cambridge Companion to Elgar
Edited by Daniel M. Grimley and Julian Rushton

The Cambridge Companion to Duke Ellington
Edited by Edward Green

The Cambridge Companion to Gilbert and Sullivan
Edited by David Eden and Meinhard Saremba

The Cambridge Companion to Handel
Edited by Donald Burrows

The Cambridge Companion to Haydn
Edited by Caryl Clark

The Cambridge Companion to Liszt
Edited by Kenneth Hamilton

The Cambridge Companion to Mahler
Edited by Jeremy Barham

The Cambridge Companion to Mendelssohn
Edited by Peter Mercer-Taylor

The Cambridge Companion to Monteverdi
Edited by John Whenham and Richard Wistreich

The Cambridge Companion to Mozart
Edited by Simon P. Keefe

The Cambridge Companion to Arvo Pärt
Edited by Andrew Shenton

Instruments

The Cambridge Companion to

MUSIC IN DIGITAL CULTURE

....

EDITED BY

Nicholas Cook
University of Cambridge

Monique M. Ingalls
Baylor University, Texas

David Trippett
University of Cambridge

CAMBRIDGE
UNIVERSITY PRESS

CAMBRIDGE
UNIVERSITY PRESS

University Printing House, Cambridge CB2 8BS, United Kingdom

One Liberty Plaza, 20th Floor, New York, NY 10006, USA

477 Williamstown Road, Port Melbourne, VIC 3207, Australia

314–321, 3rd Floor, Plot 3, Splendor Forum, Jasola District Centre, New Delhi – 110025, India

79 Anson Road, #06–04/06, Singapore 079906

Cambridge University Press is part of the University of Cambridge.

It furthers the University's mission by disseminating knowledge in the pursuit of education, learning, and research at the highest international levels of excellence.

www.cambridge.org
Information on this title: www.cambridge.org/9781107161788
DOI: 10.1017/9781316676639

© Cambridge University Press 2019

First published 2019

Printed and bound in Great Britain by Clays Ltd, Elcograf S.p.A.

Emojis used under a creative commons license, © Twitter.
Full details: Copyright 2019 Twitter, Inc and other contributors.
Code licensed under the MIT License: https://opensource.org/licenses/MIT
Graphics licensed under CC-BY 4.0: https://creativecommons.org/licenses/by/4.0/

A catalogue record for this publication is available from the British Library.

Library of Congress Cataloging-in-Publication Data
Names: Cook, Nicholas, 1950- | Ingalls, Monique Marie. | Trippett, David, 1980-
Title: The Cambridge companion to music in digital culture / edited by Nicholas Cook,
    Monique Ingalls, David Trippett.
Description: Cambridge, United Kingdom ; New York, NY : Cambridge
    University Press, 2019. | Series: Cambridge companions to music | Includes
    bibliographical references and index.
Identifiers: LCCN 2019003348 | ISBN 9781107161788 (hardback : alk. paper) |
    ISBN 9781316614075 (pbk. : alk. paper)
Subjects: LCSH: Music–Social aspects. | Digital media–Social aspects. | Music and the Internet.
    | Music and technology.
Classification: LCC ML3916 .C33 2019 | DDC 780.9/05–dc23
LC record available at https://lccn.loc.gov/2019003348

ISBN 978-1-107-16178-8 Hardback
ISBN 978-1-316-61407-5 Paperback

Contents

Figures

Contributors

Sam Aaron's research focuses on the design of novel domain-specific programming languages to explore liveness, conceptual efficiency, and performance. He is the creator of Sonic Pi which has been successfully used by teachers for computing and music lessons and also by artists to live code music for people to dance to in nightclubs.

Stephen Baysted is Professor of Film, TV and Games Composition at the University of Chichester. He has scored many AAA games, films and TV series, and has been nominated for three Jerry Goldsmith Awards, two Motion Picture Sound Editors Golden Reel Awards, a Golden Joystick Award and two Game Audio Network Guild Awards.

Alan F. Blackwell is Professor of Interdisciplinary Design in the University of Cambridge Department of Computer Science and Technology. He has been designing novel programming languages since 1983, and has a particular research interest in bringing user experience, art and craft perspectives to programming language design.

Nicholas Cook is Emeritus Professor at the University of Cambridge, and author of *Music: A Very Short Introduction* (1998), which is published or forthcoming in sixteen languages. His book *The Schenker Project: Culture, Race, and Music Theory in Fin-de-siècle Vienna* (2007) won the SMT's Wallace Berry Award, while his *Music as Creative Practice* appeared in 2018. He is currently finalising a project on relational and intercultural musicology, which was supported by a British Academy Wolfson Professorship. He is a Doctor of Humane Letters of the University of Chicago and was elected Fellow of the British Academy in 2001.

Frances Dyson is Visiting Professorial Fellow at the National Institute for Experimental Arts, University of New South Wales. She is the author of *The Tone of Our Times: Sound, Sense, Economy and Ecology* (2014) and *Sounding New Media: Immersion and Embodiment in the Arts and Culture* (2009).

Julio d'Escriván is a composer of music for visual media with a showreel that includes film, documentaries, commercials and film-trailer cues. He is also an electroacoustic composer and occasional live coder and audio-visual performer who lectures in film music composition at the University of Huddersfield.

K. E. Goldschmitt is Assistant Professor of Music at Wellesley College. Prior to Wellesley, Goldschmitt held research and teaching positions at University of Cambridge, New College of Florida and Colby College. Specialising in Brazilian and Luso-African music, the global media industries, circulation and music technology, Goldschmitt's first monograph, *Bossa Mundo: Brazilian Music in Transnational Media Industries*, is under contract. Recent publications include essays in *The Routledge Companion to Screen Music and Sound* and *Sounds and the City 2*, and a forthcoming essay in *Music in Contemporary Action Film*.

Sumanth Gopinath is Associate Professor of Music Theory at the University of Minnesota. He is the author of *The Ringtone Dialectic: Economy and Cultural Form* (2013), and, with Jason Stanyek, co-edited *The Oxford Handbook of Mobile Music Studies* (2014). Contributions to scholarly journals and edited collections address subjects ranging from Benjamin Britten, Steve Reich and Bob Dylan to musical minimalism, Marxism and music scholarship, the Nike+ Sport Kit, and the ringtone industry. Current projects revolve around sound in new and formerly new media, the aesthetics of smoothness, and the music of the Scottish composer James Dillon. Together with Anna Schultz, he received the American Musicological Society's H. Colin Slim Award in 2017.

Stéphan-Eloïse Gras is an affiliate researcher at MCC-NYU where she studies the ethical values embedded in technological design and their effects in the 'attention economy'. Her forthcoming book *Machines du goût: l'algorithme au coeur de nos sensibilités* traces the emergence of early AI patterns for emotional tracking in music recommendation engines.

Adam Harper is an Associate Lecturer in Music at City, University of London, interested in the history of popular music aesthetics and technology. As a music critic, he has written for *The Wire, The Fader, Resident Advisor* and *Dummy*, and he is the author of *Infinite Music* (2011).

Monique M. Ingalls is Assistant Professor of Music at Baylor University. Her work on music in Christian communities has been published in the fields of ethnomusicology, media studies, hymnology and religious studies. She is the author of *Singing the Congregation: How Contemporary Worship Music Forms Evangelical Community* (2018) as well as lead editor of three books on Christian music-making in global perspective. She is series editor for Routledge's Congregational Music Studies book series and is co-founder and programme chair of a biennial academic conference on Christian congregational music.

Mariana Lopez is an academic and sound designer. In 2013 she completed her PhD at the University of York on the importance of acoustics in medieval drama. She is a lecturer at York and has worked on a number of film and theatre productions as well as installations.

Lee Marshall is a Reader in Sociology at the University of Bristol, specialising in the music industry, popular music consumption, collecting, intellectual property and stardom.

Alex McLean is an artist-programmer and interdisciplinary researcher based in Sheffield, UK. He co-founded the Algorave and TOPLAP live coding movements, several international conferences/festivals, and the TidalCycles live coding environment. He is a post-doctoral researcher on the PENELOPE project at Deutsches Museum, Munich, investigating the structures of ancient weaves.

Peter McMurray is a Lecturer in Ethnomusicology at University of Cambridge. His work focuses principally on technologies of sonic difference, including cities, audio recording, musical instruments, music videos and architecture. He is currently completing a book and film project, *Pathways to God: The Islamic Acoustics of Turkish Berlin*, and has also written on the history of tape recording, orality and oral poetry, music videos, and materiality and religion. He completed a PhD from Harvard University in Ethnomusicology with a secondary field in Critical Media Practice, and he has held postdoctoral fellowships at MIT and the Harvard Society of Fellows.

Andrew McPherson is a Reader (Associate Professor) in the Centre for Digital Music at Queen Mary University of London. A composer and electronic engineer by training, his work focuses on creating new digital musical instruments, especially augmented instruments which extend the capabilities of familiar designs.

Ingrid Monson is Quincy Jones Professor of African-American Music at Harvard University. Her books include *Freedom Sounds: Civil Rights Call Out to Jazz and Africa* (2007) and *Saying Something: Jazz Improvisation and Interaction* (1996).

Paul Sanden is Assistant Professor in Music at the University of Lethbridge, where he teaches music history courses in Western art music and popular music traditions, with an emphasis on music of the twentieth and twenty-first centuries. His research regularly crosses disciplinary and musical-generic boundaries, drawing from musicology, performance studies, media theory and other disciplines to investigate meaning formation in music from Western popular and art music traditions, with a particular focus on the impact of electronic technologies on music's performance. He is the author of *Liveness in Modern Music: Musicians, Technology, and the Perception of Performance* (2013).

Steve Savage is an active record producer and recording engineer. He has been the primary engineer on seven records that received Grammy nominations. Savage is also the Executive Director of Blue Bear School of Music in San Francisco. Having received his PhD in musicology, Savage now balances a career as a producer, educator and entrepreneur.

Martin Scherzinger is Associate Professor in the Department of Media, Culture and Communication at New York University. He has been a Postdoctoral Fellow at the Princeton University Society of Fellows (2004–7), and received various fellowships (ranging from AMS 50 to ACLS). Martin's research is on sound, music, media, and politics, with a particular focus on global biographies of sound and other ephemera circulating in geographically remote regions. His research examines the poetics of intellectual property in diverse sociotechnical environments, relations between aesthetics and censorship, mathematical geometries of musical time, and histories of sound in philosophy.

Nick Seaver is an Assistant Professor in the Department of Anthropology and the Program in Science, Technology and Society at Tufts University. He researches and teaches on the ways that technologists make sense of cultural materials in the design and maintenance of software systems. He has conducted ethnographic research with the developers of algorithmic music recommender systems in the United States, and is currently studying the relationship between machine learning and attention.

Ben Sinclair has a professional background in digital music, streaming curation, music supervision and independent film production. He lives in Los Angeles with his wife, Mia, their pets Pickles and Marshall, and a record collection that has long outgrown its space. His talk-free podcast *Sound Contours* offers mixes of terrific, obscure music.

Graham St John, PhD, is a cultural anthropologist. Among his eight books are *Mystery School in Hyperspace: A Cultural History of DMT* (2015) and *Global Tribe: Technology, Spirituality and Psytrance* (2012). He is Research Fellow, Social Science, University of Fribourg, Switzerland, and Executive Editor of *Dancecult: Journal of Electronic Dance Music Culture.*

Jason Stanyek teaches at the University of Oxford, where he is Associate Professor of Ethnomusicology and Tutorial Fellow at St John's College; before that he was Assistant Professor at New York University. He pursued doctoral studies with George E. Lewis and his research on improvisation, music technology, hip-hop, and Brazilian music and dance has appeared in a range of publications. His essay 'Deadness: Technologies of the Intermundane' (co-written with Benjamin Piekut) received the 2011 'Outstanding Essay Award' from the Association for Theater in Higher Education, while a monograph on Brazilian diasporic performance is forthcoming. He is general editor for Bloomsbury's new series 33⅓ Brazil, and co-editor of *Twentieth-Century Music.*

Shzr Ee Tan is a Senior Lecturer and ethnomusicologist at Royal Holloway, University of London. While she has a regional specialism in Sinophone worlds, she is interested in how inequalities intersect with music scenes globally. To this end her research is widely focused, ranging from musical indigeneity on the Internet to Latin genres in Singapore, soundscapes of political protests in London and the sonic regimes of Southeast Asian migrant workers. Shzr Ee is current co-editor of *Ethnomusicology Forum*, and has published a monograph plus various edited volumes.

David Trippett is Senior Lecturer in the Faculty of Music, University of Cambridge. His research interests focus on nineteenth-century cultural and intellectual history, opera, posthumanism, and the scene of digital culture. His monograph *Wagner's Melodies* examines the cultural and scientific history of melodic theory in relation to Wagner's writings on music, and in 2018 he edited and orchestrated Liszt's only mature opera *Sardanapalo* (for the *Neue Liszt Ausgabe*) to critical acclaim. He currently runs a research group in Cambridge, funded by an ERC starting grant, that examines the dialogue between natural science and music during the nineteenth century.

Isabella van Elferen is Professor of Music, Head of the Department of Performing Arts and Director of the Visconti Studio at Kingston University London. She has published extensively on music philosophy, music and moving image, Gothic and horror music, and baroque sacred music. Isabella is First Vice-President of the International Association of the Fantastic in the Arts. She is member of the editorial boards of *The Soundtrack, Horror Studies*, and *Aeternum*, and guest editor for *Journal for the Fantastic in the Arts* (2013), *Horror Studies* (2016) and *Contemporary Music Review* (2017).

Acknowledgements

This book has its origins in the conference 'Creativity, Circulation, Copyright: Music in the Digital Age', held at the University of Cambridge in March 2014 and hosted by CRASSH (The Centre for Research in the Arts, Social Sciences and Humanities); we are grateful for CRASSH's support. The conference was organised by the three co-editors, who are all current or former members of the Cambridge Faculty of Music, and by Peter Webb (now at the University of the West of England), who also made a major contribution to the planning of this volume. Additional support was provided under the auspices of the ERC (European Research Council) Starting Grant 'Sound and Materialism in the 19th Century', held by David Trippett. Most of all we are indebted to Dr Ariana Phillips-Hutton, who as editorial assistant played the key role in transforming a sprawling mass of (virtual) typescripts into a deliverable book.

Introduction

NICHOLAS COOK, MONIQUE M. INGALLS
AND DAVID TRIPPETT

It is hard to think of another field of cultural practice that has been as comprehensively turned upside down by the digital revolution as music. Digital instruments, recording technologies and signal processing techniques have transformed the making of music, while digital dissemination of music – through the Internet and earbuds – has transformed the way people consume it. Live music thrives and mostly relies on digital technology, but alongside it music has become integrated into the patterns of social networking and urban mobility that increasingly structure people's lives. The digital revolution has destabilised the traditional music business, with successive technologies reconstructing it in different forms, and at present even its short-term future is unclear. (Just as this book is going to press, Apple has announced the discontinuation of iTunes, the most commercially successful response to Napster.) Meanwhile digitalisation has changed what sort of thing music is, creating a multiplicity of genres, some of which exist only online – indeed, downloads and streaming have problematised the extent to which music can reasonably be thought of as a 'thing' at all. Technology that is rapidly pervading the globe is re-engineering relationships between geographically removed traditions (including by removing geography from the equation). Some see this near meltdown of so many aspects of traditional musical culture as a harbinger of fundamental social change to come.

In short, music in digital culture is a bewildering world, most of all for those in the middle of it. This *Companion* attempts to make sense of a constantly changing field through a series of complementary perspectives: eleven chapters address topics that range from the economics of music in the digital age to relationships between technology and culture, music recommendation technologies, constructions of selfhood, the politics of protest, religion on the web, liveness, virtuality, the posthuman, and global perspectives. It also includes what we call 'personal takes' (PTs), short essays – often by digital practitioners – that focus on specific issues, genres, professional practices, and experiences, so aiming to communicate something of the specificity of life and work in the digital cultures of music. PTs are interspersed throughout the volume, not according to a regular plan but so as to throw light on the preceding or following chapters or strike sparks with adjacent PTs. Each chapter and each personal take is a self-sufficient entity when read the digital way, as a series of separate tracks, but the book is designed to offer added value when its various constituents are read together. The following is a description of the pathway embodied in the printed version of the book.

Chapter 1, Nicholas Cook's 'Digital Technology and Cultural Practice', offers a broad overview of music in digital culture, focusing in particular on the social dimensions that the technology has opened up: the aim is to set out the field that subsequent chapters populate in detail. This is followed by a PT in which Lee Marshall discusses an immediately pre-digital musical community and how it was impacted by the advent of digital technology. The main part of the book is bookended by two chapters from Martin Scherzinger that focus on the intersection of technology and economics: Chapter 2 ('Toward a History of Digital Music: New Technologies, Business Practices and Intellectual Property Regimes') provides a historical account of how the world of digital music as we know it came about, while a PT by Ingrid Monson illustrates the role played by copyright through an insider's account of the high-profile lawsuit over 'Blurred Lines'. In 'Shaping the Stream: Techniques and Troubles of Algorithmic Recommendation' (Chapter 3), K. E. Goldschmitt and Nick Seaver offer a critical overview of playlisting technologies: these represent a key interface between the streaming technologies that dominate today's music business and the practices of digital consumption and aesthetics. Two PTs offer close-up views of this world, one (by Ben Sinclair) conveying the flavour of life as a curator within a music recommendation start-up, the other (by Stéphan-Eloïse Gras) asking searching questions about the nature of taste.

Chapter 4 ('Technologies of the Musical Selfie'), by Sumanth Gopinath and Jason Stanyek, is structured around what might seem a marginal phenomenon within digital culture, in which automated facial recognition generates a personalised musical artefact, what the authors call the musical selfie – but it turns out to be a high road into a world of music as medium of self-definition and interpersonal relationships that is anticipated by but goes far beyond anything in pre-digital culture. This is followed by a PT from Adam Harper that explores the equally esoteric world of vaporwave, a digital audio-visual genre that might be described as not just *on* the web but *about* it. Peter McMurray's 'Witnessing Race in the New Digital Cinema' (Chapter 5) documents an emerging film practice whereby smartphone videos bear witness to social injustice, focusing in particular on the politics and ethics of racial violence: here digital media play a role in society that builds on pre-digital cinematic resistance but puts it in everyone's hands. A PT by Mariana Lopez explores the same issue of giving voice to the voiceless in the quite different domain of digital heritage.

Religious devotion and spirituality, the topic of Monique M. Ingalls's 'Digital Devotion: Musical Multimedia in Online Ritual and Religious Practice' (Chapter 6), represent another area transformed by digital culture, and Ingalls documents the role of music in contexts ranging from digital resources for offline devotion to online performances of personal spirituality that elide the virtual and the divine: the Internet simultaneously complements, reinforces and undermines established religions. A PT by Graham St John on EDM as a performance of the sublime is followed by two on algorave, a recent performance genre based on real-time programming, authored respectively by members of the live coding duo The Humming Wires and by Alex McLean. Like 'live' coding, 'live' performance is defined by its other – live music is what recorded music is not – and in Chapter 7 ('Rethinking Liveness in the Digital Age') Paul Sanden takes up the topic of how technology can re-create, even in a virtual environment, the sense of human presence that defines live performance. The emphasis on performance continues with the first of a group of PTs that sample the roles of digital technology across key creative practices of music: Andrew McPherson addresses performance from the perspective of instrument design, and Steve Savage reflects on the pros and cons of digital versus analogue recording, while Julio d'Escriván and Stephen Baysted focus on composition. D'Escriván reflects on how the practices of digital multimedia have led him to think about musical sound in a new way, while Baysted compares the very different natures of composition for concert listening and for the specifically digital genre of video games.

A further two chapters explore the dimension of the virtual opened up by Sanden. Isabella van Elferen's 'Virtual Worlds from Recording to Video Games' (Chapter 8) claims that music is not just an important dimension of virtual worlds, but can lead to an enhanced understanding of what virtuality is: she argues that the virtual existed in the pre-digital age (both literary narrative and recorded music create their own virtual worlds), but that virtual reality technologies are extending it in fundamentally new ways. In creating experiences located outside what we have thought of as the real world of embodied individuals and material objects, the virtual worlds of digital multimedia open up issues of how far machines and algorithms can extend human capacities, or lead to a more fundamental rethinking of the 'human'. David Trippett's 'Digital Voices: Posthumanism and the Generation of Empathy' (Chapter 9) assesses the impact of digital technology on human agency, the significance of machines that speak to us in beguiling female voices, and an opera that explores the ethical dimensions of immortality achieved through the downloading of human minds to computers. A PT by Frances Dyson traces the arc of posthuman thought from the celebratory futurism of the age before the dot-com bubble burst to the ethical and environmental potential of a human culture purged of anthropocentrism.

The book concludes with two chapters that critique contemporary thinking about music in digital culture from different directions. Shzr Ee Tan's 'Digital Inequalities and Global Sounds' (Chapter 10) emphasises the first-world, even anglophone bias of the supposedly global culture of the World Wide Web, counterposing it with perspectives drawn from elsewhere, particularly China: here, as often in digital culture, utopian and dystopian visions of technology are set in opposition, coexist, or on occasion become indistinguishable from one another. Finally, in Chapter 11 ('The Political Economy of Streaming') Martin Scherzinger complements his earlier chapter by scrutinising the current state of the digital music industry and the larger economy within which it is situated: in doing so he picks up on the concerns expressed by Tan and other contributors about the way in which, through streaming, music has become entangled in a growing culture of digital data collection and surveillance. Nothing could more clearly illustrate how music, too often thought of as just a form of entertainment, has become a key dimension of social, economic and even political life in the digital age.

1 Digital Technology and Cultural Practice

NICHOLAS COOK

There is no race, there are no genders, there is no age, there are no infirmities . . . Utopia? No, the Internet. 1997 ADVERTISEMENT QUOTED IN BAYM 2015, 39

In the last year, even as surveillance and privacy concerns peaked, music consumers migrated to streaming music services that live in the cloud in accelerating numbers. ANDREW LEONARD[1]

3,155,403,941 YOUTUBE VIEWS OF 'GANGNAM STYLE' AS OF 30 MAY 2018

7,600,000,000 CURRENT ESTIMATE OF WORLD POPULATION

According to author and educationalist Sir Ken Robinson, 'it wasn't until 2007 that the iPhone came out and has pretty much changed the way the planet works'.[2] Of course it wasn't just the iPhone: digital technology has pretty much changed how music works, and the planet remains in a state of not only technological but also social, aesthetic and commercial transition – though quite what it is a transition to is not so clear. Commentators speak freely of paradigm change, though they usually qualify this by emphasising the ways in which the new paradigm (whatever that may be) represents a continuation of pre-digital business by other means.

At one level it is quite easy to say what digital technology has meant for music. Sound – including musical sound – consists of patterns of vibrating air molecules that strike our eardrums and resonate within the ear: mathematicians represent them as continuous wave forms, and as such sound is analogue. In contrast, digital signals consist of a series of discrete numerical values, ultimately made up of 0s and 1s. Despite the difference, digital signals can replicate analogue ones in the same way that the dots of a newsprint photograph replicate the original: with photographs it is a matter of the dots being small enough, and with sound it is one of a sufficiently high sample rate. Digital recording involves measuring sound waves 44,100 times a second, and digital playback outputs numerical values at the same rate. In terms of human perception, the replication is good enough to have been the basis of the international recording industry for the last thirty-five years. And because replicating digital sounds means replicating numbers, there is no loss of quality in digital copies – unlike analogue technology, where the quality degrades every time you make a copy.

The 44,100 samples a second produce a lot of data, and in the early days of digital music this represented a challenge to processing power and storage space. Much of the early history of digital music is conditioned by various workarounds. In universities and research institutes music was generated in the digital domain – that is, through purely numerical operations – but it involved the use of mainframes and rarely worked in real time. MIDI (which goes back to 1983, the year after the introduction of the CD) was a standard for computer control of hardware devices such as synthesisers and drum machines: this offloaded the most computation-ally intensive part of the process onto dedicated hardware devices, so enabling real-time operation. Other approaches included techniques for compressing digital sound files, the most important being the MP3 format, which dates from the 1990s and was key to the development of download culture – the distribution of sound files through the Internet rather through physical carriers such as CDs.

It was rapid advances in both processing power and storage that made this possible, but analogue technologies continued to exert a ghostly influence. Recording media illustrate this. The analogue formats of shellac discs (78s, named after the speed at which the disc spun), LPs (vinyl discs allowing over twenty minutes of continuous playback on each side) and magnetic tape lie behind early digital media. DAT (Digital Audio Tape) recorders, introduced in the late 1980s, used the same magnetic tape as analogue tape recorders, but the sounds were coded in digital form. CDs retained the principle of the spinning disc, as indeed did the hard disc drives built into computers for generic data storage. These vestiges of analogue technology disappeared with the solid-state drive, which became standard in computers during the second decade of the present century, and by this time there had ceased to be any distinction between musical and generic data storage. A more radical development, around the same period, was the take-up of cloud computing, in which – just as with the earlier download culture – the physical storage medium disappeared. Of course the data are still held on physical devices, but these are relegated to server farms: out of sight, out of mind, rather like the mass export of European and American waste to India and China.

Analogue practices also retain a ghostly presence in the terminology of tracks and albums – terms derived from the physical media of the analogue era but still current today. The same applies to software. Early MIDI sequencers such as Cubase were based on the metaphor of the multi-track tape recorder, and the same remains the case with present-day applications based on digital sound: to use Ableton Live, Logic Pro or Sound Tools you lay down music in separate tracks and manipulate them on the model of the analogue mixing desk. Each also uses plug-ins that often replicate the appearance as well as the functionality of analogue sound-effect units. But running alongside these commercial products there has been, and continues to be, a variety of more abstract, experimental and flexible software for digital music creation – software that owes less to earlier analogue practices. The mainframe-based systems I referred to include the MUSIC-N series (where N stands for I, II, III etc.), which go back to the late 1950s, with Csound (1985) being a particularly influential member of the family: in essence these were specialised music programming languages with extensive libraries of functions and, as I said, not primarily designed for real-time use. At the other end of the spectrum are such programmes as Max/MSP, a visual programming language also dating from the 1980s and still in widespread use, or SuperCollider (1996), a programming environment specifically oriented to real-time synthesis.

I have sketched these basic elements of music hardware and software because they both embody basic principles of digital music and underlie many digital musicians' working environment. But I said that *at one level* it is quite easy to say what digital technology has meant for music, and that is not the level on which this book focuses. As its title proclaims, it is a companion to music *in digital culture*. Its focus is not on technology but on the social, economic and aesthetic correlates of technology, and here too we can see both new paradigms and the continuation of existing business by other means. One important point to make at the outset is that technology does not simply determine what happens in culture: as Nancy Baym (2015) emphasises, it is the belief that technological changes inevitably result in particular social consequences that lies behind both the prophecies of doom and the equally unrealistic visions of utopia (such as the 1997 advertisement quoted in the epigraph) that new technologies – not just digital technology – have always prompted. At the same time, technologies may facilitate certain cultural developments while standing in the way of others. The best way to think about this is in terms of the cultural developments that particular technologies afford: this puts the emphasis on the choices that societies make in their use of technology. Rather than asking what a new technology does to society, Baym says, one should ask how people use it, what they use it for, and why.

From the Social to the Posthuman

You cannot understand how or why people have used technology to make and consume music without setting this into the context of widespread social changes linked to the development of the Internet (perhaps an even better candidate than the iPhone for the invention that pretty much changed the way the planet works). Originally the preserve of academia and the military, the origins of the Internet can be pushed back as far as the

1950s, but until the early 1990s it was purely a medium of textual communication. That includes email, invented in the 1960s but increasingly widely adopted from the 1980s, bulletin boards (where users could read and post messages), and also a rather arcane world of text-based role-playing games that developed out of the tabletop game Dungeons & Dragons and are the remote ancestors of today's video games. However, Baym makes the important observation that these were less important as games than as 'simply creative environments in which fictional rooms and landscapes served as spaces for social interaction' (2015, 16), and that too prefigured things to come.

The Internet took on a more recognisable form in the early 1990s with the development of the World Wide Web: the first web browser appeared in 1991, bringing with it the familiar architecture of linked websites, blogs, wikis, and video or photo-sharing sites. As this implies, the World Wide Web was from the start a multimedia environment, and it was at this time that major computer manufacturers agreed a standard specification for the 'Multimedia PC' (including a dedicated sound card with audio mixing and synthesis capabilities): role-playing games were rapidly transformed into the graphically rich, explorable environments that we think of as virtual worlds. Web 2.0 (a term coined in 1999 by Darcy DiNucci) followed in the early 2000s. This was not a technical specification but rather a loosely defined design idea that revolved around interactivity and user content. Some see it as little more than marketing hype consequent upon the opening up of the Internet to commercial users in the second half of the 1990s, and – as we shall see – the idea of user-generated content lay at the heart of the commercial opportunities that a generation of entrepreneurs, most of them based in California's Silicon Valley, saw in the Internet.

So what exactly were the social changes I referred to? Even before the World Wide Web there was a great deal of talk about the Internet's capacity to afford the development of virtual communities. The classic text on this is Howard Rheingold's *The Virtual Community: Homesteading on the Electronic Frontier*, published in 1993 but largely based on his experiences from the mid-1980s as a member of the WELL (Whole Earth 'Lectronic Link), technically speaking a computer conferencing system that was based in the San Francisco Bay area but included members from much further afield. People used their real names – they were not role-playing – and the WELL accommodated a wide spread of activities: members pursued common interests (there were standing 'public conferences' dedicated to different topics from chess or desktop publishing to the Grateful Dead), discussed current issues, and in a spirit of altruism offered many kinds of mutual support, including financial. California was home to many real-world communes, as well as groups that saw themselves as communities but lacked a physical base, and among the latter were the Deadheads (the Grateful Dead fan community). Many joined the WELL, and in Rheinhold's words they 'seemed to know instinctively how to use the system to create a community around themselves' (1993, 43). The entire enterprise was pervaded by a technological version of the utopian ethos characteristic of West Coast counterculture. The Internet was seen as offering the model of a better life.

During this period sociologists and anthropologists researching the Internet largely focused on the idea of virtual community and questions of the relationship between the virtual and the real. Such communities persist to this day, partly in the form of virtual worlds such as *Second Life*, where – in accordance with the principle of role-play – participants choose their own names and rarely divulge their real-world identity. That also applies to sites like reddit, in essence online discussion groups devoted to particular topics (the reddit equivalent to the WELL's 'public conferences' are 'subreddits'): here there is no element of role-playing, but anonymity creates a freedom to express views that may be flippant or outrageous in a way that would not happen if people were interacting under their real-world names. However, the World Wide Web and in particular Web 2.0 saw the Internet taking on a quite different sort of social role, in the form of the social networking sites (SNSs) that experienced massive growth in the years after the millennium. MySpace was the largest SNS from around 2004 to 2010, when it was overtaken by the now ubiquitous Facebook.

On Facebook you are yourself (though you may be dead: Facebook sites are not necessarily deleted when you are). The basis of Facebook's architecture is the individual user, and the key action is friending. As well as your profile and photos, your personal pages include messages to or from your friends, and other friends' comments on them. Anyone can see who your friends are and how many friends you (and your friends) have: an unstated principle behind Facebook is that you are defined by the people you know and the discussions you are part of. Internet diehards with roots in the old communality may see this as symptomatic of the egocentricity and narcissism of the millennial 'Me generation', other symptoms of which include celebrity culture and 'possessive individualism' – the idea so central to neoliberalism that, in Crawford Macpherson's (2010, 3) words, the individual is 'essentially the proprietor of his own person or capacities, owing nothing to society for them'. Yet it is a widely acknowledged condition of contemporary life that none of us have fixed, stable selves, but negotiate who we are through our interactions with others. This is sometimes described as 'networked individualism', described by Manuel Castells as 'a social pattern' through which 'individuals build their networks, on-line and off-line, on the basis of their interests, values, affinities, and projects' (2001, 131). We define ourselves through the networks we belong to.

The impact of this can be seen in how people use the Internet and reflects computer use more generally. In the days when office software companies created 'turnkey solutions' – integrated software suites that did everything – you might expect to organise your working life largely around one package. That is like what members of virtual communities like the WELL used to do. In some contexts people still do it. As a resident of *Second Life* you construct your online identity – that is what role-playing means – within the context of a single platform. If your musical interests focus strongly on mashup or remixing, then you may use sites like Mashstix.com or Indaba Music in much the same way: as explained by Maarten Michielse (2016, 2013), Mashstix.com is a community dedicated to the development of technical knowhow through mutual commentary, while Indaba Music serves similar ends through its regular remixing competitions. The social networking features built into YouTube, such as user channels, comments and messaging, mean that communities linked by a common interest can exist under its umbrella too.

But networked individualism gives rise to a very different way of living on the web. Facebook or Twitter (where users interact through 280-character 'tweets' and your worth is measured by the number of your followers) are the gateways to many people's online presence, from which they navigate fluently across a wide range of different platforms. You might follow links to Instagram or YouTube, send and receive messages via WhatsApp, keep an eye on what's trending on reddit, and possibly the other eye on the office clock. You multitask between these and other communication channels (texting, email, skyping, face-to-face contact), so integrating them into what Baym calls 'one complex lifeworld' (2015, 156). And both musicians and fans do the same, using a combination of general-purpose SNSs and music-specific sites. In a study of how bands use digital communication, Danijela Bogdanovic (2016, 442) speaks of 'cross-platform interaction, whereby one's Facebook profile features links to videos on YouTube or sound files on SoundCloud and Bandcamp, where Twitter updates are synced with Facebook status updates and so forth'; Justin Williams and Ross Wilson (2016, 594) detail the complex chain of inter-platform responses that may be set off by a fan clicking the 'like' button on a musician's Facebook page. Other than video repositories such as YouTube and Vimeo, and audio repositories such as Soundcloud (which would logically have been the audio equivalent of YouTube but arrived too late), sites of particular importance to musicians and their fans include Reverbnation (aimed at musicians developing their career), Bandcamp (which enables musicians to sell their work directly to fans) and music streaming services such as Pandora and Spotify – of which more later. Each of these has at least some social networking features.

All this has many implications for music's role in society. A century ago the consumption of music was strongly tied to place. You went to concerts, or heard (and perhaps participated in) music in pubs or clubs. That changed when radio, 78s and LPs turned living rooms into major sites of musical consumption. Portable record players, battery-powered radios and ghetto blasters took it out of doors, but music on the move remained the exception until the introduction in 1979 of the Sony Walkman – the miniaturised cassette player that inaugurated the concept of personal stereo. With its digital successors such as the iPod (2001) and iPhone (2007), music became ubiquitous, as closely integrated into everyday urban (or rural) life as a soundtrack is into a film, and this further weakened its already tenuous link to place. Concerts still happen, of course – it is an irony that in the digital age live music is almost the only sector of the music business where many musicians can make money – but fans attending an event may use Twitter or phone apps such as iGroups to exchange information or live stream content to fans across the world (Bennett 2012). Or they may use their phones to record and upload videos to YouTube, creating a permanent archive that fans can access in the future; that may detract from the concert experience, but in interviews fans invoke the same kind of altruism I mentioned in relation to the WELL, explaining that they are doing it for the benefit of the larger fan community (Lingel and Naaman 2011).

With the enhanced bandwidth of high-speed data networks and superfast broadband, the making of music has also become increasingly independent of place. Building on the largely standardised design of international recording studios, the so-called 'Rocket Network' was introduced in the mid-1990s to enable multi-sited real-time collaboration between musicians across the globe; this was driven in part by a utopian vision of world musicking, and it is telling that, when the business folded, Digidesign (the company behind Pro Tools) launched its own version, now targeted firmly at the professional market and priced accordingly (Théberge 2004, 776–9). Telematic performance, where musicians across the world play together in real time, is increasingly common: as early as 1998, Seiji Osawa conducted a performance of Beethoven's 'Ode to Joy' from Nagano, Japan, in which the Tokyo Opera Singers were joined by choruses in Berlin, Cape Town, Beijing, New York and Sydney, all electronically linked. And when laptop ensembles do the same (as in the 2012 performance of a composition by Roger Dannenberg that was hosted at Louisiana State University but involved seven other ensembles across two continents), the same kind of networking is happening at two levels: in the local coordination of the individual laptop players, and in the remote collaboration of the different ensembles (O'Brien 2016). These examples of telematic musicking all involved specific audience locations. But even that disappears when Avatar Orchestra Metaverse (www.avatarorchestra .org/) – a group of collaborating musicians scattered across Europe and North America – perform on *Second Life* before an audience of avatars, digital stand-ins for real-life individuals who may be anywhere in the world. Here it is not so much that the connection between music and place has disappeared as that place has been re-created in the digital domain – as is also the case in the virtual bars, clubs and other hangouts where 'me-and-my-guitar' singers give live performances. Quite what 'live' might mean in *Second Life* has been a topic of lively discussion among its virtual residents, and in Chapter 7 of this book Paul Sanden asks the same about digital performance more generally.

Pushing still harder at the boundaries of the real is Hatsune Miku, perhaps the definitive icon of music in digital culture. The eternally 16-year-old schoolgirl began as an advertising image for Yamaha's Vocaloid voice synthesis software but developed into a virtual diva known through anime-style videos and holographic performances throughout Asia, North America and Europe. With her computer-generated voice and appearance – Louise Jackson and Mike Dines (2016, 107) speak of 'a wardrobe that could easily be used as a postnuclear school uniform' – she has been interpreted by Western commentators as a harbinger of posthuman culture, but is arguably better understood in terms of two specifically Japanese contexts. One, discussed by Jackson and Dines, is performance traditions such as the puppet theatre genre Bunraku, where issues of reality and illusion have long been thematised; the other is the system of 'idols' (real-world teenage performers whose lives and images are strictly controlled) and the corporate 'offices' that do the controlling. This creates a situation within which human performers are seen as hardly more human than Miku, and Rafal Zaborowski (2016, 123) quotes a fan saying that it is in Miku, rather than the flesh-and-blood products of the entertainment industry, that authenticity is to be found: 'This is real. This is the real freedom of expression. Look at the idols, look at the girl groups. All fake.'

There are subcultural genres that have no existence in the offline world, found mainly on Bandcamp and sustained by online cultures of discourse on platforms such as reddit and Tumblr. The outstanding example of this is vaporwave, a retrofuturist, ironical, and sometimes downright whimsical audio-visual genre often seen as the first to exist purely online (a view complicated by Adam Harper in his contribution to this book). Its musical lexicon is a collage of sometimes pastiched or reconstructed jazz, muzak, ringtones and video game soundtracks, while its visual iconography combines classical statuary (perhaps via de Chirico), obsolete computer graphics and Japanese characters. As much an aesthetic as a style, vaporwave draws on the anonymity of reddit and Tumblr (often the music is not attributed to real-world individuals), and its online presence extends as far as the darknet, the region of the Internet that is inaccessible to standard browsers; traditionally associated with organised crime, the darknet is increasingly inhabited by everyday users worried about the inexorable spread of internet surveillance (Watson 2017). It is worth adding that its online-only nature makes vaporwave the first musical genre in history whose very existence is dependent on the server farms and other physical infrastructure of a communication system whose vulnerability to terrorism or cyber warfare is increasingly a source of public concern.

At first blush this might sound simply reactionary. But Kramer's purpose is less to deplore digital culture than to address an issue that confronts many traditions under conditions of technological or social change: the repurposing of cultural heritage within new circumstances. It might be said that Kramer is just being realistic when he acknowledges that the era of 'the fully-fledged work, the supposedly timeless masterwork, was relatively brief and is now essentially over' (2013, 43). Instead of the digital download, he suggests, classical music's best hope may lie in turning itself back into the culture of performance as which it began, so recapturing some of its ritualistic value as something experienced socially, occasionally, no sooner heard than gone – something that lies at a remove from

All this adds up to a radically changed environment for both the production and the consumption of music. It affects different traditions in different ways. Lawrence Kramer has complained how download sites such as iTunes and streaming services such as Spotify fragment the works of the Western classical tradition into individual sound files: called 'songs' (a jarring term when applied to sonatas, symphonies and other classical genres), these are divorced from the context of the multi-movement compositions of which they were intended as part – and indeed from any other kind of context, given that the lavish paratexts of LP covers and CD booklets were lost without trace in the transition from offline to online culture. Kramer argues that this represents a loss of the aesthetic distance definitive of classical music as a culture of canonical works. He also argues that it represents a loss of classical music's audience, in the sense that 'the figure of the human, the fiction of "man", to which the music is addressed has become vestigial. Classical music, it turns out, is human, all too human' (2013, 45).

everyday life and so constitutes 'an exceptional event' (51).[3] And he adds, 'There could be worse fates'. As the opening chapter of a handbook to new audio-visual aesthetics, Kramer's essay has a valedictory quality, its starting point the passing of a tradition overtaken by the force of history.

Kramer remarks of his reinvented classical concert culture that the music 'would not only be "live"; it would re-mark its aliveness in a complex dialogue with the life of posthuman being' (50). This links to his characterisation of classical music as 'all too human' and opens up an issue that extends far beyond the classical tradition. The integration of music into everyday life is gathering pace through streaming, algorithmic playlisting, and – perhaps the next big thing, if it hasn't already arrived – recommendation systems based not on title, artist, or genre, but on affect. In Chapter 4 Sumanth Gopinath and Jason Stanyek describe facial recognition systems that diagnose your mood. Imagine an app that does this and streams music to reinforce positive and counteract negative mental states, amounting to a kind of personalised sonic therapy. (You can almost hear Alexa's voice: 'You're sad! Just listen.') Actually this would really be just an automated extension of what people do for themselves: Zaborowski (2016, 120) speaks of a Hatsune Miku fan who organises her MP3s into folders such as 'cheerful', 'nostalgic' or 'calm', deliberately using these categories 'in accordance with the time of day, the day's events, or her personal mood'. There are also existing apps like Brain.fm ('an innovative non-invasive digital therapy application' that styles itself 'the future of music'[4]), which generates music specifically designed for mood regulation.

Here a historian might note a precedent in mid-eighteenth-century and earlier ideas of music's capacity to both represent and affect emotions, the humours, and aspects of bodily function. The tradition with which Kramer is concerned goes back to the later eighteenth century and is the product of a new aesthetic system within which music took on the attributes of a fine art and was conceived as the creative expression of a unique artistic personality. That is a historically and geographically delimited conception of what music is that until quite recently dominated what might be called the 'official' musical culture of the historical West, but in reality coexisted with any number of different conceptions of music. By making music of all kinds accessible at the touch of a trackpad, the Internet has undermined that dominance and so reshaped the dynamics of musical culture. And in that way digital technology can be seen as a force for musical pluralism, not the vehicle of some inexorable, technologically determined advance towards Kramer's 'posthuman condition' (as I said, technology does not simply determine what happens in culture).

There is also an issue of how far what Kramer describes is properly speaking posthuman at all. He speaks of earbuds – perhaps the signature human–machine interface of digital culture – as 'prosthetic eardrums' that take music into the body cavity and so 'abolish the contemplative distance between the music and the listener' (2013, 46). He is drawing on posthuman tropes of implantation and augmentation of the human condition through mechanical extension, but whether the use of earbuds amounts to a project to exceed or fundamentally transform the category of the human is debatable. (It's like calling Hatsune Miku posthuman just because she is a hologram.) By contrast, the rapidly developing field of algorithmic composition – where creative agency is displaced to what is often the software equivalent of a black box – really does thrust music into a frontier zone where distinctions of human and machine become blurred or undecidable. Whose (or what's) music is an algorithmic composition created through unsupervised machine learning? Does the question even make sense? As discussed by David Trippett in Chapter 9, posthumanism has become an established dimension of music in digital culture, taken up, explored or simply made fun of by an expanding cadre of musicians from Tod Machover to Daft Punk.

Digital Participation and Audio-Visual Style

I said that some see Web 2.0 as marketing hype linked to the idea of user-generated content, which is business-speak for what may otherwise be called digital participation. *Second Life* illustrates this: its developers, Linden Labs, created the platform, including the tools required to create digital objects, but everything that exists within the virtual world – trees, buildings, furniture, clothes, pianos with built-in music tracks, guitars with pyrotechnical facilities – has been created by its residents. Linden Labs give their users free access (you don't have to pay to play), and in return users add value by transforming *Second Life* from a platform to a world – on the basis of which Linden Labs make money from premium subscriptions and sales of virtual land. For users this is participatory play (for a few, such as virtual land owner Ailin Graef, it is also a source of significant real-world income), while for Linden Labs it is user-generated content. Academic lawyer and public intellectual Lawrence Lessig (2008, 214–20) cites *Second Life* as an example of what he calls the hybrid economy, his new business model for the cultural industries. At the same time, such participation is key to the blurring between production and consumption that has prompted the term 'prosumer', and it is equally illustrated by people who create content on *Second Life* and by those who upload their photographs to Instagram, their audio tracks to Soundcloud, or their videos to YouTube. All of these are user-generated content.

It is above all YouTube that epitomises digital participatory culture – a culture of audio-visual creation and commentary where videos are shared within what Henry Jenkins, the pioneer theorist of internet-based participatory culture, calls 'a gift economy where goods are circulated freely for shared benefit rather than sold for profit' (2009, 119). Many internet communities have been characterised in such terms – the trail-blazing but illegal peer-to-peer downloading site Napster provides an obvious example (Giesler and Pohlmann 2003) – and in this way embody the spirit of altruism of which I have already spoken; it is only a tiny minority of YouTubers whose videos attract millions of views and who share some of the profits generated by the advertisements on the site. So why exactly do people post all this content to YouTube? Michael Strangelove (2010, 122) evades the question: 'The answer to the question "why do you'Tube?" is as broad as the answer to the question "why do humans communicate?"'. Then who are these people? In Jenkins's words, 'YouTube has become the home port for lip-syncers, karaoke singers, trainspotters, birdwatchers, skateboarders, hip hoppers, small time wrestling federations, educators, third wave feminists, churches, proud parents, poetry slammers, gamers, fans, Ron Paul supporters, human rights activists, collectors, hobbyists' (2009, 110). In short, anyone and everyone, provided of course that they have internet access (and the starting point for Shzr Ee Tan's contribution to this book is that a sizeable proportion of the world's population do not).

And what do the digital haves post? The question is unanswerable, but in the specific area of music it might encompass anything and everything from performance videos – whether for paying audiences in formal concert halls or the cameraphone in a teenager's bedroom – to the innumerable parodied or reimagined versions of canonic music videos. Versions of 'Bohemian Rhapsody' encompass the entire lexicon of digital participation (Cook 2013). There are whole websites of anime versions, including versions drawing on specific anime series such as *Neon Genesis Evangalion*; there are versions drawing on the iconographies of *Star Trek*, *Star Wars* and *Lost*; versions based on games such as Nintendo's *Megaman*, *Final Fantasy* and *Lord of the Rings Online*; versions featuring *My Little Pony* and Mount Rushmore. There are versions created using Mario Paint Composer, made out of Lego (there is a whole channel of Lego versions of Queen videos), or from obsolete digital equipment; versions by the Filipino comedy duo Moymoy Palaboy and the 'manualist' Gerry Philips; versions using puppets (not just the professionally made Muppets version); versions by the crew of *HMS Campbeltown* and by a team of BBC newscasters, with Fiona Bruce revealing an unsuspected side to her personality. Different versions are based on different performances by Queen, or on parodistic covers such as Kevin Barbare's 'Star Trek Fantasy' or

'Weird Al' Jankovic's 'Bohemian Polka', or on the 'Bohemian Rhapsody' episode from *Wayne's World*. Different versions imitate, parody or simply air their knowledge of other different versions. The list goes on and on, though this paragraph cannot.

A key to this participatory culture lies in the ease with which digital media lend themselves to visual collage, sonic remixing, video mashup, and other expressions of what is sometimes called 'redactive' creativity – what John Hartley (2008, 112) defines as the production of 'new material by a process of editing existing content'. This concept has to be understood against the traditional idea that creativity – or at any rate *real* creativity – subsists in absolute originality, creation *ex nihilo*. In reality such creativity is, if not a logical impossibility, then rare to the point of non-existence in cultural practices such as music (Boden 2004, 11; Cook 2018). Put simply, everything riffs off something else. And so the forms of redactive creation ubiquitous on YouTube follow in the traditions of quotation, direct or oblique reference, elaboration, variation, reinterpretation, paraphrase and parody that constitute the long history of music, as well as the shorter history of audio-visual media. Jenkins is at pains to stress that digital participation is a continuation by other means of the timeless practices of folk culture: 'my grandmother was a remix artist', he announces to his puzzled readers, before going on to explain that 'she was a quilter. She would take bits of remaindered cloth from the local textile mills and use them to create something new. She was able to express herself meaning-fully through the appropriation and recombination of borrowed materials' (Jenkins et al. 2016, 7–8). That, Jenkins is saying, is what mashup artists, remixers and digital participants of all stripes do. And just as in the case of the old folk culture – including such mainly religious practices as shape-note singing – so the participatory practices of digital culture contribute to the maintenance of community and social relationships (including in religious and devotional contexts, as documented in Monique Ingalls's chapter). As Strangelove writes, 'We do not merely watch online video. We engage each other in relationships through amateur online video practices' (2010, 133).

As compared to its analogue equivalents, digital technology has democratised audio-visual redaction in terms of both the necessary skills and financial outlay. Readily available and free (or illegally downloaded) software enables not only copying, editing and the layering of diverse elements – the basic elements of mashup and remix – but also audio filtering, stereo positioning, visual reframing, multiple windows, and a host of other manipulations. But as usual it is not just a matter of the technology. I can make the point in terms of internet memes, which may take the form of jokes, images or videos. (For a musical example think of

Nyan Cat, which pairs the image of a cat in the form of a poptart by American illustrator Chris Torres with the digitally manipulated version of a song originally written for Hatsune Miku, and at the time of writing has had 160 million views.) Limor Shifman sees the key attribute of an internet meme as its 'sparking of user-created derivatives articulated as parodies, remixes, or mashups' (2014, 2). And, based on an analysis of outstandingly popular memes, she sets out a number of the qualities that are responsible for this. Those that are relevant to music include simplicity (shooting a video in a single take or against a plain white background makes it much easier to imitate); repetitiveness, which enhances memorability and encourages 'active user involvement in remaking video memes' (83); whimsicality, where an ambiguous, incomplete or simply weird video 'invites people to fill in the gaps' (88); and humour, particularly in such forms as playfulness (which may 'lure user creativity by summoning viewers to take part in a game') and incongruity, 'an unexpected cognitive encounter between two incongruous elements' (79). In Jenkins's word, these qualities enhance the 'spreadability' of content (Jenkins et al. 2013).

Along with Tumblr and 4chan, reddit is the principal route through which internet memes spread on their way to Facebook and YouTube; 'many popular subreddits', Adrienne Massanari writes, 'consist entirely of conversations inspired by user-created memes' (2015, 96). So it is not surprising that the qualities Shifman sees as characteristic of memes are found more broadly in reddit. Massanari devotes a whole chapter of her book to reddit's playfulness, describing it as 'simultaneously inventive and repetitive', and often involving 'lateral leaps between seemingly unrelated topics' (in other words, incongruity). 'Puns', she writes, 'are near ubiquitous' (97), and closely related to them is what she calls 'the pile-on thread': based around a digital artefact such as an image, the thread develops through successive individuals 'remixing and playing off someone else's posting by modifying the original object in some way' (98). This is just the kind of redactive creativity we saw on YouTube, and it is at this point that Massanari makes a revealing observation: 'these pile-on threads', she says, 'are reminiscent of the Surrealist game *Exquisite Corpse*'. She is referring to the high art version of the traditional parlour game Consequences, where each player writes or draws on a sheet of paper and folds it over, leaving visible just the end of what they have done, before passing it on to the next player, who in turn does the same. (Rules stipulate a fixed grammatical structure, or the drawing of a head, body and legs.) At the end you unfold the paper and see what you have got. It is in essence a method of producing incongruous, unforeseen juxtapositions – as illustrated by the name the Surrealists gave it, based on what supposedly emerged the first time they played it: 'the exquisite corpse shall drink the new wine'.

The psychologist and creativity theorist David Feldman has spoken of Wolfgang Amadeus Mozart's 'inordinately strong tendency towards certain forms of wordplay, particularly the juxtaposition of words and meanings, a ready flow of verbal doggerel, the transposition of syntactic and semantic rules, and a playful and mischievous orientation towards written language' (1994, 53). He could have been talking about reddit, and indeed it is easy to imagine that if Mozart were alive today he would be an avid redditer. And Feldman goes on to suggest that all of these things have equivalents in Mozart's music: he played with notes in the same way that he played with words. That is the connection I now want to make. Massanari's invocation of *Exquisite Corpse* resonates with musicologist John Richardson's (2012) invocation of the surreal as a key quality of contemporary audio-visual culture. As in *Exquisite Corpse*, techniques emblematic of historical Surrealism, such as collage and montage, work through the juxtaposition of incongruous elements releasing unpredictable, emergent meaning. This is the basic mechanism behind the puns so characteristic of reddit. It is also the basic mechanism behind mashup, where the musical or semantic incongruity between two beat-matched songs or videos opens up a sometimes bewildering connotational gulf, as objects or emotions that we normally keep in separate compartments of our life world are forced into intimate conjunction with one another; Richardson speaks of the 'complicated and troubling ways' in which mashups of death-metal and Britney Spears songs reveal 'the artifice that has always existed in constructions of heavy metal rock and the brutal truths that lie under the sheen of girly pop' (171). You see and hear each through the other, giving rise to new perceptions and revealing the familiar in an unfamiliar light.

There is a widespread perception that the qualities encoded in such terms as collage, montage, juxtaposition and emergence are central to what Richardson (2012, 289) refers to as 'a digital sensibility'. Jean Burgess and Joshua Green speak of a 'logic of cultural value' embodied in YouTube videos, whose 'edits are often jarring, and the audio is manipulated through quick cuts, changing speeds, and the introduction of alternative soundtracks' (2009, 53). On the first page of her book *Unruly Media* Carol Vernallis speaks of 'the media swirl', with its 'accelerating aesthetics, mingled media, and memes that cross to and fro' as well as its 'ever-present buzzing, switching, and staccato thinking' – and she adds that across the range of contemporary audio-visual media it is generally YouTube that 'feels like the driver' (2013, 3, 15). And in this volume, composer Julio d'Escriván speaks of 'the remix mentality that pervades our culture', explaining it as a response to contemporary video editing expressed through what he calls the compositing together of blocks of sound into semantic networks that owe more to emotional topography than to traditional musical syntax. In these ways the practices of Hartley's redaction give rise to a distinctive digital aesthetic that is shared across different platforms, media types and genres.

This aesthetic – you might almost call it a style – emerges from the triangulation of technological affordances, the conditions of spreadability, and the social practices of participation. Burgess speaks of 'vernacular creativity' (Burgess and Green 2009, 25), emphasising that it has always existed but that digital culture has increased its pervasiveness and visibility to the extent that it has become something essentially new. It is perhaps this dimension of digital culture that has done more than any amount of academic or ideological critique to undermine the aesthetic exceptionalism at the heart of the hierarchical, institutionalised traditions of Western artistic practice, and it is an illustration of how the combination of multiple, local acts of continuation by other means can amount in sum to paradigm change.

New Technology, New Business

Jenkins, who uses the word 'paradigm' with considerable freedom, has distinguished between the old 'digital revolution paradigm' and the new 'convergence paradigm' (2006, 6). The first assumed that new media would displace the old, he explains, the second that the new and the old would work together in complex ways; by 'convergence' Jenkins means that formerly autonomous media are increasingly coming together as information flows freely across them. (It's like the networked way of living on the web I associated with SNSs.) But there is another major dimension to what Jenkins calls 'convergence culture' (the title of his 2006 book), which concerns the relationship between digital participants and what he calls Web 2.0 companies. *Spreadable Media* (2013), the book he co-authored with Sam Ford and Joshua Green, sets out ideas largely drawn from *Convergence Culture*, but now targeted at the business community. At the beginning of the book, the authors explain that it is motivated by 'disappointment with the way some companies have reacted to the "convergence culture" our research has examined. Some companies continue to ignore the potentials of this participatory environment, using their legal authority to constrain rather than to enable grassroots participation or cutting themselves off from listening to the very audiences they wish to communicate with' (Jenkins et al. 2013, xi). A key dimension, they explain, is the way such companies reduce the personal and social values and loyalties of their customers – such as the altruism inherent in gift economies – to the commodified concept of user-generated content, while at the same time using the courts to enforce the intellectual property rights that the law gives them.

In *Convergence Culture* Jenkins illustrates this through the examples of *Star Wars* and Harry Potter. In each case corporate rights holders (respectively LucasArts and Warner Bros) were suspicious of the activities of fanfiction writers and other digital participants to the extent of seeking to control or even close down their activities, and Jenkins comments that in these and other ways 'the media companies have shown a remarkable willingness to antagonize their customers by taking legal actions against them in the face of all economic rationality' (2006, 63–4). But the most extreme example must be the way in which the music industry responded to Napster and the demonstrable demand for online access to music by wholesale litigation against its customers: Mark Katz cites actions filed in September 2003 against a twelve-year old girl and a 66-year grandmother whose computer turned out to be incapable of downloading music files as particularly spectacular own goals (2004, 176).[5] Underlying the industry's panicked response to digital technology is something I mentioned near the beginning of this chapter: unlike analogue copies, digital copies are perfect.

At a few points in his 2006 book Jenkins contrasts American business practices with those of Japan, where media franchises 'encourage various forms of participation and social interactions between consumers'; again, 'Japanese anime has won worldwide success in part because Japanese media companies were tolerant of the kinds of grassroots activities that American media companies seem so determined to shut down' (2006, 112, 160). But perhaps the best example came the year after his book was published, when Hatsune Miku went on sale. Yes, that's right. You don't simply buy Vocaloid software. You buy Miku, 'your own personal musical idol ... not just a picture on the software package but ... a sixteen-year-old girl, 158 cm tall, weighing 42 kg, and with a passion for idol style and dance music' (Zaborowski 2016, 115). And Miku comes with a Creative Commons-style licence that allows you to 'noncommercially transform and recreate Hatsune Miku's image, and create derivative works from it at no cost' (116).

In short, as long you don't sell it, you can freely upload your version of Miku to the manufacturer's web space or to other video-sharing services such as YouTube or its Japanese equivalents. The business model is based on user-generated content – that's what motivates people to buy the software – but in a form that acknowledges the motives and values underlying its users' participation, and the importance of their retaining control over the fruits of their labour. In this way it illustrates Jenkins's new business model for the cultural industries. Conversely, companies that do not understand their customers' motives and values – that do not listen to their customers – risk alienating them and undermining their businesses. Again music provides a prime example. It is not that people stopped making money out of music, but that the established industry lost control over it. Through sticking inflexibly to the old business models and suing their customers, the major record companies lost out twice: first to Apple (whose iTunes download store appeared in 2003), and then again, with the advent of streaming, to Spotify (like Apple, a computer firm rather than a music firm: its two Swedish founders, now billionaires, came from information technology). To be sure, the record companies still make money from music: they work in partnership with Spotify. But they no longer call the shots.[6]

While digital fan culture lies at the heart of Jenkins's work, his larger approach resonates with writers in other areas. Lessig is one: I have described both his 'hybrid economy' and Jenkins's 'convergence culture' as embodying new business models for the cultural industries, and indeed they are closely related. Lessig also uses the term 'remix' culture to mean what Jenkins calls participatory culture, and his use of the term capitalises on long-running controversies – particularly in America – over the legality of sampling, the basic technology that underlies hip-hop and other forms of remix culture. A core claim of Lessig's book *Remix: Making Art and Commerce Thrive in the Hybrid Economy* (2008) is that there is a glaring contradiction between the law's attitude to practices of quotation and adaptation in literature and academia on the one hand – which simply could not operate without the principles of fair use that allow these practices – and in audio-visual media on the other, where judges have repeatedly insisted that there is no *de minimis* and that any unauthorised sampling is a crime. Other core claims are that the copying processes inherent in how computers work have had the result of extending copyright protection beyond anything pre-digital law-makers could ever have envisaged (99), and that the combined effect of the law and music industry litigation has been to 'criminalize a generation of our kids' (114). Lessig also speaks in very much the same way as Jenkins about the old folk culture in which redactive creativity was the norm, and in the American legal context this takes on a particular significance: the law's draconian treatment of sampling is based on the US constitution and its early amendments, which date from the late eighteenth century, a time when redactive creativity was taken for granted. To invoke such provisions to criminalise redactive creativity in the digital domain betrays a simple lack of historical awareness.

The other obvious parallel to Jenkins's convergence culture is what Aram Sinnreich, working in the specific context of music, calls 'configurable culture'. For Sinnreich, the production and consumption of music has for the last two centuries been subject to the 'modern framework' that has governed Western music, from Kramer's canon to the structure of its institutions. But in the digital age new technologies have opened up music to social negotiation and change, so undermining the old certainties and prompting 'a fundamental crisis' (2010, 88). Many aspects of Sinnreich's configurable culture are shared with Lessig and Jenkins, and Sinnreich acknowledges this. But he sees them as underestimating the drastic disruption of previous models that configurable culture represents: even though certain aspects of it have existed for generations, he says, 'the configurable media experiences of the present day clearly outnumber, overpower, and outpace any of these examples by orders of magnitude', and so 'I must disagree with any claims of continuity between past and present cultural practices' (71, 74).

The new paradigm that Sinnreich is proclaiming extends way beyond expressive culture. There is a parallel with Vernallis, for whom today's audio-visual media are conditioned by the conditions of life in a digital world where we are swamped by data streams, and where we constantly 'retool and reconfigure our personalities and roles' (2013, 286). More than that, 'contemporary digital media present forms of space, time, and rhythm we haven't seen before', mirroring 'work speedup, multitasking, and just-in-time labor' (26). And a few lines later she puts these thoughts together: 'I wonder if becoming more aware of the patterns of space, time, and rhythm in media and in work speedup might help us to adapt to social change'. But Sinnreich takes this thought to another level. Understanding configurable culture may give us 'a roadmap for the emergence of new social forms and institutions in the networked age', he says; it will 'both prefigure and influence the decisions we will make about how to rebuild and reshape our social institutions' (2010, 10–11, 8). The stakes could hardly be higher, for in the end 'resolution of this crisis will help to determine the organizing principles of postindustrial society for years or perhaps for centuries to come' (89).

Evidently the jury will be out on that claim for years or perhaps for centuries to come. Meanwhile musicians and the music business face more immediate problems. From an industry perspective, as Martin Scherzinger explains in Chapter 2, the golden age of the 1980s–90s – when people were replacing their LPs by CDs and digital remastering enabled record companies to monetise their back collections – was succeeded by a period of turmoil: critical factors include the exponential growth of Napster and other peer-to-peer download services, the explosion of what the industry called 'piracy', its litigation against customers, and the launching in 2003 of Apple's iTunes Store. In the following year, as dreams of an online musical utopia were fading, Katz's book *Capturing Sound* offered a balanced overview of the then current situation and a guardedly optimistic evaluation of future prospects. It is revealing to compare the future he envisaged with what actually happened. After excoriating the music industry's strategy of litigation, he suggests that 'file-sharing should actually be opened up', and that 'the industry could flourish were that to happen' (2004, 177). Copyright, which began as a strictly limited period intended to enable entrepreneurs to recoup their investment but increasingly encroaches upon eternity, should be rolled back. The application of fair use should be extended. Instead of suing their customers, the industry should do what you are meant to do with customers – sell your products to them – and this could be done through download services charged per song, through subscription, or even a licensing system administered by internet service providers in return for a flat fee: that way, Katz observes, teenagers without credit cards – a key segment of the market – could actually pay for their music. And why would the music industry ever go along with this? Because they would make money.

As a vision of the future this was at best blurred. What arrived was not enhanced and industry-supported download services but rather streaming services. These offer subscriptions, as Katz suggested, and what is more, they provide access to huge music libraries for free if you are prepared to sit through the advertisements (and for a reasonable charge if you aren't). On top of that, as described in K. E. Goldschmitt and Nick Seaver's chapter, they have opened up a new world of both humanly curated and algorithmic recommendation. The Jeremiahs may warn of creeping posthumanism and algocracy – the spread of algorithmic decision making, from personalised insurance quotations to self-driving cars and now the music you listen to – but for the rest of us, what's not to like? For many of the contributors to this volume (Scherzinger, Gopinath and Stanyek, Goldschmitt and Seaver, and Tan), the answer is something else that streaming services have brought to music: perhaps the most extreme version of the new business model that in recent years has become the norm for SNSs – a model that is nothing like what Lessig and Jenkins were talking about.

Spotify was floated on the stock market in 2018 (that is why its founders are billionaires), at which time it had yet to turn a profit. That was also true of Twitter when it floated in 2013; even Facebook had generated only small profits at the time of its flotation the year before that. And the parallels do not stop there. Through its recommendation technology, Spotify is built on big data: in the words of Brian Whitman (founder of The Echo Nest, a firm specialising in recommendation algorithms that Spotify acquired in 2014), 'every word anyone utters on the Internet about music goes through our systems that look for descriptive terms, noun phrases and other text and those terms bucket up into what we call "cultural vectors" or "top terms"'.[7] But those are not the only data Spotify collects. Like Facebook, Google (including YouTube) and other SNSs, its business is increasingly the collection of a wide range of personal data: Spotify's Privacy Policy mentions not only name, age, gender, mobile number and credit card details, but also what you listen to, when you do so, where you are when you do it, playlists you create, and your interactions with other Spotify users – and this data may be shared 'in a pseudonymised format' with Spotify's unnamed music industry and marketing partners.[8] Looking into the near future, and allowing for the rapid development of affective computing, it is easy to imagine streaming services offering exceptional opportunities for the surgically targeted, just-in-time marketing that is the advertiser's holy grail (not to mention a variety of uses by other agents of manipulation or control). After all, if Google knows you're pregnant before you do, then Spotify knows what music people play when having sex – and when they are playing it.[9]

This is the context for the Faustian bargain – Gopinath and Stanyek's term – that has become definitive of today's Web 2.0 businesses. By signing up (probably without reading the lengthy privacy policy), users gain obvious, immediate benefits. At the same time, you are agreeing to real-time collection of information that may bear upon issues as personal as your emotional state. You are contributing to a long-term but vaguely defined loss of freedom, in the form of the apparently inexorable advance towards a dystopian culture of surveillance that was troubling some far-sighted commentators a quarter of a century ago: in *The Virtual Community* Howard Rheingold was already warning that 'ultimately, advertisers will be able to use the new technologies to customize television advertising for each individual household' (it was just the television he got wrong), and a few pages later he suggests that the 'illusion of democracy' offered by the Internet 'is just another distraction from the real power play behind the scenes of the new technologies – the replacement of democracy with a global mercantile state that exerts control through the media-assisted manipulation of desire' (1993, 293, 297).[10]

Yet that is only half the story. Google Spotify and you will find any number of musicians protesting about the derisory payments they receive, or threatening to pull their catalogues from the service (as Taylor Swift and Radiohead's Thom Yorke did). Working out what artists make from

Spotify is not straightforward, partly because of the complexities of the firm's revenue model, and partly because Spotify's figures are for what goes to the rights holder – generally the record company – whereas the proportion that goes to the artist is a matter of individual contract. But after allowing for all this, the data journalist David McCandless calculated in 2010 that, in order to earn the US government's then monthly minimum wage of $1,160 from Spotify, you would need to have 4,053,110 plays per month. The Spotify site lists total historical plays of artists' ten top tracks, and the examples of three female singers with very different profiles set these figures in context. Adele's lifetime count currently stands at just under 3.5 billion, which on McCandless's calculation corresponds to 72 years on the minimum wage – and then there are other streaming services, physical sales, live performance, and licensing income. She is making good money. But for Imogen Heap, who at the age of 40 maintains a significant presence on the British scene, the corresponding figure is two years (mainly because of a single song, 'Hide and Seek', released as long ago as 2005). And in the case of Áine Cahill – at 23 one of *The Independent*'s names to watch for 2018 – the figure reduces to about two weeks.[11] Rough and ready as they may be, such figures suggest that Spotify's ostensibly successful monetisation of digital music – which resulted in a market value following flotation of some $30 billion – was achieved on the basis of a revenue model that puts even moderately successful up-and-coming artists (*The Independent* spoke of Cahill's 'breakthrough success' in 2017) practically on a par with people who upload cat videos to YouTube. Once again it's the story of monetising user-generated content. We have ended up with a situation in which most artists get practically nothing, while the corporate middlemen are bankrolled by the collection and sale of listeners' personal data. Such a possibility never crossed Katz's mind.

The Jeremiahs don't have it all. If digital technology has created the conditions for surveillance and social oppression, it has also created means for resisting them: some are documented in Peter McMurray's chapter on audio-visual witnessing and racial violence, while a timely reminder of the power of digital sound is the video of crying children at US Customs and Border Protection facilities that ended the policy of separating children from their parents.[12] And in straightforwardly musical terms the benefits of digital technology for both producers and consumers are self-evident and celebrated by our contributors. The same applies to the opening up of new stylistic and generic possibilities, especially in terms of multimedia. The world's music has never been so accessible, and classical music – in whatever form – is heard by more people around the world than ever before. The music generation apps developed within Google's Magenta project are placing sophisticated machine learning algorithms into the hands of not only professional musicians like Andrew Huang but also – in the tradition of Laurie Spiegel's 'Music Mouse' (1986) and David Zicarelli's 'OvalTune' (1989) – the kind of people who under the classical music regime would never have thought themselves capable of creating music.[13] Digital technologies also bring the pleasures (and pitfalls) of social participation to those who would otherwise be cut off from it, such as the housebound and bed-bound.

And who knows, they could even bring equity to the musical marketplace. The blogosphere is full of the potential of blockchain, the distributed database model that underlies bitcoin (discussed by Scherzinger in Chapter 11). In its most radical and much hyped form, blockchain promises a mode of revenue distribution that cuts out the middlemen and, together with smart (automated) contracts, could cost-effectively accommodate the modest but vital earnings of rank-and-file artists as well as the select company of the superstars. For all too understandable reasons Imogen Heap is actively campaigning in favour of it, and – as Jeremy Silver (2016) documents in a recent report – there are several such initiatives. But it's the old story. The issue is not whether or not blockchain has the technological potential to provide a more equitable mechanism for paying musicians than the current system. Once again, technology is not the crunch issue. It is whether there is sufficient short-term economic incentive to mobilise those who are in a position to do something about it. Scherzinger is clearly not putting his money on that one – he frames his discussion firmly in the past tense – and no more am I.

For Further Study

Baym, Nancy. 2015. *Personal Connections in the Digital Age*, 2nd edn. Cambridge: Polity.

Jenkins, Henry. 2006. *Convergence Culture: Where Old and New Media Collide*. New York: New York University Press.

Lessig, Lawrence. 2008. *Remix: Making Art and Commerce Thrive in the Hybrid Economy*. London: Bloomsbury.

Miller, Kiri. 2012. *Playing Along: Digital Games, YouTube, and Virtual Performance*. New York: Oxford University Press.

Vernallis, Carol. 2013. *Unruly Media: YouTube, Music Video, and the New Digital Cinema*. New York: Oxford University Press.

Whiteley, Sheila and Shara Rambarran, eds. 2016. *The Oxford Handbook of Music and Virtuality*. New York: Oxford University Press.

Notes

1 'Big Brother is in your Spotify: How music became the surveillance state's Trojan horse,' *Salon*, 28 March 2014. https://www.alternet.org/2014/03/how-music-became-surveillance-states-trojan-horse/. All websites accessed 28 June 2018.

2 Interviewed on the BBC's *Today* programme, 3 April 2018.

3 Ironically, Thomas Connor (2016, 142) has suggested something similar in the context of Hatsune Miku and her holographic progeny: 'Concerts could become a boutique specialty service for those wishing to be present, and a pay-per-view living-room bonus for those wishing to be telepresent'.

4 www1.brain.fm/science; www1.brain.fm/.

5 Martin Scherzinger cites other examples of the industry's 'lashing out at the wrong targets in exaggerated fashion' in Chapter 2, this volume (p. 47).

6 The tensions between content providers and streaming services are a principal theme of Scherzinger's second chapter in this volume (Chapter 11, p. 287).

7 Quoted in Leonard, 'Big Brother is in your Spotify'.

8 www.spotify.com/uk/legal/privacy-policy-update/?_ga=2.13627249.790691075.1528042793-203562537.1524838649#s5.

9 http://news.bbc.co.uk/1/hi/technology/7733368.stm; www.theguardian.com/technology/2015/feb/13/spotify-knows-what-music-youre-having-sex-to. On the more general point it is worth quoting from a speech given in April 2018 by Andrew Haldane, Chief Economist at the Bank of England: 'data on music downloads from Spotify has been used, in tandem with semantic search techniques applied to the words of songs, to provide an indicator of people's sentiment. Intriguingly, the resulting index of sentiment does at least as well in tracking consumer spending as the Michigan survey of consumer confidence' (www.bankofengland.co.uk/-/media/boe/files/speech/2018/will-big-data-keep-its-promise-speech-by-andy-haldane.pdf?la=en&hash=00A4AB2F080BDCDB1781D11DF6EC9BDA560F3D98).

10 The issue of surveillance, touched on by several contributors to this volume, is comprehensively addressed in Drott 2018.

11 For McCandless's calculation see https://informationisbeautiful.net/2010/how-much-do-music-artists-earn-online/ (the underlying figures are at http://bit.ly/DigitalRoyalty). The figures for Adele, Heap and Cahill were obtained from Spotify on 4 June 2018, while Roisin O'Connor's 'Ones to watch 2018: Our favourite new artists to listen out for next year' appeared in *The Independent* on 15 December 2017 (www.independent.co.uk/arts-entertainment/music/news/ones-to-watch-2018-new-artists-best-music-jessie-reyez-lewis-capaldi-alma-ms-banks-hardy-caprio-a8070371.html).

12 The video 'Listen to children who've been separated from their parents at the border' (www.youtube.com/watch?v=PoncXfYBAVI) was posted to YouTube on 18 June 2018 and rapidly reposted to many other sites. By 20 June it had garnered 1.8 million views. At that point Trump reversed the policy.

13 For Magenta see https://magenta.tensorflow.org/; for Huang's use of NSynth Sound Maker see www.youtube.com/watch?v=AaALLWQmCdI. Music Mouse is documented at http://music mouse.com/ and https://en.wikipedia.org/wiki/Music_Mouse; OvalTune seems to exist only in memories and in brief references scattered across the web.

Personal Take: Whatever Happened to Tape-Trading?

LEE MARSHALL

Back in the day, if you were a big enough fan of a certain kind of artist, it wouldn't take too long before you found out that there was music available other than that officially sanctioned by them or their record label. 'Sure', someone might say to you, 'that's a good album, but what about the tracks that he left off? If he'd left those on, the album would have been *really* good. I'll give you a tape.' And then a door had opened that could never be closed, a door into a room full of weird and wonderful recordings: from those killer out-takes that should never have been left off, to recordings of every concert the artist performed, to recordings of artists drunkenly messing around in a studio, fighting with other band members or recording things that no one in their right mind would want to hear again.

These recordings were all available to you, but only if you knew how to find them. You could only rely on your acquaintance's generosity so far. If you wanted to fully immerse yourself in everything that was available you had to enter into the subculture of tape-trading, in which fans would trade tapes (and later CD-Rs) through the mail, swapping copies of recordings they owned for ones that they didn't. Traders would compile lists of their recordings, often including individual sound quality ratings, and circulate to other traders via fanzines or personal networks. To help newbies get started, many traders would offer 'blanks and postage' trades, copying a number of recordings for the new collector in return for the equivalent number of blank tapes, plus a few extra to cover the costs of postage. Once you had a number of tapes that you could trade, you were away.

The other way to get hold of these recordings was to pay for them. Commercial bootlegging was the evil twin of tape-trading, disdained by many in the taping community for tainting the purity of their noble hobby. But commercial bootlegging was never more than a cottage industry run by fans and it served a key function in the unauthorised recordings ecosystem: it enabled access to recordings often unavailable to ordinary collectors. Those special studio out-takes, or early concert soundboards, had to come from somewhere; there had to be a leak in the official channel and sometimes that leak could only be sprung by financial incentive. Knowing they could sell several hundred copies of a particularly desirable recording, bootleggers were able to offer a few hundred, maybe even a few thousand dollars to someone at a studio, say, to 'liberate' a tape. In spite of the moral indignation of the purist collectors, many of the most significant unauthorised recordings would not have seen the light of day were it not for the commercial bootleggers.

The tape-trading and bootlegging subcultures existed for many years on the fringes of the music industry, part valued and part vilified by the official industry. But for many of those involved in tape-trading it was a source of immense personal value, not merely in terms of the accumulation of recordings but also in the way that tape-trading formed the basis of social bonds. The implicit trust that existed between fans willing to send tapes to strangers in the knowledge that their actions would be reciprocated, the little letters from fellow traders that accompanied the packets of tapes dropping through the letterbox, and the ability to connect with people in different parts of the world who put the same love and care into their hobby as you did, all contributed to the sense of being part of a community, participating in something more than the simple exchange of commodities.

And then the Internet changed everything.

Admittedly, it didn't change everything on its own, but the emergence of online music technologies and cultures transformed tape-trading in a number of ways. First, the boundaries between the authorised and unauthorised began to blur. Out-takes began to appear on Napster alongside normal releases with little to tell them apart, resulting in a blurring that was exacerbated by the official industry increasingly releasing 'bootlegs' of their own once sales of new releases began to decline (Bob Dylan's official Bootleg Series released by his Columbia/Legacy label now runs to fifty-three CDs' worth of material). Secondly, the 'trading' began to move online, with collectors quick to see the opportunities of BitTorrent to share recordings more quickly and conveniently than was possible with snail mail alternatives. Partly as a result of this, the bottom fell out of commercial bootlegging. New bootleg releases were shared freely online as quickly and widely as all other kinds of new releases. The fact that the bootleggers could no longer ensure a market of even a few hundred copies meant that they were unable to risk spending money on even the most desirable tapes.

There are positive elements to these changes, of course. It might be said that access to these recordings has become more democratic; the existence of these recordings is more widely known and it is now far easier for new fans to access them. They don't have to rely on someone in the know to open the door. Even experienced traders have access to recordings that they probably would have not been able to access before. Secondly, concert recordings circulate much more quickly now. In the past, even if a show was in your own country it would take at least two or three weeks for a recording to circulate, with recordings from other countries taking much longer. Today recordings can be circulating around the globe just a few hours after a show has ended, no matter where it happened. And, despite the expansion, some of the old collectivist ethos still remains, with most torrent-sharing sites maintaining strict sharing ratio requirements to ensure that users upload as much as they download.

At the same time, however, much has been lost. The social practices involved in trading have been transformed. Ironically, the shift from (offline) *trading* to (online) *sharing* has undermined some of the social bonds that were integral to the subculture, changing a one-to-one relationship into a one-to-many. There are no longer little notes accompanying a new batch of recordings in the mail; recordings can no longer be associated with a particular place they came from or were sent to, or with a particular individual who sent them. Today, often the most personal connection one receives is a plain 'thanks', written by someone using a pseudonym, listed in the comments underneath the uploaded torrent.

The shift to online sharing has also had an impact on the material that is traded/shared. For one thing, there is now just *so much stuff*. Seemingly everything is available: an online database of circulating Bob Dylan audio recordings has 13,319 different entries, while another lists 2,249 DVDs. One can download every circulating recording of the Rolling Stones (studio, concerts, interviews, obscurities) in a number of torrent files split by year. Even if one were to download the half a terabyte of data, how does one begin to make sense of it, let alone listen to it? However, while multiple recordings of concerts may be more bounteous than ever before, there is a relative lack of what many regard as the most interesting and valuable material, such as studio out-takes. The decline of commercial bootlegging has contributed to a drying up of the well. For sure, remarkable and noteworthy recordings do occasionally emerge outside official channels, but these instances are far rarer than in the 1980s and 1990s. Finally, the shift online may have made everything more convenient but it has also arguably made everything feel a bit too easy; the effort that was needed in tracking down a recording, of finding someone who had it (or who knew someone who had it), of trading for something they needed just so you could get what you needed, is no longer required. Everything is available, pretty much on tap. Crucially this means that there is *no waiting* involved. The gap between learning that an exciting new recording exists and being able to hear it is almost zero; there is no time to imagine, to fantasise, to generate desire. Delayed gratification has been replaced by instantaneous glut, and the end result is that everything just seems a bit more mundane.

In many ways, then, what has happened to tape-trading mirrors what is happening to popular music more generally. The over-abundance of recordings, the speed with which they become available, the way in which they are becoming divorced from their social origins, all contribute to a situation in which music is becoming more fragmented, harder to make sense of in a coherent way and – perhaps – more mundane. What was once understood (perhaps rather quaintly) as a subversive alternative to mainstream music consumption actually turns out to have been riding an identical wave.

2 Toward a History of Digital Music: New Technologies, Business Practices and Intellectual Property Regimes

MARTIN SCHERZINGER

There is no *document* of civilization which is not at the same time a *document of barbarism*. WALTER BENJAMIN, 1969

From Servility to Precarity: Music's Heterologous Cycles of Boom and Bust

This chapter outlines a brief history of the economics of music in an age of technological change. Instead of isolating the present as somehow exceptional, the chapter demonstrates both ruptures and continuities with the past. Drawing on methods from science and technology studies, legal theory, political economy, and musicology, it passes through a series of schematic reflections on the economics of musical production in the last two hundred and fifty years. The chapter attempts to historicise musical labour practices in the current age of technological automation, up to the implementation of lock-down technologies at the turn of the twenty-first century.

Music has long had a vexed relationship with modern economics. The industrial and agricultural revolutions of the late eighteenth and early nineteenth centuries, which had gradually created the conditions for higher material standards of living for a greater percentage of Europeans, for example, did not actually coincide with an uptick in support for professional musical composition and performance. In fact, due to the expense of music before the age of mechanical reproducibility, the changing political landscape – in particular the feudal reforms at the turn of the eighteenth century – led to a generalised *de*-escalation of paid cultural activity. Not only was music regarded as a luxury good (defined in economics as one whose consumption rises exponentially with increases in income), but it was expensive – tethered to what economists call a *derived demand* for additional goods, including instruments, teachers, sheet music, and therefore also academies of learning, publishing houses, and so on. The European courts – politically linked to various feudal principalities, local kingdoms and dukedoms after the Treaty of Westphalia (1648) – had provided significant economic support for composers and performers in the seventeenth and early eighteenth centuries. One of the consequences of feudal tenure reforms of the mid-eighteenth century was that wealthy feudal landlords and court nobility – once a significant support for musical talent – began to cut back on musical consumption. In the late eighteenth century, a host of court orchestras were shut down, for example, and a generalised ethos of frugality ensued (see Blum 1978, Moore 1987 and Baumol and Baumol 1994). According to the economist F. M. Scherer, it would take a century before the emergent capitalist class – solicitors, barristers, entrepreneurs, bankers, industrialists, government functionaries, financiers, and the like – had consolidated into a coherent enough bloc of private wealth to match the noble patronage of the previous century (Scherer 2004, 138, 141). Scherer demonstrates the way composers in the early freelance economy were enjoined to cultivate various precarious strategies for self-promotion, financial backing, press coverage and additional labours in excess of composing and performing. Remuneration varied wildly – a function of unpredictable access to commissions, performance opportunities and dedicated patrons. Piracy – including the illicit copying and theft of scores – placed an additional burden on composers in the period following the reign of the noble courts (who had hitherto owned the rights to all commissions extended to composers in their service). Wolfgang Amadeus Mozart, for example, eluded the theft of his works by giving only partial scores to copyists, forcing them to work in his apartment, and even defacing certain revisions – a kind of pre-modern *reverse-hack* in the context of rampant piracy. As a result, the livelihood of composers could be short-lived. Mozart, like many others – Franz Schubert, for example – was a well-known composer, but he was sick and debt-ridden, and he died in poverty in his early thirties. By the mid-nineteenth century, musical performance and composition had largely relocated from the noble courts to concert venues in a handful of free cities. It had also become a less servile and more precarious market-oriented economic activity – a kind of individual freelancing enclosed within large-scale cycles of boom and bust.

The various economic periods of expansion and contraction did not affect all sectors of music's economy equally. While modern boom economies are ordinarily associated with high employment and good investment returns, the reality is often considerably more complex, especially in the context of musical production and performance. Technological developments too – from innovations in instrument design and lithographic methods for music printing to infrastructure revolutions in transportation and large-scale networked communications – did not uniformly drive profitability or well-being for all stakeholders. The meteoric rise of upright piano production in the second half of the nineteenth century, for example, reorganised the way music was consumed in the context of European and American family life. New mass production methods introduced in the 1850s resulted in both improvements in the quality of pianos and a decrease in their sale prices. By economically scaling piano production (first in the United States and then elsewhere), musical performance had spread from churches, noble courts and opera houses to civic buildings, concert halls, and finally ordinary homes. By the turn of the nineteenth century, the player piano, an automatic music inscription device, had also made its mark on both European and American middle-class markets. The demand for piano music soared; arias, cavatinas, even choruses, overtures and other popular forms were arranged for piano and received widespread distribution from networked publishing houses. The distribution records for Europe's then-leading music publisher, Breitkopf & Härtel in 1823, for example, indicated that works designed to be played at home by amateurs (sonatas, theme with variations, simple piano reductions, duets, songs, etc.) dominated the publishers' inventory holdings (Scherer 2004, 190; see also Clapham 1979). On the one hand, this demand for easier music was a financial boon for composers; on the other hand, these easy pieces, the least remunerative form of composition, also proffered diminishing returns. Publishers, who often bundled these smaller works into collections, largely held the upper hand over composers in matters of compensation (Scherer 2004, 189–90; see also Moore 1987, 331–3). An impressive roster of disaffected composers – from Johannes Brahms, who complained that his publisher Fritz Simrock was overcharging for his works (hence preventing them from wide circulation) to Richard Wagner, who was constantly wrangling with both Breitkopf & Härtel and Schott – testified to the asymmetric relations between (even the most famous) composers and their publishers in the economic heyday of the modern industrial piano. To be sure, in times of evident economic growth, stakeholders in the business of music did not fare equally.

The dramatic expansion of piano production during the second half of the nineteenth century would itself enter a period of sharp decline in the early twentieth century. This was a market fluctuation that could be correlated, on the one hand, to technological change – in particular, the emergence of radio as a broadcast medium and a shift from mechanical to electric phonography – and, on the other hand, to the stark economic fallout of the Great Depression. By the end of the 1920s, the piano market had all but dried up, arguably in response to diminished consumer demand. This decline cannot be attributed to automation alone. In sync with the declining demand for pianos, for example, the delivery of player pianos had halted completely in 1932, reportedly destroyed for fuel. (It is no small irony that the last company to produce player pianos shut down in 2011, the era of algorithmically automated digital music services.) On the other hand, new habits of musical listening associated with the spread of domestic pianos had laid the foundation for the next generation of technologically enhanced passive music consumption in the domestic home, namely the (electric) phonograph and the radio. When the Marconi company first experimented with transmitting opera in June 1920, the commercial value of broadcasting was not yet widely understood. In fact, the shift from wireless telegraphy to radio seemed to mark a *reduction* in technical functionality – from an interactive (sender/receiver) communication technology to a non-interactive (broadcast) technology – which initially dissuaded investors. In the United States, the Westinghouse Electric Corporation first offered (free) broadcasts on KDKA in Pittsburgh as a marketing tool for delivering consumers to hardware – the purchase of their radio sets. 'Toll broadcasting' was only considered profitable in itself when AT&T established WEAF in New York City two years later. This was an era in which radio reception also became dependable – the result of various technological improvements, including high-power transmitters, vacuum tubes, and in-built loudspeakers (instead of headphones). By 1927, radio sets had reached one-quarter of American households; three years later, nearly half the population owned one. A period of passive, or relaxed, musical listening had become normative and widespread (Starr 2004).

Although the structural arrangements and legal principles regulating radio differed from nation to nation, music transmission played a large role in the early days of broadcasting. The dissemination of radio had brought with it new political and legal regimes for the social management of sensory engagements with sound. In the United States, for example, radio was regarded as a scarce resource, grounded in a licensing system for private broadcasters, while, in Europe, radio was a largely government-run broadcasting system, financed by tax regulation. The legal construal of radio as a *public* service (on both sides of the Atlantic) placed certain restrictions on broadcasting content. In the Radio Act of 1927 in the United States, for example, the Federal Radio Commission (FRC) spelled out that licences could be granted to broadcasters only if the 'public convenience, interest or necessity will be served thereby', a position that oversaw the removal of purportedly controversial content – including anti-Semitic preaching, fortune-telling and fake science as well as birth control advocacy, opposition to lynching, and defence of civil rights (by, for example, the American Civil Liberties Union). One organic outcome of these legal regulations was a shift in content toward inoffensive, conventional and standardised broadcasts. The ethnic nationality hours, labour news and church services that characterised programming in the early

1920s were replaced by variety shows, soap operas, and above all *musical* performances directed toward a broad consumer market in the 1930s. Large networks removed anything potentially controversial or offensive for fear of alienating either their southern station affiliates or their advertisers (who refused to sponsor shows that did not align with their market brand). Aside from their ability to balance diverse political and cultural allegiances, the promotion of standardised songs (by lucrative stars) was also linked to new modes of financing culture within the legal contours of a new technological medium. This shift concerned the underwriting of radio broadcasts by sponsorship and advertising. Initially, advertising on the radio came under the same moral censorship as certain kinds of programming, but by the 1930s, radio became even more reliant than newspapers on advertising. By this time, advertising on radio had become direct and insistent – a kind of pervasive parallel auditory exposure to commercial products that inter-rupted (at regular intervals) both the 'sustaining' content (paid for by the network) and 'sponsored' content (paid for by advertisers) (Marchand 1985). Listeners came to experience radio music as a free service, under-written by aural billboards that were linked either to corporate sponsors of the programme or advertising agencies (hired by corporations).

As a vehicle for financial returns, music was an ideal medium for early radio transmission. First, as a largely non-informational medium (and therefore uncontroversial practically by definition), music readily eluded the censorious dimensions of the Radio Act of 1927 (and its various revisions throughout the twentieth century). It should be noted, however, that music by black Americans, construed as 'obscene' and 'indecent' in the early days of radio, was the notable exception to this basic principle. Second, music was an ideal vehicle for product placement in the context of early prohibitions on radio advertising. Brand names were frequently inserted into dialogue, while songs and performers were often named after their sponsors. Examples of branded performers in the early Tin Pan Alley era included the Palmolivers (Frank Munn and Virginia Rea, known as Paul Oliver and Olive Palmer) and the Vicks Vaporub Quartet, whose music included light jazz, show tunes and easy opera. Third, music doubled as both the content of the programme and an advertisement promoting itself as a commodity. The dissemination of music on the radio thereby delivered listeners to a second-order (albeit more traditional) distribution network for both sheet music and (eventually also) gramo-phone record sales. Importantly, the sales figures for records actually decreased in the first two decades of the radio era. This dip reflected the perceptual elision of promotional material with owned content during straitened economic circumstances. As a result, the early struggle between the American Society of Composers, Authors and Publishers (ASCAP) and

the National Association of Broadcasters (NAB) involved selective references to the meaning of radio music – understood, on the one hand, as
commercially purchased content, and, on the other, as a promotional
vehicle for content. In other words, ASCAP sought a fee for licensed music
that was programmed for radio, while the NAB argued that radio provided
free exposure for music, thereby bolstering (sheet) music sales. By the mid-
century, however, the tables had turned: far from soliciting a fee, record
labels were actively soliciting (and even illegally paying for) airtime from
radio executives and DJs. Phonograph production had burgeoned into a
large-scale industry, underwritten by a business model that basically
remained intact until the end of the twentieth century. Each technological
shift – from the long-playing record (LP) to the compact disc (CD), by way
of the cassette tape and a host of additional (often failed) formats –
disrupted some aspect of the industry as much as it amplified another
aspect. The wholesale shift to digital formats in the late 1980s, for example,
produced an artificial boom in music sales, whereby consumers were
enjoined to expand – and often duplicate – their existing vinyl collections
on CD. But not all technological changes heralded sales increases. After the
Second World War, it was sheet music sales that dipped, for example,
emerging by the end of the century as a minor (if robust) sector of the
music industry.

The meteoric rise of radio broadcasting in the 1920s would not have
been possible without the advances made in recording technology some
twenty years earlier. Emile Berliner's refinement of Thomas Edison's
phonograph (talking machine) in the late nineteenth century – substituting Edison's tinfoil/wax cylinder with a flat metal disc, for instance, and
etching the recording on both sides of the disc – greatly improved the
recording quality of music, and furthermore cast the music in a more
robust and reliable material form. The modern gramophone was now
fixed, durable, affordable, mobile, and above all readily reproducible.
Recorded music and sound became raw material for a host of additional
industries, quickly migrating into cinemas, cafés, dance halls, and department stores, and, of course, onto radio. The traditional coordinates of
musical culture had radically shifted. If the late nineteenth century marked
a traditional period characterised, on the one hand, by amateur music-
making in a domestic setting, and, on the other, by the rarefied ritual
attendance of specialised musical concerts, professional operas, operettas,
vaudeville, and so on, then the early twentieth century marked a musical
culture that had transformed into a ubiquitous, commercially amplified
soundscape of recorded music.

Over time, the de-skilling of a music-performing class of musical
amateurs simultaneously produced a new class of skilled recordists,

songwriters, publishers, lyricists, arrangers, promoters, cover illustrators, brokers, broadcasters and businessmen. Commercial songwriting, for example, once a semi-skilled hobby involving meagre financial returns, became a lucrative business in the era of recorded sound (Suisman 2009). Stephen Foster, a well-known songwriter in the era before recorded sound, earned a meagre sum for his well-known songs, while Irving Berlin was heralded as a kind of superstar in the context of Tin Pan Alley a few decades later. This is because publishers, still the centre of economic power in the industry, strategically stimulated demand for recorded music by promoting a select group of branded songwriters (such as Berlin, Jerome Kern and George Gershwin) and performers (such as James Aldrich Libby and Virginia Rea), using novel techniques of distribution, repetition and promotion (or 'plugging') at baseball games, train stations, parks, dances, nickelodeons, restaurants, department stores and cafés. The standardised verse-chorus structure of popular songs was itself a calculated transformation of (largely chorus-free) vernacular song forms, designed to enhance sales (Suisman 2009). The mechanism was simple: Aided by 'boosters' (paid claques integrated into groups, crowds and gatherings) that burst 'spontaneously' into the chorus of the song in public, commercial music could be promoted in the seemingly de-commercialised context of communal singing. By the late 1920s, boosters were largely replaced by radio transmission, which became a natural conduit for analogously promoting and amplifying a targeted set of songs by intermittent repetition.

In sum, in the early twentieth century, music – seemingly dematerialised by recording technologies – was actually radically *re*materialised as a durable commodity, a fixed entity for private consumption. The legal insistence on a tangible medium to secure the benefit of copyright protection (about which more below) was extended from musical scores to phonograph recordings. Music's modern materially documented form thereby dramatically expanded the archival scope and economic authority of its circulation. A once-ephemeral experience was transformed into a widely disseminated repeatable one, captured in a tangible medium that was legally vested in a host of property rights. The convergence of sound recording and radio broadcasting, which played a considerable role in disseminating commercial music into both domestic and commercial spaces, completely altered the contours of musical consumption and distribution. In America, the various Radio Acts of the 1920s, followed by the Communications Acts of the 1930s, became foundational pillars for media policy. Broadly speaking, though they were nationally owned, the radio airwaves were ultimately privatised on a model of trusteeship, which meant that networks could largely control the new electronic portals to the American public. In Europe, broadly speaking, radio was a government-run broadcasting system, while in Britain, a quasi-independent public broadcast model was developed. In general, therefore, radio in America (and elsewhere) was primarily characterised, first, by a model of federal licensing and regulation; second, by monopolised network domination such as the National Broadcasting Corporation (NBC) and, by the late 1920s, also by the Columbia Phonograph Broadcasting System (CPBS, forerunner of CBS) in America; and, third, by the integration of programming with the interests of advertisers, sponsors and advertising agencies. Of course, the details were often more complex than this brief sketch permits. For instance, though they were largely private independent entities, American radio networks occasionally overlapped with music content providers as well – CBS, for example, was financed by the Columbia Record Company – thereby streamlining the dual economic imperatives of music recording and distribution.

To remain within the American context, the Federal Communications Commission (FCC – successor to the FRC) in the era of the New Deal adopted two important policies that reshaped the structure and content of radio for decades to come. First, the commission renounced the ban on editorials, adopting instead the Fairness Doctrine (which required broadcasters to offer reply-time for disagreement about controversial news or public affairs programming); and, second, the commission placed restrictions on radio ownership, effectively limiting each network to a single station in any geographical area. In 1943, for example, the Supreme Court upheld the FCC ruling, and NBC was forced to sell its 'blue' network to the American Broadcasting Company (ABC). It was in the context of radio regulations that emphasised localism, public interest and competition that rock 'n' roll came to flourish. But the pressure toward radio monopolies would persist until the end of the century. With the passing of the 1996 Telecommunications Act, restrictions on radio ownership were lifted once more. Within a few years, deregulated radio became vertically concentrated and horizontally integrated to an unprecedented degree. By 2002, Clear Channel Communications and Viacom alone controlled over 40 per cent of the US radio market. Clear Channel was also the world's largest broadcaster, concert promoter and billboard advertising firm.[1] The record industry, too, had become one of the most concentrated global media markets: six leading firms – PolyGram, EMI, Warner Music Group (a unit of AOL Time Warner), Sony Music Entertainment, BMG (a unit of Bertelsmann) and Universal Music Group (a unit of Vivendi) – controlled between 80 and 90 per cent of the global market (Herman and McChesney 1997, 43). Corporate consolidation between these firms had continued unabated in the years following, and by the end of the first decade of the twenty-first century, the six major labels had dwindled to three. But by then, the Internet had ushered in an entirely different music delivery system, which would challenge the authority of music's centralised corporate blocs in an unanticipated new way – not by way of regulative measures passed by Congress or the FCC, but instead through social networks that took hold on the borderline between the legal and extra-legal.

Tragedy of the Commons: From Torrent to Stream

As with the radio spectrum in the 1920s, the early Internet was also regarded as a public resource, initially developed in the context of American military strategy and thus funded by tax revenues. Unlike radio, however, the Internet was not considered as a medium marked by spectrum scarcity. Although it had the capacity to broadcast and disseminate information, the Internet was therefore legislated less by principles regulating radio and more by those regulating the telephone. The legal classification of the Internet actually intersected two technologies – telephony (characterised by bi-directional one-to-one communication), on the one hand, and radio (characterised, at least by century's end, as unidirectional one-to-many communication), on the other. As a result, online expression was protected by the First Amendment (and hence less censoriously handled than it was on radio or television) and broadband Internet access was classified on the model of 'common carriage' – a bedrock historical principle attendant to telephone signals. Due to the sheer volume of information and data aggregated online, it was impossible for any internet service operator to offer direct and complete end-to-end transmission between content providers and consumers, adopters, and end users. As a result, most content requested by users traversed several different networks, which potentially became a chokepoint for the flow of data. However, since the Internet was initially grounded in the telephone infrastructure, there was a prohibition on any form of broadband discrimination between either network operators, who offered hosting services to content providers, or internet service providers (ISPs), who offered internet connections. The common carriage principle – rooted in legal understandings of telephony, and later dubbed 'net neutrality' by Tim Wu (2003) – persisted until 2018, when the FCC, and then the US Congress, eventually voted to dismantle it.

The combination of open access and free speech protections brought with it the promise of a decentralised and disintermediated digital architecture (i.e. an economy in which middlemen are removed) grounded in new efficiencies of peer-to-peer (P2P) connectivity and search functionality. The record industry boom of the 1990s, aided by monopolist collusion in the context of the aforementioned shift from analogue (LPs) to digital

(CDs) – no less than the re-monopolised radio airwaves – reached a tipping point in 2000, after which it slid into a seemingly terminal economic decline. Within a single decade, an entire generation of young listeners was ripping, burning, downloading and sharing music files outside traditional circuits of exchange. Widespread downloading – dubbed 'musical piracy' by detractors – became associated with an entirely new cultural logic of music-making. The established music industry was being undermined on various fronts. For example, the legally indiscriminate use of samples in the form of remixes and mashups became a distinctive compositional practice in the early 2000s. At the same time, official industry releases were often pre-empted by leaks, excavated by insiders associated with digitally networked underground internet 'scenes' (sometimes known as the 'darknet'). By 2002, for example, albums by Metallica, Tupac Shakur, Lil Wayne, Dr Dre, Jay-Z, Queens of the Stone Age, 3 Doors Down, Björk, Ashanti, Ja Rule, 50 Cent, Kanye West and many others had been leaked by Rabid Neurosis (RNS), an internet chat group associated with music piracy (Witt 2015, 73, 140, 220).

Artists and labels took various approaches to this new reality, often paradoxically benefiting from giving away music free, and paying the price for withholding it. One approach was a kind of reverse-hack, recalling some of the peculiar antics for undercutting piracy in the age before copyright protection – Mozart's defacement of his own scores, for example, or his release of only partial scores to copyists. Likewise, in 2003 Madonna would upload a decoy MP3 onto some file-sharing networks, carrying a recording of her voice asking, 'What the f*** do you think you're doing?' When users attempted (illegally) to download the song, they heard the scorning voiceover instead. In response, enraged music fans mounted an anti-Madonna campaign featuring an online contest for the best techno, trance or house remix of Madonna's voiceover. One hacker even managed to post tracks from *American Life* for free download from Madonna's own website (Scherzinger and Smith 2007). In stark contrast, Lil Wayne simply capitulated to the new reality of illegal downloads, and made his entire output available online for free download. In addition to legitimate album releases, Wayne then also released several free 'mixtapes' as ends in themselves. The mixtape had historically been a kind of demo tape crafted to secure a contract with a label; Wayne was using it to secure his freedom *from* a label. His strategy paid off, and by 2006, Wayne was earning accolades from established critics, less for his albums than for his mixtapes (Witt 2015, 201). While the informal trading of files initially produced a spike in record sales (indicating the promotional value of early online piracy in the absence of widespread portable MP3 players), the traditional music industry lost half of its mass within seven years. The devaluation of recorded music in the first decade of the twenty-first century thereby recapitulated the decline in sales figures for phonograph records in the early era of radio a hundred years earlier; and, as it was for the radio era, the economic decline would turn out to be temporary.

The common narrative describing the emergence of online music circulation generally emphasises a period of crowdsourced mass piracy in the context of independent and open networks. The actual reasons for the decline of the traditional music industry, however, are complex and over-determined – the result of contradictory actions and reactions from a range of technical and social actors, on the one hand, and political and economic stakeholders, on the other. Networks of regulatory agencies, legal personnel and standards bureaus confronted innovations by computer programmers, audio researchers and signal-processing specialists; while a new generation of online hackers, netizens and ordinary internet adopters confronted restrictions imposed by music industry executives, security officers and legal personnel. For example, one of the most forward-looking techno-logical breakthroughs for transmitting high-fidelity music files using min-imal data was initially deemed a commercial *failure*. In the early 1990s, the Fraunhofer Institute for Integrated Circuits developed a rule-governed system for compression-decompression that could transmit digital record-ings using less than one-tenth of the bandwidth associated with the com-pact disc. Fraunhofer deployed a combination of psychoacoustic masking techniques (computational protocols for evacuating inessential frequencies of a sound signal) and a Huffman coding technique (an algorithmic routine for reducing pattern redundancy). This kind of low-bandwidth transmis-sion was designed for the Internet-enabled personal computer market, which had grown considerably in the 1990s – a decade not unlike the 1920s, marked by the meteoric rise of household radio sets. The new technical format, known as the Moving Picture Experts Group, Audio Layer 3 (or MP3), was met with some limited success – MP3-bearing 'Zephyr' boxes, for example, broadcast the National Hockey League, and then about 70 per cent of all sports by the late 1990s – but, throughout the decade, the MP3 remained locked out of its target PC market. Large players in the record industry (such as BMG) rejected Fraunhofer's vision of an online 'digital jukebox', and a rival format (the Philips-designed MP2) was favoured by the standards committees in the early 1990s. As a result, Fraunhofer designed a floppy disc encoder in 1995, known as L3Enc, which they promoted by giving it away *free* online, with the option of leaving a donation (Witt 2015, 21, 55; see also Sterne 2012).

As with MIDI-enabled keyboards in the 1980s, Fraunhofer's was a 'free' product aimed at creating technological path-dependency for users and adopters. The first MP3 player for Windows, known as WinPlay3, was released in 1995, also free, but disabled after a limited number of plays. By 1996, L3Enc software had been hacked and was being used to share (illegal) music files online; WinPlay3 was also hacked to enable full functionality; and serial numbers for L3Enc and WinPlay3 had been intercepted from links to the Fraunhofer FTP server (Witt 2015, 50). Newly networked online communities were deploying Internet Relay Chat (IRC) channels – privately operated servers using hashtags to indicate different interest groups – to disseminate pirated software (known as 'warez') and musical files (including pre-releases) online. RNS, mentioned above, was one such community involved in the dissemination of pirated music and software as well as various album leaks. In 1997, WinPlay, a derivative of the official Fraunhofer MP3 player, had been downloaded several million times, and by 1999 a single website, Napster, had connected twenty million users to a centralised library of songs. Downloading music online and file-sharing had moved from IRC channels into the main-stream. This presented a dramatic challenge to the classical economic model for the music industry and unleashed a series of lawsuits against all manner of potential lawbreakers – including individual users, P2P operators and hardware suppliers. For example, the Record Industry Association of America (RIAA) sued Diamond Multimedia Systems, the MP3 device makers; and a conglomeration of record companies sued Napster for copyright infringement across its P2P network. Napster lost their case, but – because of Section 512 of Title 17 of the US code, known as the 'safe harbour' provision of the 1998 Digital Millennium Copyright Act (DMCA) – Diamond won their case, and portable MP3 players could still be sold. Fraunhofer might have failed to secure official international recognition for the MP3 as a technical standard, but the sale of portable MP3 devices in the wake of *RIAA* v. *Diamond* brought the company considerable success.

In 2002, Apple's online iTunes Store also took advantage of the court's ruling, and began to offer legal downloads of songs (sold on a per-unit basis) for their portable devices. Napster, still operating in a kind of networked gift economy, had effectively laid the groundwork for Apple's rise to market dominance, forging the way toward an efficient and inter-active new model for musical listening. As it was for Westinghouse in the 1920s, Apple was as vested in delivering consumers to hardware as it was in promoting and selling music. Two key points illustrate this additional economic prerogative. First, Apple tailored the launch of iTunes with a business plan aimed at creating a 'balance between the industry and music listeners', tethered to a marketing campaign deploying the cool rhetoric of interactivity and freedom (Cosentino 2006, 196). The first Apple advertising campaign, revealingly titled 'Rip, Mix, Burn', was thus able to gain traction on the tactile, mostly illegal, behaviour of a generation of online users (already habituated to P2P sharing, free downloading, and self-curated playlisting). Apple thereby channelled an informal, but widespread, millennial *habitus* of (illegal) online music stockpiling toward the purchasing of licensed music. As a result, they also cornered the early market on a generation of mobile music devices that operated on the basis of downloads instead of CDs. Second, Apple initially disabled the MP3 format, locking users into the AAC format instead, and even deploying a DRM system called 'FairPlay' to block MP3s from playing on their devices. However, they eventually capitulated to the widespread demand for MP3 functionality – no less than repeated attempts to disable their DRM system, including the infamous 'PlayFair' hack – in the context of vast online reservoirs of MP3s.

The second major entity to take advantage of the safe harbour ruling was Google, a 'web crawler' that had by then become the world's leading search engine. Between 2002 and 2007 Google had grown by a factor of forty with annual revenues reaching into tens of billions of dollars. Indeed, the word 'google' had transformed into a verb, synonymous with online search itself. In 2006, the company purchased YouTube, an online video community platform launched as a small start-up in 2005. The purchase marked a turning point for Google, who were expanding their operations from a search-based delivery system to curated online content provision. This evolving structure recalled alliances such as that between CBS and the Columbia Record Company, one of only two great monopolies effectively controlling music distribution in the late 1920s and the 1930s. Just as radio ownership had consolidated in a few years into a monopolised structure, so too was the Internet of the early 2000s coalescing around a handful of powerful companies. A few years later, industry commentators increasingly recognised the rising value of gigantic, easily searchable databases for music: 'Eventually, the most successful music companies may not be the ones that create, play, or sell music. Rather, they may be the ones to collect the most music data.'[2] But back in 2006, YouTube – a kind of Napster for video – was still a small start-up, fast growing a reputation for the non-commercial hosting of user-generated content (UGC). Within a year, the site was delivering over 100 million video views per day, and hosting tens of thousands of daily uploads (Wasko and Erickson 2009, 374). YouTube was perhaps the *locus classicus* of online services that characterised what came to be known as Web 2.0. Web 2.0 described a set of internet applications – enabled by new technologies, such as RSS, Wiki and Flash – that facilitated interaction, sharing and exchange among users. Internet users during this period increasingly shared files, uploaded videos, edited encyclopaedias, forwarded information and socialised online. This kind of UGC upended the traditional distributor model for content provision – largely controlled by intellectual property rights – to a network model that operated in a kind of parallel gift economy. Again, as with early radio in the 1920s, YouTube was, at first, an advertisement-free and community-driven content provider. With the purchase by Google, however, advertising soon became the central model for financing the platform. Furthermore, YouTube soon began to integrate its operations with music labels and other media industries. By 2008 YouTube had signed licensing deals with many major players in the content industries – including Universal, Sony BMG, EMI, Warner, CBS, NBC and others – but its business model was primarily tethered to a rapidly expanding internet audience that provided vast swaths of self-generated, *free* content.

Individual users whose videos went viral – early examples included Lonelygirl15 and Happyslip – were signed by YouTube directly, and paid a percentage of the advertising revenue associated with their views. For musicians, the platform held the advantage of bypassing the traditional contractual dependence on the music industry. Artists ranging from Ingrid Michaelson, White Stripes, OK Go, Jonathan Coulton, Arcade Fire, Cactus Cuties and Samantha Morton in the first decade of the twenty-first century to Macklemore, Ryan Lewis, Gotye, Justin Bieber, Carly Rae Jepsen, Milly Rock and The Weeknd in the second decade testified to the success of self-launched musicians in the twenty-first century (Espejo 2009, 7; LaPlante 2009, 28). Not surprisingly, musicians like David Byrne (lead singer of Talking Heads) offered an upbeat assessment of the changing circumstances for creative musicians in the context of Web 2.0 applications such as YouTube. Musicians, Byrne argued, were no longer beholden to producers, promoters, marketers and managers (such as the '360', or equity, deal), but could function entirely independently – their music could be 'self-produced, self-written, self-played, and self-marketed'. Byrne concluded: 'For existing and emerging artists – who read about the music business going down the drain – this is actually a great time, full of options and possibilities.'[3] The sentiment was echoed by Michael Bracy of the Future of Music Coalition, a nonprofit organisation dedicated to the livelihood of musicians: 'Who needs major labels, and Rolling Stone, and MTV? . . . Hundreds of bands, not a single superstar among them, all have significant followings and fanbases thanks to technology' (quoted in LaPlante 2009, 29).

In the early years of Web 2.0, an ethos of decentralised, disintermediated and democratic cultural production came to be understood as a genuine technical possibility. Yochai Benkler, for example, argued that the decrease in computational costs, enhancements in digital signal processing, and network architecture would issue a new model of production sustained by sharing and collaborative volunteerism (2006, 87, 59). Benkler labelled this model 'commons-based peer production', characterised by a digitally networked environment that 'makes possible a new modality of organizing production: radically decentralized, collaborative, and nonproprietary; based on sharing resources and outputs among widely distributed, loosely connected individuals who cooperate with each other without relying on either market signals or managerial demands' (60). In 2006, the jury was still out as to whether platforms like YouTube were a democratising force for culture or a massive reservoir of economic exploitation.

Following the shutdown of Napster, a series of additional P2P networks emerged, including Grokster, KaZaa, eDonkey, BearShare, Gnutella, Limewire and Oink. Aside from services like Oink – a sophisticated and exclusive index of pirated material run by audiophiles – most of these services failed to match the scope and quality of Napster. However, the lawsuits against both networks and individuals intensified. In 2003, over 200 individuals were targeted (and fined $150,000 per song); and by 2005, the RIAA had bought lawsuits against tens of thousands of individual file sharers. Mostly, the heavy-handed nature of the punishment was self-defeating and the RIAA was condemned for its arbitrary and vindictive approach to litigation. In one infamous case – *Capitol Records* v. *Jammie Thomas* (2007) – the defendant (a single mother) was fined $222,000 in damages for sharing twenty-four songs via KaZaa. These individual lawsuits mostly targeted relatively innocent and naïve offenders, thereby evoking sympathy for the accused and antipathy for the record label. A download on Napster, for example, also involved a simultaneous upload (linked to an IP address) by default – a preset that could easily be disabled by tech-savvy users. In the manner of pre-modern punishments, following Michel Foucault's analysis, the music industry was lashing out at the wrong targets in exaggerated fashion. Nonetheless, file-sharing and downloading persisted throughout the first decade of the twenty-first century. Indeed, the introduction of an open-source technology known as BitTorrent – which broke up and distributed files into hundreds of small 'bits' – alleviated some of the bottleneck problems associated with traditional P2P traffic. New sites emerged (such as Mininova, Pirate Bay and BTJunkie) hosting torrents linked to thousands of computers across the globe; Oink too shifted its protocols for file production to BitTorrent. These sites were also eventually taken down or raided. But by then the CD had become obsolete and online music distribution had become the norm. Record labels, which had long resisted new models for generating revenue, finally began to cut licensing deals for streaming media, a form of musical consumption that, from the perspective of the user, resonated with the decade-long practice of building personalised playlists from file-sharing and downloading.

Dialectics of Rights Management: An Allomorphism of the Law

For all the appearance of anarchic circulation of free culture, however, this period also witnessed the unprecedented arrogation of cultural practice by major multinational corporate entities in two – mostly contradictory – senses. On the one hand, the rapacious capacities of search engines, social networks, retail outlets and other online platforms for the surveillance and collection of free data supplied by the public reflected a novel way of instrumentalising capacities that were historically considered non-instrumental. In other words, the very act of musical listening, associated in the twentieth century with affective enjoyment and leisure time, was transformed, in the twenty-first century, into a revenue-generating resource for large corporations – a new form of digital labour, extracted by technical interfaces designed for the capture of data. Far from simply enhancing efficiencies in search functionality, social networking, recommendation algorithms, and so on, the gathering and mining of big data (ravaged from an unprotected public domain) cast light on the paradoxical financial investment corporations had in the *free* flow of culture. Curiously, the progressive embrace of distributed free content (no less than the resistance to the enclosure of the commons) marched in uncanny step with the demands of these economic stakeholders. Designed to externalise every desire, maximise access, proliferate consumption and hasten click-rates, platforms controlled by this corporate sector reflected a vested interest in a friction-free flow of information, grounded in affect. Datasets, in short, were enriched by unbounded subjectivity. One might call this the era of free culture for schizophrenic capital.

On the other hand, the increased institutionalisation of permission-based distribution and access controls undercut the cornucopian image of free content, shared by freely interacting and contributing users, however deftly the apparently unimpeded cornucopia was actually monetised in the age of big data. Once again, the paradox of the Internet – its potential for the surveillance of seemingly friction-free digital traces – had simultaneously intensified the scope and reach of digital rights management (DRM) of copyright-protected culture. Just as the Internet enabled high-speed copying with little quality loss, it also enabled enhanced detection of copying and new opportunities for control and enforcement.

Here, too, music lent itself especially well to this kind of legal encroachment on its public circulation. Most obviously, music – generally consumed by way of repeated listening – opened lucrative opportunities for companies offering pay-as-you-go listening services tethered to access-control protection systems. This rental model offered an opportunity to monetise affective investments – effectively commodifying intangible experience and sentiment in *real time*. In fact, with the passing of the DMCA, the use of technological protections facilitated a system of pay-per-use (view/listen/install), thereby linking access itself to an automatic debit mechanism. In their representations to Congress, the copyright lobby argued that, barring a set of precise circumstantial exceptions, any reproduction of a work was the exclusive right of the copyright holder. Since exceptions had not been enumerated for internet-based copies in the 1976 Act, copyright owners were entitled to monetise all digital copies online. Remarkably, copyright owners argued that this right should be extended to reproductions found anywhere on a computer, including the volatile Random Access Memory (RAM) (Litman 2006, 22–32). The policy manoeuvre was a transformation of traditional copyright law, which distinguished between fixed reproductions (such as phonograph records and books) and unfixed ones (such as broadcasts and exhibitions). Ephemeral copies, such as those found on radio or television broadcasts, reduced what economists call the 'option value' of the reproduction, and were not protected by copyright law. Since a reproduction of a work found in RAM could technically be saved to a hard drive, stakeholders in copyright protections argued that the copy was essentially fixed in a tangible medium. Concomitantly, its option value had become blurred. The fundamental right associated with the copyright owner was the right to authorise the reproduction of protected work that had been *fixed* in a sufficiently stable tangible medium. In the open network, therefore, ephemeral uses of a work were concretely transformed into traceable fixed ones. Consumption could now be regulated in accordance with the fundamental operation of computers. In a context of metered usage (or pay-per-use), music was now potentially becoming an enticing financial prospect for the industry.

It is important to note that the forms of enclosure upon cultural work outlined above were in fact in a contradictory relation with one another. If content industries were invested in cementing access-control protection systems and copy-control protection systems into technological devices and communicative platforms, service providers were invested in the opposite – the friction-free flow of unfettered data points. It is possible to describe the legal outcomes of this inter-industry struggle as a series of detailed negotiations between lobbyists for content industries, on the one hand, and ISPs, on the other. Indeed, with the passing of the DMCA in

1998, service providers were granted an exemption from liability for their users' uploads and posts on condition that they agreed to remove or block access to copyright-protected material when alerted to infringing files by content providers. The safe harbour was the direct result of a negotiated agreement during the 105th Congress on the question of liability for copyright infringement online. But it reflected a pattern of copyright-law-making in the United States that had long taken the form of negotiated settlements between powerful private parties, with sometimes competing vested interests. In the first decade of the twentieth century, for example, the interests of copyright holders (musicians, composers, publishers, and so on) conflicted with those of the then-new 'talking machine' (phonograph), motion picture and piano roll industries. Since the latter were absent from the negotiations in 1906, the bill that emerged did not favour them. As a result, in ensuing conferences, the proposals were modified to better reflect the operations of these industries: compulsory licences were granted for mechanical reproductions of musical compositions, on the one hand, and all jukebox operators were granted a complete exemption, on the other (Litman 2006, 70–7).

For all the appearance of balancing the conflicting demands of copyright law by way of negotiated concessions, these conferences historically facilitated interactions between copyright-intensive businesses and institutions increasingly at the expense of publicly oriented institutions of learning, public domain advocates, and the like. One may speak here of the inertial tendencies of copyright laws passed in the previous century, which generally bore the marks of a relatively narrow set of interests. The occasional benefits to the public (such as the broadcasting provision in the 1909 Act, or, arguably, the safe harbour provision in the 1998 Act) accrued as if by accident; they often represented the symptomatic fallout of an inter-corporate struggle more than a genuine confrontation within a public sphere. In this scenario, public interest was only served in the gaps opened by conflict between powerful industry players. In fact, the tendency to exclude direct discussion of public interests in the lead up to statutory action intensified in the age of the Internet. The decade leading up to the DMCA, for example, witnessed a marked increase in copyright-related campaign contributions to politicians, with the aim of gaining leverage over IP policy in Congress. Perhaps it was not surprising that the provisions of the DMCA witnessed the de facto erosion of a host of exemptions that had been historically granted to under-represented interest groups, public and private alike – jukebox operators, record companies, cable television systems, radio and satellite broadcasters, music stores, restaurants, libraries, educational institutions (such as schools and universities), and so on. The exemptions came under threat because the DMCA included language prohibiting the manufacture and use of *any* device or service that could circumvent copyright protection. The underlying logic of this legal manoeuvre was ensnared in a *non sequitur* known as the *fallacy of the undistributed middle*. Simply put, just because all infringements involve copies does not mean that all copies involve infringements.

But the seemingly accidental legal benefits carried traces of the contradictory forces that brought them into being. It would not be difficult to list an array of logical problems with the provisions of the DMCA, insofar as it renovated the meaning, scope and authority of copyright protection with frequently contradictory effects in actual practice. Take, for example, the case of Napster discussed above. Recall that Napster's technology facilitated access to music collections of geographically remote users. Napster had a central search function, but, since collections were not posted online directly, the model for sharing was effectively decentralised. Napster's model thereby posed a direct challenge to the basic economic principles underlying the legal distribution of commercially valuable information, which had hitherto been controlled by corporate intermediaries (record labels, film companies, etc.). After the largest record labels brought suit against it in 1999 (*A&M* v. *Napster*), Napster was ordered to shut down its then-current operations and reconfigure itself as a commercial platform. The kind of defence that characterised the 1984 'Betamax' case (*Sony* v. *Universal*) failed in this new context primarily because it was argued that Napster had the technical capacity to circumvent infringing uses whereas Sony, in the 1980s, did not. In the case of the videocassette magnetic tape recording format, deployed in relatively closed social networks, infringing uses could not be as readily detected, which led the court to protect the substantial potential for non-infringing uses. Although the question concerning the illegality of non-commercial file-sharing was itself hotly contested and in doubt, *A&M* v. *Napster* effectively opened the door to the pre-emptive circumvention of *any* sharing. One logical consequence of this decision is that, de facto, *all* non-commercial exchange was judged illegal until proven legal. One can detect here not only a case of the fallacy of the undistributed middle, but also the logical impossibility for Napster, in practice, to divert users from infringing/non-commercial behaviour. This was a particularly surprising interpretation given the reluctance of the music industry in the late 1990s to move their retail operations to the Internet.

As Napster rose to prominence, the music industry, under the auspices of the Secure Digital Music Initiative (SDMI) coalition, was formulating technical rights management systems that could be incorporated into devices (MP3 players, CD or DVD drives, flash memory devices) and networks (internet or wireless networks, set-top boxes or modems). The approach was multipronged, including both watermark and encryption technologies. Digital watermarks are sequences of binary digits (bits) associated with a work that enable its identification and tracking. A digital watermark could trigger a technological device to behave in certain ways. For example, it could prompt a device to offer a software upgrade. The upgraded version of the software could, in turn, technically distinguish between SDMI-protected content and non-compliant (unmarked) content, and disable playback for the latter. Even if an artist had released unmarked content, the SDMI upgrade could potentially restrict its playback. By using technological artefacts as themselves a site for legal intervention, DRM of this sort both perpetuated a syllogistic fallacy and automated its enforcement. Unable to register the situational domains that distinguish what was legally permissible to do with a copyrighted work from what was not legal, this kind of automated enforcement asymmetrically expanded the rights of some stakeholders and diminished, if not obliterated, the rights of others. It pre-emptively placed constraints on reproduction and distribution of digital information by embedding copy-protecting technical watermarks, digital locks, licence agreements and encryption technologies, effectively circumventing access controls or authorisation on specified devices, as well as preventing the copying, distribution, viewing, pausing, transferring, or syncing of copyright-protected material.

By shifting the focus from the adoption or *use* of content to the *design* of technical conduits for content, traditional copyright protection was thereby extended from the present into the future, speculatively circumventing *possible* infringement. Such auto-policing undermined uses formerly enabled by the copyright framework, which traditionally balanced the rights of authors and their publics. For example, DRM prevented uses that were in accordance with the 'first sale' doctrine (which permits the re-sale and sharing of works), the religious services exemption (which waives the public performance right in religious contexts), and the 'fair use' doctrine (which exempts a range of educational, domestic and other types of expressive uses of works). This kind of enclosure on sanctioned cultural uses of music paradoxically undermined the proper functioning of other aspects of the law. It had become a kind of *law-disabling law*. The fundamental character of copyright was thereby altered; its operational meanings metamorphosed into different forms even as it retained its justifications *under the auspices of the same basic law*. Like a chemical compound whose composition remains while its crystalline form alters, some of its guiding principles were quietly amplified, others were diminished, and still others abolished entirely. In short, DRM produced an *allomorphism* of the law.

As the details of the law mutated, it became less clear which institutions could appropriately be called upon to ensure its proper functioning. For example, the idea of a 'broadcast flag' – a copy protection system designed for digital televisions and receivers – was considered and assessed by the FCC in 2003 (Gillespie 2007). The traditional role of the FCC was to monitor content for broadcast media (such as radio and television) and to oversee the granting of licences for slices of the spectrum. The broadcast flag, however, was designed to be a government-mandated form of encryption that could detect and monitor the redistribution of television content in a networked environment. At stake in assessing the flag was not the type or quality of content that could be broadcast, but rather the technical character of a technical conduit for content. The commission was becoming caught up in issues that were historically beyond its remit. In the past, the FCC had never been tasked to arbitrate either the legality of technological functionality or the logic of algorithmic computation, such as that associated with the broadcast flag. Indeed, in 2005 the American Library Association (ALA), in conjunction with a collection of consumer and digital technology advocate groups, challenged the FCC's ruling on the flag (*American Library Association et al.* v. *Federal Communications Commission and United States of America*). The ALA argued that the ruling, which pertained to copyright, was beyond the FCC's jurisdiction, and, after some debate, the regulation was officially eliminated in 2011. Nonetheless, as computing and broadcasting converged (and thereby distribution increasingly coincided with consumption), DRM technologies continued to be assembled directly into networks and devices.

Scaled to the level of society as a whole, if technical barriers could be built directly into the communication platforms, devices and networks that were central to contemporary social life – participation in community, commerce, conversation, etc. – then social life itself could be pre-emptively regulated to prohibit circumvention of the law. For example, if manufacturers of DVD players were legally mandated to omit a recording function on their playback devices, or if DVDs encoded a 'regional' restriction on the playback of DVDs, circumvention of copyright protection could not, as a technical matter, take place on those devices. Basing the compensable unit of copyright protection on the *copy* itself – however ephemeral its actual distribution, or however volatile its term in a memory chip – entailed disabling (what many considered to be) a fundamental operation of networked computers: reproduction of files in stable digital form. Under this reading, a new construal of a law undermined a basic technical principle of a new technology.

This is not the only view. Some theorists argued that, far from proliferating copies by operational definition, the digital network in fact rendered copies redundant. In this view, the fundamental principle of the global Internet necessitated the existence of only *one* file. Online streaming services for music and films operated on the basis of this idea: companies like Netflix and Spotify began to deliver content by granting access to a kind of master file in real time over a network (Lanier 2010). In the context of the open network, the need for multiple copies became technically redundant. Of course, this principle was fundamental only to the extent that the system was fast, fluid, widespread and openly accessible. DRM undermined the fundamental aspects of such a system. For all their conceptual differences, then, these interpretations of the digital architecture coincided on the question of DRM. Whether the Internet was construed as a 'giant copy machine', or its inverse, a zero-copy machine, DRM disabled its fundamental method of operation (Kelly in Lanier 2010, 221; Nimmer 2003, 157).

The disabling of technical functionality concomitantly disabled legal defences (such as fair use) which were recognised by a lengthy copyright tradition and a history of case law. Programming the machine to perform below capacity, copyright owners were thereby able to wall off legitimate uses of cultural information and also to remove from the public the very public domain material that was inevitably incorporated into protected works. Lodging the power to disable technical functionality in the hands of a subset of commercial actors, therefore, had significant implications for the future of cultural freedom, legal transparency and social equity. For example, *encoding law* pre-emptively in devices and platforms illegitimately expanded the legal scope of copyright, and even contradicted a fundamental principle of the law itself – the presumption of innocence. Under these conditions, it became quasi-mandatory for all cultural expression and exchange to be structured on the commodity form; music's overtly experiential and social values necessarily shoehorned into commercial terms. With automatic technical controls effectively substituting for legal controls, social life became increasingly operationalised to conform to market values.

Despite the evident encroachment of DRM in the early decades of the twenty-first century, the track record for its successful implementation was, in fact, strikingly mixed. As the *ALA et al.* v. *FCC & USA* case in 2011 indicates, the industry faced considerable setbacks when it came to the direct encoding of law in devices and networks. In the case of the broadcast flag, the pushback emerged from consumer and technology advocacy groups in an alliance with librarians. But the overall countervailing figures of agency actually cast a much wider net. From self-conscious activism and critical academic commentary to the deployment of circumvention technologies supplied by software engineers, wiki contributors, free software advocates, and hackers, the attempt to impose technical restrictions on open networks frequently met its match in the general practice of the unruly everyday. It would not be an exaggeration to say that collaborative P2P networking and sharing, demonstrably indifferent to its legality, had become a dominant sociocultural technique in the first decade of the twenty-first century. The actions of a critical mass of listeners seemed to indicate an interest in music's affective, sentimental and experiential values over and above its monetary ones. As if locked in a constitutive dialectic with the encroachment of DRM itself, the efficiencies in distribution systems, search functionality, P2P connectivity, and so on – the conditions for the possibility of DRM – produced its antithesis, the encroachment of a free zone of decentralised everyday cultural practice. In short, the very attempt technologically to lock down an open network produced a host of unanticipated social effects that paradoxically undermined it.

The decrease in computational costs, enhancements in digital signal processing and networked architectures arguably ushered in a period of cultural production sustained more by collaborative volunteerism than by commodity exchange, market signals, or managerial strategies. Some of this activity operated by way of a strategic incorporation of the law. Examples included the institution of free, or open-source, software, which deployed copyright and licensing law (the GNU General Public License) to undermine its deleterious effects and to foster collaboration, as well as open, peer-produced online reference tools, such as Wikipedia, whose content was likewise released under a GNU Free Documentation License. But the vast majority of P2P production and sharing was simply set adrift from the institutionalised economic structures that were conceived to guide it. While this widespread anthropological reality challenged the economic interests of various content industries, new commercial interests actually capitalised on it. Indeed, the decentralised and nonproprietary practice of sharing and downloading information objects became ubiquitous, practically defining the fundamental features of major corporate sites like YouTube, MySpace, Facebook and Google+. Music played a prominent part in this transformation. In the first decade of the twenty-first century, MySpace integrated their platform with major music labels, Facebook built a partnership with the Spotify streaming service, Google built an online music store linked to Google+, and YouTube became the largest platform for music uploads. The new models for music consumption were built on the success of music in the context of early forms of online networking in the 1990s. Of all the informal exchange that characterised the early days of the Internet, music was perhaps the most successful example of commercial culture that began to circulate outside its market imperatives.

It is instructive to compare the attempts to impose DRM by the music industry with those of the film industry. When DVDs came to the market, the mainstream motion picture studios introduced a content scrambling system (CSS) to restrict their play on licensed DVD players. Manufacturers of DVD players were forced to license the key to unlock CSS descrambling software in their players. The licence specifications included restrictions on the geographical regions in which DVDs could be played and disabled the skipping function for commercials, trailers and copyright messaging that appeared before the movie. While it restricted access, digital encryption like CSS did not actually prevent copying. Manufacturers of hardware were thus additionally compelled to exclude a 'record' function on their players. In short, the DMCA successfully ensured that CSS was implemented as a matter of law. In contrast, recall that the RIAA responded to the rise in amateur file-trading in the late 1990s by introducing the Secure Digital Music Initiative (SDMI). SDMI sought to embed rights management information in musical works via digital watermarks, which could be detected by playback devices to make it impossible to play copies of an illicit file that was once SDMI protected. To ensure that devices were SDMI-compliant, the music industry argued that playback hardware needed to be standardised to trigger the disabling upgrade. The consumer electronics industry had no direct financial interest in imposing proprietary security solutions on their portable digital devices. And yet, despite the inter-industry conflict, an agreement was in fact reached in 1999, which outlined rights management specifications for mobile devices.

Nonetheless, SDMI did not succeed the way CSS did. The failure can be attributed to the unexpected rise of the MP3 as a dominant format for music, as well as the increasing importance of internet-enabled computers doubling as playback devices. The computer and software industries were faced with a different set of business opportunities from those of both the content industries and the consumer electronics manufacturers, and they emphasised the importance of open networks, efficient formats for content delivery, and optimal functionality. The agency of the music-listening public was another important factor contributing to the failure of SDMI. As mentioned, even advertising campaigns by computer manufacturers indicated an allegiance to a new kind of musical culture, characterised by P2P sharing, downloading and collaboration. It is noteworthy in this regard that Apple's relatively low-level digital rights restrictions played an important role in the initial success of iTunes in the early 2000s. Recall that Apple's FairPlay DRM system was eventually abandoned in favour of increased functionality (enabling the conversion of files to MP3 formats, and so on). In sum, music escaped the restrictions of DRM for a variety of intersecting reasons: unstable business models for different industrial sectors; widespread adoption of new digital technology that allowed the public to communicate with a vast audience; the repeated hacking of encryption technologies; and a netizen worldview that emphasised the importance of equal citizens, free information and resource sharing in an open network. For a brief moment in the contemporary history of musical listening, public interest arguably trumped a narrowly proprietary one. The triumph of this kind of public interest, however, was short-lived. By the end of the first decade of the twenty-first century, a moment marked by the onset of streaming media – where online *habitus* was characterised less by interaction between users and more by interaction between algorithms and adopters – the era of Web 2.0 itself reached a turning point. Music's labour relations had mutated into new relations of power: the political economy of musical streaming.

For Further Study

Gillespie, Tarlton. 2007. *Wired Shut: Copyright and the Shape of Digital Culture.* Cambridge, MA: Harvard University Press.

Meinrath, Sascha D., James W. Losey and Victor W. Picard. 2011. 'Digital Feudalism: Enclosures and Erasures from Digital Rights Management to the Digital Divide'. *Advances in Computers* 81: 237–87.

Scherer, F. M. 2004. *Quarter Notes and Bank Notes: The Economics of Music Composition in the Eighteenth and Nineteenth Centuries.* Princeton: Princeton University Press.

Snickars, Pelle and Patrick Vonderau, eds. 2009. *The YouTube Reader.* Stockholm: Mediehistoriskt.

Sterne, Jonathan. 2012. *MP3: The Meaning of a Format.* Durham, NC: Duke University Press.

Witt, Stephen. 2015. *How Music Got Free: A Story of Obsession and Invention.* New York: Penguin Books.

Notes

I would like to thank Monique M. Ingalls, Ariana Phillips-Hutton and, above all, Nicholas Cook and David Trippett for their encouragement and generous engagement with this work. Sections of this chapter draw on, and update, aspects of previous publications, including 'Du téléchargement à l'écoute en ligne: les économies de la musique numérique', *Transpositions: Musique et Sciences Sociale* 6 (2017), and 'Alchemies of sanctioned value: Music, networks, law', in *The Handbook of Artistic Citizenship*, edited by David J. Elliott, Marissa Silverman and Wayne D. Bowman, 359–80, Oxford University Press, 2016.

1 Stephen Marshall, 'Prime time payola', *In These Times*, 5 May 2003, http://inthesetimes.com/article/575/prime_time_payola. All websites accessed 18 September 2018.

2 Chris Faraone, 'How The Echo Nest is powering the Internet's musical brain', *Fastcompany Magazine*, 14 September 2011, www.fastcompany.com/magazine/159/music-database.

3 David Byrne, 'David Byrne's Survival Strategies for Emerging Artists and Megastars', *Wired*, 18 December 2007, www.wired.com/entertainment/music/magazine/16-01/ff_byrne?currentPage=all.

Personal Take: On Serving as an Expert Witness in the 'Blurred Lines' Case

INGRID MONSON

In the summer of 2014, I was engaged by the Marvin Gaye family to serve as an expert witness in *Williams et al.* v. *Bridgeport Music, Inc., et al.* (LA CV13–06004 JAK (AGRx)), a copyright infringement lawsuit more popularly referred to as the 'Blurred Lines' case. I collaborated with Judith Finell, a forensic musicologist with decades of experience as an expert witness in music cases, and the legal team representing the Marvin Gaye family – Richard Busch and Mark Levinsohn. After a highly publicised trial, the jury found that Pharrell Williams and Robin Thicke's song 'Blurred Lines' had infringed Marvin Gaye's copyright of 'Got to Give It Up' and awarded the Gayes $7.4 million. This was a victory for authorial copyright in popular music, but was denounced in many corners of the music industry as something that would hamper the creativity of younger artists.[1] Though I disagree strongly with that assessment, my purpose here is not to respond to criticism, but rather to describe the experience of serving as an expert witness and the main issues that interested me as a scholar.

I accepted the case because it was obvious to me on first listening that there were substantial similarities between the pieces that could not be accidental. In addition, I found it unbelievable that the songwriters would claim their piece was not based on 'Got to Give It Up', after they had given many media interviews in 2013 that marketed 'Blurred Lines' as inspired by it. One of the most common misconceptions about the case is that the Gaye family sued Williams and Thicke when the opposite was true: after a licensing negotiation failed, Williams and Thicke sued the Gayes. The impression that the Gayes had sued Williams and Thicke was created by misreporting in the press.[2]

My initial duties were to transcribe and analyse the similarities between 'Got to Give It Up' and 'Blurred Lines'. In the midst of my preliminary analysis the plaintiffs (Williams and Thicke) filed a Motion for Summary Judgment: this in effect asked the court to rule that there were no triable points of similarity between the pieces, and meant I had to respond to a long list of very detailed claims made by their expert about the dissimilarity of the pieces. Serving as an expert witness means having to respond to detailed arguments made by the other side, no matter how absurd they seem to be, often under severe time constraints. The Motion for Summary

Judgment was denied in late October 2014, clearing the way for the trial. I was deposed for seven hours in December 2014 by opposing counsel. The discursive strategy seemed to be to ask questions designed to get me to say things that conflicted with my own report. One technique was to keep repeating the same question until you equivocated or stumbled. Isn't it true that a half step motion from C to C♯ is completely generic? Isn't it true that there are only twelve notes in music and so you'd expect to have overlap between pieces? The most exasperating moment of my deposition occurred when the opposing attorney misquoted my expert witness report as saying the very opposite of what I had said. He wanted me to respond as if he had quoted me correctly (and have that on record), but fortunately one of the attorneys from our team pulled out my report and helped me to show that I had been misquoted.

The opposing side based their case on the Copyright Act of 1909, which governed 'Got to Give It Up', since it was recorded one year before the Copyright Act of 1976 came into effect in January 1978. The 1909 law required a musically notated copyright deposit (after 1978 a recording automatically registered a piece for protection). Since much popular music was aurally composed, what was filed was generally a stripped down version of the piece containing only melody and chords: in other words, a lead sheet. The 'Got to Give It Up' copyright deposit included an eight-bar bass line, as well as the melody and chords. The copyright deposit for the song was made *after* the recording. The song itself was aurally composed. Our side argued that the truest representation of the piece was the recording.

The 'Blurred Lines' attorneys argued that the Gaye children owned only the copyright deposit, not copyright in the recording. They consequently stressed notational rather than aural evidence as grounds for the existence of similarity. They even petitioned to have the recording excluded from the trial. Judge John Kronstadt initially granted their petition and forbade us from playing the recording in court. A few days later he amended his ruling and allowed us to play only those parts of the recording that were represented in the copyright deposit. Our musical examples, consequently, were limited to bass, melody and keyboard. The jury heard no percussion whatsoever. The testimony of the two expert witnesses was not allowed to overlap, and so the main burden of presenting the musical examples fell on Judith Finell.

My testimony centred on the question of why the combination of accompaniment parts to 'Got to Give It Up' was not generic but rather part of Marvin Gaye's composition. Since Gaye played the bass, keyboard and hand percussion himself, his creative contribution to the accompaniment was not in question. I noted that the bass line had a stop and start rhythmic profile that was related to Motown but not like that of a generically expected Motown bass line. I pointed out that the off-beat keyboard part was similar, but not identical, to a reggae accompaniment rhythm. But I also noted that in neither reggae nor Motown would you expect to find these two rhythms combined. I had listened to hundreds of pre-1977 recordings to make sure. I would have been able to make an even stronger case had I been able to talk about the hand percussion, because there are actually three different rhythm families combined in this very original accompaniment. The opposing side's musical expert cited many examples where one line of the musical texture was similar to one of the tunes, but the remaining parts were different. Our side argued that what made the copying in 'Got to Give It Up' so striking was its *combination* of musical similarities.

My interest as a scholar lies in how, in a Foucauldian fashion, the Copyright Act of 1909 created the object of which it spoke: a definition of popular song as being comprised simply of the melody and the chords. Everything else was considered to be *arrangement*. Adding walking bass lines, drum rhythms, harmonisations and counter-lines was not viewed as compositional, but rather as the application of generic styles to a melody. The law, in other words, encoded a bias against aural composition and groove-based music, which served as the basis of the Williams and Thicke side of the case.

In my work as a scholar of African-American musics, I know that some of the most innovative musical creativity in the genres of jazz, R&B, soul, gospel and hip-hop has taken place in the composition of exactly these accompaniment parts, which musicians call grooves or rhythmic feels. They are not mechanical styles but living, breathing complexes of melodies, rhythms and harmonies that artists have woven and re-woven into the extraordinary recorded archive that forms the lifeblood of African-American and other American popular music. The question of when an innovation in a groove becomes standardised and, hence, generic seems to me to be a fundamentally historical question, requiring careful comparison of specific examples. In the 'Blurred Lines' infringement case, we showed that its authors were 'channelling' not a late 1970s feel, as Pharrell Williams argued, but, rather, a specific piece that served as a template. The audibility of those relationships to the jurors, in my opinion, is why we won.

I do not believe that defending authorial copyright in this matter hampers younger musicians in the ways that some popular music scholars and journalists have argued.[3] Most artists don't brazenly copy multiple parts from one tune. However, the music industry finds it much more profitable to encourage their younger artists to freely borrow from the less protected pre-1978 recordings than to defend its earlier artists. This, too, could happen to today's artists after time passes and their popularity wanes, although they will benefit from being judged by the later law. The recording industry will no doubt try to do to them what, in this case, the 'Blurred Lines' attorneys tried to do to the Marvin Gaye family.

The Williams and Thicke attorneys appealed the trial verdict to the 9th Circuit Court of Appeals. Fourteen musicologists signed an amicus curiae brief outlining the musical merits of the case for the Gayes. The Institute for Intellectual Property and Social Justice also filed an amicus brief on behalf of the Gayes outlining the history of the application of copyright law. Ten musicologists signed onto the brief on behalf of Williams and Thicke. On 21 March 2018, the appeals court upheld the trial verdict in a 2–1 decision. The majority ruled on narrow procedural grounds; the dissenting judge criticised the majority for 'uncritical deference to music experts'.[4] The Williams and Thicke attorneys subsequently applied for an en banc rehearing of the appeal. On 11 July 2018, the request for an en banc hearing was denied.[5] The losing side can still appeal to the Supreme Court, but, since the case turns on evidentiary issues rather than a major point of law, acceptance of the case by the high court is considered unlikely.

In the end Williams and Thicke have only themselves to blame for the decision. It was they and their attorney Howard King who decided to sue the Gayes. They could have simply licensed the song in advance of the release of 'Blurred Lines' or come to an agreement after the Gayes' attorney Mark Levinsohn requested a licensing conversation in the summer of 2013.[6] They responded, instead, by suing the Marvin Gaye family.

Notes

1 Noah Feldman, '"Blurred Lines" copyright verdict creates bad law for musicians', *Chicago Tribune*, 17 March 2015, www.chicagotribune.com/news/opinion/commentary/ct-blurred-lines-robin-thicke-court-perspec-0317-20150316-story.html.

2 *Billboard*, 'Robin Thicke and Pharrell's lawyer to appeal "Blurred Lines" verdict', 12 March 2015, www.billboard.com/articles/news/6495271/robin-thicke-pharrells-lawyer-to-appeal-blurred-lines-verdict; *Boston Globe*, 'Jury finds Pharrell, Thicke copied for "Blurred Lines" song', 11 March 2015, https://www.ksl.com/article/33771659/jury-finds-pharrell-thicke-copied-for-blurred-lines-song?print=1; Alex Stedman, '"Blurred Lines" jury orders Pharrell, Robin Thicke to pay $7.3 million to Marvin Gaye family', *Variety*, 11 March 2015, variety.com/2015/music/news/blurred-lines-verdict-pharrell-robin-thicke-ordered-to-pay-7-3-million-to-marvin-gaye-family-1201450117/.

3 Robert Fink, 'Blurred Lines, ur-lines, and color lines', *Musicology Now*, blog of the American Musicological Society, 15 March 2015, musicologynow.ams-net.org/2015/03/blurred-lines-ur-lines-and-color-line.html; Jacob Gershman, '"Blurred Lines" verdict a "dangerous" threat to creativity, musicians warn appeals court', *Wall Street Journal*, 31 August 2016, blogs.wsj.com/law/2016/08/31/blurred-lines-verdict-a-dangerous-threat-to-creativity-celebrity-musicians-warn-appeals-court/; *Guardian*, 'Pharell Williams and Robin Thicke to pay $7.4m to Marvin Gaye's family over Blurred Lines', 11 March 2015, www.theguardian.com/music/2015/mar/10/blurred-lines-pharrell-robin-thicke-copied-marvin-gaye; Victoria Kim, Randy Lewis and Ryan Faughnder,

'"Blurred Lines" ruling stuns the music industry', *LA Times*, 11 March 2015, www.latimes.com/local/lanow/la-me-ln-blurred-lines-ruling-roiled-the-music-industry-20150310-story.html.

4 Colin Stutz, 'The "Blurred Lines" appeal failed – now what?', *Billboard*, 22 March 2018, www.billboard.com/articles/news/8257580/blurred-lines-appeal-pharrell-robin-thicke-marvin-gaye-legal-analysis.

5 Eriq Gardner, 'Appeals court won't rehear "Blurred Lines" case', *Hollywood Reporter*, 11 July 2018, www.hollywoodreporter.com/thr-esq/appeals-court-wont-rehear-blurred-lines-case-1126253.

6 Tim Keneally and Pamela Chelin, '"Blurred Lines" trial was avoidable: Read Marvin Gaye family's statement', *The Wrap*, 18 March 2015, www.thewrap.com/blurred-lines-trial-was-avoidable-read-marvin-gaye-familys-statement-exclusive/.

3 Shaping the Stream: Techniques and Troubles of Algorithmic Recommendation

K. E. GOLDSCHMITT AND NICK SEAVER

Introduction

In 2005, music futurists David Kusek and Gerd Leonhard proposed treating music as a utility as part of a radical solution to the problem of listeners' increasing unwillingness to pay for recordings. The previous decade had seen a rapid contraction of the recording industry even as other music-related sources of revenue publishing and concert attendance grew (Preston and Rogers 2013). Many listeners were already treating their illegal downloads like a stream of musical information, sometimes downloading more files than they could possibly listen to, sampling music to incorporate into their regular listening (Andersen and Frenz 2008). For Kusek and Leonhard, the metaphor fits: like clean water, listeners should pay a monthly fee for their access to music downloads (2005, 8–12). A decade later, their idea seems to have been realised.

The music streaming market is now globally outpacing sales of physical media and digital downloads, with subscriptions and advertising revenue displacing purchases.[1] After its launch in 2005, the online video streaming service YouTube had become so popular as a place to listen to music via music videos that in 2009 it launched Vevo, a dedicated music video service, and within another year, its own branded music discovery service.[2] YouTube's dominance as a music discovery destination was validated in 2012 when the Nielsen survey showed that young people in the United States were using it more than radio to find and listen to new music.[3] Four months later, Billboard announced it would include YouTube plays when ranking a track's popularity. With most new music available to stream on demand from YouTube's seemingly infinite catalogue, many people no longer downloaded and instead managed their music files between devices that, by the end of the decade, included a smartphone and a computer. Now, companies like Rhapsody, Spotify and Deezer offer on-demand access to large libraries of music for a monthly fee. Although the spread of music streaming has been tied closely to the spread of devices and connectivity, thus tracking with global inequities, the dramatic rise of streaming subscriptions has led to the utility model dominating visions of the future of the music industry (even as 'new' and 'old' media continue to coexist).

As music streaming services have grown their catalogues, they have sought to differentiate themselves not through the music they provide, but through the techniques by which they mediate between users and the catalogue (Morris and Powers 2015). These include interface design, branding and, increasingly, algorithmic recommender systems that direct listeners' attention to narrower selections from the music these services make available.[4] Digitisation decoupled the distribution of music from the limitations of retail floor space, which supposedly enabled niche tastes to flourish in 'the long tail' (Anderson 2008) of deep catalogues – the large amount of music that makes up just 1 per cent of user listening. The notion of the 'long tail' reinforces the widely held belief that it is increasingly difficult for listeners to find new music they like and has driven research into recommendation techniques to aid these listeners (Celma 2010).[5]

Industry and academic researchers have produced a range of techniques for recommending music to listeners, drawing on diverse sources of data, kinds of labour and visions of listening subjects. This chapter explores these efforts in the contemporary terrain of music streaming services, their ties to discovery and taste, and the underlying assumptions about listeners, listening and music embodied in the techniques many of these services employ. We base our perspective on experience – K. E. Goldschmitt was employed by Beats Music as a world music 'expert curator' in 2014 and Nick Seaver is conducting an ongoing ethnography of the developers of music recommender systems. Through a close examination of these techniques and the issues they raise, we argue that the discourse of music recommendation reveals core concerns about music's social role in the early twenty-first century. These concerns revolve around a long-lived anxiety about the relationship between humans and machinery in music.

Consider one predecessor for the metaphor of music 'on tap': Muzak, which by the 1980s represented everything 'uncool' about corporate music. Throughout the last half century, Muzak offered programmed music targeted for work and retail environments through telephone cables, and later broadband, cable and satellite (Lanza 2007). Although Muzak was founded in 1954 as a tool for managers to increase the productivity of workers, by the 1980s it offered clients a customised experience through its famed 'audio architecture'. With the exception of a study by Tia DeNora and Sophie Belcher (2000), critiques of Muzak are often alarmist responses to late capitalism with its emphasis on corporate manipulation and consumerism (Goodman 2009; Attali 1985; Radano 1989). Today, background music in retail environments is more popular than ever as 'music becomes part of the consistency of [retail] space' (Sterne 1997, 23). Playlist design is so important for retail that it functions as a type of branded ubiquitous music taking part in a company's sonic brand (Goldschmitt forthcoming; Kassabian 2013; Powers 2010). Now, online streaming services and programmed music in retail are merging, with many smaller outlets and restaurants using on-demand music streaming recommendation services for their sonic branding.

Although contemporary music streaming services tend to advertise their services as either human, relying on expert curatorial work, or algorithmic, relying on scientific guarantees of precision and scale, in practice all of these services blend human and machine components.[6] This cyborg condition characterised the production of music well before digitisation, whether in the use of instruments, recording technologies, or technologies of circulation (cf. Loughridge and Patteson 2015; Sterne 2003; Katz 2004). As will become clear, these music discovery tools should not be understood in terms of the popular opposition between people and algorithms, but rather as sociotechnical systems that rely on and reinforce particular ideas about human and machine capacities in relation to music.

In early incarnations, streaming music depended upon software that listeners installed on their personal computers. The most common applications were Real Audio Player (from RealNetworks, Inc., founded in 1994) and the QuickTime media player (from Apple, launched in 1991), which could play both audio and visual content from the web. The difference between these two applications was the relationship the user had with the format: QuickTime allowed some content (WAV and MPEG files) to be downloaded directly to the computer for future use when access to the Internet might not be readily available, while Real Audio depended on an active internet connection. Of the two, Real Audio's format most resembles how streaming works today; it broke up the content of large audio-visual files into smaller files that would transmit more easily over a modem and then reassembled them on the user's computer. By the early 2000s, Apple's iTunes had a 'radio' function that consolidated already existing streaming content to one outlet. In the years before portable MP3 players, smartphones and podcasts, these early attempts to stream content showed the potential to work within the constraints of limited network capacity, hard-drive space and mobility while still maintaining audio fidelity.

An early example of server-based music recommendation was Apple's 'Genius', first premiered as a feature of iTunes 8 in 2008. Genius made recommendations based on a listener's local library (with tracks either ripped from CDs or downloaded from a variety of outlets, including the iTunes Music Store). Even then, Genius only worked effectively if the user had an internet connection: the recommendations were computed on

Apple's servers. Like the recommenders to come, Genius was predicated on the information that users allowed Apple's centralised servers to see – in this case a user's library and data about the listening history. As of 2016, the service continues as 'Genius Shuffle', alluding to the iPod's popular 'shuffle' function from a decade earlier (see Powers 2014).

One of the longest-lived music streaming services is Pandora Internet Radio, which, since its launch in 2000 as Savage Beast Technologies, has promoted itself on the basis of its algorithmic recommendations. Soon thereafter came Last.fm in 2002, which allowed listeners to log their listening activity, connect with other 'similar' listeners, and stream music recommended by algorithms on the basis of their listening history. From their beginnings, streaming services have relied on algorithmic recommendation to contour the musical flows they provide, while the availability of the services themselves has been contoured by the vagaries of licensing agreements with the recording industry: Pandora is currently only available in the United States, as it relies on government-guaranteed licences; Last.fm discontinued its streaming offerings in 2014, citing the challenges of licence negotiations, and instead focused on recommendations based on listening histories collected from other services. These other services – Spotify, Deezer and Apple Music are large examples as of this writing – have grown in popularity, although they are generally revenue-challenged, relying on venture capital (Spotify) or profitable parent corporations (Apple Music, Amazon Prime Music, Google Play Music) to keep the musical streams flowing.

As Jeremy Wade Morris and Devon Powers note, the metaphor of 'streaming' implies that listeners gain more freedom and a virtually limitless supply of music while glossing over drawbacks. They show that the dual nature of the services comes down to the word's competing definitions: streams imply the possibilities of 'flowing freely' as well as 'dividing the precious from the worthless' or 'streamlining' to produce improved results (2015, 107). Further, they demonstrate that although streaming is often applied to interruption-free digital media playback practices, the concept has a lengthy history. Now that broadband internet access and smartphones are more widely available, streaming mainly functions in two ways: either the website or application temporarily downloads the file in small chunks to play it remotely, or the file is transmitted from a remote server leaving no local copy. The second version is called 'true streaming' and, as Morris and Powers show, it is the preferred format for music services since it transforms music from a durable good to a single-use product in the name of efficiency and content abundance (2015, 108). This is a radical change from previous values about music consumption such as ownership, fidelity and intimacy of listening in the privacy of the domestic sphere (see Straw 2002; Keightley 1996; Hosokawa 1984; Katz 2004; Taylor 2012; McCracken 2015).

Changing notions of listener privacy draw the sharpest contrast between broadcasting and streaming services. Providers of streaming content collect data about not just the speed and ease with which consumers receive the content, but also what content users access, and even minute data such as whether they listen to an entire track or album and at what point they decide to switch to something else. This contrasts with radio, where stations can only access such information through direct listener feedback through telephone correspondence (e.g. requests and questions about songs) or voluntary surveys such as those conducted by Nielsen. Thus, alongside changing notions of ownership and access, streaming has upended expectations of privacy. The changing role of user data is one of the major compromises that listeners tacitly accept for the allure of seemingly unlimited content.

Techniques of Music Recommendation

Promotional and critical discourse on music streaming recommendation generally rehearses the longstanding divide between machines and humans: while some services advertise the power of their algorithms for making recommendations, others emphasise that they employ human 'curators', hired experts who assemble playlists. Journalists covering this industry often frame new developments in terms of a struggle between humans and machines; for example, John Paul Titlow's 2013 article 'Screw algorithms! The new music service from Beats uses celebrity curators to show you new music'.[7] However, as already stated, all recommender architectures, by virtue of their existence in computers maintained by people, involve both algorithmic and human components. In practice, then, recommendation is not an either/or decision between humans and computers, but a question of how human and computer work is arranged. Thus, in what follows, we do not ask whether a given technique is algorithmic or not, nor do we concern ourselves with locating services along a spectrum from human-centric to machine-centric techniques. Humans and machines are complexly interrelated in all sorts of musicking, and ideas about their strengths and weaknesses are both dependent on each other and historically specific (Seaver 2011). As a result, critics must engage empirically with particular recommender configurations, looking at how they distribute work across humans and computers, and how the capacities of humans and computers are imagined within them.

Here, we investigate the landscape of music recommendation, illustrating the diversity of recommender techniques and their arrangements of humans and machines. Above all, we show how contemporary music recommendation is a heterogeneous affair, often blending many different techniques and data sources.

Curation

With the growing use of algorithmic recommender systems, a number of music streaming services have sought to differentiate themselves as essentially 'human', employing people to produce playlists 'by hand' rather than constructing playlists or radio streams algorithmically, as noted above.[8] Services like Beats Music (now acquired and incorporated into Apple Music), Songza (now acquired and incorporated into Google Play Music), or Tunigo (now acquired and incorporated into Spotify) maintain stables of experts to produce themed playlists organised around genre, activity or mood. The human origin of these playlists is sometimes highlighted: when Beats Music was launched in 2014, for example, it featured playlists composed by celebrities such as Ellen DeGeneres, while PR materials boasted that its curatorial team was staffed by former music critics and radio DJs (under VP of Programming and Editorial Scott Plagenhoef, who had been hired from a position as Editor-in-Chief of the online music magazine *Pitchfork*). Although the humanness of playlist curators is a common trope, their identities are only occasionally revealed. On services like Songza and Beats, when it launched, playlists were not credited to their assemblers but instead subsumed under genre headings: a playlist like 'Inspired by Bossa Nova', for example, was credited to 'Beats World', the identity of its creator subsumed under the corporate banner. Eventually, Beats would reveal the names of its playlist makers, encouraging them to build personal 'brands' that might entice users into browsing more playlists. Upon its acquisition by Apple, these playlists were returned to corporate authorship, under names like 'Apple World'. At the time of writing, Spotify's human-curated playlists (built from the acquisition of Tunigo) are generally credited to 'Spotify', with some exceptions for programming divisions like 'Spotify Latino'. (These do not include user-generated playlists, for which Spotify provides a platform, and which make up the entirety of material on sites like the online radio service 8tracks.)

Timothy D. Taylor (2013; 2016) has argued that both 'the commodification of taste' and the rise of digital music recommendation services incorporating algorithms are part of the broader cultural trends of neoliberal capitalism. He posits that the rising power of Music Supervisors in visual media is a result of their expertise in consumption, a role not dissimilar to playlist creators at services such as Apple Music;

recommendation is part of the broad cultural changes that have also produced multiple approaches to 'search' and 'discovery' for music. We add that these 'hand-picked' curation efforts in subscription music streaming services also show how expert consumption is heavily tied to algorithms on many levels. Once completed, these playlists become material to be recommended by algorithms. While they are being compiled, human playlist makers are aided by a variety of technical supports: most explicitly the charts and analytics of the streaming service, which can let the playlist makers know which songs are popular on a service in order to feature them, or that reveal at which song listeners often stop, suggesting that a particular track should be removed or replaced. (Stories of such analytics-driven insights are commonly related by people working in the industry: irregularities in the logs draw attention to a track with a vocalist inadvertently placed in an otherwise instrumental playlist, or to a jarring segue that rouses the listener to re-attend to the player and change tracks.) In some cases, human playlist makers are assisted by algorithmic browsing aids like Spotify's 'Truffle Pig', which suggests tracks similar to those already in a playlist or filters the large catalogue according to algorithmically induced features.[9]

Collaborative Filtering

Algorithmic recommenders can be broadly divided into two types: *collaborative filters* analyse patterns in listening activity across users, while *content-based* recommenders parse representations of the musical content to generate recommendations. A third type, which is becoming increasingly popular with the spread of smartphones and their attendant capacities for data collection, is *context-based* recommendation, which suggests music based on one's listening location, time, and so on (Seaver 2015).

Collaborative filtering is the most widespread recommender technique, with its origins in 1990s research in the field of information retrieval. Although twenty years of research attention have resulted in a diverse array of technical variations, the basic premise of collaborative filtering is much the same as it was at the start (Goldberg et al. 1992; Resnick et al. 1994; Konstan and Riedl 2012): given a set of users, a set of items, and a set of ratings that link some of them together, try to discern a pattern that allows future ratings to be predicted. This is the commonplace 'Users like you liked items like this' mode of recommendation, and it is considered by researchers to be 'domain-independent': because a collaborative filter needs no special data about the items or the users other than the interaction history represented by the ratings, it does not matter what those items are. With minor tweaks to accommodate different usage patterns, the same collaborative filtering architecture can be used to recommend items as diverse as music, movies, newspaper articles, hotels or recipes. In some cases, the ratings are explicit: users of movie rental service Netflix, for example, may have rated movies on a five-star scale. For music, ratings are typically implicit and usually based on listening history – actions such as repeat listens, adding tracks to a personal playlist, or skipping tracks can be interpreted as kinds of ratings and aggregated together. Once predicted, ratings can either be displayed to the user directly ('We think you will rate this movie 4.5 stars') or used as inputs to other product features: displaying the top twenty predicted ratings in a special 'Recommended for you' section or playing them in personalised radio streams, for example (see Seaver 2012 for a longer discussion of collaborative filtering).

Content Analysis
Dissatisfied with the narrow scope of collaborative filters and persuaded by the idea that the content of objects (how music sounds) is relevant to people's preferences for them, some researchers have attempted to incorporate representations of materials into recommender architectures.[10] These methods are considered 'domain-specific' in that a technique for representing materials in one domain may not be useful in another: a system for parsing the sonic content of a piece of music will not be useful for a hotel recommender, for example. For this reason, general recommender systems research continues to focus on enhancements to collaborative filtering, while work on content-based recommenders is differentiated by the object to be recommended.

Music has invited perhaps the widest range of efforts at content-based recommendation. The most well-known is Pandora's 'Music Genome Project'. Inaugurated in the early 2000s, this project aimed to represent the musical qualities of tracks in a set quantity of discrete 'genes': features such as the gender of the vocalist, the most prominent instrument, the relative tempo, and so on. To determine a piece of music's 'genome', Pandora trains 'musicologists' to listen to and evaluate every track added to the service. The resulting data are used to determine whether tracks are similar to each other, and these similarity evaluations are used to ascertain listener preferences and produce recommendations. Thus, the service may indicate to the user that it is playing a particular track 'because it features busy beats, unsyncopated ensemble rhythms, use of tonal harmonies, a slow moving bass line and a variety of synth sounds' (as it did during one of the authors' recent listening sessions).

While Pandora's personalised radio stations are a well-known exemplar of algorithmic recommendation in the music streaming industry and technology press, they are crucially dependent on human processing that provides the data on which the recommender relies. Corporate competitors have blamed this human processing bottleneck for the relatively small catalogue available on Pandora: while other services boast enormous catalogues limited only by the extent of their licensing agreements, Pandora's catalogue is limited by the listening time of its human experts. Pandora has sometimes adopted the language of curation to defend this catalogue size: the human processing step is presented as a moment of judgment that ensures the service only hosts 'good' music, unlike the massive catalogues of on-demand streaming services such as Spotify.

Other companies and academic researchers have sought to supplant this human evaluation by using algorithmic techniques to process musical sound. Where expert tagging systems like the Music Genome Project rely on trained judgment to assess musical qualities, these other systems use a variety of computational strategies (generally known as 'machine listening') to parse audio data for musically salient features. One of the better-known commercial examples of this work comes from The Echo Nest, a music infomediary company (Morris 2015a) acquired by Spotify. The Echo Nest's machine listening system breaks audio data into sub-second 'segments' that are analysed for their harmonic content; these data are then aggregated at higher and higher orders into information about rhythm, key, tempo and other musically salient features; finally, using machine learning techniques and survey data collected from company interns, these features are mapped on to 'subjective' attributes such as 'danceability' or 'energy'.[11] Thus, The Echo Nest can provide, with numerically scored confidence, not only a track's tempo, but also its danceability (at least according to a system trained by human graders).[12]

Pandora, too, has begun to use machine listening to supplement the efforts of its human experts, providing preliminary algorithmic guesses informed by the correlations between Music Genome data and the audio data they represent.[13] So again, we find a distinction marked as human/algorithmic adopted for rhetorical purposes: Pandora's humans are aided by machines and The Echo Nest's machines are aided by humans.

Ensemble Methods

The various techniques we have described so far are unevenly distributed across the music recommendation industry. Often, particular techniques have played large roles in branding particular companies: Pandora stands for human-annotated music data, while The Echo Nest stands for large-scale algorithmic processing, and Beats Music stands for expert, human curation. However, as we've demonstrated, these companies all rely on humans and algorithms working in conjunction to produce their recommendations. There are no wholly algorithmic nor wholly human music recommendation infrastructures.

The interrelation of humans and algorithms is not limited to the socio-technicality of particular techniques – the people necessary to train machine learning systems or the software that supports the work of expert curators. As streaming services grow and consolidate, they increasingly depend on a wide range of techniques to produce recommendations. Spotify, for example, provides a range of recommendations to its users, who can choose from curated playlists, algorithmically powered radio (which relies on both collaborative filtering *and* content analysis), and an ever-growing set of tools meant to facilitate music discovery such as 'Discover Weekly' and 'Fresh Finds'.[14] These latter are regularly updating playlists that attempt to help listeners find 'new' music: Discover Weekly finds music that is new to the listener, while Fresh Finds highlights music that is newly released. The precise composition of these services is a trade secret, but reportedly draws on a variety of data sources and analytic techniques.

To describe this situation, we can adopt a term from machine learning: the 'ensemble model'. Ensemble models are techniques for aggregating the outputs of many different algorithms. Instead of choosing the single best-performing algorithm for a task, a company might instead employ an ensemble of algorithms, combining their outputs in a custom weighted average. This allows a system to use algorithms with diverse strengths and weaknesses, adjusting their balance such that their performance on average is better than the performance of any algorithm in isolation. So, a recommender system might combine collaborative filtering and content analysis, using data about both consumer listening histories and audio content in a balance that might vary depending on some other variable. A service like Spotify, then, is essentially heterogeneous, offering a variety of recommendation products that depend on a variety of techniques; those techniques are heterogeneous, too, composed out of human and algorithmic parts that are constantly reconfigured into arrangements that make it difficult to distinguish between the human and the algorithmic at any level. While ensemble methods technically refer to the aggregation of algorithmic outputs, we suggest that, given the human–machine collaboration outlined here, the term might be usefully adopted to refer to the whole ensemble of people and algorithms that make up a recommender. Thinking of them in this way usefully reconfigures our attention: Who is conducting this ensemble? According to what principles? What terms govern admission to the group?

Algorithms beyond Music

These musical applications prove useful to make sense of broader algorithmic developments. The rise of music recommendation is part of a larger trend in personalisation: news sites, movie streaming companies and social networking sites all employ algorithmic systems designed to help users find material of interest to them with the goal of keeping their attention. While media industries revolve around algorithmic filtering, other applications of algorithms have also surfaced into popular and critical discourse: computer programs identify potential terrorists, direct police attention to particular neighbourhoods, trade stocks faster than humans can perceive, and evaluate loan applications. While these various algorithms are not all related to one another, they have contributed to a sense that the contemporary moment is defined in large part algorithmically. This 'black box society', as Pasquale (2015) names it, is marked by the operation of hidden computational processes that sort and rank from centres of power. If music recommendation seems relatively innocuous, these other practices indicate the scope and potential impact of increasing reliance on algorithmic processes.

With the newly prominent role they play in cultural life, algorithms have become objects of concern for people outside computer science and mathematics. A steady stream of popular press books is dedicated to revealing how algorithms shape our world (e.g. Dormehl 2014; Steiner 2012; MacCormick and Bishop 2013). Across the humanities and social sciences, a loosely affiliated set of scholars have taken up the task of 'critical algorithm studies', the discourse of which is split between wonderment and fear, echoing the larger trend in writing on technology and culture. This work investigates the biases, power relations and epistemological presuppositions that permeate the supposedly objective and straightforward machinery of algorithms. Legal scholars have focused on the question of accountability and obscurity, i.e. who to hold responsible when a hard-to-access algorithmic system has undesirable effects, such as a disparate impact on minority groups (Granka 2010; Barocas and Selbst 2015; Sweeney 2013). Critical theorists have engaged with the relationship between power and knowledge produced algorithmically, critiquing the popular claim that algorithms offer a less biased and more accurate way to understand human life (e.g. Beer 2009; Mager 2012). Others in the social sciences have highlighted the sociocultural life of algorithms – the human settings in which algorithms are constructed and operated, and on which they rely (van Couvering 2007; Ensmenger 2012; Bucher 2012; Ziewitz 2016).[15]

Scholars have also been concerned with the effects that algorithmic processing might have on culture. Striphas (2015) has outlined the emergence of what he calls 'algorithmic culture', culture that is shaped not only for human participation, but also for computational audiences. The criteria by which Netflix orders movies in its user interface (Hallinan and Striphas 2016), for example, may result in the production of movies with this processing in mind. In music, analogous claims hold that recommender criteria might influence artists to alter their work. Although these influences on cultural production are at the moment speculative, it is clear that algorithms constitute a new audience for cultural materials, decoding them according to potentially novel criteria (Hall 1980). While they may not (yet) determine what musicians do, they play a growing role in boosting the profile of some musicians at the expense of others. Popular music history has seen a relationship between the development of recording formats and musical style: the length of records shaping pop song composition, notions of the rock album as a work of art, and most recently the priorities of recording engineers shaping the MP3 (Sterne 2012). Format shifts have consequences for the political ecology of music (Devine 2015) and point to the potential for algorithmic recommendation to influence musical production – another way that capitalism shapes music (Taylor 2016).

Algorithmic recommendation joins a long history of human and technological interrelation in music, dating back to the heyday of mechanical musical instruments.[16] Music has been a site for anxiety about human and machine capacities, at once a mode of expression considered essentially 'human' and dependent on technical apparatuses. We can consider the contemporary situation as an emerging 'musical assemblage' in Georgina Born's sense: 'a particular combination of mediations (sonic, discursive, visual, artefactual, technological, social, temporal) characteristic of a certain musical culture and historical period' (2005, 8). Like previous musical assemblages, this one involves human and technical components, and to borrow another phrase from Born, we might say that across history, music destabilises the 'cherished dualism' between people and technology (2005, 8). While many critics of algorithms rely on a human/machine dichotomy to express their concern about ostensibly dehumanising algorithmic processes, the case of music troubles this common sense, offering a critical vantage point on similar concerns in other domains.[17]

Troubles in Streaming Recommendation and Consumption

As these different services proliferate, so too do potential problems. The main focus of scholarly and media coverage of streaming services such as Spotify is artist remuneration, spearheaded by lawsuits and threats by high-profile artists to remove their content from the service's offerings. The streaming service Tidal went so far as to harness this discourse of improving artist remuneration and streaming bit rate from its launch.

However, the inviting graphical user interfaces of these services obscure a range of other problems, of which we will consider challenges for niche tastes, privacy and transparency in industry deals.

Metadata Inaccuracy and Challenges for Niche Tastes

Listeners interested in discographical data such as recording dates, composition details and genre accuracy encounter numerous problems with digital distribution, problems that are amplified by streaming recommendation services. The source of these problems is the metadata – the data about the data – that the record companies process during the mastering phase of record production and then bundle into the digital file. As Morris puts it, these metadata 'provide the information backbone of the digital music industry' (2015b, 24) by including such details as sampling bit rates, recording date, artist, track name, album artwork, composer and genre – information that casual listeners ignore but that matters to enthusiasts. In the 1990s, these metadata were largely compiled by fans invested in the CDDB (compact disc database), an open-source online database designed as a hobby by two engineers. Fans volunteered to enter the information themselves, sometimes with errors about who or what counted as genre, artist and composer. These decisions had long-term consequences for artists seeking to expand their audience and users seeking to expand their listening. When the CDDB was purchased by a consumer electronics manufacturer in 1998, those early efforts by fans and volunteers formed the foundation of what the database would be. In 2001, the company shifted direction to a closed-source, profit-making venture named Gracenote (Dean 2004).

Ever since the advent of digital recording and distribution, many of the major record companies have not attended to their metadata, with the result that much of the information in the Gracenote database is inconsistent. This is especially the case for so-called 'world music' recordings and remixes. Prior to the slow decline of physical products like the CD, metadata errors were obscured by the availability of more explanatory liner notes. However, the richness of that information has yet to make the leap to streaming services, and this leaves fans and enthusiasts working with a system that, when it comes to the fine details of recording, is full of errors. The problems that stem from the compromises in metadata are considerably worse for what are largely considered niche music markets that automated services have difficulty reconciling.

In 2015, Anastasia Tsioulcas dedicated a National Public Radio feature to the problems of classical music in streaming services: 'If that metadata is wrong, or – as is so often the case – incomplete, then there's a big problem. Call it the "tree falling in a forest" conundrum: If classical recordings can't be found and heard, they functionally cease to exist.'[18] The author compared her experiences of trying to find a good recording of pieces by well-known composers on a variety of streaming services; she discovered that she could not effectively search for a famous classical music recording on a first try. On Spotify and Pandora recommendations often started in the middle of larger pieces (e.g. the second movement of a concerto). These problems show how basic search and design features of streaming services are incompatible with key values and practices of classical music. Streaming services rely on searching for a single track title and/or artist; in practice, titles aren't standardised, and the artist heading can apply to soloist, ensemble or composer. The result is that the design alienates invested listeners. Such issues are not unique to the present moment but rather are a symptom of new distribution and performance technologies.[19] They also underscore just how problematic it is to use applications designed for popular music in the service of niche genre recommendations – which many of these services purport to be doing.

Jazz is also incompatible with streaming recommendation services due to difficulties in mapping core jazz values onto a track-based interface. In a review of Spotify, Gregory Camp used the example of searching for specific recordings by Ella Fitzgerald to demonstrate the shortcomings of the service for jazz scholars. He stated that searching for a specific recording is considerably easier if listeners recognise album artwork due to the service's 'near-complete lack of discographical information' and 'often inaccurate search function' (2015, 377). The problem is that discographical data such as musicians and recording dates – which are crucial for jazz musicians, researchers and fans seeking a specific solo or arrangement – are not readily available in the interface for most music streaming services and are not a priority for automated recommendation and playlists. It is no wonder, then, that between 2012 and 2015 Blue Note records attempted to rectify these challenges for jazz through a dedicated third-party app that ran within the Spotify interface, allowing users access to the kinds of information dedicated to special edition releases.[20] But of course this discographical information was only available for Blue Note, which is far from the only record label with an extensive jazz catalogue. The need to release that information in a separate app underscores how unwieldy streaming service search facilities and the recommendations based on them are for minority genres.

Metadata accuracy is considerably worse for 'world music', where typos in names and track titles, errors in genre names and inconsistent transliterations replicate across music streaming formats. Often those informational gaps occur when world music tracks are licensed for compilations and mixtapes, but they can also happen when a smaller label hires a digital rights consolidation service to broker licensing and distribution deals (see Luker 2010; Goldschmitt 2014). With so many steps between recording and international distribution, it is no wonder that accuracy gets lost in translation, thereby exaggerating the imbalance in what kinds of music streaming services recommend. In a world music context, metadata inaccuracy is just one example of the ways in which artists continually lose control of how their recorded output is presented, accessed and monetised. In contrast to casual listeners, specialist users who enjoy these genres have to show considerable dedication to make the services work for them; Taylor notes that on Pandora, a user-directed pruning process can lead to a 'precious playlist' that will work with world music genres, but one has to 'keep at it' (2016, 72). Moreover, world music recommendations are based on tracks from compilations by larger labels, and this results in revenue losses for musicians because of the greater number of intermediaries involved.

However, these artists do not always face challenges finding listeners in streaming services; indeed, many niche genre enthusiasts previously relied on specialist retail outlets in large cities, mail catalogues and magazines. When music made the leap to digital distribution, niche record label owners viewed the transition with measured optimism despite the overall bleeding in revenues across the industry. This optimism was due to the opportunities afforded by Anderson's 'long tail': record labels could sell fewer copies of more artists over a much larger geographic area. But this was counteracted by the fact that genres like jazz, classical and world music typically relied on releasing liner notes of considerable heft in comparison with pop music, and, as of yet, this information is not included in the interface. This is troubling given the potential for recommender systems' development to help listeners find more obscure music. Instead, their design aids the discovery of certain kinds of obscure musics to the disadvantage of others. Such challenges reveal the contradictions at the core of these discovery services.

Privacy and Payola

Another issue that arises from extensive use of recommendation services is the loss of user privacy.[21] As noted above, online digital music services keep track of every play, pause and skip to improve their recommendations, part of a larger trend for retailers to better match consumers with content. Some technology futurists and critics have used the concept of the 'Little Brother' to describe such recommendation services. The concept of the Little Brother includes recording and surveillance by individuals and corporations; it first emerged when home movies by private citizens began to effect major political consequences, the first example being Abraham

Zapruder's film of the Kennedy assassination. Its name compares it to Orwell's 'Big Brother' of pervasive state-run surveillance. As Lawrence Lessig points out, the Little Brother of customer service has an incentive to monitor consumption habits effectively and guard those data so that we 'listen' when it makes a recommendation (2001, 132–3; 2007, 132–7). While some privacy advocates urge more protections for consumer data (Solove 2001; Bustillos 2013), the larger consequence of Little Brother is an increase in day-to-day monitoring so that these recommendation services can get the 'context' they claim they need to guide their customers.

Apps on computers and mobile devices are collecting data about users each time we agree to 'terms of service'. Spotify claims to know what kinds of music people use for a wide variety of activities, including such private ones as exercise, sleep and sexual intimacy, through playlist titles and patterns of user behaviour.[22] But these changes to privacy are part of a broader trend and demonstrate a shift in discourses of control, especially as they relate to technology and copyright. There are links between the Little Brother of recommendation services and the effect that surveillance through technology is having on values surrounding privacy. Turkle argues that the constantly changing 'terms of service' agreements with application updates contribute to the growing sense that there is no privacy, and accompany a heightened likelihood of anxiety among the most vulnerable users (2011, 255). Further, she cites anxiety among teenagers who fear the long-term consequences when every choice about culture happens in public, what she calls 'the anxieties of always' (256).[23]

As legal scholar Jessica Litman (2006) argues, change in privacy expectations accompanies larger shifts in how the media industries attempt to control digital content. In analogue models of listening, copyright owners had no ability to monitor how their content was used; today, the ability to collect those data for owners and content providers is assumed without protections for privacy. Given that musical taste correlates with other demographic data, the potential for abuse looms large – especially as it relates to data over invisible characteristics such as mental health, emotional well-being, sexuality and even sleep (Crary 2013). It is not a stretch to imagine how abuses of these data can lead to consequences for individuals across employment and financial services. A different kind of context indeed.

Ironically, curation services that rely on knowledgeable insiders can be even less transparent than algorithmic 'black boxes'. For example, from its launch, Beats gained the trust of record labels that were initially suspicious of online music services by offering them playlists that highlighted their labels – in short, a return to an older record industry promotional model. Since the dawn of popular music publishing in the late nineteenth century, the music industry has relied on various forms of 'payola' to curators in order to promote their products (Suisman 2012; Sanjek 1996). While payola came under congressional suspicion in 1960, the practice of back-room deals to promote artists was 'a process that was already old news' (Wald 2009, 207) a century ago.

Even as new curation services raise ethical issues about industry influence on taste, the configuration specific to this digital musical assemblage obscures their potential for abuse. Record labels regularly find ways to encourage distribution outlets like radio and music streaming services to promote their products (through on-air appearances, exclusive content, product giveaways, and so on). The relationship between curators and record labels is arguably as problematic as that between lobbyists and politicians: when there are incentives to protect one's friends, it is difficult to separate the choices that fall outside these influences. Rather than being the fault of listeners wanting recommendations, the problem is that the mechanics behind these recommendations are covert and only serve to reward those who already exert disproportionate influence on listening. Fundamentally, the issue is that the processes that go into so-called 'human' curation are invisible, making it impossible to know what exactly is going on.

As we have demonstrated in this chapter, the issues raised by music streaming services and their recommender systems are not new. Apocalyptic or celebratory appraisals of these new technologies miss their variety, complexity and historical trajectories. While music streaming services may exacerbate some problems for audiences and musicians, it is important to remember that they are part of a larger trend in the relationship between industry, money, technology and musicking. Further, we hope that a careful examination of how these systems interact with niche genres and users' data will allow us all to be better equipped to tackle the sacrifices inherent in these new listening experiences. When critics desire a return to purity in music discovery (e.g. Ratliff 2016), we must recognise this as nostalgia for a nonexistent past. Now, as then, the forces that filter what music reaches listeners are a complex assemblage of technical and human parts, influenced by capitalist demands and with unevenly distributed effects across the world of music. The builders of these new tools are human, and while algorithms and 'big data' are not unbiased, they often reflect, emphasise and even amplify power differences that already exist.

For Further Study

Drott, Eric. 2018. 'Why the next song matters: Streaming, recommendation, scarcity'. *Twentieth-Century Music* 15 (3): 325–57.

Morris, Jeremy Wade and Devon Powers. 2015. 'Control, curation and musical experience in streaming music services'. *Creative Industries Journal* 8 (2): 106–22.

Razlogova, Elena. 2013. 'The past and future of music listening: Between freeform DJs and recommendation algorithms'. In *Radio's New Wave: Global Sound in the Digital Era*, edited by Jason Loviglio and Michelle Hilmes, 62–76. New York: Routledge.

Seaver, Nick. 2018. 'Captivating algorithms: Recommender systems as traps'. *Journal of Material Culture*. https://doi.org/10.1177/1359183518820366.

Striphas, Ted. 2015. 'Algorithmic culture'. *European Journal of Cultural Studies* 18 (4–5): 395–412.

Notes

1 'IFPI Global Music Report 2016', http://ifpi.org/news/IFPI-GLOBAL-MUSIC-REPORT-2016.
2 Jack Schofield, 'YouTube adds a music discovery / playlist feature, and offers Sundance movies for rent', *The Guardian*, 22 January 2010, www.theguardian.com/technology/blog/2010/jan/22/youtube-playlist-discovery-sundance-rental.
3 The Nielsen 'Music 360' report showed YouTube's dominance among teenagers: 64 per cent of teens listened to new music through YouTube and 56 per cent through radio. 'Music discovery still dominated by radio, says Nielsen Music 360 report', 14 August 2012, www.nielsen.com/us/en/press-room/2012/music-discovery-still-dominated-by-radio–says-nielsen-music-360.html.
4 Although streaming services claim to offer 'all the music you'll ever need' ('Music for Everyone', 2016), these catalogues have limits and are contoured by nationally specific licensing agreements, the global circulation of recordings, and, of course, what music is recorded in the first place (Kassabian 2013; Meier 2011; Hesmondhalgh 2008).
5 This assumption has many flaws that often only apply to niche markets in popular music; Cortney Harding, 'The fundamental "why" of music discovery: Everyone seems to be betting big on music discovery. What if they're wrong?', *Medium*, 17 September 2015, https://medium.com/cuepoint/the-fundamental-why-of-music-discovery-4ab9a1b33665.
6 For an insider discussion of artisan curation, including its relationship to algorithmic playlisting, see Ben Sinclair's Personal Take, this volume.
7 *Fast Company*, 10 October 2013, www.fastcolabs.com/3019830/screw-algorithms-the-new-music-service-from-beats-uses-celebrity-curators-to-show-you-new-mu.
8 Razlogova (2013) shows how 'hand-picked' discourse affects public radio stations that employ it to maintain a veneer of 'liveness' (e.g. Auslander 1999; Sanden, this volume) in broadcasts even as the sources of those 'hand-picked' decisions are unknown.
9 Josh Constine, 'Inside the Spotify–Echo Nest Skunkworks', *TechCrunch* 2016, https://social.techcrunch.com/2014/10/19/the-sonic-mad-scientists/.
10 Loeb 1992; cf. Brian Whitman, 'How music recommendation works – and doesn't work', *Brian Whitman*, 2013, https://notes.variogr.am/post/37675885491/how-music-recommendation-works-and-doesnt-work.
11 Tristan Jehan and David DesRoches, 'Analyzer documentation', *The EchoNest*, formerly available at developer.echonest.com/docs/v4/_static/AnalyzeDocumentation.pdf; Jason Sundram, 'Danceability and energy: Introducing Echo Nest attributes', *Running with Data*, runningwithdata.com/post/1321504427/danceability-and-energy.
12 For further discussion of The Echo Nest see Stéphan-Eloïse Gras's Personal Take, this volume.
13 Enrique Cadena Marin, 'AI-driven data could be the music industry's best marketing instrument', *Venture Beat*, 26 March 2018, https://venturebeat.com/2018/03/26/ai-driven-data-could-be-the-music-industrys-best-marketing-instrument/.
14 'Introducing Discover Weekly: Your ultimate personalised playlist', *Spotify Press*, 20 July 2015, https://web.archive.org/web/20150721120218/https://press.spotify.com/us/2015/07/20/introducing-discover-weekly-your-ultimate-personalised-playlist/; 'Introducing Fresh Finds',

Spotify News, 2 March 2016, https://web.archive.org/web/20160308062044/http://news.spotify .com/us/2016/03/.

15 For an extensive reading list see Tarleton Gillespie and Nick Seaver, 'Critical Algorithm Studies: A Reading List', *Social Media Collective Research Blog*, 25 November 2015. https://social mediacollective.org/reading-lists/critical-algorithm-studies/; see also Shzr Ee Tan's discussion of algocracy in Chapter 10, this volume, pp. 258–60).

16 Dierdre Loughridge, 'The robot's mixtape', *Even*, evenmagazine.com/the-robots-mixtape/.

17 David Trippett provides a broader discussion of the relationship between digital culture and posthumanism in Chapter 9, this volume.

18 'Why can't streaming services get classical music right?', *NPR.org*, 4 June 2015, www.npr .org/sections/therecord/2015/06/04/411963624/why-cant-streaming-services-get-classical- music-right.

19 As Nicholas Cook (2013) has shown in his work analysing early recordings, the information that classical music audiences considered relevant was at odds with what recording companies thought they would want (including recording date), a judgment in opposition to other media in the period (such as book publishing).

20 Spotify phased out its third-party apps between 2014 and 2015. In 2013, Blue Note released a dedicated app for iOS devices that linked directly to the iTunes Store.

21 For further discussion of the user data and surveillance within a commercial context see Martin Scherzinger, Chapters 2 (especially p. 48) and 11, this volume.

22 Alex Hern, 'Spotify knows what music you're having sex to', *The Guardian*, 13 February 2015, www.theguardian.com/technology/2015/feb/13/spotify-knows-what-music-youre-having-sex-to.

23 For more on this topic see Eric Drott (2018).

Personal Take: Being a Curator

BEN SINCLAIR

Curation offers listeners a human touch, a guiding hand to the vastness of streaming libraries of twenty-million-plus songs, of which users really only want to hear a small sliver. Streaming services contain entire worlds of playlists, labyrinths of personalised digital spaces, automated discovery pages promising a fresh experience with each impression, but the stacks need help being read and the algorithms need help understanding what good music is.

Now as in the past, magazine or web editors and writers, radio programmers, and real-life touring DJs bring new music to fans, and it is from their ranks that many curators come. There is also the kind of curator who comes from the label side of the industry, who understands A&R and PR. These people are involved in taste-making from the back end, and are used to trying to bring taste-makers' attention to an artist. But constantly sifting and hunting through new releases, following the genre trades (blogs, charts and newsletters) to keep in touch with where the labels, the music journalists and the culture are at – all with the burden of pleasing not only listeners but also record labels – is like being the middle child in a family full of people who won't speak to one another. People who have curated in a corporate context have said to me 'It almost killed my love of music, so I quit', or 'I never knew what I would be doing in four years. It felt like there was no plan'.

It is partly the corporate context: at the start-up where I began work in 2011, under a certain pay grade we weren't allowed to know how the product we were developing was actually going to work. But mainly it was the tension between two different ideas of what music recommendation should be. The holy grail among the engineers and programmers is the perfect algorithm that promises a wholly individualised experience where you simply pick up your phone, open an app, press a button, and the right music for your location, time of day or mood starts playing. You're immediately satisfied. You never had to go out of your way to hear great music. And the brand behind the algorithm gets the credit for helping you hear what you *really* wanted to hear. But the engineer's holy grail is not the curator's. For artisan playlisters the dream is that listeners will discover their next favourite song or artist through them, to recommend great music that other curators have missed, to get the credit for it, and so carve out a space for yourself as an individual. It's the same dream as the record store guy, the music journalist, the über-cool around-town DJ, or the record collector homie who can't move anymore because of all his vinyl.

At the top of the company, they were clearly betting on the best of both worlds – a kind of hybrid media player – but it felt like an internal competition between curators and engineers on what kind of product we would become. Curators worried about representations, legitimacy and gaining the consumer's trust. At the same time we knew we were generating a database that algorithms would dip into and spit out in ranked recommendations. So we weighted tracks, albums and artists by hand, providing a numerical weight to each in the database and even tagging the very best tracks; at the very least, we would teach the algorithms how to present consumers with good music, the right music, instead of random tracks that no one cares about. But the engineers saw things differently. They prophesied that in the end, no matter what, the algorithms would outperform artisanal playlists or handmade discovery features. For them, the curator's role was a temporary one, teaching the algorithms that would do your work in the future; the ultimate goal was to replace the human taste-maker with code. Tech companies see it the same way. They would rather use a curators' cultural IQ to build the foundation of a product, then cut deals with high-profile artists to do marketing-level curation, like celebrity playlists or radio shows. Ultimately, they want the broadest base of consumers so that they are hitting the largest number of people at once.

There was even a geographical dimension to the division between curators and engineers. In our company, curation mainly happened at the Los Angeles office, where marketing was based. There, every conversation and every reference to music was geared toward exhibiting cool, demonstrating relevance to consumers, offering perspective on whatever's trending right this second on social media, having the right kinds of opinions on the latest albums by the biggest stars or the coolest songs by whichever fresh young bands the major labels are pushing this week. I preferred the tech-focused departments of our north office, where I could hire, train and edit the hell out of some terrific lists in different genres, offering my voice to each. I wanted to work with collegial adults who obsessed over records like I did, who knew all the best tracks to recommend in all scenarios. So we built libraries for deep genres, the farther reaches of the record store: Classical, Smooth Jazz, International, Experimental Rock, Experimental Electronic, Minimalism, Ambient, New Age, sometimes drifting into areas like Alternative, Indie and slightly more mainstream Electronic. We felt we had the freedom to choose quality above all else.

As we got closer to launch, we continued weighting albums, artists and songs so they could be picked up by the recommendation algorithms, trying to make sure they wouldn't put crap in front of our users. But we still didn't know what we were doing. Would there be a master algorithm and would it use marketing profiles based on set genres or the overlaps between them? Would the master algorithm grab from song buckets associated with each of these profiles? Would anyone ever be recommended a Boredoms list? Would they keep getting David Bowie records recommended just because they had them in their library already? How was this going to work? We had to trust our expertise and our instincts, and make decisions in the moment based on where we thought the culture was. We looked forward to a future after the new app went public when we would have a set editorial schedule and life would get easier.

Instead, our company succeeded in doing what all start-ups want to do: it got sold. It was folded into another, larger company, and by the time I was working on the latest product, they had decided to sunset the previous ones. The feudal struggle for dominance between companies continues, and the endgame will likely see a few deep-pocketed distributors – the top handful of tech corporations – consolidate power, raking in the bulk of the market while the rest die off or survive as boutique services.

Being a curator means a lot of things.

It means being able to pick tracks for the right real-life contexts, but it also means being able to sequence a playlist the way an artist or a DJ might sequence an album or a mix. It means being able to please an audience that you (for the most part) imagine from a desk, and doing so on a gut level, rather than making purely data-driven decisions in a team of engineers. It means not just knowing a library of music, but having the ability to shape it to give the most visibility to its very best parts. It means not just staying on top of new releases, but knowing which tracks to watch, and what contexts they should be played in. It means teaching computers about what good music is, what great tracks are, perhaps directly contributing to a future where machine DJs replace you. It means being able to communicate with artists and DJs and labels that have established brands and working with them on making unique playlists or other content. It means being able not only to commission a list from someone, but also to come up with ideas for lists in volume, assign and edit them, and when necessary add or subtract songs and completely re-sequence them so they flow better. It means knowing the difference between a good piece of music that people should hear, and something people can discover for themselves. It means knowing that some kid who doesn't look like you or come from your background might discover a new or rare artist or a terrific deep cut they wouldn't otherwise have come across, because you were the one who curated a service they use.

The frightening implications of teaching machines how to seem cool crumble when you consider how much better it makes you feel to simply listen to a new record with a friend, or hear something someone with good taste is excited about, or pick up something with a cool cover and experience it yourself when you get home. So, more than anything, being a curator means listening.

Personal Take: Can Machines Have Taste?

STÉPHAN-ELOÏSE GRAS

In September 2014, I created an account for the philosopher Theodor W. Adorno on the online music platform Rdio.[1] I wanted to see how Rdio's recommendation engine would analyse Adorno's 'taste profile'. This experiment was a bit tongue-in-cheek: Adorno was apprehensive, at best, about the effects of emerging technologies on musical taste. He despised radio and recorded music for offering a 'culinary listening' based on sensuous experience, which tended to favour 'light music', and he thought they undermined what he called 'structural listening' by decontextualising music from its original conditions of production. Instead, he preferred classical music by male German composers such as Bach, Beethoven, Wagner, Schoenberg and Berg. To get his Rdio station started, I created a playlist of thirty-seven excerpts from works by these composers, all of which he had cited as his favourites during a radio programme in 1965.[2] Despite his concerns, Adorno focused on short and 'beautiful' passages in this show: in other words, he used the media to prompt the very 'culinary listening' that he blamed on the media. This paradox framed my experiment.

As I was creating this fictive Rdio account based on the personal tastes and real subjectivity of one of radio's most famous philosophers and critics, I was struck by some intriguing possibilities. Would my twenty-first-century Adorno share his disapproval of Wagner on Facebook? Would he sing the praises of Alban Berg or Beethoven within their own Spotify or Pandora stations? How would he react when, in response to his enjoyment of the 'beautiful passages' from Alban Berg's *Suite Lyrique*, Rdio's recommendation engine – 'powered by Echonest', as the Rdio website had it – suggested that he listen to a track called 'Keep It Simple' by the electronic musician Schlomi Berg? Peter Szendy (1994) has spoken of Adorno's 'discophony', a discourse based on listening to recorded music. What would the German philosopher say about a 'webophony' 'powered by Echonest'?

Acquired by Spotify in March 2014, The Echo Nest was the recommendation engine used by the majority of music streaming platforms in the world (e.g. Rhapsody-Napster, Rdio, Spotify, iHeartradio), providing the listening experiences for millions of users by collecting data and generating their taste profiles. The Echo Nest claimed to '*power all of today's best music experiences by automatically knowing everything about music.'* How can a technology know everything about music? Born in 2007 out of the merger of two PhD dissertations from the MIT Medialab's Music Information Retrieval (MIR) research group, The Echo Nest is a complex technical object through which we can consider the evolution of musical spaces online. Equally a search engine for music information, a recommendation software and a semi-open dataset and programming interface, The Echo Nest combined artificial listening via analysis of the sound signal with monitoring of consumers' behaviours via collection of their data; this contrasts with, for example, Pandora's strategy of manually or semi-manually indexing and aggregating music data.

In this way, The Echo Nest did something that no previous technology had done. Their Application Programming Interface (API)[3] allowed profiling users' tastes and predicted their preferences by bringing together the analysis of listener behaviours and that of the audio signal. For The Echo Nest, it seems, taste is a reflection both of the formal and acoustic characteristics of the music tracks and of the subjectivity and social history of the listener. In this sense, MIR-based machine learning algorithms represent a new paradigm for analysing and understanding musical language and listeners' experiences. By automating music interpretation and analysis, and by extracting and projecting patterns of listeners' behaviours, these algorithms do more than recommend items that consumers might like: they turn into 'taste-maker' machines and become generators of taste (Gras forthcoming). Such machines are both a digital extension of the cultural industry's traditional recommendation systems (such as Top 50 lists) and arbiters of a deep change in the ways we understand and analyse music as a cultural artefact. The possibility of taste profiling based on automatic music recommendation can be seen as a dispossession of human subjectivity by its mechanical correlate – against which the Frankfurt School warned. Yet, at the same time, it has the capacity to create something new: the experience of listening to Schlomi Berg after Alban Berg is otherwise inconceivable, yet potentially enriching for Adorno.

Such an outcome calls into question the very idea of 'taste' as formulated by Enlightenment thinkers. Trees, flowers, bugs, particles and cells do not have taste: it seems so profoundly human that we don't interrogate it as a category. Ever since Kant's *Critique of Judgment*, taste has been understood as either the subjective manifestation of the universal or else an expression of cultural, social or technical milieux. Historians and sociologists have studied how our preferences and opinions are constantly being framed by societal factors such as the globalisation of production and distribution, class inequalities and reproduction or the social treatment of bodies. But they have barely imagined the possibility that people might not be exclusive possessors of taste: the concept is such a crucial expression of modern subjectivity that we could almost categorise it as a *belief*.

The emergence of automatic music recommendation over the past decade shifts our expectations of how music can make sense, even in its most ineffable ways. Taste-maker machines underlie a change in the aesthetics of music that demands a reconsideration of the Frankfurt School heritage. Today's digital industries are technologically driven and pervasive, but fulfil some of the same functions as the cultural industries critiqued by Adorno and his colleagues: they are shaping new conditions for the production of meaning and taste. In other respects, however, they are very different. For instance, machine learning algorithms using artificial neural networks enable analysis of the exponential amount of data generated by music-related activity online, and can be used for complex pattern recognition problems involved in the recognition of musical emotion or melody and rhythm. Such approaches are based on autonomous or pre-trained processes that no longer refer to classical music theory. Identifying tastes and preferences – such as the 'beautiful passages' that Adorno singled out – no longer relies on the traditional approaches built into the twentieth-century cultural industries. This shift from taste-maker machines to what could be thought of as 'machine taste' interrogates both whether we need to invoke the concept of taste in order to think about musical listening and subjectivity, and whether taste really defines us as human. In this way it opens up new perspectives on music and language.

Notes

1 Until its acquisition by Pandora in December 2015, Rdio was an online music streaming service that offered both free and subscription services. They claimed to have 500,000 subscribers in 85 countries.
2 The programme, called 'Beautiful Moments', was a montage of his favourite musical passages broadcast by Hessische Rundfunk in Frankfurt-am-Main. It was about two hours long and contained fifty-two musical examples from thirty-seven different compositions by fourteen composers; Adorno chose all the recordings. The text was subsequently published in Adorno 2009.
3 An API is an open or partially open interface and set of functions that allow the creation of applications and programs which access the features or data of an operating system, application or other service. APIs are crucial to the business models of most web platforms and aim primarily to generate value via allowing the development of new services and applications.

4 Technologies of the Musical Selfie

SUMANTH GOPINATH AND JASON STANYEK

Prelude: The Lincoln Music Selfie Experiment

'Celebrate your individuality by turning your selfie into sound.' Thus goes
one of the taglines for the 'Music Selfie Experiment', an award-winning
marketing campaign for the Lincoln Motor Company that launched
during Grammy Week 2015 in Los Angeles.[1] The Experiment, developed
by the advertising agency Hudson Rouge, uses facial analysis software to
derive information from photographic selfies – information that, in turn,
helps to create individualised musical tracks algorithmically generated
from an extensive database of audio recordings ('more than 4 million
facial-recognition audio track variations are possible', touts Lincoln's website).[2] An instance of 'experiential marketing', one of the Experiment's
goals was to create a novel form of engagement and participation akin to
what the influential marketing theorist Bernd H. Schmitt calls 'Strategic
Experiential Modules': sensory, affective, creative-cognitive, physical, lifestyle and social-identity experiences that 'get customers to sense, feel,
think, act, and relate to' specific companies and brands (Schmitt 1999, xiii;
also Gopinath and Stanyek 2013; Spurgeon 2008).

By the time of the launch of Lincoln's Music Selfie campaign, numerous
ads had already capitalised on the selfie phenomenon. But Lincoln offered
a new twist by sonifying the visual selfie: 'What does a face sound like?' was
the campaign's primary slogan. The 'multisensory expression of one's self',
as Lincoln's website put it,[3] is created in the following manner: after the
user uploads a photo, the software analyses 'facial features: (shape, chin,
mouth, nose, cheeks, eyes, eyebrows)'. The algorithm runs its course and
then we hear, in layered sequence, different instrumental tracks generated
by different facial features: 'lips forming guitar tonality'; 'eyes arranging
keyboard elements'; 'nose setting rhythmic percussion'; 'eyebrows defining
ambience'; 'jawlines establishing bass'. Using the vernacular instrumentation of an extended Western rock/pop ensemble, each newly composed
piece lasts around thirty seconds and is ringtone-like in length and formal
design (Gopinath 2013). Stylistically, the music includes ambient, instrumental rock, soul, pop, smooth jazz and more, but this is all nonetheless
sufficiently consistent to convey a vaguely urbane, cosmopolitan sensibility. As the track is 'composed' layer-by-layer, a button appears on the

screen: 'Share Your Music Selfie'. Like any other selfie, the musical selfie isn't truly a selfie until it is sent out into the world.

Using music selfies to sell an automobile might seem a slightly orthogonal marketing strategy (what does a sonified face have to do with a luxury town car?). But it wasn't such a surprising one in 2015. Facebook had already entered its second decade of life and had become – along with WhatsApp, Twitter, Instagram and Snapchat – a virtual clearinghouse for selfies. Google announced that twenty-five billion selfies were uploaded to Google Photos that year, while a widely circulated 2016 report claimed that the average millennial would take 27,500 selfies in their lifetime.[4] Commenting on this phenomenon, Allan Metcalf wrote that the '*selfie* reflects the Millennials' immersion in technology and social media; lives sometimes lived more comfortably online than in person; concern for their image; and generosity in offering their best selves to friends and the world. For Millennials, the selfie is the conjunction of technology with desire' (2016, 182). Celebrations of the selfie have been met with criticisms that highlight its links with sexting, loss of control over personal identity, body dysmorphic disorder, vanity and narcissism, and braggadocio and self-promotion.[5] Prominent cultural critics have weighed in. Sherry Turkle condemned selfies for making us 'accustomed to putting ourselves and those around us "on pause" in order to document our lives', and views selfies as symptomatic of social media's tendency to consistently pull us out of the here-and-now, making users 'less accustomed to reflecting on where you are and what you are thinking'.[6] For Henry Giroux, selfie culture shows how 'the ideological and affective spaces of neoliberalism have turned privacy into a mimicry of celebrity culture that both abets and is indifferent to the growing surveillance state and its totalitarian revolution'.[7]

In some senses, the Lincoln Music Selfie Experiment is a party trick that harnesses common digital technology and a ubiquitous aesthetic practice to generate anodyne music that hardly illuminates the complexities of human selfhood. Yet Lincoln's Experiment stands out as an evocative illustration of specific aspects of the production, consumption, promotion and monetisation of music in the age of the digital selfie. As Nick Mizroeff (2016, 22) puts it, 'The selfie is the first visual product of the new networked, urban global youth culture', and Lincoln's marketing team sought to capitalise on this reality. Indeed, the prominent appearance of the term 'music selfie' is only one component of a naked attempt to reach out to that youth culture. Other conspicuous factors include the participatory design of the Experiment; its discursive emphasis on the individuality of the participant-consumer; the centrality of music in conjunction with a specific brand to produce an affective response; and the heavy involvement of a marketing company in a relatively sophisticated digital music project. All of these are of a piece, with the ultimate goal being the targeting of millennials as a new market demographic. As for the project's media production components, which were created by Canadian design firm Jam3 and the Swedish audio production company Plan8, especially striking is the automated, algorithmic generation of sound, which is increasingly used in music production and of which Lincoln's effort is a relatively compelling example. The project makes extensive use of massive music production libraries – databases searchable by genre, mood, theme, instrumentation, and other parameters – that are now routinely accumulated by production firms servicing video and film production projects.

Beyond that, the multimodal/multisensory aspect of the Lincoln experiment is absolutely characteristic of the current moment. The matching of image to sound and the dissemination of both in digital video files has become widespread through well-designed video editing suites, while increased bandwidth means that digital files in compressed formats are readily distributed through an array of social media and video platform services. But perhaps the most striking feature – in 2015 a relatively novel gambit, now increasingly prevalent – is Lincoln's use of facial analysis technologies in combination with digital music production tools. That these are now being harnessed for the creation of music is a remarkable phenomenon that should not go unnoticed.

Musical Selfiehood

Referencing Michel Foucault (1988) and Tia DeNora (1999), our chapter's title registers changing techniques and technologies (Agazzi 1998) of musical experience at the millennial moment, when the Internet had only recently begun to transform the music industry and music consumption (Morris 2015). DeNora's 'Music as a Technology of the Self' – in which radios, cassette tapes, vinyl records and compact discs are the primary means by which her interlocutors listen to and make use of music in their everyday lives – marks the end of a particular era and the beginning of a new one. What Vincent Mosco (2005) calls the 'digital sublime' first hit music in 1999 and mushroomed over the following decade: the period witnessed the emergence of peer-to-peer file-sharing; the normalisation of digital audio formats; the stabilisation of digital audio production hardware and software; the inception of music streaming services; the launch of the iPod and a resulting boom in ubiquitous music listening; the augmentation of headphones to include the input capabilities of microphones as well as noise cancellation algorithms; the creation of YouTube; and, finally – and crucially – the mobilisation of social media that coincided with the arrival of the smartphone and its immensely variegated and powerful software ecosystem. These factors continued to develop and consolidate over the 2010s. Increasingly, musical bodies link up with bits, musical acts are tied to apps, and musical selves are musical selfies.

The twining of the selfie with music – which extends well beyond the isolated example of Lincoln[8] – indexes the development of what we call *musical selfiehood*. The '-ie' makes a difference. Unlike in Foucault's and DeNora's investigations of the relationship between technology and *self*, there is no implicit subject/object divide between technology and the *selfie*. Instead of being tied up with the problem of selfhood per se, the '-ie' points to small, easily produced data representations – digital bits that reflect upon, proliferate from and circulate beyond the material apparatus that creates them. If selfhood is 'more an aim or a norm than a natural given' (Rose 1996, 4), an 'ongoing project that serves as a response to the question of how to be' (Jopling 2000, 83), then selfiehood is a distributed sociodigital undertaking that involves the recursive generation of data and its mass accumulation for a variety of economic, governmental and social purposes. Selfiehood involves feedback processes with numerous inputs and outputs operating at multiple timescales from the infinitesimal to the temporally distended. It entails the intersection of human activities with automated processes including recommendation engines and other sites of algorithmic creativity and generativity. It is buttressed by imperatives for participatory, user-generated content, and prioritises the accumulation and rendering of networked information into tradeable consumer profiles and biopolitical databases. As part of the big data economy, selfiehood is a commercial and political project of vast proportions that has acute ramifications for the lived experiences of individuals and the constitution of communities.

In the three sections below, we explore musical selfiehood through three paradigmatic examples: the playlist, headphones and self-produced video recordings of musical performances, respectively illustrated by Spotify ('You are what you stream'), Beats by Dre ('Hear what you want'), and YouTube ('Broadcast yourself').[9] Each example corresponds to one of three common practices that have become ever more pervasive in everyday life since 1999: 'curation', 'enclosure' and 'broadcasting'. Examining these can clue us into the broader dynamics of musical selfiehood. In the first section, 'Curation of the selfie', we consider the extensive forms of self-tracking and self-quantification that condition how individuals reflexively take care of themselves when interacting with the vast archive of musical content available through cloud-based services; as an extension of the 'constant practice' of 'taking care of oneself' that Foucault addresses in 'Technologies of the self' (1988, 21), curation is manifested musically in the playlist. Care, the etymological source of 'curation', however, does not only occur between and by individuals. Rather, it is the broader, marketised system of musical data tracking – perhaps as a vast, digital *curate* that 'cares' for the souls it manages – that automates and generates a kind of care that deeply entangles the playlist with the self-care of users. The second section, 'Selfie enclosure', points toward listening itself, and signals the new forms of relation between interiors and exteriors that emerge as headphones are fitted with microphones. It marks the production and management of the boundary conditions of listening, figured through algorithms that loop musical selfies in never-ending recursions of bodies, ecologies and sounds. Key to selfie enclosure is the wide availability of consumer products that include active noise cancellation, a process of destructive interference that superimposes a sound wave with its inverse in order to manage unwanted sound. This makes for a theoretically rich corollary between sonic and visual realms, given that taking a selfie with a front-facing camera typically involves monitoring a mirror image that appears to be flipped in the resulting photo. Finally, 'Broadcasting the selfie' highlights the performative dialogues that emerge between musical self and other in the wilds of social media. The key term here is the *otherie*, which conventionally refers to the images or videos of others (i.e. of those who are *not* the self of the selfie).[10] In our rendering, however, the otherie is not only the other of the self/ie, but also the very process of producing an image or video that circulates within a system of differences: any selfie in juxtaposition with another image causes each to become the other's otherie. This includes selfies themselves, when juxtaposed with other selfies of the same person or different people. The self-produced music video is central here, as are the platforms and the apps that allow the selfie to create new forms of aggregation with its otheries and allow for the emergence of a kind of corporate Big Otherie (the psychoanalytic interpretation of the curate, perhaps).

The projects of selfie-curation, selfie-enclosure and selfie-broadcasting go far beyond the mere presence of the photographic selfie in the musical domain – for example, a selfie taken while listening to or making music. Likewise, these projects are not equivalent to relatively traditional musical (self-)portraits like those of Virgil Thomson (Walden 2018), to 'deeply personal' compositions put forward as 'a kind of musical selfie', or to songs that use '(private) confession' as a staging ground for 'mini-thinkpiece[s] on selfiehood'.[11] Yet, when it comes to the projects of musical selfiehood, there are striking continuities between the musical and visual realms. For example, both musical and visual selfies involve recursive processes of looping, feedback and mirroring; they facilitate the easy generation of new files, tags and metadata; they involve production via algorithmic, highly automated processes and interfaces that encourage – even demand – direct human participation and creativity; and they rely upon the aggregation and networked interrelation of information as part of the construction of finely tuned histories and profiles that weigh upon future activity. These features are generally characteristic of the early-twenty-first-century world of networked, digital information. In the story we tell here, however, the musicalisation of the selfie hinges upon the assumption of the uniqueness of individual identity and expression, which seems at odds with the anonymity and generality of the network processes described above. The Music Selfie Experiment was based on the idea of 'a unique song that only that user's face could produce', but the Experiment's songs were not unique: rather, an ideology of uniqueness and individuality was central to its marketing pitch, as it perhaps is to the rhetoric of selfiehood in general. In identifying trends, patterns and tendencies within networked, digital music cultures of the 2010s, we necessarily attend to the non-unique and reproducible dimensions of musical selfiehood. It turns out that there are many.

1. Curation of the Selfie

Your face will pick your next playlist.[12]

The minimalist web page for the face-generated-playlist app, Peekabeat, includes a few well-placed words in white Arial font on top of a fifteen-second video loop colour-filtered by a vertically (and temporally) varying cyan–violet gradient. In the video, a bearded white male puts on a pair of earbuds and begins to bounce his head to the music he hears – presumably the blues-based instrumental garage rock that streams from the site. Quickly the man's demeanour shifts into frenetic air-guitaring and air-drumming, and the loop ends by his giving us the clichéd sign of the horns with both hands, affirming that he has indeed rocked out. The words superimposed upon this little spectacle read, 'let your face / tell what music suits you', and invite us to press the 'start experience' button. If users accept the invitation, they are asked to either use their computer camera or upload a selfie. Either way, facial analysis of the sort found in the Lincoln Music Selfie Experiment determines their mood, and a corresponding song is streamed from the site (see Figure 4.1). If you download the app to your phone, you find a more extensive set of correspondences produced through an entire playlist of songs drawn from multiple online sources, including the listening data contained in your own Spotify account.

The name of the app itself inspires numerous associations, not least of which is its source in the game peekaboo. A Freudian *Fort-Da* (Gone-There) game of hiding and showing the face, peekaboo is performed by an

Description

The right playlist in a glance.

Your face will pick your next playlist. How? With some magical nerdy tricks, of course!

You just have to take a picture, our App will do the rest. Peekabeat uses the Facial Action Coding System to recognize the emotions shown by your expression

Figure 4.1 Peekabeat: 'Your face will pick your next playlist'.
Screenshot used courtesy of AQuest.

adult or older child for the amusement of an infant, often with the phrase 'Peekaboo, I see you!' being intoned when the face is revealed: a self encounters or performs as an other. With Peekabeat, however, the app acts as a kind of mirror to the infantilised consumer/user, re-presenting the self through a digitally curated collection of pre-recorded music. The application effectively says 'I hear you' – or better, it sees you and speaks back with a popular song. And how does it do this? The Peekabeat site explains that it 'uses the Facial Action Coding System to recognize the emotions shown by your expression and suggests you some songs on Spotify'. Popularised by Malcolm Gladwell (2005), the Facial Action Coding System (FACS) was developed by psychologist Paul Ekman and Wallace Friesen in 1978, and breaks facial expression down into dozens of unique facial 'action units' (AUs): Erika Rosenberg's (2005, 13) historical background states that there are forty-four unique AUs, while the Wikipedia entry on FACS increases the number, adding codes for facial movement, head movement, eye movement and visibility.

Mapping the algorithmic analysis of facial geometry onto AUs using software of the sort found in the Lincoln project is one piece of the story. Another is the correlation of AUs with widely known theories of emotion by Silvan Tomkins, Ekman and others that posit between six and eleven discrete emotional states. The result has been a ballooning of emotion-analysis tech entrepreneurship. In 2015 a report described the existence of over twenty application programming interfaces (APIs) for algorithmic analysis of human emotion, supporting an industry at that time worth

$2.77 billion and expected to grow substantially.[13] Companies have produced their own introductory texts on FACSs and emotion recognition, some of which claim to offer 'Everything you need to know to elevate your research with emotion analytics' (iMotions 2016, 1). The final piece of the puzzle is the well-known human or machine encoding of music-analytic data via projects like the Music Genome Project (used by Pandora) and The Echo Nest (used by Spotify): this makes it possible to scan tracks for affective markers (e.g. tempo, mode, energy and loudness), and link this with the automated analysis of song texts through affective content analysis. Part of a larger movement within computer science called affective computing (Picard 1997), the combination of these techniques with the analysis of a Spotify user's listening histories and taste/genre preferences provides a glimpse of a viable method for generating playlists according to face-analysed mood (Dureha 2014).

Peekabeat is not the only application that uses emotions identified by facial analysis to generate musical playlists. The HTC Mood Player, a now-defunct project sponsored by the Taiwanese mobile phone company HTC and Spotify, worked on similar principles, while in 2011 a coder named Benjamin Gleitzman used Facebook's face-recognition software to identify individuals and the Hunch API to text-mine their profiles for clues as to what songs would likely be of interest to them; this application, called AutomaticDJ, also made use of The Echo Nest and Spotify's metadata API.[14] These applications form just a small part of the broader computational endeavour of automatic playlist generation.[15] The web page Playlist Machinery illustrates the range of approaches available just through Spotify; they involve keyword searches (The Playlist Miner), places you visit (Roadtrip Mixtape), morphing between artists of different genres (Boil the Frog), artists' most recent live shows (The Set Listener), and textual acrostics (Acrostify).[16] Other generators build playlists by genre or mood (Magic Playlist), by popularity of songs (Spotibot), by using one song to find related artists and songs (Soundtrack), by using new releases from your favourite artists (Release Radar), by appropriating existing playlists (Playlists.net), or, in the case of Discover Weekly, by automatically generating lists based on your Spotify listening habits.[17] In addition, Spotify's Your Time Capsule produces a two-hour-long 'personalized playlist with songs to take you back in time to your teenage years', while for the exceptionally lazy there is the Lazify app, which automates much of this data-labour at the press of a single button ('Being lazy is fun!').[18] The possibilities seem endless.

The applications discussed above look like speculative interventions in a marketplace that prizes the automatic, artificially intelligent generation of content. But this 'content' is really a (re)arrangement and selection of pre-existing content from a database – the massive and quickly growing sound file catalogues of streaming, cloud-based services, which, like online platforms in general, have radically decreased distribution costs (displacing them to internet service providers). The ramifications include the decreasing significance of hits and blockbuster sellers, the increased potential for marketing entire catalogues to niche consumers, and the need for guides and routes through the database. It is in this last role that the playlist has become a pre-eminent vehicle for musical experience. Endlessly fungible and automatically generated, easily stored, widely shared, and reified as 'word of mouth taken to an industrial scale' (Anderson 2008, 34), the playlist has morphed from its origins in concert programming and performance setlists, radio and discotheque DJ playlists, the track order of original LPs and reaggregated compilation albums, and end-user-created analogue or digital 'mixtapes', into a valued form that can, on the one hand, be sponsored by stars and, on the other hand, be constructed at the press of a button (or through the analysis of a selfie).

Playlists are one of the principal musical forms of the current moment – Jeremy Wade Morris (2015, 162) calls them 'metacommodities' – but what do they have to do with selfhood and selfiehood? Certainly the playlist serves a 'curatorial' function that involves the selection, ordering, shaping and presentation of content for others (Bruno 2011). Morris notes that in their generation of playlists, 'iTunes employed users as curators and packagers of digital music commodities', appropriating their free labour and so 'increasingly encroaching on previously uncommodified practices' (160). The same might be said of social networking sites in general.[19] However, in a remarkable article on streaming services and user-data collection, Eric Drott (2018, 262) cites Danielle Lee, Vice President of Global Partner Solutions for Spotify, arguing that music streaming is different from other aspects of social media. As Drott points out, in a fiercely competitive marketplace for consumer data, the idea that music provides access to the authentic self constitutes the central sales pitch for data collected from music listening. This idea is problematic, to say the least, and it raises troubling questions about the enthusiastic use of services that track people's actions and thoughts to an unprecedented degree.

Awareness of data tracking ranges from ignorance to tacit acceptance to unqualified embrace (think FitBit), and links to the growing 'quantified self' movement in which participants track and log many sorts of data about themselves, including their music listening. The voluntary aspect of this phenomenon is perhaps its most alarming dimension; consumers/ users passively accept or actively court the tracking of data for various purposes, from the mere agreement to use the service to employment of its self-tracking mechanisms. Our argument about 'selfiehood' attempts to capture the voluntary, subjectively affirmative nature of this data-based condition, in which users merely shrug their shoulders at the notion that they are being carefully and comprehensively tracked: Big Brother may be watching, but it's no big deal, and potentially even fun.[20] Drott's Deleuzian argument is that postmodern, dividuated selves (that is, selves broken down into elements such as affects, drives and habits) are constructed and reproduced by the data-tracking industry, and this raises questions for the musical self and selfiehood: to what extent do multiplied and dispersed acts of curation and sharing shore up fictions of selfhood, anchoring them to juridical identity, a limited number of IP addresses and phone numbers, and the seeming coherence of personal experience? Contradictions and antinomies abound and will not be resolved any time soon – particularly given iPhone X's incorporation of face-recognition technology into its Face ID system, which makes automated face recognition (and potentially face analysis) a routine presence in the lives of millions.[21]

2 Selfie Enclosure

The selfie. Reinvented. . . . #BeatsByDre[22]

On 25 January 2016 Rihanna tweeted a selfie.[23] The accompanying three-word text – 'listening to ANTI', with a red balloon emoji thrown in for good measure – was sparse, utilising just a smidgen of characters to set the stage for the release of the superstar musician's new album a few days later. The accompanying photo, however, upped the ante: Rihanna is bedecked in Dolce & Gabbana's $8,895 Napa Leather Rhinestone Headphones with Crown, a lavish accoutrement clearly meant to echo the crown that covers the eyes of the child depicted on artist Roy Nachum's embrailled album cover for *Anti*.[24] In the selfie, the D&G headphone crown is sense-enhancing – a clear sign of augmented hearing, of the longstanding but increasingly ubiquitous ability to channel the world through small loudspeakers on top of, or inside, one's ear canal.

Studded with Swarovski crystals and pearls and 'compatible with MP3 readers, smartphones and audio playback devices', as the D&G website tells us, Rihanna's headphones push the limits of conspicuous consumption.[25] Yet, there's more to the selfie than that. Rihanna's eyes practically take on the golden hue of the crown's colours, as if her face and the headphones were inextricable parts of the same entity. We see her personal motto tattooed across her upper right chest: 'Never a failure always a lesson', written backwards so that she can read it in the mirror (ironically, the tattoo is not selfie-friendly as smartphones 'un-mirror' images taken with the front-facing camera).[26] And she's obviously listening intently – why would her bejewelled left hand be brought so close to her mouth if not to show focus and attention? Her far-away, downturned eyes, too, with their lack of visual focus, seem to be saying 'I'm listening, not looking.' She *is* looking though, right into the screen of her smartphone: she's looking at herself listening to herself. Instead of 'listening to ANTI', the tweet could have read: 'look at me looking at myself listening to myself performing ANTI'. It's a document of a peculiar, recursive looping of the self.

And people did look at her. As of 17 September 2018, the tweet generated 178,000 retweets, 289,000 likes, and 11,000 comments. It has become one of the quintessential musical missives of the Twitter age, making numerous 'best selfies' lists and appearing as one of the 'Most Iconic Celebrity Selfies' chosen by *US Magazine* for its photo spread to celebrate 2017 'National Selfie Day'.[27] When Rihanna first posted her selfie, her album *Anti* hadn't been released, so the selfie's initial impact was as contingent upon what was missing from the photo as it was upon its representation of opulence and celebrity. Soon after her tweet went out, first-responder tweeters chimed in:

> @NathanZed: 'lemme listen too 🙈 🙈 '[28]
> @thisisamplify: 'Can we have a listen? Thanks'[29]

But once the album was officially released a few days later, Rihanna's listening experience could be accessed, and a 'listening to ANTI 🎤' meme began to develop, with her fans mimicking her *Anti* selfie – sometimes in adulation, sometimes in jest (a few users on Instagram used #Listening-ToANTI to post pictures of themselves in self-made paper crowns, striking the same contemplative listening pose as Rihanna). While the meme often appeared without an attached selfie (@pixieitzel: 'I've been listening to ANTI all day someone make me stop'[30]), some fans took rather mundane pictures of themselves listening to Rihanna's music through their own modest headphones, a show of allegiance to their beloved singer (@Prince0fChina: 'Listening to ANTI (with my cheap headphones 😂😂😂🧑🏿) @rihanna 🎤'[31]).

The phenomenon of the 'headphone selfie' cannot be reduced to the *Anti* meme. It is widespread, with thousands of selfies posted to Instagram and Twitter (and beyond) showing headphoned individuals selfigraphically documenting their own listening experiences. No track listing or playlist is necessary; the headphones can do all of the semantic heavy lifting, their very presence signifying a communion between ear and sound, between self and musical other, between consumer and product. This phenomenon is on full display in 'Solo Selfie' for Beats by Dr Dre Solo2 headphones, a video ad campaign that launched in November

2014.[32] Parading on the screen is an almost endless succession of celebrities – from Kendall and Kylie Jenner to hip-hop stars Funkmaster Flex, Big Sean, Jadakiss, Nicki Minaj and Fabolous – each taking a video selfie of themselves wearing the wireless Solo2 headphones. A painfully saccharine song – 'Something New' by Axwell A. Ingrosso, with the anthemic hook 'We belong to something new' – places the headphone-enclosed celebrity listener within the broader public sphere, echoing the Beats corporation's hyped-up claim that their Solo2 headphones are 'a symbol of individuality as much as they represent a connection shared by millions of people across the globe'.[33] The campaign had its didactic side as well: witness the tutorial video that teaches #SoloSelfie lovers how to take their very own video selfies while wearing their Beats headphones ('start with one "b"... bring it around, hit that selfie pose ... make that selfie face ... come around to the other "b"'). The tutorial ends with the on-screen text 'SHOW YOUR #SOLOSELFIE', an unsubtle command to post the resulting video.[34] Or as the brand's Twitter feed put it when the product launched, 'The Selfie has been reinvented. Enter Solo Selfie or #SoloSelfie – a new movement of self-expression. Share yours and tell the world your story.'[35]

The #SoloSelfie campaign has a particular choreography that asks consumers to perform two very specific, yet interlocking, moves of enclosure. The first is found in the form of the Solo Selfie video itself: the sweeping, encircling motion described above, from the brand logo ('b') on one earcup, across the face (quite literally, the front of the head), to the brand logo on the other earcup. It follows the same trajectory of the eye-covering crown on Rihanna's *Anti* album cover – but here, it is the very enclosure of head by headphone that is meant to signify. (As an article in *Fast Company Design* pithily puts it, 'The headphones are designed to turn your head into a billboard for Beats by Dre.')[36] The second move involves taking user-produced data – the headphone selfie itself – and sending it off to the wilds of social media. This move encloses as well; individual users are caught in a tight loop with the Beats corporation, their selfies quantified in the service of multinational capital.[37]

A third move of enclosure plays out in what has become perhaps the most significant Beats marketing campaign: 'Hear What You Want'. The 2013 campaign's flagship commercial features the US American football player Colin Kaepernick, lately notorious as the athlete who triggered the 'taking the knee' protest movement.[38] The commercial begins with an announcer's voice: 'Can he handle it? Can he handle the pressure? This is the big question with quarterback Colin Kaepernick. I've been talking to a lot of fans, and they keep saying: "We can get to him, we can get to him."' The video cuts to Kaepernick looking out of the window of a bus taking him to the stadium. We hear 'You suck', the first salvo of almost a full minute of vile (one could certainly say racist) diatribes against Kaepernick; they culminate in a near riot as an anti-Kaepernick contingent of football fans surround his bus (with one male literally taking a piss on the bus tyre), throw an ice-filled beer cooler against the bus's windshield, and threaten Kaepernick with physical violence.

Kaepernick's solution? To calmly place his Beats by Dre Studio Wireless headphones over his ears. The violent din is immediately reduced to a faint murmur, with Beats's adaptive noise cancellation filtering out the external world.[39] A few seconds later, Kaepernick presses play on his MP3 player, Aloe Blacc's 'The Man' comes on, and there's no further trace of the violent mob, they've been reduced to silent screaming faces. We hear the opening lyrics of Blacc's song, 'Well you can tell everybody . . . I'm the man, I'm the man, I'm the man', with the clear reference to Elton John's 1970 hit 'Your Song' – itself a paean to the song as gift and to selfhood as intersubjective – reduced to a solipsistic, me-generation discharge, snugly encased in the headspace between the Beats cans. Yet, as Kaepernick makes his way from the bus to the stadium, the noise of the crowd finds its way in. We're reminded that no enclosure is complete. Even the encircling move from the #SoloSelfie campaign – the sweep from right 'b', to face, to left 'b' – can't keep the enclosure intact.

Selfie enclosure is thus performed simultaneously on a number of different registers. Let's name three. It is an economic form, allowing capital to seize and monetise the selfie-generated data putatively shared in the 'digital commons'. As Mark Andrejevic claims: 'the model of digital enclosure suggests that ubiquitous interactivity also has the potential to facilitate unprecedented commodification of previously nonproprietary information and an aggressive clamp-down of centralized control over information resources' (2007, 297; see also Lametti 2012). Selfie enclosure is also a sonic form conditioned upon a longstanding (yet always aspirational) affordance of headphones: the ability to keep the outer sonic world at bay. Headphone enclosure has a history almost as long as that of sound recording itself (Sterne 2003, 155–67), but the capability to seal off the world has been intensified in the age of active noise cancellation – an age which not insignificantly began, on the mass-market consumer level, at that millennial moment when music was going fully digital. Finally, selfie enclosure has implications for the commonsensical (yet problematic) notion that each self emerges as a form of distinction from other selves – not least because, as Slavoj Žižek points out, 'self-enclosure is *a priori* impossible . . . the excluded externality always leaves its traces' (2012, 845).

It is practically a truism to say that musical *selfhood* is generated and sustained through externalities. As Naomi Cumming puts it in her 2000 book *The Sonic Self*, 'Musical selfhood . . . is not, then, surrounded by irremediable boundaries, isolating the individual "self" as the origin of insight, but is formed in shared activities, which ensure modes of connection with others' (60). Yet, as Arild Bergh and Tia DeNora have pointed out, the invention of the phonograph – and later the Walkman and iPod – prompted shifts in 'the psycho-culture of listening', one being 'listeners' increasing ability to isolate themselves, both from other listeners and from the performers' (2009, 108). Indeed, at the dawn of the Walkman in 1979, commentators were quick to call attention to the isolation produced when you 'clap on a pair of stereo headphones for the first time': what you hear is music like it's 'going on right inside your own head' (Emmerson 1979).

It's not a stretch to suggest that one of the allures of this heightened form of enclosed listening is that it directly intersects with everyday conceptions of selfhood, described by Charles Taylor as 'modern inwardness, the sense of ourselves as beings with inner depths, and the connected notion that we are "selves"' (1989, x). The longstanding material concern with the efficacy of the 'seals' afforded by different types of headphone enclosure (open-back/closed-back; over-ear, on-ear, in-ear, etc.) has had the effect of reproducing this 'inwardness'. As a 1979 article in *Popular Science* put it, 'Headphone enclosures influence how much ambient sound you can hear' (Free 1979, 111). The phrase 'you can hear' is, of course, akin to the Beat Corporation's 'hear what you want', indicating a particular relationship between the headphoned listener and the sounds beyond the enclosure. But it's a two-way street, and seals are only ever partially effective at maintaining separation between the worlds inside and outside headphones. There are leaks between domains, and these leaks often reveal the social contours of material culture. 'Of all the daily discourtesies', Ray Rivera wrote in the *New York Times*, 'none to me is more irksome than headphone leak. You know, that treble-drenched drone emanating from iPods half-way down the subway car' (2009, see also Marshall 2014).

Musical *selfiehood* emerges out of algorithmically managed relationships between interiors and exteriors. The new forms of management that have allowed for the development of the selfie – musical and otherwise – are an intensified control of the various inputs and outputs that flow between domains within complex systems. Since the release of the first mass-marketed consumer-noise-cancelling headphones by Bose in 2000, headphones have increasingly been fitted with both output capabilities (via loudspeakers) and input capabilities (via microphones); passive forms of noise control have been supplemented or even supplanted by active electronics that consistently monitor one's ambient acoustic surroundings. They condition the sonic world of the self in much the way that a thermostat conditions the self's thermal world (Chalmers 1996, 293–7). The latest Beats headphones (the Studio3 Wireless, released in September 2017) use what the company calls 'pure adaptive noise cancellation' [Pure

ANC], software that 'compares the ANC-altered music with the original sound file on your device . . . 50,000 times per second'.[40]

Such recursive processing upends conventional understandings of what a listening self is. The Beats website gives a fuller overview:

> Pure ANC is a form of noise cancellation that uses advanced algorithms to monitor the sounds around you and adjust the level of noise cancellation to best match your environment. Pure ANC also evaluates fit and adjusts for leakage caused by hair, glasses, the shape of your ears and movement of your head as you go about your day. Additionally, Pure ANC simultaneously checks what you're hearing while noise cancelling is applied against the original music content to adjust and ensure optimal audio fidelity.[41]

Much like the sonifying facial analysis systems described above, the selfie-enclosures of active noise cancellation are evaluative, responsive and generative. 'Hearing what you want' becomes a function of persistent monitoring and data-processing, with the data consisting of the twinned sonic environments inside and outside the headphones. Remarkably, the algorithms also 'evaluate' the head's protrusions (ears, hair, glasses) as well as its movements, an anatomical and choreographic mapping that gets injected into listening itself. In a world in which a great portion of consumer audio devices (whether smartphones or headphones, smart speakers or automobile sound systems) rely on algorithmically driven forms of noise cancellation, listening to music and 'hearing what you want' has become a performance of selfiehood.

3 Broadcast your Selfie

SING! SELFIE! SHARE![42]

Of all the gadgets that signal the musical selfie as an epochal form of digital selfhood, the SelfieMic is, perhaps, the most quintessential. Created by UK-based toy manufacturer Worlds Apart and first released in August 2016, the SelfieMic harnesses the selfie stick – that ubiquitous device which allows selfie takers to mount their smartphones onto an extendable rod, removing the phone from the user's hand and thereby 'solving the problem of one's deictic arms' (Bollmer and Guinness 2017, 164).[43] With the SelfieMic, the rubberised handgrip at the end of the standard selfie stick is replaced with a microphone, an inert grip transformed into an active input. The full kit – microphone, selfie stick, earpiece, smartphone clamp – enables you to 'Sing like a star and create your own music videos with SelfieMic', as the product website puts it. And it works in tandem with StarMaker, a 'karaoke app' developed by StarMaker Interactive Inc. 'so that anyone and everyone could know what it feels like to be the lead singer of their favorite song'.[44] StarMaker currently boasts a catalogue of over three million licensed songs, and touts its ability to offer users the chance to 'perform, publish and monetize on YouTube, Facebook, Vine, Instagram and more' (StarMaker 2017). That is, the main affordance of StarMaker (whether used with the SelfieMic or just with one's own smartphone or personal computer) is not the enabling of a private form of surrogate stardom, a contemporary slant on singing in the shower or singing along to the radio in the car; rather, it provides 'rising social music talent' with 'the opportunity to publish videos to their own YouTube channels as part of the StarMaker Network', so helping 'undiscovered talent achieve the fame they deserve'.[45]

The StarMaker YouTube channel does indeed provide a platform for some very talented young singers (most appear to be teenagers), with many of the uploaded videos revealing polished renditions of contemporary hits. But the spectacle and dazzle of broadcast television shows like *American Idol* and *The Voice* is completely absent. Singers are typically in their bedrooms, the inner sanctum of middle-class teen privacy. Fully in selfie-taking mode, they sing directly into their computers or smartphones, looking at themselves on the screen as they perform. Many use Apple earbuds, which function both as a monitor (helping to avoid feedback) and as a microphone. It's strange to witness virtuosic, full-voiced performances being sung into the small mic built into the Apple headphone cable: many StarMaker singers bring the mic close to their mouths, as if they were holding an SM58. Yet many of these videos only reach audiences in the hundreds or low thousands, and retain a degree of intimacy in terms of both venue and size of viewing audience. Of all the content on the StarMaker YouTube channel, it is the 'Collab Lab' videos that are most widely watched. But even these, which 'feature StarMaker artists', command rather modest audiences: the most popular receive views numbering only tens or low hundreds of thousands (as of 8 October 2017). For example, a mashup of songs by the The Weeknd and David Guetta by Andrew Garcia, a singer who 'kicked off his path to stardom by joining the StarMaker Network' ('and so can you!'), has only garnered 220,000 views – a relatively low number when star performers can count on YouTube views in the hundreds of millions or even billions.[46]

There are other apps that seek to merge selfie with karaoke, and some reach far more viewers than StarMaker. The app-maker Smule, for one, offers Sing! Karaoke, an app that is like StarMaker in some respects ('We all have a voice. Find yours with Smule Sing!') but significantly more advanced in others. For example, Sing! Karaoke's 'Duet with the Artist' series allows amateur singers to collaborate with stars such as

Shawn Mendes, Nick Jonas and Jessie J, with a split-screen view showing side-by-side singing selfies.[47] Shawn Mendes's Smule duet video for his hit song 'Treat You Better' represents a typical case. Mendes, a young singer who first achieved notoriety in 2013 when he began posting cover songs to the video-sharing app Vine, is in what appears to be his own bedroom, staring into the front-facing camera of his own shaky smartphone, and wearing the obligatory earbud/microphone combo. It's quite a homely scene for a musician whose first two albums debuted at number 1 on the *Billboard 200* chart, both before he was eighteen years old. His performance is designed to seem interactive and responsive, with Mendes adding spoken lines such as 'What's up guys? Ready to sing "Treat You Better" with me?' at the opening, and instructions such as 'sing it out'' and 'alright, sing this with me' at moments when the duet partner is supposed to enter. He also offers flattering interjections such as 'beautiful!', 'you got this down!', 'yeah!' and 'you crushed that, very proud of you'. Of course, these are 'static' compliments and will be heard in every duet, no matter whether the amateur singer actually 'crushes it' or not. In the best instances – for example eleven-year-old Julie Bella's Smule duet with Mendes (which has no fewer than 4.5 million views) – the amateur singer responds, genuinely, to Mendes's calls: 'Ready to sing ... with me?'/ 'Yeah, I love that song'; 'You crushed that, very proud of you'/ 'Thank you'; 'I love you'/ [surprised, smitten] 'Oh ... OK'.[48]

Performing music with a distant, non-responsive other has numerous historical precedents. In 1936, eighty years before the release of the selfie mic, NBC Radio introduced its 'Home Symphony', designed for amateur performers to play along in real time with radio broadcasts. During its first year or so on the air, hundreds of thousands of people were able to 'play with an orchestra in their own homes', during which time NBC sold 240,000 orchestra parts to radio listeners (Hill 1937, 92). Beginning around 1940, a similar (yet non-real-time) version of 'playing along' also emerged: Columbia Records released its 'S' series of 'Add-A-Part' recordings, chamber music recordings missing one part. The advent of the LP enabled a new version of this format called 'Music Minus One', with a much-praised version of Schubert's Trout Quintet from 1950 launching a lauded (though also ridiculed) recording series that exists to this day (Schonberg 1953). Yet despite, or perhaps because of, the popularity of such activities, they received hefty criticism from contemporary observers. Discussing the NBC Home Symphony, Adorno labelled it a 'pseudo-activity' and called attention to each player's 'illusion that he is taking part in a performance when he is really not; and that he is doing something for his own sake when he really only imitating what is being played to him'. In short, 'the home-participant's real achievements do not count'. Eight decades after

Adorno, Sherry Turkle offered a similar diagnosis of the 'virtual worlds' of the 2010s, opining that '[t]echnology proposes itself as the architect of our intimacies. These days, it suggests substitutions that put the real on the run' (2011, 1).

But what of Julie Bella's earnest, twitterpated reaction to Mendes's canned 'I love you'? One might anticipate an Adornian or Turklian criticism of the encounter between two young singers who have never met in person (or in real time) and yet engage musically to such a degree that a pre-recorded, generic 'I love you' at the end of an impassioned duo performance elicits an undeniable warmth and intensity of feeling. If Adorno would label this a 'pseudo-activity' (standardised, limited, illusory) and Turkle would call it evidence of 'the real on the run', we would rejoin that cotermineity, whether spatial or temporal, cannot in itself provide any guarantee for the *affectiveness* of any human interaction. The intimacies generated through musical performance are not necessarily a function of fleshy co-presence; to believe otherwise is to disregard the outsized role non-cotermineity plays in human life, from mundane daydreaming to digital performances that bring together far-flung participants. This is not to argue for a flattening (or exaggerating) of the politics or ethics of such encounters. But the critiques offered by Adorno, Turkle and others rule out the potential of performing with or simply *being with* non-present others. In the performative realm of the selfie, co-presence – as selfie-presence, as otherie-presence – holds no assurance for particular forms of relation. Susan Sontag said it best in *Regarding the Pain of Others,* her book on photography: 'Images have been reproached for being a way of watching suffering at a distance, as if there were some other way of watching. But watching up close – without the mediation of an image – is still just watching' (2003, 117).

The side-by-side performance of Mendes's and Bella's singing selfies is but one example of a widespread form of distributed performance that relies upon very particular arrangements of selfiehood. A number of observers have noted that selfies are not just 'self-portraits' but necessitate exchange. Allan A. Metcalf maintains that '[j]ust taking a picture isn't enough to make it a true selfie . . . the technology of social media also was needed, making it easy not only to take pictures of the self but also to send them' (2016, 182). The Mendes/Bella performance is a case in point. The Smule Sing! app allows users to post their videos on social media, and Bella posted hers on her own YouTube page. As of May 2018 the video garnered 5,778,346 views and over 7,850 comments. The vast bulk of these are positive ('OMG beautiful !!!!!', 'So GOOD'), with some of them calling attention to the interaction between the two singers. Or the lack of interaction, depending on how you see it. A comment by 'Shawn Mendes

Fan' – 'Shawn is so sweet to the girl' – elicited a range of replies, with quite a few pointing out that Bella and Mendes weren't actually singing together:

NAHIDA ZAMAN: '. . . it's a pre recording. if you download smule you can sing with different artists'

MOMIO LOVE: 'it's fake you can sing with him on smule right now if you wanted he would say the same things'

And icecreamgirl678 offered a subtle perspective on the difference between real-time and non-real-time online interaction:

> I think [Bella] thinks this is FaceTime haha ;) I cracking up the beginning and end sooo funny.[49]

Icecreamgirl678 is right: it's not FaceTime. But it is still about faces. Singing faces. Face-voices.

YouTube's arrival in 2005, coupled with the expanding availability of webcams and mass-market video-editing software, gave amateur musicians the tools to create and broadcast self-produced music videos. A distinct subcategory of these take the form of performances stitched together from the user-generated selfie performances of multiple musicians. These non-real-time 'virtual ensembles' are fairly widespread, with those led by musicians such as MysteryGuitarMan (Joe Penna) and Eric Whitacre counting among the most conspicuous. MysteryGuitarMan's Mystery Symphony performance (2010) of Edvard Grieg's *In The Hall of the Mountain King* and the various instantiations of Whitacre's 'Virtual Choir' are created through the meticulous editing of hundreds or even thousands of user-generated selfie videos sent in by amateur musicians. While musically interesting, the principal impact of these videos is visual, with a sea of side-by-side faces coming face-to-face with the viewer. 'The intimacy of all those faces' made Whitacre 'tear up' when he first saw the final version of the virtual choir performance of his 'Lux Aurumque'.[50] Of course, one could as easily become teary-eyed when thinking of the uncompensated labour – the literal *face-work* (Goffman 1967) – of the thousands of musicians who contribute their time and skills to the quite lucrative videos uploaded to YouTube. As Emily Bick has said of 'Lux', 'Whitacre controls all relationships within this network, and manipulates them to embellish his own brand.'[51] If, as Erving Goffman (1967, 5) tells us, '*face* may be defined as the positive social value' one claims for oneself, then we might say that, in pieces like Whitacre's – as in the Lincoln Music Selfie Experiment – *sharing* one's face modulates social value into economic value.

Yet not all of these stitched-together video performances are crowd-sourced. Another burgeoning subcategory of the musical selfie involves individual users working alone, typically in their bedrooms, to create split-screen, multi-tracked videos that feature selfies of themselves playing or singing as an ensemble. Again, these are not real-time performances and, as such, are thus distinct from classic one-man-band or more recent loop-pedal performances, both of which require a sustained form of self-coordination (not unlike juggling) and both of which manifest layered sonic selves out of a single visual one. The selfie ensembles that begin to be prevalent around 2007 with Connor Berge's 'One Man Band' video *multiply* the self through a binding together of separate audio-visual performances; each discrete audio track has its concomitant visualisation.[52] This practice might be placed within a genealogy that goes back to the 1910s and 1920s, when actors performed with themselves in 'double-exposure scenes' (Bode 2017): for example, Mary Pickford kissing her (other)self on the cheek in the 1921 film *Little Lord Fauntleroy*, or Lawrence Tibbett singing a duet with his own ghost in the 1931 movie *The Cuban Love Song* (a scene that might be regarded as the inaugural moment of overdubbed musical performance). But whereas these on-screen performances typically had actors playing multiple characters, many selfie performances are visually homogeneous, with the sole performer multiplied identically, flaunting selfie-sameness. A provocative example can be found in Mike Tompkins's 2011 a cappella version of Coldplay's 'Paradise', in which, at one point, he has twenty-six identical versions of himself singing on the screen (see Figure 4.2).[53] The relative complexity of the self-other relationship in the Home Symphony or the Mendes/Bella performance is distilled and intensified. The multiplied selfie becomes constellated as otherie.

It perhaps shouldn't be surprising that the *selfie a cappella* – or the *selfie choir* – has been one of the key formations in the universe of selfie performance. The commonsensical understanding of the voice as that which communicates 'the true, vital, and perceptible uniqueness of the

Figure 4.2 Mike Tompkins × 26 (Coldplay 'Paradise' A Capella Cover). Screenshot used courtesy of Mike Tompkins.

one who emits it' (Cavarero 2005, 5) is exaggerated by the presence of so many identical faces which, in their accumulation, create what might be called a face-voice, a hybrid entity reducible to neither the aural nor the ocular. In the selfie choir, the face-voice is spatially distributed across the screen, typically with each singing face corralled into its own separate box (rather like the old television show *The Hollywood Squares*). A vast number of these selfie performances utilise the box as a framing device, with the visual result coming close to the ubiquitous selfie photo collages found on social media platforms.[54] Templates abound, with almost all offering some form of rectilinear arrangement. As spectacles of selfie-sameness, the multiplied face-voice simultaneously renders legible the relative continuity of the person (we know that it's a unique person responsible for the entire performance) and brings the selfie 'face-voice-to-face-voice' with its otherie (we know, through variations in facial expression and vocal line, that none of the face-voices is identical to another).

A case in point is the videos produced via Acapella, an app that its parent company Mixcord calls 'the only place to create engaging multi-frame music videos and download an Apple lossless copy of the audio'. A 2015 article in the *Boston Globe* summed it up like this: 'With the new app Acapella, you can record and arrange up to nine short video clips into a selection of foxy sharable layouts, allowing you track rich harmonies or serve some serious one-man-band realness.'[55] The article appeared under the headline 'On singing selfie app Acapella, it's all you', with *all you* functioning as a snide yet perceptive comment on both the continuities of selfiehood (it's *just* you) and the nature of cumulative selfiehood (each selfie has its otheries). Lawrence Kramer has provocatively suggested that music 'has served as the preeminent measure of the self's relation to a generalized otherness' (1995, 54). But in an age when more than four billion people are connected to the Internet,[56] music is also a measure of the self's relation to a highly specific otherness, an otherness that often takes the form of otherie.

Postlude: Selfie Surveillance

Encrypt your Identity in Sound.[57]

First, we see lines. Horizontal lines of equally small width on a greyscale continuum from black to white, stacked on top of one other and together constituting a rectangle that covers the middle section of the screen. The rectangle stands against a black backdrop. Two words – 'Sound Selfie' – in white and rotated 90 degrees extend along the left-hand side of the rectangle, and what appears to be a username, also in white and rotated 90 degrees, is visible on the right. Viewing the image and text, it dawns upon us that the rectangle stands in for a photograph of a face; it also looks quite a bit like a barcode. Then we press 'play'. The image seems to move, to vibrate and throb, due to shifts in the greyscale continuum that are imposed on some, but not all, of the lines – at times veering towards the white and at others the black end of the spectrum. Accompanying these visual changes is an FM-synthesis-generated soundtrack that blurts out a very fast stream of seemingly random notes – atonal blips and bleeps within a relatively limited range (around an octave below middle C to an octave above it). Sometimes the image freezes at one of its altered states; at such moments, the soundtrack 'freezes' too, fixating on a single note that it repeats irregularly. In addition to these synthesiser bleeps, a glitchy click track – apparently a programming error,[58] but one that provides an interesting effect – taps along at about 120 BPM. It seems as if a person whose face is obscured is attempting to speak, but in a language that is incomprehensible or perhaps encrypted by some nefarious scrambling device. The video lasts only sixteen seconds, and its terseness seems to mirror the spatial and temporal compactness of the commonplace photographic selfie as well as that of a product or face-identification scan.

Such is the effect of Jasmine Guffond's remarkable multimedia participatory artwork *Sound Selfie* (2014–15).[59] The project involves participants in an art gallery sitting in front of a computer that uses a facial analysis program called FaceOSC to generate raw data from the scanning of their faces.[60] The raw data are a stream of numbers, which are converted via Max/MSP into the black and white lines and the soundtrack, together captured in a video file. Mirroring the circulation of photographic selfies, the *Sound Selfie* videos are then automatically uploaded to Facebook. The disturbing effect of the videos is part and parcel of the project's critical thrust, which recalls 'contemporary modes of participatory surveillance that are often based on the intentional disclosure of personal information by users of social media, mobile apps and online platforms'.[61] Guffond's project thus articulates an important dimension of selfiehood – participatory surveillance – that is central to the work of Henry Giroux cited above and to current discourses on 'dataveillance' (Lupton 2016, 102), but has not been foregrounded in the musical selfie analyses we have offered so far.

Guffond's *Sound Selfie* prompts us to consider how 'participatory surveillance' characterises musical selfiehood. We can consider this problem in relation to each of the three core practices of musical selfiehood discussed above: curation, enclosure and broadcasting. With respect to the curation of the selfie, Drott (2018) explains how Spotify profiles are multiply subdivided, including by time of day, geographic location, activity, and, crucially, listening habits. Such profiles are minutely compiled and analysed in order to enhance the user data marketed to advertisers. In one particularly disturbing example, Spotify executives blithely comment that, based on the use of showering playlists, the company knows when their users are showering. However, such musical surveillance is also beginning to account for listeners' emotions, with MIR researchers increasingly using machine learning and text mining to facilitate emotion recognition (Drott 2018; see also Kim et al. 2010; Yang and Chen 2012; Han et al. 2016). And as we've seen (with our analysis of Peekabeat, for example), the facial analysis used by musical selfies is also a means of ascertaining a user's affective state (Patel et al. 2016; Ghule et al. 2017). The holy grail of such an approach would be real-time emotion detection on a mass scale. Such technologies would potentially allow numerous powerful entities – including marketing firms, policing institutions and political polling companies – to gain affective information from and, in so doing, propose forms of participation and consumption to every individual on the planet. This is one possible future that Guffond's vision of musical selfiehood discloses.

As of early 2018, such systems are still nascent. But real-time facial analysis and recognition are beginning to surface in musical contexts, with the profoundly racialised attempt to use facial recognition software by police forces at the August 2017 Notting Hill Carnival being one controversial example.[62] This emergent surveillance of musicking faces resonates with Deleuze and Guattari's claim that '[f]aces are not basically individual; they define zones of frequency or probability, delimit a field that neutralizes in advance any expressions or connections unamenable to the appropriate significations' (1987, 168). And that is what both facial analysis and facial recognition software do: they reduce individuals to zones of probability, gleaning information that can be added at any given moment to one's 'data double' (the abstract representation of an individual that aggregated personal data construct). The impulse here is curiously, and disturbingly, reminiscent of older, now discredited race-scientific practices of phrenology, anthropometry, and physiognomy. That such information could be used for race-based marketing, including for marketing music, would surprise no one – though its reliance on types and categories for classifying humans would give the lie to inflated claims about personalised or individualised marketing and the uniqueness of the consumer.

Surveillance in the context of the selfie enclosure is a somewhat different matter (even though many of the mechanisms of data collection are the same). Here the crucial problem is the honing of the technical system to the shape and lifestyle of the individual user and environment. If the most recent forms of noise cancellation now incorporate perpetually repeated measurement of a user's head in order to maximise the tightness of the sonic enclosure created by the headphone-listener loop, this process can be seen as part of a more generalised dynamic in which listening machines employ control systems that feed output back as input. Machines like headphones or loudspeakers are now also listening devices fitted with microphones and sensors, as we've seen, but they represent only one example of increasingly prevalent feedback and feed-forward systems. Here the endgame is the smart device and smart house, in which the constant monitoring of user and environment both responds to and produces a user's desires. Numerous such devices became widespread around 2015; smart speakers are one prominent example.

In all such technologies, the internal monitoring system is linked to an external monitoring system, whereby corporations gain highly detailed information about user–device interaction. In these domains, complex user agreements rife with legalese are a crucial mechanism for allowing information to be shared with 'third parties'.[63] The interrelation between internal and external monitoring thus creates the dilemma that Hicham Tahiri describes as 'the privacy/convenience tradeoff', as exhibited in a recent class action complaint brought against the Bose Corporation for 'secretly collecting, transmitting, and disclosing its customers' private music and audio selections to third parties' via its Bose Connect app.[64] As a lawyer representing the plaintiff said in interview, 'people put head-phones on their head because they think it's private, but they can be giving out information they don't want to share'.[65] With headphones being increasingly plugged into larger musical ecosystems that extend beyond the user/device dyad, the assumed privacy of the classic headphone enclosure is compromised.

And what of broadcasting the selfie and its relationship to surveillance? At one level, the fact that users record videos and upload them to mega-platforms like YouTube, which is integrated with Google and its immense suite of apps and services, means that all of the data gleaned from those videos are also shared between different apps and services and hence, presumably, with Google's own tracking mechanisms. These data usually take the form of tagging information and metadata but also increasingly include data drawn from automated image recognition applications such as Google's Video Intelligence API.[66] Moreover, any additional apps that users employ to make their musical selfies, such as Acapella, will have their own, additional networks of data sharing – pinging one's data between numerous servers and data-processing centres all over the globe. Funda-mental to this reality are, again, the typically unread user agreements that participants accede to once they employ any particular app or service. For example, Mixcord's user agreement makes easily transgressed distinctions between personally identifying and non-identifying (aggregated) information, describes extensive tracking of data, and authorises sharing of content on multiple platforms that 'uniquely identify the user'.[67] In this way a self-made bedroom music video syncs up with other user-generated data, entering a tangled network of interfirm partnerships (the infamous 'third parties' we just mentioned).

But data tracking is not only occurring at the level of the firm. Such data are also central to contemporary modes of individual petty accumulation that inspire dreams of celebrity and success in the minds of aspiring musicians. Paralleling the optimisation modalities of the quantified self movement, petty digital entrepreneurship is so commonplace in the digital music business that one can almost miss claims like StarMaker's to 'perform, publish and *monetize*' user-generated content (our emphasis). After all, the tracking undertaken by Google is not only in the corporate behemoth's interest but also that of individual users who monetise videos for their personal financial benefit and track revenue through easily acquired apps and plug-ins. With performances monetised through tracking, rather than through watching or listening per se, listeners/watchers pay not with money but with clicks. Surveillance is fundamentally selfie-tracking here – a voyeurism metamorphosed into clicks, but with the promise of public appearances, ticket and recording sales, and the lucrative creation of an artistic brand. For emerging musicians, fantasies of celebrity and financial success are written into increasingly ubiquitous data analytics as part of a broader informatic entrepreneurialism. Encrypting your identity into sound, as Guffond puts it, is a Faustian bargain, simultaneously a promise of capital accumulation and the unruly digital distribution of your personal information – something against which only a relatively small number of economic elites (including celebrities) can protect themselves.

These processes of musical selfiehood, especially when perceived through the refractive power of Guffond's *Sound Selfie*, seem profoundly machinic, tied up less with the production of unique individuals and senses of self than with repeatable acts that generate tiny fractions of surplus value – fractions that can however accumulate into a worthwhile investment. The paradox of repeatable individuality takes on a particularly neoliberal cast in the current moment: the curating of self and self-image is part of an entrepreneurial imperative that requires face- and image-work (and increasingly sound- and music-work) in order to make oneself viable within a marketplace of shrinking opportunities. As Peter Kelly compellingly says in *The Self as Enterprise*: 'Individualisation processes increasingly locate the self as the space/site in which the tensions, risks, contradictions, paradoxes, ambiguities and ambivalences of globalised, rationalised capitalism are to be resolved and managed – or not' (2016, 14). And that is part and parcel of what we mean when we displace the discourse of the self by the notion of the selfie. If music continues to define the self in the digital-network era – through playlist creation, headphone listening and self-made musical videos – it may be harnessed to these projects of entrepreneurial self-construction (as it already is for many aspiring musicians). At the same time music also exists as an irreducible remainder. Its projections of daydream-like utopias point towards a world beyond this one, in which everyone gets to make and share music that matters to them.

Guffond's artwork helps us to rethink what is at stake in apparently innocuous musical selfies and the new social condition – selfiehood – they index. What we term selfiehood impinges upon the construction of the self, but not in a crudely deterministic way.[68] How could it? Senft and Baym (2015) note that the selfie is readily associated with pathology, ultimately obscuring the deep economic links between selfie-making and neoliberalism. (We remain undecided on whether pathologies associated with visual selfies are entirely applicable to musical selfies.) We might point to Wendt's notion of the selfie as central to the construction of an 'ideal self' (2014, 45), the social pressure for which could be seen as a product of precariousness, of the retracted promise of economic stability in times of growing scarcity. This leads us to a still more vexing matter: the relationship between the self and the selfie is not easily divined. It is striking that writers on the selfie seem to avoid investigating this relationship, instead taking the notion of the self as a given while examining the selfie's multifariously complex appearances in society, culture and politics.[69] Certainly it is an open question as to whether and to what degree the selfie has transformed the self in contemporary modernity; thus far it is apparent that the musical selfie has not fundamentally altered the material and formal properties of music. But although the music on offer in the musical selfie may not be particularly novel in its sonic configurations or structural traits, it is exceptional in its socio-technological imbrication, in the circulatory spirals and webs within which it is found.

For Further Study

DeNora, Tia. 1999. 'Music as a technology of the self'. *Poetics* 27(1): 31–56.

Drott, Eric. 2018. 'Music as a technology of surveillance'. *Journal of the Society for American Music* 12(3): 233–67.

Foucault, Michel. 1988. 'Technologies of the self'. In *Technologies of the Self: A Seminar with Michel Foucault*, edited by Luther Martin, Huck Gutman and Patrick Hutton, 16–49. London: Tavistock.

Gopinath, Sumanth and Jason Stanyek. 2013. 'Tuning the human race: Athletic capitalism and the Nike+ sport kit'. In *Music, Sound and Space: Transformations of Public and Private Experience*, edited by Georgina Born, 128–48. Cambridge: Cambridge University Press.

Rose, Nicholas. 1996. *Inventing Ourselves: Psychology, Power and Personhood*. New York: Cambridge University Press.

Senft, Theresa M. and Nancy K. Baym. 2015. 'What does the selfie say? Investigating a global phenomenon'. *International Journal of Communication* 9: 1588–606. (Introduction to featured section on 'Selfies', 1588–872.)

Notes

The authors would like to offer our heartfelt thanks to Nicholas Cook for his astute and patient editing; to Eric Drott for his valuable feedback on an earlier draft; to David Trippett, Monique M. Ingalls and Ariana Phillips-Hutton for their contributions at various stages of writing; and to Jasmine Guffond and Heather Phenix for their helpful insights into their work.

1 Basic documentation for the project, including an explanatory/promotional video, was formerly available at 'A Song for a Certain Few', http://now.lincoln.com/a-song-for-a-certain-few/. The image bearing the tagline is widely available on the web at the time of writing, e.g. https://i.pinimg.com/originals/3d/79/a3/3d79a378bdd20c55049314362ff6e58a.png. All websites accessed 27 September 2018.

2 Lincoln, 'Lincoln digital campaign introduces Music Selfie Experiment', 9 February 2015, https://media.lincoln.com/content/lincolnmedia/lna/us/en/news/2015/02/05/lincoln-digital-campaign-introduces-music-selfie-experiment.html. As we learned in correspondence with Heather Phenix (2 October 2018), one of the producers of the Experiment, it incorporated an open-source facial analysis javascript library called clmtrackr. In this chapter, we rely on the distinction between facial recognition (identification of an individual through face-examination algorithms), facial analysis (the algorithmic examination of facial actions and behaviours) and face identification (the much more basic identification of the presence of [unidentified] faces within images). Confusingly, these terms are often used interchangeably. For further details see Navin Manaswi, 'Difference between face detection, face recognition and facial analysis', *MantraAI*, www.mantra.ai/difference-between-face-detection-face-recognition-and-facial-analysis/.

3 Excepting a few videos and a well-hidden working version of the site (at http://musicself.jam3.net), most traces of Lincoln's experiment have vanished from the web.

4 Richard Gray, 'Create a playlist with your FACE: Spotify tool scans selfies to see how you're feeling and makes music mixes to suit your mood', *Daily Mail*, 18 September 2015, www.dailymail.co.uk/sciencetech/article-3240152/Create-playlist-FACE-Spotify-tool-scans-selfies-feeling-makes-music-mixes-suit-mood.html; Frames Direct, 'How to Take a Good Selfie Infographic', www.framesdirect.com/landing/a/how-to-take-a-selfie.html?AID=10584984&PID=7793420&SID=81222X1532592X3225d2a7d807d49eaaaa8537bb27cb96&AFFILIATE=5&medium=7793420.

5 BBC, 'Self-portraits and social media: The rise of the "selfie"', BBC, 7 June 2013, www.bbc.co.uk/news/magazine-22511650.

6 Sherry Turkle, 'The documented life', *New York Times*, 15 December 2013, www.nytimes.com/2013/12/16/opinion/the-documented-life.html.

7 Henry Giroux, 'Selfie culture at the intersection of the corporate and the surveillance states', *Counterpunch*, 6 February 2015, www.counterpunch.org/2015/02/06/selfie-culture-at-the-intersection-of-the-corporate-and-the-surveillance-states/.

8 For example, the Japanese skincare company IPSA launched their (now-defunct) Face Melody website in 2016 on the premise: 'Your face is one of a kind. The color and texture of your skin, your expression, and your features. These are all unique to you and you alone', www.dailydot.com/debug/selfie-sound-face-melody/. Mea Mobile's iDNAtity uses both facial recognition and 'phenotype profiling' based on user input to convert 'your unique genetic code into musical notes', http://idnatity.com/the-science-behind-idnatity/. Approaching the problem from an academic research-driven perspective rather than a marketing one, Gascia Ouzounian, Georgina Born, Christopher Haworth and Peter Bennett have created Echo-Snap, the purpose of which is to create mobile apps for generating musical 'selfies'. See www.echo-snap.com.

9 Spotify, 'You are what you stream', http://spotify.me/en-GB; Beats Electronics, 'Beats Electronics, LLC Trademarks List', www.beatsbydre.com/company/trademark; Alex Hudson, 'Is Google taking the "you" out of YouTube?' *BBC News*, 16 May 2011, http://news.bbc.co.uk/1/hi/programmes/click_online/9485376.stm.

10 Urban Dictionary, 'Otherie', www.urbandictionary.com/define.php?term=Otherie.

11 Shondiin Silversmith, 'This is what a "musical selfie" sounds like', *PRI's The World*, 15 December 2016, www.pri.org/stories/2016-12-15/what-musical-selfie-sounds; Eric Harvey, 'St. Vincent: "digital witness"', *Pitchfork*, 15 December 2014, https://pitchfork.com/features/lists-and-guides/9555-the-100-best-tracks-of-2014/?page=8.

12 Peekabeat, Apple App Store, https://itunes.apple.com/us/app/peekabeat/id1230901779?mt=8.

13 Bill Doerrfeld, '20+ emotion recognition APIs that will leave you impressed, and concerned', *Nordic APIs* (blog), 11 August 2016, https://nordicapis.com/20-emotion-recognition-apis-that-will-leave-you-impressed-and-concerned/.

14 See https://github.com/gleitz/automaticdj.

15 See Chapter 3, this volume.

16 'Smarter playlists', www.playlistmachinery.com.

17 Elise Moreau, '8 Awesome Tools for Better Spotify Playlists', *Lifewire*, 15 March 2017 [updated 3 May 2019], www.lifewire.com/awesome-tools-for-better-spotify-playlists-4091942.

18 'Your Time Capsule', https://timecapsule.spotify.com/; 'Discover Lazify for Spotify, the app for the lazy', http://lazify.nl/lazify/.

19 It is indeed a basic principle of so-called Web 2.0 businesses as described by Henry Jenkins: see Chapter 1, pp. 15, 21.

20 See Ann-Christine Diaz, 'Facial recognition technology makes marketers a fun Big Brother', *AdAge*, 18 September 2013, http://adage.com/article/news/brands-facial-recognition-campaigns/244233/.

21 Russell Brandom, 'The five biggest questions about Apple's new facial recognition system', *The Verge*, 12 September 2017, www.theverge.com/2017/9/12/16298156/apple-iphone-x-face-id-security-privacy-police-unlock.

22 Beats by Dre, 27 November 2014, 10.05am. https://twitter.com/beatsbydre/status/538030751128621056?lang=en.

23 Rihanna, 25 January 2016, 6.22am, https://twitter.com/rihanna/status/691627277940080640?lang=en.

24 Elsie Taylor, 'Roy Nachum, the artist behind Rihanna's Anti cover, explains what it all means', *Vanity Fair*, 14 October 2015, www.vanityfair.com/culture/2015/10/rihanna-anti-cover-what-it-means-roy-nachum.

25 Jamieson Cox, 'Rihanna is listening to her new album with insanely luxurious headphones', *The Verge*, 25 January 2016, www.theverge.com/2016/1/25/10826314/rihanna-anti-trolling-dolce-gabbana-luxury-headphones.

26 This means that while Rihanna would have seen the mirror image of her tattoo on her smartphone screen, the image she sent out into the world shows the tattoo's reversed text.

27 CNN, 'Look at me! Selfies of the year', CNN.com, 2 December 2016, http://edition.cnn.com/2016/12/02/entertainment/gallery/year-in-selfies-2016/index.html; Nicholas Hautman, 'Happy National Selfie Day! Revisit 10 of the most iconic celebrity selfies', *Us Weekly*, 21 June 2017, www.usmagazine.com/celebrity-news/pictures/happy-national-selfie-day-revisit-10-iconic-celebrity-selfies-w489066/.

28 NathanZed, 25 January 2016, 7.50am, https://twitter.com/NathanZed/status/691649350599098368.

29 Thisisamplify, 26 January 2016, 6.34pm, https://twitter.com/thisisamplify/status/692173834431107072.

30 Pixieitzel, 7 February 2016, 4.06pm, https://twitter.com/pixieitzel/status/696485166022160384.

31 Prince0fChina, 5 February 2016, 2.13pm, https://twitter.com/Prince0fChina/status/695732116143874048.

32 Montagesvideofr, 'Beats Solo2 TV commercial, "Solo Selfie" song by Axwell Ingrosso', YouTube, 01:02, 25 December 2014, www.youtube.com/watch?v=whI9eK4PuZQ.

33 Danel Eran Dilger, 'Apple, Inc. Beats promotes Solo2 headphones with new celebrity-packed #SoloSelfie campaign', *appleinsider*, 26 November 2014, https://appleinsider.com/articles/14/11/26/apple-inc-beats-promotes-solo2-headphones-with-new-celebrity-packed-soloselfie-campaign.

34 GQFrance, 'Beats by Dre Presents_ #SoloSelfie - The Tutorial', DailyMotion, 01:11, n.d., www.dailymotion.com/video/x2b7cts.

35 'The selfie. Reinvented', 27 November 2014, 10.05am, https://twitter.com/beatsbydre/status/538030751128621056?lang=en.

36 Devin Liddell, 'Beats by Dre isn't great design, just great marketing', *Fast Company*, 10 March 2015, www.fastcompany.com/3042776/beats-by-dre-isnt-great-design-just-great-marketing.

37 See e.g. Glam Barbie, 'Beats by Dre presents: #SoloSelfie', YouTube, 0:39, 29 November 2014, www.youtube.com/watch?v=PcR56z6tsAU.

38 Beats By Dre, 'Beats by Dre x Colin Kaepernick: Hear What You Want Commercial (Director's Cut)', YouTube, 2:47, 8 December 2013, www.youtube.com/watch?v=5G9tusbzEhM; Kaepernick is also discussed by Peter McMurray in Chapter 5, 141–43.

39 Alex Blue V (2017) refers to the Beats Solo2s as 'racism-canceling headphones' and provides a poignant, intricate analysis of the racial dimensions of another one of the 'Hear What You Want' commercials (featuring the basketball star Kevin Garnett).

40 Elizabeth Stinson, 'The new Beats headphones cancel noise better than ever', *Wired*, 4 September 2017, www.wired.com/story/new-beats-headphones-cancel-noise-better-than-ever/.

41 Beats by Dre, 'Noise cancelling vs. noise-isolating', n.d., www.beatsbydre.com/uk/support/info/noise-canceling-isolating.

42 SelfieMic, https://web.archive.org/web/20180201141541/https://selfiemic.co.uk/.

43 On the relevance of deixis to the selfie, see Frosh 2015.

44 Kelby K. Clark, 'Amateur singers can show off their inner star with top-rated karaoke and vocal coaching apps', *[App]ddicted!*, 9 April 2013, https://appddicted.wordpress.com/2013/04/09/amateur-singers-can-show-off-their-inner-star-with-top-rated-karaoke-and-vocal-coaching-apps/.

45 Business Wire, 'StarMaker launches music video network', *Business Wire*, 14 October 2014, www.businesswire.com/news/home/20141014006156/en/StarMaker-Launches-Music-Video-Network; StarMaker home page (section: 'STARMAKER ORIGINALS'), The Internet Archive, Wayback Machine (Archive date: 17 October 2017), http://web.archive.org/web/20171017192523/http://www.starmakerstudios.com:80/.

46 StarMaker, 'The Weeknd (Can't Feel My Face) + David Guetta (Hey Mama) Mashup - Andrew Garcia and KRNFX', YouTube, 3:05, 27 August 2015, www.youtube.com/watch?v=M4LntIcY-f8; Taylor Weatherby, 'YouTube's 10 most-watched music videos', *Billboard*, 12 July 2017, www.billboard.com/articles/news/magazine-feature/7709247/youtube-most-watched-videos.

47 Sing! by Smule, Apple App Store Preview, https://itunes.apple.com/us/app/sing-karaoke-by-smule/id509993510?mt=8.

48 Julie Bella, 'Treat You Better - Shawn Mendes and 11 Year Old Julie Bella (Smule Duet) #SingWithShawn #SingWithLG', YouTube, 3:08, 28 October 2016, www.youtube.com/watch?v=usMHGHgxmFw.

49 Comments to Julie Bella, 'Treat You Better - Shawn Mendes and 11 Year Old Julie Bella (Smule Duet) #SingWithShawn #SingWithLG', YouTube, 3:08, 28 October 2016, www.youtube.com/watch?v=usMHGHgxmFw.

50 Eric Whitacre, 'The Virtual Choir: How we did it', 23 March 2010, https://ericwhitacre.com/blog/the-virtual-choir-how-we-did-it.

51 Emily Bick, 'Collateral damage: Emily Bick on crowdsourced choirs', *Wire*, July 2014, www.thewire.co.uk/in-writing/collateral-damage/collateral-damage_emily-bick-on-crowdsourced-choirs.

52 Connor Berge, 'One Man Band', YouTube, 1:25, 14 February 2007, www.youtube.com/watch?v=mHwV2JuwZls.

53 Mike Tompkins, 'Coldplay - Paradise - A Capella Cover', YouTube, 5:27, 8 November 2011, www.youtube.com/watch?v=K2YSo8Z_-a4.

54 Sam Robson, 'The Lion King - Circle of Life acapella arrangement!' YouTube, 4:57, 29 July 2015, www.youtube.com/watch?v=s_um4Qj4aJA.

55 Michael Andor Brodeur, 'On singing selfie app Acapella, it's all you', *Boston Globe*, 27 November 2015, www.bostonglobe.com/arts/2015/11/27/apps/uEwsTLhJpfQpKZiT0f6LOP/story.html.

56 Internet World Stats, 'World Internet usage and population statistics', 31 December 2017, www.internetworldstats.com/stats.htm. The figure for 31 December 2017 was 4,156,932,140.

57 Jasmine Guffond, 'Sound Selfie', http://jasmineguffond.com/art/Sound+Selfie.

58 In correspondence (16 January 2018) Guffond told us, 'This project is 2–3 years old and actually that glitchy click track isn't intentional, I guess it is some artifact related to the process because

when I test the max patch out now on my computer there are no glitches.' Even if not intentional, we'd argue that the clicks are aesthetically effective and communicative.

59 See the Sound Selfie Facebook page, www.facebook.com/soundselfie/, and 'Sound Selfie', http:// jasmineguffond.com/art/Sound+Selfie.

60 Personal correspondence, 16 January 2018.

61 Guffond in Georgie McVicar, 'Algorithmic gaze: Jasmine Guffond', *Stray Landings*, 1 August 2015, http://www.straylandings.co.uk/interviews/the-algorithmic-gaze.

62 Rashid Nix, 'The decision to use facial recognition software at Notting Hill Carnival is another example of racial profiling by the police', *The Independent*, 27 August 2017, www.independent.co.uk/voices/notting-hill-carnival-racial-profiling-facial-recognition-stop-and-search-a7915401.html; see also Harris 2018. These systems are not racially neutral, and a number of commentators have discussed their racial biases, especially their misrecognition of faces of colour. See Clare Garvie and Jonathan Frankle, 'Facial recognition software might have a racial bias problem', *The Atlantic*, 7 April 2016, www.theatlantic.com/technology/archive/2016/ 04/the-underlying-bias-of-facial-recognition-systems/476991/; Phoebe Weston, 'Is face ID racist? Apple's iPhone X is slammed by Chinese users who claim its facial recognition system can't tell them apart', *The Daily Mail online* (UK), 21 December 2017, www.dailymail.co.uk/sciencetech/ article-5201881/The-iPhone-X-slammed-RACIST-Chinese-users.html; Steve Lohr, 'Facial recognition is accurate, if you're a white guy', *New York Times*, 9 February 2018, www.nytimes .com/2018/02/09/technology/facial-recognition-race-artificial-intelligence.html.

63 The problem of user or terms of service agreements is also discussed in this volume by Goldschmitt and Seaver (Chapter 3, p. 78) and Scherzinger (Chapter 11, p. 291).

64 Hicham Tahiri, 'Understanding user privacy in the age of smart speakers', *VentureBeat*, 27 November 2017, https://venturebeat.com/2017/11/27/understanding-user-privacy-in-the-age-of-smart-speakers/; Rochelle Garner, 'Bose is spying on us, lawsuit alleges', *CBS News*, 20 April 2017, www.cbsnews.com/news/bose-is-spying-on-us-lawsuit-alleges/.

65 Jonathan Stempel, 'Bose headphones spy on listeners: lawsuit', Reuters, 19 April 2017, www.reuters.com/article/us-bose-lawsuit-idUSKBN17L2BT.

66 Nadine Krefetz, 'Google Video Intelligence analyzes images in videos', *Streamingmedia.com*, 21 July 2017, www.streamingmedia.com/Articles/Editorial/Featured-Articles/Google-Video-Intelligence-Analyzes-Images-in-Videos-119488.aspx.

67 Mixcord, 'Privacy Policy', www.mixcord.co/privacy-policy.html. As Karl Bode notes, 'using data from roughly 400 volunteers, the researchers found that they could identify the person behind an "anonymized" data set *70% of the time* just by comparing their browsing data to their social media activity'. 'One more time with feeling: "Anonymized" user data not really anonymous', *Tech Dirt*, 26 January 2017, www.techdirt.com/articles/20170123/08125136548/one-more-time-with-feeling-anonymized-user-data-not-really-anonymous.shtml.

68 Which is not to say that the self isn't a contested notion; Zahavi notes that in several fields it has been common to dismiss notions of the self as a 'neurologically induced illusion' (2005, 1).

69 See the numerous essays summarised and introduced in Senft and Baym 2015.

Personal Take: Vaporwave is Dead, Long Live Vaporwave!

ADAM HARPER

A grand dichotomy sometimes emerges around the role of early-twenty-first-century digital technologies in cultural life, all too stark but nevertheless deeply ingrained, vividly observed, and acutely revealing: online or offline? A host of similar discriminations line up in parallel: digital or analogue, physical or virtual, user or bot? One formulation tellingly folds authenticity into ontology: URL (that is, a web address) or IRL ('in real life')? Supporting all of this is that monolithic construction, 'the Internet', singular and definitive, discussed not as a network of servers and devices but as if it were a shared geographical space to be visited or lived in, an alternative (and often lesser) plane of reality, a new Wild West peopled by exotic subcultural aliens, conmen and other dangerous sorts.

Such narratives have significant consequences for the production and reception of music, but then they always did. Concerns over the worth and survival of 'real music' in relation to its urban, mechanical or electrical antagonists extend as far back as John Philip Sousa's fulminations against recorded music (1906) – quoting Wagner on the importance of sincerity in 'the expression of soul states' (279) – and beyond that to late-eighteenth-century literary Romanticism. More recently, rock musician Jack White has banned phones from his gigs in pursuit of a '100% human experience' and enjoyment of the music 'IN PERSON'.[1] There have also been strong statements about the benefits or dangers of opening the doors of cultural production to technologically enabled amateurs, whether using digital platforms as discussed by Astra Taylor (2014), or, in the 1980s, the cassette (the enthusiasm of grass-roots 'cassette culture' versus the industry's 'home taping is killing music').

These are the values that participants in digital cultures must reckon with, especially if they find themselves following in the footsteps of earlier countercultures: young, weird and rebellious. The backlash against Silicon Valley's techno-utopianism, expressed by Taylor and others, echoes the anxieties of mid-twentieth-century counterculture over the 'machine' of technocratic society, even in their debts to Romantic notions of archaism and escape.[2] In the mid-2000s indie subcultures, observing a latest iteration of this aesthetic preference for archaic musics and technologies by reviving vinyl and cassettes, found themselves using the Internet extensively: it superseded paper fanzines as a medium for news and networking. Websites such as the blog *Gorilla vs. Bear* disavowed their digital nature in a visual design of blurred, grainy, analogue photography and even, at one point, wood panelling, as they provided their listeners with MP3s of guitars and old-fashioned synthesisers. The aesthetic was as offline as online could be.

It speaks to this treatment of the Internet as incidental that when one of the earliest musics to emerge in sight of this milieu was christened 'blog house', it seemed to make sense. The faintly derisory term alludes to the fact that the music – a hard-edged disco with basic analogue synthesiser sounds for an indie audience – was celebrated and disseminated on blogs. Today the term might imply too broad a form to refer to so specific a content – imagine 'vinyl jazz' or 'CD techno' – but then the appellation 'SoundCloud Rap' (named after the streaming platform rappers had uploaded to) became common currency in 2017, even in the upper echelons of music journalism.

Since blog house's nominal acknowledgement of the digital sphere, online musicians and listeners have begun to grapple more directly with their existence within impersonal, digital-commercial superstructures that their countercultural superegos might be telling them they should be wary of. Many underground musicians began to turn away from archaic idioms and technologies towards more comprehensively electronic ones. This move, represented most prominently by artists Oneohtrix Point Never and James Ferraro and later taken up by Holly Herndon, Arca and artists of the PC Music collective (Harper 2017; Waugh 2017), can be read as indicative of a new interest in digital modernity.

By this point the growth in speed and infrastructure had made it easy to maintain every level of a complex musical culture from networked digital devices, even the live streaming of concerts. Though widely heard as a satirical representation of the propaganda of digital living with its ersatz timbres and restlessly upbeat mood, Ferraro's *Far Side Virtual* (2011) was nevertheless released on a vinyl LP for an underground audience of attentive listeners – a fact which introduces an irony into the work it might not otherwise have had. Yet around the time *Far Side Virtual* was released, artists were beginning to exchange music with like-minded others without releasing it (as the parlance goes) 'physically'. This music, later known as vaporwave, offers an archetypical case of a musical style and subculture being digital not just in form but in content.

A typical vaporwave track either is made up of a single looping sample of smooth adult-contemporary pop or jazz produced in the newly digitised studios of the late twentieth century, or offers a close pastiche of it. Often the samples are altered slightly: slowed in time and pitch simultaneously, effects added. Releases are almost always album-like collections; initially these were free zip files downloadable through MediaFire (a common way to pirate MP3s at the time), but the SoundCloud and Bandcamp platforms later provided a structure of dissemination, which has sometimes required payment and even enabled physical purchases. As Born and Haworth (2017) and Glitsos (2018) have detailed, the genre soon developed a fan community based on social media websites such as reddit and Tumblr.

A very significant – perhaps definitive – dimension of the vaporwave experience lies in its paratexts, almost all of which are part of the fiction: the album cover and name, the video, the track titles, the blurb, and even the marked location and social media presence, with text frequently incorporating Unicode symbols or East Asian characters. All of it contributes to the suggestion that the release was produced by some corporation as mood music for a lifestyle of business, shopping or luxurious downtime. While a few genuine biographical details are known about a handful of the most famous vaporwave producers, the majority are deliberately anonymous, and this impersonality is a part of the intriguing alienation vaporwave courts.

One popular talking point about vaporwave has been that it is 'dead', in the typical subcultural narrative of an underground scene killed off by outside observers.[3] Given the amount of material released in the mid-2010s that looks and sounds like vaporwave, this can only be true for the first artists to make it, who have since explored other styles – in fact, the continual description of vaporwave as a 'microgenre' seems at odds with its vast representation on Bandcamp and the fact that it has spawned several offshoot styles. Another possible reading is that vaporwave has always been 'dead' inasmuch as it is not 'live' music, and enshrines a bittersweet exploration of what is impersonal, absent and defunct. The musical idioms and audio-visual quality of some vaporwave releases (especially those produced early on by INTERNET CLUB and 情報デスクVIRTUAL) suggest a world that, though tired, could still pass for contemporary. But a degree of archaism in music and visuals that connotes the era of the worn VHS tape has become commonplace. Academic accounts of vaporwave given by Trainer (2016), Born and Haworth (2017), Glitsos (2018) and myself (2017) emphasise this. Glitsos develops the point most fully, seeing in vaporwave 'a kind of "memory play"... a process of audio-visual collage that deploys the act of remembering as a central feature and concern' (2018, 100, 114). Born and Haworth observe 'a reflexive and politicized material and aesthetic play with the very historicity of the Internet' and 'an extraordinarily acute awareness of the historicity of the Internet as an unfolding medium' (2017, 74, 79); Trainer pithily calls vaporwave 'the muzak of the dawning of the digital era' (2016, 419–20).

In this respect, then, vaporwave offers archaism within a contemporary frame, just as *Gorilla vs. Bear* and blog house did – the difference being that vaporwave's medium was broadly speaking continuous with rather than separated from its technological past, so bridging the analogue/digital divide. A notable example of this is INTERNET CLUB's hosting of zip-file albums such as *NEW MILLENNIUM CONCEPTS* on an Angelfire website laid out in Times New Roman, suggesting an online setting at least a decade out of date. The same might be said of their moniker, quaintly recalling a time when the Internet could be a hobby rather than a ubiquitous aspect of everyday life.

The Internet itself, however, is less often directly represented in vaporwave than the sounds and imagery of personal computers and operating systems (especially Windows 95). Still more common are digitally ripped VHS tapes of advertisements, particularly from Japan. And perhaps the most recognisable index of vaporwave as a subculture, the ancient Greek or Roman bust, has a far from obvious relationship to the early Internet prior to vaporwave's own semiosis. It is best explained as a period reference, an opulent cliché of 1980s interior design and neoclassical public spaces, glaring quizzically from the cover of what is by far the most famous vaporwave release, Macintosh Plus's *FLORAL SHOPPE* (which, at the time it was reviewed by YouTube critic Anthony Fantano, was not a recent or particularly representative example of vaporwave, but has since come to symbolise the genre, perhaps partly as a result of that exposure). This association might not wholly account for the persistence of marble bust imagery: the reference became its own self-reflexive cliché, only further emphasising the 'deadness' of the music. But as a metaphor, it has much in common with the ancient ruins that mesmerised the Romantics (in Shelley's 'Ozymandias', for example), and cheekily agrees with Sousa's complaint that mechanical music is 'as like real art as the marble statue of Eve is like her beautiful, living, breathing daughters' (1906, 279).

Indeed, although vaporwave might present a key example of compelling combination of the form and content of digital culture, it cannot be reduced to a uniquely 'online' culture. Though it may have dared to leap across the grand dichotomy of URL and IRL, vaporwave nevertheless displays the same exoticism and archaism that previous generations hesitant about technocratic, commercial modernity displayed, in this case inheriting it from indie and alternative musics.[4] My original reading of vaporwave as a music critic situated it in an imaginary 'virtual plaza', ambivalently mirroring late capitalism's play of virtuality, technological acceleration and planned obsolescence.[5] That some artists and listeners complained that this read vaporwave as too dispassionate and calculated only underscores the aesthetic commitment of its community to sincerity, even when living in the belly of the digital beast and suited in corporate imagery.

Thus in this case, the paradigm shift represented by a culture in digital rather than analogue surroundings can be cast all too dramatically. Traditional constructions of authenticity have not collapsed in the digital setting, but find a new arena in which to be negotiated. Online or offline, musicians and listeners still explore the complex relationships between self and other, modernity and history, just as they once did with the synthesiser, the electric guitar and the recording studio. Few of us talk of 'personal computers' or 'surfing the web' nowadays: similarly, it seems probable that with time, the tendency to reify multifarious digital technologies as an 'Internet', a locus of narrow cultural and aesthetic values one might participate in, reject or even comment on, will wane. Certainly, vaporwave scholarship is 'dead' – and thriving as a result.

Notes

1 Luke Morgan Britton, 'Jack White bans phones at gigs for "100% human experience"', *NME*, 24 January 2018, www.nme.com/news/music/jack-white-bans-phones-gigs-2227093.
2 In his critique of 'the digital age', Powers (2010) invokes Thoreau throughout; in his seminal text on 1960s counterculture and technocracy, Roszak (1969) invokes Blake and Wordsworth.
3 Leor Galil, 'Vaporwave and the observer effect', *Chicago Reader*, 19 February 2013, www.chicago reader.com/chicago/vaporwave-spf420-chaz-allen-metallic-ghosts-prismcorp-veracom/Content? oid=8831558.
4 Taylor's exploration of the 1990s lounge revival (2001) and Dolan's analysis of kitsch in indie pop (2010) provide instructive 'offline' comparisons with vaporwave.
5 Adam Harper, 'Comment: Vaporwave and the pop art of the virtual plaza', *Dummy*, 12 July 2012, www.dummymag.com/features/adam-harper-vaporwave.

5 Witnessing Race in the New Digital Cinema

PETER MCMURRAY

I can't breathe! ERIC GARNER, JULY 2014, BYSTANDER VIDEO OF ARREST

I can't even hear. He just slammed my f**king head into the ground ... Thank you for recording! SANDRA BLAND, JULY 2015, BYSTANDER VIDEO OF ARREST

Stay with me! We got pulled over for a busted taillight in the back. And the police, just – he's covered ... They killed my boyfriend! [Discussion with police officer; phone falls to ground as speaker is handcuffed.] They threw my phone, Facebook! DIAMOND REYNOLDS, JULY 2016, FACEBOOK LIVE VIDEO OF SHOOTING OF PHILANDO CASTILE

In March 1991, Rodney King was pulled from his car and beaten by officers of the Los Angeles Police Department. A nearby resident, George Holliday, shot a homemade video of the event that would become one of the most important pieces of American forensic media since the Zapruder film made at the time of John F. Kennedy's assassination. That importance was recognised immediately by police administrators, news broadcasters and academics. In popular media, the video was played on a seemingly endless loop in the immediate aftermath as well as during the trial of the police officers. For instance, a 7 March 1991 broadcast by ABC News opened with anchor Peter Jennings introducing the case and video as follows: 'Now the story that might never have surfaced if somebody had not picked up his home video camera. We've all seen the pictures of Los Angeles police officers beating a man they had just pulled over. The city's police chief said today he will support criminal charges against some of the men.'[1] In one of the most provocative academic articles written on video as a medium, Avital Ronell argues that the video clip functioned as a form of truth-telling testimonial relative to the mythologies of television. In particular, she sees the depiction of police (especially the Los Angeles Police Department) as the epitome of television programming: 'the Rodney King show is about television watching the law watching video' (1994, 295). Writing shortly before the officers' acquittal, Ronell presciently describes a judicial and cultural apparatus that would likely acquit them anyway, highlighting how easily such video can be ignored because it records everything indiscriminately – a kind of machinic excess that is 'simply present while at the same time devoid of presence' (297).

Yet for all the commentary about the Holliday video from so many quarters, the tape was considered largely self-explanatory, save for the question of whether King took a step toward the police or charged them. (This same debate has been central in several recent police shootings of African-Americans, especially that of Michael Brown in Ferguson,

Missouri, in 2014.) Ronell underscores that video serves a testimonial function that television – literally, a distant viewing – never can, even if it is often disregarded in legal proceedings. But the Holliday video is also a distant viewing: despite the appearance of close proximity, the video is actually shot at a distance, with Holliday zooming in on King and the police officers. I remember seeing the Holliday clip on the news when I was growing up – always a kind of mute presentation with voiceover interpretation by newscasters. In the clip I mention above, for example, Peter Jennings turns to a reporter for ABC, Gary Shepard, who then simply speaks over the Holliday video. This video was frequently dredged up again in spring 2017 as part of twenty-five-year commemorations of the Los Angeles riots. Watching it again – and more closely – I am struck by the effect of the zoom on the video. And more to the point: for the first time in my life, I listened to the audio recorded with it. The actual sound of violence in the moment is relatively minimal. At certain points, I hear the voices of police officers yelling at King, but language is indistinct. It's simply the sound of authoritative commands. I never hear any sound of impact, despite the revulsive image of police repeatedly hitting King's body with batons and kicking him.

Instead, I hear something less obvious, but perhaps more systemically ominous: a helicopter hovering just overhead. In the aftermath of this event, apologists for the police force (including Los Angeles Police Chief Darryl Gates) argued that this event was an aberration. Yet the inescapable chopping of the helicopter's rotor blades evokes a much broader assemblage of police machinery, in this case hovering overhead audibly but not visibly. State-sanctioned violence, it seems to imply, is not accidental but by design. (All that's missing is Wagner's 'Ride of the Valkyries' in the spirit of *Apocalypse Now* as a final exclamation point.) Although the low thudding drone of the helicopter is relatively subdued in the video, it emits a higher-pitched whistle that slowly rises and falls as the chopper circles. Only when the helicopter leaves (after about 04:30) is it possible to hear anything clear from the scene: police scanners and radios, doors slamming, and a few more orders being barked out. The helicopter not only provided technological cover, it provided audio cover too, masking sounds of police violence that might have further intensified the affective power of the video.

Occasionally the sound of voices near the camera becomes audible too. While the helicopter is present, these voices are unclear. Once it leaves, it's possible to hear at least two different groups of people discussing what has just happened, with one group describing how the police had been beating King and another speaking in Spanish about the event more generally. In a sense, these are the first documented analysts of this violence, embedded in the video record as eyewitness interpreters. In addition, I hear handling noise on the camera. Holliday is often described as an amateur videographer, and these noises confirm that claim. The camera was primarily a tool of visual documentary; its microphone was an automatic but useful supplement, documenting audio traces of the event from a distance without recourse to an audio equivalent of video zoom technologies. As a result, we have two distinct audio-visual spaces: visually, we inhabit the space of the police violence; but aurally, we remain in conversational, close (and safe) proximity to Holliday, though with the looming sonic apparatus of police force circling overhead.

Sound and image have been disjoined. Given the horrific nature of the moment, it would be distasteful to call this disjuncture 'productive'. But attending to both the audio and the visual, and how they overlap or document separate and asynchronous sensory spaces, allows a kind of mediated witnessing by potential viewing audiences – by which I mean, quite literally, those that see and hear. In recent years, media theorists have increasingly begun to raise the question of what it means to bear witness to an event – especially a traumatic or violent incident – that a person encounters only through indirect means like a recording (Peters 2001; Rentschler 2004; Frosh and Pinchevski 2009; Krämer and Weigel 2017). In the United States these questions have taken on a greater urgency in the past few years as police violence against black people (and especially black men) has come more forcefully into public consciousness beyond communities of colour – in particular as a result of the Movement for Black Lives (including Black Lives Matter activists), which connects the current predicament to the Los Angeles riots a quarter century ago. And indeed, writing a decade before Black Lives Matter emerged as a movement, Fred Moten traced a sonic history from the beating of Rodney King to the killing of Emmett Till, whose brutal death was immortalised in a photograph of his open-casket funeral, as events demanding audition in order to be understood properly: 'This means we'll have to listen to it along with various other sounds that will prove to be nonneutralizable and irreducible' (2003, 196). And Moten's aural witnessing itself fits into an even older tradition of 'bearing witness' as a critical and collective sonic practice in African American religion and politics that remains highly relevant today (Ross 2003; Floyd-Thomas 2016). Indeed, these sonic forms of participatory witnessing that grow out of the Black Church and the Civil Rights Movement augment less race-conscious forms of media theory in which witnessing is in many ways a visual and individualistic practice.[2]

In the past few years, a recurring set of commentaries has highlighted connections between the video documentation of police violence in the

Rodney King beating and the increasingly common (and deeply disturbing) digital recordings of more recent police violence. Headlines such as 'The viral video that set a city on fire' (Young 2017) have circulated online, while several film-makers have released documentary projects about the riots, including *The Lost Tapes: LA Riots*, composed almost exclusively from audio-visual footage from 1991–2. Throughout these discussions, music and sound have often emerged alongside the more obvious aspect of the visual. For instance, in his 2016 op-ed piece for the *Los Angeles Times*, James Peterson opens by connecting questions of music, documentary media, and race: 'The rapper KRS-One famously posed this question to law enforcement: "Who protects us from you?" Exactly 25 years after Los Angeles police officers beat up Rodney King near a 210 Freeway offramp, the answer is the same as ever: The camera does, but only to a point.' Peterson continues by noting that Holliday was 'armed with an analog video camera', nodding to the technological shifts that have taken place in the past quarter century. He then proceeds to discuss the recent deaths of Eric Garner and Walter Scott, victims of police violence who have been central to the Black Lives Matter movement. Although Peterson does not return to rap music, he easily could have, given the prominence in recent protests of rapper Kendrick Lamar's 2015 song, 'Alright'.[3]

In this chapter, I explore the sonic and musical aspects of digital screen culture. A near infinitude of possible directions for such an essay exists, spanning music videos and animal videos, whispered 'ASMR massages'[4] and chanted hate speech, soundmaps and audio-visual museum installations. Moving beyond such content-based themes, one might also write about the massive infrastructure that supports digital audio-visuality in its many manifestations, including the political-economic and environmental impact of server farms, smartphones (and their planned obsolescence), energy grids and the labour forces that are hidden behind these already-hidden infrastructures. But the questions of race, sound, digital transmission and power that swirl around the admittedly American-centric question of police violence and Black Lives Matter not only illustrate the breadth of contemporary media practices, but also point to a kind of media-cultural reckoning that is taking place today. If YouTube and other forms of new digital cinema previously offered a kind of expansive, quick-to-go-viral form of entertainment, the recent spate of video documentation of police violence reminds us of Friedrich Kittler's dictum that 'the entertainment industry is, in any conceivable sense of the word, an abuse of army equipment' (1999, 96–7). In this case, however, we might invert this idea: in recent years, the do-it-yourself entertainment industry of homemade video has increasingly paid attention to the abuses of military-grade equipment passed along to American police forces. Online video services can no longer pretend to be simple distribution hubs for cat and music videos (though music videos will play an important role here). Rather, these technologies offer important new possibilities for addressing the trauma of such violence.

In particular, reconfiguring relationships between audio and video – as well as our expectations of those relationships and our abilities to 'read' them – may allow for new forms of witnessing that are expressly mediated. Nicholas Cook has written of the critical 'perceptual interaction between [multimedia's] various individual components, such as music, speech, moving images, and so on: for without such interaction there is nothing to analyse' (1998, 24). Generic conventions or technical limitations may lead us to assume that the 'perceptual interaction' of a particular (multi) media piece is fixed: in the case of the Rodney King video, one may well assume there is no audio or that whatever it may include is unnecessary for understanding the video. As I've written above, I disagree. Those perceptual interactions are subject to manipulation (whether intentional or not) by artists and media forms. But they also allow for an audience to exercise what Ingrid Monson calls its 'perceptual agency' (2008): we can choose to attend to certain musical (or audio-visual) aspects more or less than others. And while Cook and Monson are concerned with things we would readily identify as 'music' or 'musical multimedia', I hope here to extend their models of interactive, dynamic sensation to include other forms of audio more generally, whether speech/recited poetry, ambient environmental sound, or the particularly violent sounds of police brutality. Experiencing those audio-visual media and perceiving – or more aptly, choosing to perceive – the ways they witness about the world, especially when relayed on further by 'sharing' or commenting on them, quickly moves beyond just analysis (though analysis remains critically important) and into a realm of mediated co-witnessing.

Thus, after offering some theoretical background, I focus in this essay on three case studies in which the interplay between additional images creates new opportunities – as well as pitfalls – for digital witnessing: Beyoncé's 'visual album' *Lemonade*; recordings of the killing of Philando Castile by police; and to conclude, protests at American football games against 'The Star-Spangled Banner', the national anthem of the United States. These examples, as well as related forms of music video and documented police violence, show some of the divergent uses of audio-visual media today, while underscoring the acute political forces at play within them and giving rise to them. These media offer an opportunity, in particular, to rethink longstanding notions of witnessing and mediation: bystanders can readily become activists with the push of a button, and distant viewers are invited to view decimated black bodies, both as cultural witnesses and/or as voyeurs of violence. At the same time, these videos and crowdsourced documentary practices also raise unsettling questions about technocapitalism and the companies like Google (parent company of YouTube), Apple and Facebook that profit – whether inadvertently or, perhaps, by design – from violence against black bodies and the repeated viewings of media documenting that violence. In an age full of new forms of technological mediation, witnessing and gazing, producing and consuming, activism and spectatorship blur with one another, and the political consequences can be significant.

Musicians as Multisensory Witnesses

Let me proceed with a YouTube clip. At a concert in Seattle's Key Arena in December 2014, Stevie Wonder prefaced his 1973 song 'Living for the City' with a short speech while he and his band played the vamping synthesiser ostinato over a bass pedal point that opens the song. As documented by YouTube user 'Zoltan Grossman' on what appears to be a camera phone, Wonder said:

> I want you to know truly sincerely, I love sincerely each and every one of you. [*audience cheers*] You can put your heart on that. You know, I've always seen all of us, no matter what our ethnicities are, no matter what our color, are seen as one family. [*cheers*] And I'm not saying it just because I'm on stage. I'm saying it because that's how I really feel.
>
> Can you believe that within one month, two grand juries – *secret* grand juries – declined to indict two policemen for the killing of two Black men? I just don't understand that.
>
> Let me just say this also: I don't understand why a legal system would *choose* secrecy when there's so much mistrust of what they're saying. [*cheers*] I don't understand why there could not have been a public trial where we would be able to hear all sides to this deal. [*cheers*] I just don't understand.
>
> I tell you what I do understand. I heard Eric Garner say, with my own ears: 'I can't breathe!' And as much as he's apologized, I don't understand why he [the police officer] did not stop . . . You see, I feel that – when people say to me – and you know, I've heard this from various politicians as well, 'You've got all this black-on-black crime'. But my feeling's that guns are too accessible to *everybody*. [*cheers*]
>
> I do, I do – I do understand that something is wrong, real wrong. And we as family, Americans, all of us of all colors, need to fix it – with a quickness, real soon. [*cheers*]
>
> I love you. And I really love you, you know that. And this is why this song unfortunately is still relevant today. If you know the words you can sing along with me.[5]

Several aspects of this performance bear on the question of audio-visuality, witnessing and screens. First, Stevie Wonder is functioning as a sensory witness of sorts, challenging the secret (and thus impossible-to-perceive) proceedings of the grand juries in question. In the American legal system, grand juries stand as a preliminary legal proceeding. Although Garner had been killed nearly six months earlier, Wonder's remarks came immediately on the heels of the grand jury non-indictment on 3 December, which led to a wave of protests around the United States, as well as the recirculation of a video made by Ramsey Orta showing police choking Garner to death while he sputters, 'I can't breathe!'[6] Wonder emphasises that he has personally listened to the audio from that same clip: 'I heard Eric Garner say, with my own ears: "I can't breathe!"' Presumably Wonder is referring to the experience of hearing Garner's recorded voice. Yet this mediated experience has an unmediated quality for Wonder, as he witnesses Orta's technological witnessing and then attests to it as his own experience, no less authoritative for having been based on an audio-visual recording. This question of mediated sensation is heightened all the more because Wonder is himself blind: the key action here was *hearing* Garner speak in that fatal moment.

In some sense, Wonder's statement fits neatly into a longstanding tradition of protest music, especially among African-American musicians. One strain of that tradition, ranging from spirituals and blues to contemporary hip-hop and R&B, places the musician him- or herself in a personalised role, as a kind of aesthetic witness. If a witness is generally understood to play a role as an epistemological medium – to transmit *knowledge* about a person or event, as Sybille Krämer emphasises (2015, 144–64) – this musical form of witnessing trains its focus on the affective dimensions of knowing, or what Tomie Hahn calls 'sensational knowledge' (2007). One might argue that Wonder's performance, with musical accompaniment during the speech, followed by a song – all the while surrounded by dancers, bright lights and a cheering audience – is hardly the place for a nuanced transmission of knowledge. But this kind of knowing-affective mediation seems to be precisely Wonder's aim, as he concludes by encouraging those who know the words to 'Living for the City' to sing along. The song's lyrics chronicle the difficulties of life for a poor, young black man from the American South moving to New York before getting falsely arrested and imprisoned. Much of the dramatic action of the piece is told not so much through the lyrics but rather through a kind of micro-radio-play with the sounds and speech of a bus and driver, police sirens and handcuffs, a courtroom verdict and the clang of prison bars.

The song's concluding stanzas recount how the protagonist, wandering the city (after release from prison?), is nearly dead from breathing the city air. In stark contrast to the magical kind of 'world breath' that Friedrich Kittler imagines as animating operatic heroes (1987), Wonder conjures instead the image of a gritty lack-of-breath that leads slowly but inexorably toward death – all too resonant with Eric Garner. The final lines shift to a first-person narrator – perhaps the protagonist, perhaps the singer – with a particular injunction for listeners: 'I hope you hear inside my voice of sorrow / And that it motivates you to make a better tomorrow.'[7] The voice is explicitly figured as a means of conveying not just words or semantic content, but feeling. Audition is a kind of burrowing-into: hear *inside* the voice, let its affective qualities resonate around the listener. And do something about it. Empathic hearing becomes a kind of testimonial action, even when displaced from the original circumstances in question. Wonder's audiences can't be there alongside the song's protagonist; but precisely *because* of that displacement an ethical burden remains on them to hear-inside, to listen with care, and to respond accordingly.

Fittingly, Wonder's speech was transmitted to the world as a multi-layered, sedimentary testimonial. The video's creator, Zoltán Grossman, describes his actions as follows:

> I started filming him when I guessed from a few chords that he was starting 'Living for the City' – one of my faves. At first I was disappointed that he started talking instead, but then realized that he had spoken about Ferguson before, and his remarks about Eric Garner's death in New York could be valuable. They sure were, and I'm glad that I filmed it.[8]

Smartphone video not only serves as a bulwark against police violence, it also can transmit other acts of witnessing, as in this case. Of course, Ramsey Orta's video of Eric Garner, which he alleges led to his own imprisonment, cannot fairly be compared to a bootleg video of a concert, not least because of the risk Orta took on while filming (some of which is captured in the confrontations with police during the filming itself). But both perform a similar kind of work as testimonials in the sense that Wonder's lyrics suggest: they are not simply documents that capture an event, but rather invitations or even demands to be circulated and heard. Although witnessing traditionally shuns extra layers of mediation, in these somewhat paradoxical cases, the greater number of mediations – repostings, shares online, embeddings – the more effective the witnessing has been. Mediation – and, specifically, remediation – becomes a form of amplification in the digital age. That amplified witnessing is, of course, subject to the technical constraints and (sometimes whimsical) human preferences of social media. But it amplifies nonetheless.

Digital Video and Its Transformations

Years before the invention of YouTube, the rapper Chuck D of the group Public Enemy famously described rap music as a kind of mass medium like a news broadcast: 'For the first time, a kid from New York can understand how a kid from Los Angeles lives … You've got to understand, Public Enemy and rap music are dispatchers of information. We're almost like headline news … the invisible TV station that black America never had' (Jones 1989). Again, music has long served as a vehicle for communicating and transmitting ideas – including but not limited to ideas of protest – across considerable geographies. Internet-based platforms like YouTube offer a new set of possibilities for such transmissions but, as with any medium, those transmissions are constrained and facilitated by the particularities of that medium.

We might theorise YouTube and the digital video platforms that have emerged in its wake in any number of ways: as a site of physical inter-activity and bodily re-performance in which aurality borders on touching, as I have explored elsewhere (McMurray 2014); as the 'unruly' heart of a new digital cinema (Vernallis 2013); or as a physical infrastructure, including the glass and plastic of screens, silicon wafers, server farms storing petabytes of 'cloud' data, as well as the human labour used to assemble the latest iPhone (Peters 2015; Kirschenbaum 2008). But, of course, YouTube and its competitors are not fixed entities; they have histories and are changing at this very moment. We might imagine a 'golden age' of YouTube, dating roughly from the purchase of YouTube by Google in 2006 to around 2012, when certain changes in scale and market became clear: Psy's 'Gangnam Style' reached one billion views; Facebook bought the photo and video-sharing site Instagram; and smartphones became nearly ubiquitous (van Dijck 2013; Burgess and Green 2012).

In the wake of that golden age of YouTube, a major rupture has taken place, one that appears to be tied closely to the rise of the Black Lives Matter movement and especially the acts of digital witnessing that accompany it. The ubiquity of portable recording devices and options to share media made on those devices has given rise to new forms of political accountability. Digital cinema has taken on a certain social gravitas, and these 'new media' demand – returning to Stevie Wonder briefly – a hearing-inside that embraces the hypermediated audio-visual testimonial of events like protests and police violence. Journalist Stereo Williams has written about the kind of maturing that has come along with these musical – and I would add, audio-visual – testimonials. In a 2015 article entitled 'Is hip-hop still "CNN for Black people"?', riffing on Chuck D, Williams suggests that 'this contemporary wave of social conscious music seems to be reflective of what the public is feeling, and that public doesn't really seem to want it to be anything else ... These guys [and all of Williams's examples are men] are asking questions as opposed to acting as though they have the answers', in contrast to previous generations of political artists.[9]

The following examples give a sampling of what audio-visual media – especially in the United States, but not limited to any single geography – have become in light of current tensions surrounding not just police violence but broader questions of race and justice, and to a certain degree gender, as well. They may seem like marginal or exceptional examples in unpacking what digital screen culture means today, but following Stereo Williams I argue that they raise critical questions (while not always providing complete answers) about the stakes of audio-visual media and their circulations. And again, they pose these questions through expressions of witnessing – but expressions that are always tinged in multivalent ways by capital, violence and other forms of institutionalised power.

Case 1. Beyoncé's *Lemonade*: Video as Amplification
As is so often the case with multimedia work, Beyoncé's (2016b) release, *Lemonade* – a self-described 'visual album' that premiered as an hour-long television show – raises a number of questions about definitions. What is a *visual* album? (And what is an *album* in the digital age?) Does that terminology mean that visuals take priority over music? Or vice versa, since Beyoncé is a singer? Or does she fit into a broader category of 'entertainer' given how she incorporates dance and video into her work? And what about live performances of the album's material? Once again, Nicholas Cook's formulation of tensions *between* media in multimedia (1998, 103) is helpful analytically: to what degree do the album's audio and visual elements complement or contest one another? Or to reframe the question once more in terms of the audience, what does it mean for an audience to attend to certain components of this album more than others? As if Beyoncé had planned it precisely that way, these questions consumed the popular press and academic online spheres for months in the wake of *Lemonade*'s release (e.g. McFadden 2016, Pareles 2016, Vernallis 2016, among many others). Central to this reception was a further question: how should this material be positioned relative to Black Lives Matter?[10] In a sense, the answer to all these questions seems to be: Yes. That is, the album indeed seems designed to provoke many (or perhaps all) of these questions. In so doing, it maximises its own self-amplification, with critics serving as the channel for that response. The degree to which that is a savvy business decision or an act of social conscience – or both – is less clear. But whatever Beyoncé's internal motivations, *Lemonade* tapped into

the same kind of amplifying channels as she had with earlier, single-song music videos like her 2008 hit, 'Single Ladies'. What seems different to me is precisely the massive tear in the American cultural fabric that had emerged since the late 2000s because of the visibility of police violence. And in many ways, the unfolding of *Lemonade* as an album follows that same progression.

Before tracing what *Lemonade* does internally, it bears mention that *Lemonade* did not arrive on the scene fully formed. Prior to its debut on HBO on 23 April 2016, shorter fragments were released, focusing on the song 'Formation'. On 6 February, the song and its music video (from the full-length *Lemonade* visual album) were released, one day before a live performance of the song at the half-time show of the Super Bowl, the American football championship game. 'Formation', which serves as the finale of *Lemonade*, also includes some of the most overt political commentaries and imagery of the whole album – especially in contrast to the earlier segments, which focus more on questions of personal relationships and specifically on fidelity and betrayal (Beyoncé 2016a). The Super Bowl performance is notable not least because, as I discuss below, American football has been drawn into the audio-visual performance of race and anti-racism in surprisingly central ways. And Beyoncé appears to have taken full advantage of that platform, perhaps most strikingly in the outfits worn by her dance troupe. In the 'Formation' video itself (which, again, comments quite directly on questions of race in America), the dancers performing with Beyoncé wear multiple outfits, including old denim and white T-shirts. But at the Super Bowl, they donned outfits that were suggestive of the Black Panthers, the American black nationalist group formed fifty years earlier in 1966 – the same year the Super Bowl began (Caramanica et al. 2016). While audiences' response to the costuming varied, it offered a compelling reminder of the possibilities of amplifying certain qualities of *Lemonade* (or specifically of 'Formation') through visual elements: first, through the video itself, with its striking imagery of post-Hurricane-Katrina New Orleans as well as anti-police protest; and, secondly, through the additional costuming of the Super Bowl half-time show, itself one of the most important multimedia events in the United States.

But these officially released videos were not the only video precursors to *Lemonade*'s formal release. In May 2014 after the Met Gala in New York, silent video footage from a security guard's phone filming a closed-circuit surveillance camera leaked, showing Beyoncé's sister, Solange Knowles, hitting and kicking Jay-Z, Beyoncé's husband, while Beyoncé stands by. Several critics and other media pundits weighed in on whether this incident was connected to the tale of infidelity that dominates the first half of

Lemonade. Most have rightly dismissed the idea that Beyoncé is required to tell the truth about her life – as though she lacked the creativity to imagine something beyond the 'authenticity' of her own lived experience (Tinsley 2016; Als 2016). But by the same token, it does raise questions about how an audience should know when to flip on/off an authenticity filter. This kind of uncertain disjuncture is amplified by Beyoncé's posture during the Solange/Jay-Z scuffle: she stands more or less motionless (at least as shown from above by the camera). Furthermore, when she exits the elevator, she seems poised for the paparazzi, smiling calmly, unlike the others leaving with her.[11]

More broadly, *Lemonade* is a series of music videos that feature Black women centrally throughout. These individual music videos are then connected with a mix of (often abstract) imagery accompanied by voice-over of Beyoncé speaking, often reciting poetry by Somali-British poet Warsan Shire. In addition, each song has a title, but those titles never appear in the visual album. Instead, they're replaced by single-word titles ('Intuition', 'Denial', 'Anger' and so on) that evoke multiple stages of grieving. This thickly layered media constellation has proven to be a boon for interpretation, making nearly every moment of *Lemonade* overdetermined with possible meanings.

Unsurprisingly then, debates sprung up regarding several aspects of the visual album, including: the depiction of intersections of race, gender and sexuality; the respective roles music and visuals play in the album; and the economics of Beyoncé's storytelling.[12] For many fans and critics, Beyoncé's depiction of the complex entanglements of race, gender and sexuality was thrilling. But at least one prominent author, bell hooks, challenged Beyoncé on the way she brought these two issues together, criticising in particular Beyoncé's apparent embrace of violence as a response to oppression – most memorably in 'Hold Up', as she walks down the street with a baseball bat smashing cars, fire hydrants, a CCTV security camera, and (it appears) even a camera operator.[13] (This track shows the most explicit self-awareness of media in the album – and perhaps the most direct violence comes at the expense of an imagined human holding the camera when Beyoncé hits both with the bat to bring the track to a close.) Significantly, hooks responds to the audio-visual album primarily as a set of moving images, barely commenting on its aural aspects. In contrast, a certain set of music critics insisted on evaluating the album first and foremost as music – reviewing it like any other album (including earlier Beyoncé releases). For them, the cinematic version was secondary, much like any other music video would be relative to an album or song. Robin James helpfully summarises the various positions taken on this debate, but makes the compelling case that attempts to interpret the album primarily (or solely) as 'just music' enact 'epistemic violence', demanding that it conform to standards of beauty and value developed for Western visual and musical arts.[14] James's point seems obvious but it underscores the fact that *Lemonade* sits between media, genre categories and critical discourses; there are no clear criteria or metrics for evaluating it, despite important audio-visual precedents from Prince to Beyoncé's own 'Single Ladies' video.

If *Lemonade* has largely drawn acclaim for its audio-visual depictions of race, gender and sexuality, its connection to capitalism is more complex, if less commented upon – perhaps because that connection is so obviously present for a professional artist who makes money from her art. After premiering on the American cable television channel HBO, *Lemonade* was available only on Tidal, a music streaming service owned by Jay-Z (Rys 2016). The audio-visual material of the album itself suggests a deep-seated but ambivalent relationship with capitalism, most notably in the memorable line from 'Formation', that she 'just might be a black Bill Gates in the making'. But beyond this kind of brash entrepreneurialism, which was normalised years ago by rappers, the album's audio-visual 'text' (i.e. the album itself) and the context of its release (choices about record labels, streaming, etc.) begin to blur into one another. Stephen Witt (2016) describes the political economics of *Lemonade* as follows: 'As art, it was an unforgettable act of public shaming. As business, though, it was a gift of surpassing value, suggesting a kind of Clintonian marital bargain, in which pride is sacrificed in service to dynasty. The irony is rich: the man whose presumptive philandering provided the subject matter for this album now stands to profit most from its distribution'. The comparison to the marriage and simultaneous careers of Bill Clinton and Hillary Clinton underscores the fact that the personal is political here and vice versa. Some critics, including Greg Tate, focused on the potential for profiteering from more obvious socio-political issues, suggesting that Beyoncé's embrace of Black Lives Matter and race-related issues was in many ways a business decision.[15]

More broadly, Beyoncé is bearing witness to a cultural moment that extends beyond just the questions of love, race, gender and power she explicitly addresses, yet her witnessing is also marked by a kind of excess, sedimented with other cultural accretions: perhaps unintentionally, she is also documenting the broader neoliberal regime of music production she and we inhabit. But rather than argue the merits of that embrace of capitalism – whether as a taint on the album's politics, a necessary evil, or even the successful 'hustle' of her musical entrepreneurialism – I would suggest that this complexity gives listeners/viewers greater perceptual agency in determining what exactly *Lemonade* means and to what issues it bears witness. Again, witnessing becomes highly mediated through legions of fans and critics (including those who dislike the album); they too are part of that witnessing. As such, Beyoncé's ability to elicit responses from those audiences is integral to her ability to witness on her own terms. She gets us to talk, and we selectively amplify her audio-visual act of witnessing, itself an act of audio-visual amplification of resistance to police violence.

Case 2. Philando Castile's Death: Audio as Amplification

On 6 July 2016, Philando Castile was driving with his girlfriend Diamond Reynolds and her young daughter in Minneapolis, Minnesota. He was pulled over by officer Jeronimo Yanez and his partner, ostensibly over a broken tail light. Yanez then approached the driver's side window and began talking to Castile. In less than a minute, Castile had been shot seven times. Castile was a registered gun owner and had properly disclosed to the officer that he had a gun in the car. The precise details of what happened in the next three seconds is subject to disagreement, but Yanez claims that Castile was reaching for his gun despite the officer's warnings not to move. Reynolds in turn claims Castile was reaching for his driver's licence, as instructed by the officer. What is clear is that Yanez began to shoot at him point-blank through the open window while yelling loudly. Reynolds then picked up her phone and began using Facebook Live to stream live video of what was unfolding (Reynolds 2016).[16] That video is a chilling mix of grief, chaos and technological savvy. It is a compelling, if disturbing, act of witnessing – paradigmatic of digital video tools that have greatly expanded the affordances and meanings of video, while also greatly expanding access to video-making technologies. This expansion affects phones especially, thanks to a handful of massive tech companies (Apple, Google, Facebook) that are reaping profits from these technological 'disruptions' in video and media production.[17]

The video begins with Reynolds apparently addressing Castile, crying out, 'Stay with me!' She then begins addressing the generic Everyone of the Internet, saying:

> We got pulled over for a busted taillight in the back. And the police, just – he's covered . . . They killed my boyfriend! He's licensed to carry [a firearm]. He was trying to get out his ID in his wallet out [of] his pocket and he let the officer know that he had a firearm and he was reaching for his wallet. And the officer just shot him in his arm. We're waiting for a back–   (Reynolds 2016)

At this point, Reynolds is interrupted by Yanez, who has been repeatedly cursing in the background ('F**k!'). In one of the most telling moments of the exchange, he yells at Reynolds to keep her hands where they are. With tremendous poise, she replies, 'Don't worry, officer.

I will.' Before she can finish her words, Yanez screams out again: 'F**k!'
Reynolds and Yanez then begin rehearsing events. Yanez, whose voice is
raspy and panicky, says:

[YANEZ:]   'I told him not to reach for it. I told him to get his hand up.'
REYNOLDS: 'You told him to get his ID, sir. You told him to get his driver's licence.
           Oh, my God, please don't tell me he's dead. Please don't tell me
           my boyfriend just went like that.'
YANEZ   (still pointing his gun through the window): 'Keep your hands where
           they are, please.'
REYNOLDS: 'Yes, I will, sir. I'll keep my hands where they are. Please don't tell me
           this, Lord. Please, Jesus, don't tell me that he's gone. Please don't tell
           me that he's gone. Please, officer, don't tell me that you just did this
           to him. You shot four bullets into him, sir. He was just getting his
           licence and registration, sir.' (Reynolds 2016)

The tragic cinematography of the scene intensifies as Reynolds is
instructed to get out of the car with her hands up and visible to the officer.
She begins asking about her daughter, who was riding in the back seat of
the car and had been pulled out of the car immediately after the shooting
by Yanez's partner. Reynolds is told to walk backward, and responds by
filming behind herself – suddenly we see the officers standing behind her
with guns drawn, telling her repeatedly, 'Keep walking!' She is wrestled to
the ground and, as she is handcuffed, her phone falls beside her, pointing
up to the sky as a small child's cry is heard, sirens approach, tyres squeal,
and Reynolds begins wailing. But before doing so, she speaks to her still-
livestreaming phone: 'They threw my phone, Facebook.'[18] Reynolds then
began broadcasting her plight again from the back of a police car, retelling
the story and also commenting that her phone battery was about to die. In
a particularly poignant moment, we see that her daughter is sitting with
her in the back. Reynolds continues to switch between audiences, speaking
to her daughter and then the world (at least that subsection of it that had
access to her Facebook stream): 'I don't know if he's OK or if he's not OK.
I'm in the back seat of a police car, handcuffed. I need a ride. I'm on
Larpenteur and Fry. They've got machine guns pointed. [inaudible from
child] Don't be scared. My daughter just witnessed this. The police just
shot him for no apparent reason. No reason at all.' As Reynolds breaks
down, her daughter in turn comforts her: 'It's OK, Mommy. [Reynolds
cries out.] It's OK, I'm right here' (Reynolds 2016).

In many ways, there is nothing that can be said about a video like this.

But something must be said about a video like this. So let me say that it
is a masterpiece of audio-visual witnessing: it is impressive in its physical
and technical execution, it is emotionally riveting, and it conveys the
gravitas and profound loss that comes with such a traumatic death. That

Reynolds manages to film at all after the shooting, let alone while walking backwards and while handcuffed in the back of a police car, is remarkable in itself. That virtuosity, if such a word can apply in such grim circumstances, is intensified by the rhetoric of hands: keep your hands where they are, keep your hands in the air, and implicitly, keep your hands cuffed behind your back. Needless to say, these are not the standard hand positions for shooting video. But beyond the presence of mind Reynolds shows to use these tools in real time in the midst of trauma, her ability to cogently narrate what she has seen and heard – and what she is seeing and hearing, even when we as viewers can no longer see her after her phone is thrown to the ground – demonstrates a deep commitment to the art of witnessing. Even when her body and camera/phone are forcibly displaced from one another, she continues to witness acousmatically as a voice without a visible body, a kind of violation of the most basic (old) rule that witnessing demands bodily presence. On account of the ubiquity of such audio-visual media devices, witnessing is changing. Nevertheless, the importance of a commitment to witnessing, even of such a brutal act, is central to what Reynolds's actions mean in our current (social) media ecology. And that ecology quickly extends to encompass others beyond Reynolds, most painfully evident in her comments in the back of the police car with her daughter: she too witnessed this killing. Her daughter becomes a co-witness and an interlocutor, offering comfort while also coming to terms with extraordinarily complex circumstances.

On 16 June 2017, Yanez was acquitted of all charges, unleashing a wave of protest around the country. A few days later, a second video was released publicly, filmed from the dashboard camera of his police vehicle. This dash-cam video, which had been used as evidence in the trial, was the centrepiece of a cluster of official, police-generated audio-visual fragments that documented various moments in the shooting and its aftermath. As I mention above, while it documents an act of police brutality, it inverts the audio-visual relationships found in the Rodney King video: it features a static wide shot instead of a tightly zoomed image, while the close-miked audio records Yanez, amplifying his spoken interactions with Castile, then the gunshots, and finally his anguished (perhaps panicky) vocalisations after shooting Castile. These vocalisations attracted considerable commentary: do they indicate that Yanez knew immediately he had made a mistake? A lack of professional composure? Two responses from police/criminology commentators underscore the affective impact of his voice crying repeatedly, 'F**k!':

Analyst 1, David A. Klinger, professor of criminology and former Los Angeles police officer:

'Afterwards, he's in a very emotionally wrought place. He's screaming into his mike. There's no composure. He did not present a very professional demeanor.'

Analyst 2, Paul Butler, law professor and former federal prosecutor:

> 'Part of what may have made a difference to the jury was the officer's very emotional reaction after the shooting. He's somebody who realizes that he's made a grievous mistake. It's certainly an argument for a manslaughter conviction rather than a murder conviction. People who do harm in the heat of the moment still deserve punishment.'   (Bosman and Smith 2017)

In other words, Yanez's vocal timbre matters for legal purposes. From a purely technical perspective, we hear Yanez's voice overmodulate the microphone repeatedly, resulting in distortion as he curses about the predicament. The use of audio-visual recording media became a central part of the internal police investigation that followed the shooting, and the police force has gradually begun to police itself through the use of audio-visual equipment as a kind of auto-witnessing. (This is part of the move toward having police wear cameras on their bodies and mounted in their vehicles.) Yet there are many ifs and buts. The police investigation noted Yanez's standard use of such media (e.g. having the dashcam running whenever pulling someone over) as well as deviations from this (the second officer to arrive did not do this). Yet the dashcam footage from Yanez's vehicle was not released to the public until a few days after the trial (nearly a year after the shooting). Again, Yanez didn't radio the general police radio dispatcher but rather contacted another officer directly; the only recording of that conversation – in which Yanez gives his dubious reasoning for deciding to pull over Castile, based solely on racial profiling, including the size of Castile's nose – was made not by police but by a local citizen who was independently monitoring and recording the police scanner (Mannix 2016). In this way Yanez circumvented the technologies designed to police the police. And another key audio recording, an interview with Yanez as part of a state investigation into the killing, was disallowed from the court proceedings (Xiong and Mannix 2017). Juvenal's aphoristic question, 'Who will watch the watchmen?', seems apt, if sensorily incomplete. (The same holds for the word 'witnessing' itself, with its etymological emphasis on vision.) The shooting of Philando Castile reminds us that acts of witnessing, especially today, also demand a careful listening.

If Rodney King's beating and trial and the Los Angeles riots that followed mark a starting point in mediatised witnessing about and against police violence, the shooting of Castile and its livestreaming by Reynolds marks a kind of climax. Other killings had been filmed on smartphones, including Eric Garner's death-by-choking, discussed above.[19] But in the case of Castile, the immediate aftermath of the shooting was streamed in real time. The relationship of audio and video also connects King and Castile, in an inverted way: like the King beating, Castile's death was filmed from some distance, leaving certain actions illegible, but whereas the audio in King's case clarified almost nothing about the specifics of police actions, the audio from Yanez's microphone gives an intense feel of proximity to this fatal act of violence. When viewed and heard together, this bundle of media – Reynolds's live video broadcast, the police video and other media (from police and other citizen bystanders/recordists) – bears a striking witness to Castile's killing. And yet the legal results were the same: acquittal of the police officer(s) involved. On the one hand, we might read the acquittal of Yanez as the perennial failure of all media to effectively witness; as Ronell (1994) writes, these technical witnesses fail to analyse themselves – they fail to say what they mean, as it were. And on some level that seems apt in this case: even with audio-visual media produced by both parties, the evidence was found inconclusive. But I would interpret this case slightly differently. Those media were never designed to lead to justice. They are far too malleable, especially in the hands of a legal system that has shown little inclination to punish officers for the violence they commit. Instead, as Diamond Reynolds clearly understood in her snap decision to start broadcasting Castile's death, they are better suited to witnessing through amplification, aimed at a broader public that may take – but hasn't yet taken – steps to bring about structural change in society in order to minimise such violence.

Conclusion: Oh Say, Can You See?

Some readers of this essay may find it too American-centric. These problems, the thinking goes, are unique to the United States, with its peculiar mix of a history of slavery, lingering racism, a massive prison system, and a vast media infrastructure that can readily amplify (or stifle) all kinds of performative utterances. Instead, a topic like the role of media in the Arab Spring or something about YouTube music more generally might have more obvious relevance to a wider readership. Unsurprisingly, I disagree: racism may be more visible (and audible) in the United States, but it would appear to be part of a larger global trend, both in overt politics (e.g. the re-emergence of global populism) and in more subtle manifestations through ethnic and religious conflict (e.g. the expulsion of the Rohingya from Myanmar or the Syrian Civil War and its fallout). And so I conclude briefly with an example I believe has broader relevance, despite the appearance of being the most American of examples.

Case 3. Football Players Protest 'The Star-Spangled Banner'

Since 2016 a new practice of protest has become common: American football players kneeling, sitting or holding a fist in the air while the American national anthem ('The Star-Spangled Banner') is played at the beginning of games. It began in fall 2016 as a response by football player Colin Kaepernick to police killings of black Americans. Without any fanfare, Kaepernick would quietly sit on the bench alongside the field while his teammates would stand at attention in front of him. In the United States, as in many other countries, when the national anthem is played at sporting events, people – players, fans, officials – are expected to stand at attention and face the flag. Many put their hand over their heart. This is the stuff of national anthems everywhere – musical nationalism performed in highly public settings, especially those tied to sports.[20] Kaepernick described his motivations as follows: 'There are a lot of things that are going on that are unjust ... There's a lot of things that need to change. One specifically? Police brutality. There's people being murdered unjustly and not being held accountable.' He continues, with a more sonic allusion: 'I'm seeing things happen to people that don't have a voice, people that don't have a platform to talk and have their voices heard, and effect change ... No one's tried to quiet me and, to be honest, it's not something I'm going to be quiet about. I'm going to speak the truth when I'm asked about it.'[21] Teams declined to hire him for the 2017 season, leading Kaepernick to file a lawsuit alleging that team owners and the National Football League were conspiring together to fire a warning shot at other players who might be similarly inclined (Belson 2017). Unsurprisingly, with Kaepernick gone, the practice intensified, all the more so after Donald Trump commented repeatedly about how such players should be fired for what amounts to their exercising of free speech, a guaranteed right in American constitutional law.

The fallout of these exchanges is not yet clear but at risk of triteness I want to close with the question posed in the opening lines of that national anthem: 'Oh say, can you see ... ?' As it turns out, Kaepernick had been sitting on the bench for the anthem for several weeks before news outlets noticed and reported on it. Whether Kaepernick wanted the media to notice or not (he hadn't said anything about it prior to that first wave of reporting), media – and in this case, 'the media', including television, newspapers and online media platforms – amplified his protest and the responses to it, both negative and positive. Tellingly, almost all reporting on these protests has been mute: still images circulate widely showing players kneeling. The music is almost never shown with these images – perhaps because a national anthem is the kind of musical object that everyone assumes everyone knows intimately. Intentionally or otherwise, the effect is to eliminate an entire sensory register – music, sound, speech, hearing – that might lead to players being allowed to speak out about their concerns and be heard. Some broadcasts now simply skip the national anthem.[22] As an exception, one sound-sensitive news piece on 11 September 2016 included not only audio-visual footage of the anthem as sung by firefighter Keith Taylor, but also an unprompted analysis of hearing and listening by Doug Baldwin, a player on the Seattle Seahawks: 'There is a message that needs to be heard. And so, you heard us. Now listen to us'.[23] Baldwin suggests it was not the singing firefighter but the kneeling (effectively silent) players who needed to be heard. Furthermore, the relationship between hearing and listening is not a theoretical question, as it might be understood in academic debates, but rather an invitation for participatory engagement by an audience. Collective witnessing calls for receptive listening.

This example may be quintessentially American but it recapitulates the broad question: how do people use media to witness in a time of violence, and what are the sensory ecologies of that witnessing? Following on from that, how do the audiences of such acts of witnessing then play a role in that witnessing? As audio-visual media become more readily shareable, the creation of digital cinema falls not only to those who produce those media but also to audiences who watch/listen, evaluate, debate about and perhaps share them. In an age where online circulation is so visibly quantified – how many times was *Lemonade* streamed in its first week, or how many times was the hashtag #Blacklivesmatter used on Twitter after a given police shooting? – witnessing becomes a distributed act. Viewer/listeners are pulled into a constellation of media, offering a reminder that those media choices have concrete political and social consequences. 'New media' may not be so new in this regard: from memorials to early religious martyrs (who combined death and witnessing in defence of the propagation of a message) to the Rodney King video, hearers can readily re-tell and viewers can otherwise inscribe, record and share images as well. But new media certainly heighten the impact of (some) individuals within that broader media ecology. And, of course, these 'individuals' need not be actual people, as seen in the rise and impact of 'bots' that automatically engage with humans in these media ecologies to, say, influence an election or replace telephone-based customer service lines. But these post-human extensions of media are precisely the point. What is at stake here, both in the filming and circulating of dramatic recordings of police violence and in the banal retweets generated by artificial intelligence, is the status of the human, and especially the human body. Witnessing has long had a close connection to bodily presence; in the digital age, that connection has been distributed but has not disappeared. Although the distinctions between human and machine continue to blur increasingly quickly, basic functions like breathing, seeing and hearing remain critical.

For Further Study

Alexander, Elizabeth. 1994. 'Can you be BLACK and look at this? Reading the Rodney King video(s)'. *Public Culture* 7 (1): 77–94.

Beyoncé [Knowles]. 2016. *Lemonade*. Kahlil Joseph and Beyoncé Knowles Carter, directors. Columbia Records. Premiered 23 April, Home Box Office (HBO). Visual album.

Chang, Jeff. 2016. 'Making Lemonade'. In *We Gon' Be Alright: Notes on Race and Resegregation*, 159–68. New York: Picador.

Krämer, Sybille and Sigrid Weigel, eds. 2017. *Testimony/Bearing Witness: Epistemology, Ethics, History and Culture*. London: Rowman & Littlefield International.

Lamar, Kendrick. 2015. 'Alright'. Directed by Colin Tilley. Aftermath/Interstellar. Music video.

Taibbi, Matt. 2017. *I Can't Breathe: A Killing on Bay Street*. New York: Spiegel & Grau.

Notes

I'm grateful to Braxton Shelley and John Durham Peters, as well as the editors of this volume, for their feedback on earlier versions of this text.

1 ABC News, 'Video of Rodney King beaten by police released', *ABC News*, 7 March 1991, abcnews.go.com/Archives/video/march-1991-rodney-king-videotape-9758031. All websites accessed 20 March 2019.

2 This is not to say, however, that particular sensory modes map neatly onto race. In fact, Moten's reading of the infamous Till photograph begins by citing Elizabeth Alexander's powerful but explicitly visualist 1994 essay in *Public Culture*, 'Can you be BLACK and look at this: Reading the Rodney King video(s)'.

3 See Greg Tate, 'How #BlackLivesMatter changed hip-hop and R&B in 2015'. *Rolling Stone*, 16 December 2015, www.rollingstone.com/music/news/how-blacklivesmatter-changed-hip-hop-and-r-b-in-2015-20151216; and Jamilah King, 'The improbable story of how Kendrick Lamar's "Alright" became a protest anthem', *Mic*, 11 February 2016, mic.com/articles/134764/the-improbable-story-of-how-kendrick-lamar-s-alright-became-a-protest-anthem#.GzoCjXdiB.

4 Autonomous Sensory Meridian Response (ASMR) refers to the practice of listening to close-miked, whispered audio recordings that make use of the binaural space of headphones to elicit intense physical responses, often described as a 'tingling' sensation. See Pettman 2017, 20–1.

5 Grossman, Zoltan [Zoltán Grossman], 'Stevie Wonder on Ferguson & New York grand jury verdicts', YouTube, 4 December 2014, www.youtube.com/watch?v=VX6lJmxVLtY. Transcription adapted from video description. Special thanks to Zoltán Grossman for the video, transcription and correspondence.

6 The video history of this clip is, like so much phone-based footage, a complicated web of partial publications, republications and repurposings. The video was first posted in a partial version (duration 02:49) by the New York-based *Daily News* (Ramsey Orta, 'Staten Island man dies after NYPD cop puts him in chokehold', *Daily News*, n.d. (c.18 July 2014), video.nydailynews.com/

Staten-Island-man-dies-after-NYPD-cop-puts-him-in-chokehold–26426042), followed by an article with the same video excerpt posted two days after the shooting (Annie Karni, Rocco Parascandola and Larry McShane, '2 cops pulled off streets, Staten Island DA looking into man's death after NYPD chokehold', *Daily News*, 19 July 2014, www.nydailynews.com/new-york/nyc-crime/staten-island-da-man-death-nypd-chokehold-article-1.1871946). A year later, Ken Murray, a *Daily News* photographer, described how he acquired Orta's footage for publication on the day of Garner's killing ('How the Daily News acquired the Eric Garner video', *Daily News*, 11 July 2015, www.nydailynews.com/new-york/video-shows-fatally-choking-eric-garner-graphic-content-article-1.2289271), and the *Daily News* published an 'Unedited version' on YouTube around the same time (Ramsey Orta, 'Eric Garner video – Unedited version'. YouTube, New York Daily News, 12 July 2015, www.youtube.com/watch?v=JpGxagKOkv8), which specifies in its notes that it includes four separate video files edited together (duration 11:08). For broader accounts of how the recording was made, as well as subsequent police retaliation against Orta, see Mathias 2016 and Taibbi 2017. In many ways, the cluster of footage produced by Orta and its subsequent publication calls for, among other things, a more traditional ('positivist') historiography – a kind of digital source studies coupled with ethnography that traces in detail the circulation of these media fragments. For an example of the video as embedded in media around the time of Wonder's performance in early December 2014 and the protests that followed the decision not to indict, see Laughland et al. 2014.

7 Stevie Wonder, 'Living for the City'. *Innervisions*. Motown Records, 1973.

8 Zoltán Grossman, personal correspondence with author, 24 September 2017.

9 'Is hip-hop still "CNN for Black people"?', *Daily Beast*, 24 March 2015, www.thedailybeast.com/is-hip-hop-still-cnn-for-black-people.

10 See Chang 2016 and Zandria F. Robinson, 'How Beyoncé's "Lemonade" exposes inner lives of Black women', *Rolling Stone*, 28 April 2016, www.rollingstone.com/music/news/how-beyonces-lemonade-exposes-inner-lives-of-black-women-20160428.

11 Several authors have commented on how Beyoncé remained 'silent' in the elevator (literally) and afterward, or questioned whether she was in fact silenced by the combination of technologies (CCTV cameras) and cultural constraints (e.g. Nicholas Hautman, 'Jay-Z Addresses Solange Knowles elevator fight for the first time: "We had one disagreement ever"', *Us Weekly*, 21 August 2017, www.usmagazine.com/celebrity-news/news/jay-z-opens-up-about-elevator-fight-with-solange-knowles-w498636/; Priscilla Peña Ovalle, 'Resounding silence and soundless surveillance, from TMZ elevator to Beyoncé and back again', *Sounding Out!*, 15 September 2014, soundstudiesblog.com/2014/09/15/resounding-silence-and-surveillance-from-tmz-elevator-to-beyonce-and-back-again/).

12 Hannah Giorgis, 'All the best pieces about Beyoncé's Lemonade', *BuzzFeed*, 29 April 2016, www.buzzfeed.com/hannahgiorgis/i-aint-sorry?utm_term=.deXwDmkA7M#.wc2Pq6ObXx; *The Atlantic*, 'Beyoncé's *Lemonade*: The week in pop-culture writing', 30 April 2016, www.theatlantic.com/entertainment/archive/2016/04/beyonces-lemonade-the-week-in-pop-culture-writing/480525/.

13 bell hooks, 'Moving beyond pain', *bell hooks Institute*, 9 May 2016, www.bellhooksinstitute.com/blog/2016/5/9/moving-beyond-pain. hooks's commentary sparked its own wave of intense discussion and response, e.g. Melissa Harris-Perry et al. 'A Black feminist roundtable on Beyoncé, and "Moving beyond pain"', *Feministing.com*, 11 May 2016, feministing.com/2016/05/11/a-feminist-roundtable-on-bell-hooks-beyonce-and-moving-beyond-pain/.

14 Robin James, 'How not to listen to Lemonade: music criticism and epistemic violence', *Sounding Out!*, 16 May 2016, soundstudiesblog.com/2016/05/16/how-not-to-listen-to-lemonade-music-criticism-and-epistemic-violence/.

15 Greg Tate, 'Review: Beyoncé is the rightful heir to Michael Jackson and Prince on "Lemonade"', *SPIN*, 28 April 2016, www.spin.com/2016/04/review-beyonce-lemonade/.

16 Reynolds's video was initially recorded and broadcast on Facebook Live but has since been disseminated widely through news outlets and other digital video repositories like YouTube. I cite the original video here as Lavish Reynolds 2016 (her Facebook username) with Jeronimo Yanez's dashcam video as Yanez 2016. As digital 'versions of record' I would highlight YouTube uploads of both videos by Ramsey County, Minnesota (username: Ramsey County), though the Reynolds video does not include footage from the back of the police vehicle. See DeLong and Braunger 2017 for a synchronised edit of both videos with analysis.

17 See Moon and Volz 2016 and Roberts 2016 on the ethics of Facebook Live in response to the Castile shooting. Intriguingly, the *Star Tribune*, which provided the most extensive local

newspaper coverage of the shooting, ran an opinion piece just weeks earlier on the ethics and possibilities of using livestream video, including in encounters with police (Blanchette 2016).

18 Reynolds highlights the social aspects of social media in her vocative cry addressed to 'Facebook'. The plea and physical gestures of recording that surround it underscore what Paul Frosh has called 'kinesthetic sociability': 'selfies' are above all bodily gestures that foster social networks (2015). The same holds here, but the stakes are significantly higher.

19 As one example that exceeds my scope here, Regina Bradley's discussion of Sandra Bland – who was pulled over, had her arrest filmed by a bystander, and then subsequently died in jail – recounts how central a role sound, voice, and loudness played in Bland's death. 'SANDRA BLAND: #SayHerName Loud or Not at All', *Sounding Out!*, 16 November 2015, soundstudiesblog.com/2015/11/16/sandra-bland-sayhername-loud/. Ashon Crawley also places Garner's death front and centre in his account of 'Blackpentecostal breath' (2017).

20 National anthems as musical and social objects played an important role in ethnomusicology fifteen to twenty years ago, as seen in Turino 1999, Guy 2002 and Daughtry 2003.

21 Nick Wagoner, 'Transcript of Colin Kaepernick's comments about sitting during the national anthem', *ESPN*, 29 August 2016, www.espn.com/blog/san-francisco-49ers/post/_/id/18957/transcript-of-colin-kaepernicks-comments-about-sitting-during-national-anthem. Wagoner has 'affect' in place of 'effect', but this is clearly a transcription error.

22 David Z. Morris, 'The reason why Fox Sports isn't airing the NFL's national anthem today', *Fortune*, 1 October 2017, fortune.com/2017/10/01/fox-sports-nfl-national-anthem-protest/.

23 ABC News, 'National anthem protests grow at NFL games', *YouTube*, 12 September 2016, www.youtube.com/watch?v=ZT1EN-s6C0s. Baldwin's listening practices in their own right have attracted media attention ('Now his eardrums are much more receptive', writes Matt Calkins, 'Want real change?', *Seattle Times*, 18 October 2017, www.seattletimes.com/sports/seahawks/want-real-change-get-seahawks-doug-baldwin-involved/).

Personal Take: Giving History a Voice

MARIANA LOPEZ

As a researcher and sound designer I am fascinated by the use of digital technologies to study and interpret cultural heritage. The use of sound installations in heritage sites is one of my main fields of interest as it allows us to explore how people's engagement with venues and objects changes through these digital mediations while also challenging the dominance of visual experiences.

In 2009 I assisted (mostly by carrying cables, moving speakers and ushering people) in the *I-Hear-Too: Live* event that took place in the UK cathedral known as York Minster. The aim of the event was to encourage visitors to rediscover the space by focusing on sonic experiences. Among the various installations, two of them captured my imagination. The first was *Minster Voices*, a sound montage played through loudspeakers in the Zouche Chapel and designed by the media production company History-works. A combination of voice recordings and sound effects (including keys, footsteps, bells and stonemasonry) allowed listeners to familiarise themselves with the stories of those who look after the Minster, while also inviting visitors to reassess their own relationship with the space. The second was *Octo: Sotto Voce* by sound artist David Chapman, which demonstrated a very different but equally engaging approach. Chapman's piece was a sonic mosaic of whispers, reminding us of the association between hushed voices and religious spaces. The piece was designed as an eight-channel installation to emulate the octagonal shape of the Chapter House. Listeners could walk around the space and approach individual loudspeakers to experience the piece at different positions, challenging the idea of an aural sweet spot. The artist used dry recordings, that is, recordings with no spatial information, relying on the acoustic characteristics of the installation space to modify the piece.

In 2014 I took part in the Festival of Medieval Arts in York with my installation *Hearing the Mystery Plays* in All Saints Church, Pavement. The installation explored the impact of acoustics on the York Mystery Plays, a series of medieval plays with religious themes performed in the streets of York on wagons designed for the occasion. The installation was based on my research on the acoustics of Stonegate, one of the performance sites, as well as the acoustical impact of different types of wagon structures, wagon orientations, and performer and listener positions. I chose to focus on

Stonegate because it still retains its medieval dimensions as well as its original timber-framed structures. In relation to the wagons, the scarcity of written documentation makes it necessary to explore a multiplicity of possible staging techniques as we cannot know for certain which ones were used at the time. The sound installation explored these unknowns and made this multiplicity of acoustical options available to the public. The aim was to avoid a simplistic representation of the past that presents the designer's interpretation as 'historical truth'; on the contrary, it put at the forefront the fact that all re-creation of sounds and acoustics from the past is faced with a myriad of possibilities.

The sound installation comprised three different soundscapes based on the plays of *The Resurrection*, *Pentecost* and *The Assumption of the Virgin*, all including speech and music auralisations. The term 'auralisation' describes a computer-aided process that allows us to hear the way sound is modified by the characteristics of a space. The musical extracts included plainchant, the predominant style for worship in medieval times, as well as polyphonic music notated as part of *The Assumption of the Virgin*.

The soundscapes played in a loop over headphones. A screen displayed images of the virtual models used for the acoustical re-creations as well as the names of the plays and characters. The computer models presented two alternatives of wagon structures, one open on all sides with columns supporting a pitched roof, the other a multilevel structure with a main deck closed on three sides representing Earth and an upper deck representing Heaven. Listeners were also able to hear the difference between a wagon with an orientation towards one of the sides of the street and another one towards one of the ends of the street. Moreover, the auralisations included a variety of performer and listener positions to demonstrate the acoustical impact of such changes. Participants were encouraged to use QR codes to access web pages that included information on the research behind the creative work.

Throughout the duration of the installation I collected data on the interaction of approximately one hundred participants. I found out that the average time spent listening was four minutes, which exceeded my expectations. Although the installation had a total running time of thirteen minutes it was designed so that people could start listening from any given point. Only 8 per cent of visitors interacted with the web pages through a mobile device; such a low percentage raises questions on the suitability of this method to provide the general public with information on research. However, this low percentage was not due to a lack of interest in learning about the subject, as 69 per cent of listeners approached the research team on site to express their thoughts on the project, ask questions and leave comments. The data collected showed that even though the installation was set up with simple technology, non-specialist visitors found the experience engaging and accessible. Furthermore, their reception indicated that the communication of several possible versions of the past is welcomed and should be considered for future installation work.

The variety of approaches to sound experiences at heritage sites not only allows designers and researchers to rethink the ways technologies can be applied to the communication of cultural heritage, but also draws attention to the importance of sound as intangible heritage, and its key role in understanding, interpreting and communicating history. Traditionally, heritage studies have been silent, focusing on written documents and visual aspects. Even the study of heritage acoustics often falls into the trap of concentrating on numerical data, without acknowledging the importance of listening. The proliferation of sound installations in recent years is starting to challenge such tradition and, consequently, returning History its voice.

6 Digital Devotion: Musical Multimedia in Online Ritual and Religious Practice

MONIQUE M. INGALLS

Digital technologies and online networks have transformed religious faith, practice and experience in the twenty-first century. The Internet both communicates and mediates; it is a means for sharing and evaluating religious ideas and a space where religious experience takes place. The Internet not only enables engagement in established forms of religious ritual brought online, but also makes possible new forms of ritual practice. The online environment is both a medium for expressing and experiencing religion and a mode of religious production in its own right, generating powerful religious experiences for those who approach its digital offerings in a devotional posture, and, in the process, challenging certain religious authorities and official traditions. In particular, online media challenge the historical connections between ritual acts of worship and discrete geographical places, types of social interaction, and 'live' or 'face-to-face' modes of passing on religious tradition. Just as online media have enabled new forms of human sociality to flourish, so also have they opened new ways for individuals to experience direct connections to the divine, often without recourse to religious authorities or to traditionally established ways of accessing the divine.

Exploring the ways digital technologies and religious practice have mutually shaped and influenced one another has formed the basis of much scholarly reflection since the late 1990s, part of the general 'media turn' within religious studies (Engelke 2010). This resurging interest in processes of mediation within religion – and in religion as a form of mediation – has spurred the development of interdisciplinary subfields such as media and religion and 'digital religion' (see especially Dawson and Cowan 2004; Campbell 2005, 2010, and 2013; Engelke 2010; Wagner 2012). Scholars working at the interface of digital culture and religious practice have developed and applied a range of methods for analysing and interpreting textual and visual components of digital religion; however, sonic, musical and audio-visual elements remain comparatively under-theorised despite their prominent role within digital rituals and online resources.

To show the crucial role of music and, more generally, sacred sound[1] within digital religious practice, this chapter examines music's role in three types of devotional ritual, synthesising case studies from scholarship in media, music and religious studies. These case studies include those from my own research on music in digital devotion within evangelical Christianity, as well as scholarly research on other religious traditions. They facilitate exploration of several interrelated questions, including how and in what contexts music is used in online ritual; how engaging in music as part of participatory digital technologies is changing how people experience and practise their religious faith; and to what extent music in particular connects online and offline religious practices. Addressing these questions through the lens of musical and audio-visual experience will help scholars understand and assess the implications of the new digital apparatus on religious authority, religious experience and the formation of religious communities. It will also bring scholarship on music and digital religion into a more sustained dialogue, enabling these conversations to further enrich one other.

Ritual in Digital Religion: Definitions and Key Issues

Devotional rituals, though not exclusive to religion, are acknowledged to be central components of most religious traditions as the key means of imparting religious experience and forming a united community.[2] Literary critic Marie-Laure Ryan offers a succinct description of the relationship between religion and ritual: 'in its religious form, ritual is a technique of immersion in a sacred reality that uses gestures, performative speech, and the manipulation of symbolic objects ... to [establish] communication between the human and its Other' (2003, 293). Online digital platforms serve as both '*resource* and *space* for devotional practice' (Vekemans 2014, 132, emphasis mine). In other words, digital online media provide a marketplace or gift economy for resources that support religious devotional rituals offline (particularly audio and audio-visual materials), in addition to an immersive ritual environment where people may encounter the sacred. The transfer of religious practice online, as well as the use of the web for individual religious experimentation, has spurred numerous debates within religious communities worldwide about what kinds of online rituals (or offline rituals with online components) can be considered 'authentic', and to what extent they are efficacious. In other words, how far can these activities themselves be considered rituals versus merely computer-mediated representations of rituals? Is taking part in a Buddhist ritual in *Second Life* a substitute for attending one offline? Is the experience of congregational worship as meaningful when one is in front of a large screen at a 'satellite' church venue, singing along with a band that is playing 'live' at a different venue across town? Can a Jewish worshipper joining a prayer group over Skype comprise part of the quorum of ten individuals necessary for corporate prayer? Are YouTube videos that juxtapose digital Qur'anic text with sacred sound a help or a hindrance to a believer's devotion to the divine word?

The study of media and religion[3] shows that these questions are not new; rather, questions of authenticity, authority, and the moral, social and spiritual shaping of community inevitably accompany media and technological change within religious groups and the societies of which they are part (see Hoover 2006; Schofield Clark 2007; Lynch 2007; Engelke 2010; Lynch et al. 2012). Such tensions and debates within religious traditions have sprung up with the introduction of various technologies at other points in history (e.g. graphic writing, mass-mediated printing, musical notation, microphones and cassettes), as people within these traditions debate whether the possibilities afforded by new technologies are in line with their beliefs, practices, ethics and aesthetics.

So what actually *is* new about how people use digital technology in relationship to religion and ritual? What difference does digital culture make to religious practice? The academic field of digital religion (sometimes also referred to as 'cyber-religion' or 'online religion') has emerged to answer this key question and to lay out related questions for scholarly exploration. According to Stewart Hoover, what is different about digital media 'is the extent to which it encourages new modes of practice', its 'generativity' (2013, 267). New modes of practice that digital media enable have generated liminal 'third spaces' for religious practice;[4] digital practices enable 'small sphericals of focused interaction' and entail unique aesthetic logics that 'hail' the user and point toward social action (268).

Scholarship on digital religion generally includes in-depth analysis of texts and images; however, it rarely examines sonic and musical components in any detail.[5] Music is a key element in much audio-visual devotional media, as well as a communicative, affective medium in its own right. Sacred sound and music are key elements in the connective tissue between 'religion online' and 'online religion' (Helland 2000) – in other words, resources for religious practice made available online, and religious devotion practised online. And music's use within new online digital rituals brings along with it many aspects of older debates about how music should function within religious devotional practice (see especially Echchaibi 2013, Engelhardt 2018). It is my contention that close attention to music and sacred sound can illuminate many of the key questions digital religion scholars are asking about how authenticity and authority are variously established, challenged, deposed or maintained. The case studies in this chapter show how music variously facilitates, enhances, comprises and authenticates online religious practice, and focus in turn on different types of digital devotional practice: (1) ritual in online virtual worlds; (2) devotional resources for use in offline ritual that are shared online; and (3) audio-visual materials that serve as both resources and spaces for devotion. These are arranged in a general progression from digital rituals that are relatively conservative (in that they reflect or seek to simulate offline devotional practices) to transformative rituals that challenge religious authority and influence devotional practice offline.

Music and Ritual Online: Shaping and Authenticating Sacred Soundscapes in Virtual Worlds

Virtual worlds, as Ryan conceives them, are created from a deep immersion in narrative that creates an experiential break with ordinary time and space. She notes that 'the presence of the gods can be compared to the telepresence of VR, because it breaks the boundary between the realm of the human, located *here*, and the realm of the divine, located *there* in sacred space' (2003, 295). Often in direct contradiction to religious authorities and traditions which seek to preserve the distance between worshippers and the divine, mediated virtual realities create proximity, resulting in 'the participants in the ritual experienc[ing] the live presence of the gods' and attaining 'a status that may be properly described as co-authorship of the cosmos' (295). Devout practitioners of religions have often recounted intense, immersive experiences in sacred 'virtual worlds' as part of ritual devotional practice (see Wagner 2012; Garaci 2014). Participating in devotional music-making – whether through chanting prayers, 'deep listening' to a cantor or choir, or lifting one's voice together with others in congregational hymn-singing – often facilitates this kind of deep immersion into the narrative of religious tradition by evoking a complex set of associations, memories and emotions (Rouget 1985 [1980]; Becker 2004). In online 'virtual' rituals, from tours of pilgrimage sites and interactive ritual simulations to religious services in virtual gaming worlds, music serves as a mechanism for structuring time and transforming online space into ritual space.

Perhaps the best-documented virtual religious ritual is the online pilgrimage or 'cyberpilgrimage', facilitated by venerational websites that enable practices common in shrine worship (Brasher 2001). Connie Hill-Smith defines 'cyberpilgrimage' as 'the practice of undertaking pilgrimage on the internet', online journeys that are 'hugely diverse in scale, complexity, content, design and purpose, ranging from technologically "simple" web pages displaying photographic galleries and explanatory text, to more sophisticated websites that attempt to reconstruct and repackage iconographic, structural and sensed aspects of the experience of "real-life" pilgrimage' (2011, 236). Traditional sites of Christian pilgrimage, including Lourdes, St Peter's Basilica, Jerusalem's *Via Dolorosa* and Croagh Patrick, have become popular sites for online pilgrimage (MacWilliams 2004; Hill-Smith 2011; Wagner 2012). While early cyberpilgrimage scholarship occupied itself predominantly with studies of Christian sites, recent studies examine sacred online journeys within Hinduism (Jacobs 2007), Buddhism (Connelly 2013), Jainism (Vekemans 2014), Judaism (Radde-Antweiler 2008) and Islam (Derrickson 2008). Players have populated the MMORPG (massively multiplayer online role-playing game) *Second Life* with numerous real-world physical sacred sites, including well-known mosques, temples and churches, many of which give users the option to stream or download devotional music as their avatars explore the virtual sacred sites (Radde-Antweiler 2008). Some places of worship on *Second Life* also host live (virtual) devotional musical performances, and occasionally avatars can join enactments of sacred journeys, including a virtual *hajj* to Mecca.

Just as programmers can arrange constellations of pixels on a screen to create recognisable ritual objects, so also do they use music and sound to imprint soundscapes, transforming virtual space into sacred space. Numerous sites devoted to prayer rituals demonstrate how music structures, frames and sacralises virtual ritual. For example, Hindus, Jains, Sikhs and some Buddhists practise an individual prayer ritual called puja ('adoration', 'worship'), which involves presenting various offerings to the image of a particular deity and can be performed at either domestic or temple altars. Devotional songs (bhajans) and mantras are a common accompaniment to devotional acts offline and are frequently present in online practice as well. When users visit spiritualpuja.com, they can click on the image of a Hindu temple to enter the main site. Once 'inside', you are greeted with the words 'ONLINE PUJA' along with a brief explanation of elements of the Hindu devotional ritual. You can scroll down and choose from fifteen different puja rituals (including three tantric rituals with 'adult content' warnings). When you enter each puja in honour of a particular deity, a new bhajan begins. You can view a video compilation or devotional images, or scroll down to the virtual altar, where you can make virtual offerings of flowers, incense or a candle to a central image of the god/dess or guru. A 'guide me' button to the side of the altar reminds you to ring the virtual bell to begin the ceremony. Similarly, the Jain informational and devotional website jainuniversity.org, sponsored by a coalition of Jain leaders in Vadadora City (in northwestern India) offers a virtual puja ceremony to the Lord Mahavir, with simulation of eight different offerings. When you click on each offering, a new bhajan begins playing.[6]

In her study of online Buddhist practice, Louise Connelly writes that visual and auditory dimensions of online ritual must compensate for the lack of the remaining senses to combat the sensory limitations of the online platform (2013, 131). Ambient sounds are common features of the *Second Life* experience and, tellingly, even the silent meditation ritual (*zazen*) at the Buddha Centre on *Second Life* is far from sound-free: the 'silence' idealised in this virtual environment is created not by the removal of all sound, but by the presence of certain sounds, including running water and windchimes. A gong and singing bowl are sounded to mark the start and end of the ritual, and chanted scriptures often form the focus of the ceremony itself. Further, social roles at the gathering are established sonically, creating continuity between religious authority online and off-line: it is the avatar of one of the rotating meditation leaders – all of whom are religious specialists, including monks, priests or teachers in offline temples – who chimes the singing bowl to signify the start and end of the meditation session, and who leads the chanting and intones the mantras (Connelly 2013, 130).

Hill-Smith (2011) observes that 'the overlaying of tradition-preserving, tradition-transmitting media material on to the basic experience (i.e. culturally specific music, doctrinally based text explaining or enhancing imagery, iconographic "hotspots", etc.)' is a common feature of nearly all cyberpilgrimages. The examples sketched above suggest that this observation can be extended to most rituals that take place within virtual worlds, whether on websites created and hosted by religious institutions or within gaming platforms like *Second Life* (see also Miczek 2008; Kluver and Chen 2008; Jenkins 2008). Sonic architecture helps to constitute spaces for religious devotion, and in the same way religiously marked sounds and genres enclose and authenticate certain virtual spaces and activities as sacred, suggesting a generally conservative orientation where online 'ritual patterns replicate offline forms with limited innovation' (Hutchings 2013, 164). Hutchings argues here that ritual online is essentially dependent on religion offline: that the transfer of offline ritual practices to online ritual spaces relies on the transfer of their associated meanings. But not all uses of music in online ritual are conservative. We shall see that some of the practices of digital devotion pose a formidable challenge to religious institutions and structures.

Reinventing Tradition: Online Musical Tools for Offline Devotional Practices

The Internet constitutes a vast marketplace for devotional resources, particularly audio recordings for accompanying public or private worship. Scholars working across religious traditions have noted how readily many religious communities use the online marketplace to share and purchase audio and audio-visual resources for devotional practice, including recordings from music labels and distributors, music-related discussion forums and blogs, music streaming sites, livestreamed or pre-recorded religious services and concerts, online radio stations, sound recordings and music videos uploaded to social media sites such as YouTube (Echchaibi 2013; Engelhardt 2018; Hagedorn 2006; Ingalls 2016; Summit 2016; Weston and Bennett 2013). This section engages these academic case studies to highlight the ways the vast array of online musical resources shape and condition offline devotional practice.

The ready availability of religious musical materials online has in some cases encouraged a 'pick 'n' mix' spirituality (Campbell 2013, 6) in which individuals draw from a variety of disparate materials to meet their self-defined spiritual needs – so bypassing sources of authority and communities of interpretation that condition the meaning or constrain the use of these materials. This is an intensification of a trend noted before the advent of digital technologies: religious items proliferated on the globalising commodity marketplace, enabling the rise of powerful religiously oriented commercial music and media industries.[7] In the same way, musical recordings of global sacred traditions, now readily accessible via the online marketplace, have become popular resources for such individualised spiritual practices. In analysing online comments from listeners, Katherine Hagedorn writes that the online marketplace facilitates an engagement with 'exotic' sacred traditions like Cuban Santería and Indo-Pakistani *qawwali* that allows Western listeners to 'gain access to some of the spiritual capital of these religious traditions without investing in the religious practices themselves' (Hagedorn 2006, 489).

What begin as idiosyncratic practices may, however, aggregate into more standardised forms shared by far-flung communities of practice. Weston and Bennett (2013) note that the vast array of musical resources and ideas available via the internet marketplace, including instructional videos, internet radio stations, blogs, forums and online stores, helps spread and standardise practice within the virtual community of neopaganism. Music forms the central node of discourse and practice in 'the one place that unites nearly all Pagans: online' (4). In the case of a relatively new religious movement like neopaganism, listening to and discussing shared music provides a meeting place for community and in turn establishes connections between individuals which extend to offline relationships. Further, these increasingly dense interconnections entailed in shared practice and discourse work to create norms from an array of eclectic practices and beliefs.

In the cases of sacred world music and neopagan devotional music, online pedagogical tools and resources encourage spiritual practice beyond the purview of religious institutions. Such tools are indispensable within some organised religious traditions, enabling greater access to once-specialised training and sometimes sparking renewal of interest in certain musical or devotional practices. In the process, online digital mediation can subtly alter, or even completely overhaul, received meanings and essential aspects of the religious practice by bypassing traditional sources of authority and enabling new ways of practising religious music. In his recent book chronicling the resurgent interest in cantillating Scripture within American Judaism, Jeffrey Summit (2016) discusses how digital technologies for teaching Torah cantillation are changing how the tradition is transmitted and authority is structured. According to Summit, the proliferation of cantillation software and audio and audio-visual recordings available online has raised issues of 'the validity of authority, a dislocation of learning from a specific place and time, a shift from community oversight and control to individual direction and personal agency' (221). Educators and students based in local synagogues often use online pedagogical materials to learn tropes, or musical motifs, applied to each word of scripture as indicated by symbols above the text. Students learning cantillation from online resources often encounter simplified and standardised versions, bypassing traditions from their local synagogues replete with variations passed down from cantor to student. Yet the democratisation of technology to record and transmit cantillation practices can also have the opposite effect. Summit notes that it is spurring many Jewish cantors and educators to record their personal trope styles in order to preserve local traditions (238). Again, students sometimes learn cantillation from Jewish traditions on the opposite end of the theological or political spectrum from their own, thus blurring denominational lines. These technologies enable a private, individualised learning of Jewish tradition, unmoored from both traditional authority and local community. Summit notes the near-unprecedented situation in which 'it is possible to become a "technician of the sacred" without being an actively engaged member of a worship community' (238).

In the case of devotional music genres with well-established commercial industries and circulation networks, as in that of sacred world music, online access accelerates trends that began in prior decades with the growth of commodity markets for devotional recordings. Within evangelical Christianity, for instance, the online saturation of popular commercial worship music further erodes the authority of denominations and church networks as gatekeepers of congregational worship music. But there are other gatekeepers. While individuals have instant access to thousands of new worship songs, the Christian commercial recording industry plugs the music of a handful of popular brands and so increasingly constrains their choices. Evangelical worship music evidences the seemingly contradictory trend noted by Jenkins wherein new media technologies enable individuals to 'archive, annotate, appropriate, and recirculate media content in powerful new ways', even as media content – commercial devotional music, in this case – becomes even more tightly concentrated in the hands of a few dominant corporations (2006, 18). Since the early 2000s, owing in large part to online circulation, contemporary worship music (a pop-rock-based repertoire intended for congregational singing and often simply called 'worship music') has become a transnationally circulating genre sung in weekly services by tens of millions of evangelical and pentecostal-charismatic Christians. The music's ready availability on the Internet further fuels the dominance of a handful of influential worship 'brands' who produce the music.

One of the major influences on the digital market for evangelical congregational songs over the past two decades has been Christian Copyright Licensing International (CCLI). CCLI is a private, for-profit company that provides licences for churches to reproduce song lyrics in their services by serving as a copyright clearinghouse for most of the Anglophone contemporary worship music industry. It also provides a range of paid online services for churches, including the digital library SongSelect, which the company bills as 'the best place to find licensed audio samples and lyrics along with vocal, chord and lead sheets from more than 300,000 songs of worship' (us.ccli.com). CCLI collects detailed statistics twice per year from a proportion of subscribing churches – now totalling over 250,000 – which it uses to distribute royalties to songwriters and publishers. The company began publicising its 'Top 25' charts in the 1990s, listing the most frequently sung worship songs among their subscribing churches.

Due to the surveillance into local practice enabled by this powerful digital platform, the CCLI worship charts not only reflect but also to a great extent drive the production and adoption of new worship music. During my three years of field research within the Nashville-based Christian music industry, music executives and recording artists told me story after story about attempts to identify, promote and market songs that would top the CCLI popularity charts, which they called the 'church charts'. New songs shared online on social media – whether 'legally' through publishers and recording labels' official channels or informally by fans recirculating the recordings via social media – amass hundreds of thousands and sometimes millions of views within weeks of their release, facilitating their quick adoption into local worship contexts. The average age of contemporary worship songs on the CCLI charts has decreased rapidly as local music directors at churches increasingly use paid online services like CCLI's SongSelect and social media, in addition to Christian commercial radio, to discover and access new songs, rather than denominational resources, record clubs or music conferences.[8] In 1997, the average song on CCLI's top twenty-five worship songs list was seventeen years old, and the newest of the songs on the list was eight years old. By 2006, the average song on CCLI's list was ten years old, and six songs on the list were five or fewer years old. By 2016, the average top 25 CCLI song was seven years old and over half the songs on the list (thirteen songs) had been written in the last five years.

Both the examples of Jewish cantillation and of evangelical Christian worship music demonstrate how increased autonomy provided by digital technologies poses serious challenges to traditional religious authorities. However, in other cases, digital tools for musical devotional practices work hand in hand with and even help to shore up religious authority. Jeffers Engelhardt recounts such a case in his examination of how digital musical media has helped Orthodox practitioners in Greece establish what they call a 'Christocentric everyday': 'a worldly Orthodox milieu of ethical action and Christ-like becoming' (2018, 72). Rather than focusing on one media form, Engelhardt uses thick description of the digital audio and audiovisual resources that four devout followers of Orthodoxy in Thessaloniki use in their devotional practice. These include: digital recordings and broadcasts of sermons and chant; YouTube video channels devoted to liturgical chant and daily hymns; mobile ringtones using chant intonation formulas; and mobile apps that produce an electronic vocal drone for accompanying Byzantine chant (73). While Engelhardt's Orthodox informants found these resources useful for private devotion and musical pedagogy, they drew a firm distinction between what he terms 'natural media' and 'marked media': in other words, those analogue forms that comprise the received Orthodox tradition and new digital forms seen as outside it. Natural media, such as 'incense-laden air, human voices and bodies, and bells' (76), are those thoroughly enculturated media forms understood as central to Orthodox practice that, over time, have been rendered immediate within liturgy and theology. Marked media, which include broadcast and digital media, are those which operate outside the boundaries of worship and thus call attention to themselves and their 'sense of remove from the sacramental life of the church' (76). Rather than individualising practice and challenging traditional Orthodox belief, these media have participated in a widespread Greek 'push back to the church', a popular move to embrace traditional religious authority in the wake of widespread political and social change in the context of Greek neoliberal austerity.

Examples from across established religious traditions and new spiritual movements show that the influence of digital technologies is neither predictable nor unidirectional, and that there are a variety of ways in which religious practitioners use online musical tools in offline devotional practices to (re)invent and reinvigorate their traditions. In some cases, their use can forge closer links with traditional authorities and religious hierarchies, while in other cases it encourages a transfer of power, mediated through the agency of individuals, from religious institutions to media industries. The next section continues in this latter vein, describing how digital media transform religious practice, sometimes blurring the line between online and offline devotional practice. In these instances, online digital musical and audio-visual resources move beyond being merely resources or ingredients for religious practice, instead serving as the very spaces where religious experience occurs.

Online Devotional Resources: Muslim and Christian YouTube Videos as Audio-Visual Icons

Music plays perhaps the most formative – and transformative – role within the third type of devotional practice: the use of audio-visual resources for rituals experienced online. Exploring case studies from Muslim and Christian devotional videos on YouTube illustrates how audio-visual media draw together images, text, and music and sacred sound in a manner designed to produce powerful religious experiences for devoted viewers. Further, these religious practices online challenge established authorities – and sometimes even key tenets of religious orthodoxy – shaping expectations and religious experience in a way that spills into offline religiosity.

Sound is recognised as the dominant sense within Islamic religious devotional practice, and its strategic use has been key to the success of revival movements within contemporary Islam (see Hirschkind 2006). Both listening practices and communication styles within contemporary Islam have shifted markedly due to the introduction and widespread use of audio and audio-visual technologies. In his research on popular cassette sermons in Cairo, Charles Hirschkind writes that catering to devotees whose listening practices have been shaped by the media and entertainment industries has altered both sermon rhetoric and the aesthetics of oral delivery. These rhetorical innovations 'combine classical sermon elements with languages and narrative forms rooted in such diverse genres as modern political oratory, television dramas, radio news broadcasts, and cinematic montage' (2006, 11).

Expanding Hirschkind's work on cassette sermons to digital audio-visual media, Nabil Echchaibi analyses the rhetorical and stylistic innovations within Islamic communication that have resulted from popular

Muslim preachers' use of various digital online technologies. Using Egyptian televangelist Amr Khaled[9] as an example, Echchaibi notes that his sermons involve 'a creative triangulation of the physical, the visual, and the digital' (2013, 445), and that his embrace of the integrative potential of digital technologies has introduced new aesthetic possibilities: 'Khaled has moved beyond aural media and therefore expanded the sensorium his followers draw from to build pious identities in a world of confusing sounds, images, and digital bytes' (448).

As a spoken form, Khaled's sermons often use dramatic, evocative visual imagery; online, some of his videos feature superimposed images and many include background music. On one video sermon posted to Khaled's YouTube channel in June 2016, a recording studio forms the central source of images during the minute and a half of opening credits.[10] The opening video segment features a hand turning a knob; as a tape reel starts to rotate, soft arpeggiated piano music with heavy reverb begins. As the song continues, a rapid succession of images from the recording studio (hands turning dials and knobs, cassette decks, analogue equalisers, and a pianist's hands on a keyboard synthesiser) are interspersed among images of sacred texts, illuminated light bulbs and the imposing wooden door of a mosque. The instrumentation quickly thickens, as violin, 'ud, a full string section, and a male voice are added to the texture. The musical highpoint (01:13) features lush string orchestration and a male vocalist singing a melismatic line as several dynamic video segments flash in quick succession: a written script descends, a male worshipper falls prostrate in worship, two hands are shown on an electronic keyboard, a hand grasps prayer beads, and an unseen hand writes on parchment as the camera pans back from a library shelf covered in well-worn texts. After the credits and the opening song end, Khaled, a smiling, dark-haired middle-aged man, appears in a brightly lit, lavishly furnished room seated cross-legged in front of a large microphone. Soft instrumental music continues to play under most of his sermon. At the end (19:00), as Amr Khaled closes his eyes, lifts his hands in a prayer posture, and begins an impassioned prayer, a soft, low synthesiser drone begins and the melismatic male voice returns once again to sing a florid line.

The juxtaposition of music, sacred text and images in online sermons like this also appears in other genres of devotional videos centred on sacred sound. In Islam, Qur'anic recitation and *anasheed*, a vocal devotional song genre sometimes accompanied by percussion, enjoy widespread circulation online. Examples of both can be found on 'The Merciful Servant', which claims to be the largest Islamic YouTube channel, with over 700,000 subscribers and over 170 million views of its videos.[11] With the stated goal 'to educate, inspire and motivate muslims and guide everyone in the world to a better understanding of islam [*sic*]', this YouTube channel features informational videos on such topics as jinn, prophets, and basics of Muslim belief and practice, together with devotional videos that feature chanting combined with still and moving images, frequently with translations into English superimposed. Merciful Servant bills these videos as 'emotional,' 'POWERFUL', 'heart touching' and 'motivational', clearly intending them to be affective, to stir the heart and the emotions towards greater devotion to God.

Though Islamic tradition prohibits the use of images in public devotion, Merciful Servant's devotional videos include numerous still and moving images of various kinds. 'Quran chapter 76: Al-insan (The Man)', a Qur'anic recitation video by Egyptian muezzin and recording artist Omar Hisham al Arabi, illustrates the way images are used in these videos. An English translation of the chapter's text is superimposed on a series of changing images as al Arabi chants in Arabic. The text comprises several distinct parts, beginning with a first-person account written in God's voice and describing the divine purpose in creating humanity; this is followed by a detailed description of paradise in the afterlife that awaits the righteous as a reward for their just deeds. The chapter ends with a series of commands related to proper devotional practice. Throughout the recitation, marked by reverb so heavy it sometimes gives the impression of polyphony, a series of moving images appears on the screen, generally changing every six to ten seconds. Many of these images are clearly intended to depict the sacred text. Images of human statues and a human foetus appear at the beginning of the chapter as God narrates humanity's creation. The image of a vast ocean accompanies the portion of the passage describing 'a fountain that flows abundantly'. During the textual description of the garden of paradise, the viewer visits a computer-generated garden. When the topic of divine cosmic judgment arises, the viewer takes a virtual trip through outer space.

Not all images used in the video correspond exactly to the sacred words; some introduce added meanings or associations. Many majestic images from nature (nearly all computer-generated) do not directly relate to the text. These include a snow-capped mountain flanked by clouds, a boat on the ocean at sunset, and a forest whose trees are on fire but not consumed. A human eye brimming with tears is shown as the text describes how devotees' love for God motivates their care for the poor, orphan and captive. When the text points to the coming transformation of humankind, a moving image appears of human figures made from what looks like flowing computer code, as in *The Matrix*. Depictions of public devotional practice are interspersed throughout, including an aerial view of a mosque, followed by the depiction of a lone worshipper prostrating himself on a tiled floor.

Scanning other videos on The Merciful Servant, five basic categories of images predominate: images of nature (still and moving, photographic and CG); depictions of worship spaces and sacred architecture; men engaging in acts of devotion (mainly in *sujud*, the prostrate prayer posture); cosmic scenes featuring the universe or solar system; and abstract patterns of light that seem to depict flowing currents of energy. Several of these same image types emerged in my research into evangelical Christian devotional lyric videos on YouTube (see Ingalls 2016, 2018). I examined the musical and visual content of fifty worship videos (ten settings each of five popular contemporary worship songs) in tandem with online surveys and phone interviews with creators of twelve of the videos. Three image types predominated in this sample: nature images, used in more than two-thirds of the videos; depictions of worshippers, used in slightly more than one-third; and depictions of Jesus, used in one-third. I shall outline each in turn.

Occasionally the nature photos corresponded directly to the song lyrics, but they were usually unrelated. When discussing why they chose nature photos, Christian video creators told me they used images of nature to point to God as creator, and to create an atmosphere conducive to worship that would not distract the viewer from the song's message. In other words, nature images were intended to function as both subtle theological statement and as a pleasing, but innocuous, visual wallpaper.

Depictions of worshippers in worship videos generally feature a single worshipper or a group of worshippers with arms outstretched in prayer.[12] In analysing music, lyrics and visual elements together, I found that worship video creators commonly placed worship depictions at the musical climaxes within the song, especially at the beginning of a song's chorus where the instrumental texture, melodic height and volume increase. Worshipping bodies are generally featured as silhouettes against a plain colour or natural background, thus resembling the silhouetted bodies from Apple's iPod advertising campaign. Justin Burton describes why the dancing silhouettes were key to the overwhelming success of the campaign: the dancers were 'blank [human]-shaped spaces that could be filled with whatever identity a particular audience most wanted from [the iPod]' (2014, 319). By modelling the posture of worship at musical climaxes during these devotional videos, the worship video creators demonstrate that they have internalised certain expectations of evangelical devotional practice and gesture and invoke the bodily posture in which a devout viewer should be receiving the video.

Within the third category, depictions of Jesus, YouTube worship videos include evangelical popular art, Orthodox and Catholic icons, and still or moving images from films about the life of Jesus. US evangelicals, as heirs of Protestant iconoclasm, rarely use divine images in public worship;

however, religious historian David Morgan has shown mass-mediated images of Jesus to be central objects for private evangelical devotion. Morgan asserts that for pious viewers, these representations of Jesus 'make visual, and therefore in some sense embody, the personal savior, who "saves, comforts, and defends" them'. Through images of Jesus, 'Christ's personal significance for one's life is made visual: the face that one sees belongs to the divinity who cares personally for one's welfare. This visual personification of Christ clearly serves the evangelical imperative for a personal relationship with Jesus. Christ is encountered face-to-face' (1996, 193).

The religious work performed by the three image types common within Christian worship videos – two of which have direct counterparts in the Muslim devotional videos discussed earlier – suggests that in the online worship space images, sacred texts, and music are coming together to form a new and potent experiential whole. Within the YouTube comment boxes, some viewers testify how these videos invoke a personal experience with the divine. The video reminds some of powerful offline worship experiences they've had. Others narrate their real-time physical responses when watching the worship video, which range from being inspired to sing along loudly, to being moved to tears, to experiencing chills or goose-bumps, to feeling moved to spontaneously raise their hands in worship in front of their computer screen.[13] If we take these narratives at face value, it appears that, at least for some viewers, these videos mediate a sense of divine presence and evoke the same worshipful responses that characterise offline evangelical worship. Worship videos model a particular devotional posture and invite their viewers to adopt it.

These case studies of Muslim and Christian videos show how the affordances of digital online media have inspired new devotional practices with elements – in both cases, religious images – considered heterodox by many religious authorities and prohibited within public worship. Will these technologies drive a wedge between online and offline devotional practice, or influence the latter to become more like the former? In the case of contemporary mainstream evangelical Christianity, I have elsewhere suggested that online audio-visual devotional practices enabled by 'small screen' media are driving the incorporation of screen media in offline worship (Ingalls 2016). In *The Wired Church* (1999) Len Wilson, one of the first evangelical writers to address the use of digital technologies for worship, asserts that the screen is becoming 'the stained glass, and the cross, for the electronic media age . . . Icons were the Bible for the illiterate, and the screen is the Bible for the post-literate' (41). By synthesizing the devotional practices associated with sacred sound, images and text, audio-visual icons on small and large screens alike serve as markers of sacred space, potent religious symbols, foci for devotional meditation and conduits for divine encounter. They become emerging examples of what Birgit Meyer has called 'sensational forms': religious media 'exempted from the sphere of "mere" technology ... and attributed with a sense of immediacy through which the distance between believers and the transcendental is transcended' (2009, 12). As ways that religious traditions 'invoke and organize ... access to the transcendental', new religious sensational forms like audio-visual devotional videos can influence not only practice, but also deeper structures of belief and ethics (13).

Conclusion: The Musical Shaping of Ritual and the Sacred Everyday

This chapter has demonstrated that music and sacred sound are essential components of many types of online ritual. From virtual pilgrimages to shared audio-visual resources to devotional screen media, music works to authenticate the online space as a sacred space even as it challenges – sometimes subtly, at other times overtly – what beliefs and practices are considered orthodox, efficacious or acceptable. Engaging in music as part of participatory digital technologies has the potential to change how people experience and practise their religious faith. Following Michel-Rolph Trouillot (2003, 116), online resources and spaces for digital devotion help fuel the 'production of [religious] desire ... [T]he expansion and consolidation of the world market for consumer goods' create a sense of lack where once there was none, and expand the range of possibilities for devotional practice beyond the control of religious authorities. The Internet serves as a one-stop shop to find a vast array of resources across religious traditions: a marketplace of commoditised elements that can serve as resources for the conservator of tradition as well as for the 'spiritual-but-not-religious' person seeking out a mix of elements to further her quest for transcendence. It allows users to access information about musical and devotional practices from around the world, connects them to religious communities online and offline, and provides a relatively anonymous space for individual experimentation.

For practices whose authenticity or authority is likely to be questioned, music helps to sacralise the virtual world, grounding it in the associations of sacred practice offline. As Hirschkind reminds us, sound's sensuous aspects act powerfully on the body even as they shape ethical priorities, 'recruit[ing] the body in its entirety' and inciting moral passion in the devout listener (2006, 12). Arguably, at the level of sensation, it makes little difference whether the sound's source is live performance or a recording, or whether it originates offline or online. But music-infused audio-visual rituals online do not merely serve to simulate or imitate offline practices; as demonstrated by YouTube devotional music videos, online ritual practices can convey divine presence in their own way, synthesising existing practices into new 'sensational forms' (Meyer 2009) that are not readily available – and sometimes not even replicable – offline. Music can either provide continuity between online and offline religious practices, or form part of a composite resource for devotional practice that synthesises and transcends its offline counterparts.

Using audio and audio-visual online media, this chapter has suggested that examining music and sound is crucial for religion and media scholars who seek to understand and assess the implications of digital culture for religious authority, experience and community. And for music scholars interested in digital culture, online ritual and religious practice provide an ideal site for examining how music participates in contemporary debates about the nature of online community, the global commodity marketplace, and the interface between musical and extra-musical media. Digital multimedia technologies enable new intermedial relationships among music, images and text, and the audio-visual experience that is produced is increasingly irreducible to each of its component parts. The type of media convergence demonstrated within online religious devotional resources has the potential to profoundly shape how people experience, share and make music. If online media continue to be important conduits for transmitting religious audio-visual content, will they reshape music industry structures in the process? Will they form religious traditions into increasingly networked communities who congregate around shared participatory audio-visual practices as much as common beliefs? One thing is clear: music and sacred sound, as an essential component of religious audio-visual practice, insert themselves into the structures of daily life and, in conjunction with offline religious practice, shape embodied ways of listening, viewing and worshipping.

For Further Study

Berger, Teresa. 2017. @ *Worship: Liturgical Practices in Digital Worlds*. London: Routledge.

Campbell, Heidi, ed. 2013. *Digital Religion: Understanding Religious Practice in New Media Worlds*. London: Routledge.

Cheong, Pauline Hope, Peter Fischer-Nielsen, Stefan Gelfgren and Charles Ess, eds. 2012. *Digital Religion, Social Media and Culture: Perspectives, Practices and Futures*. New York: Peter Lang.

Engelke, Matthew. 2010. 'Religion and The Media Turn: A Review Essay'. *American Ethnologist* 37 (2): 371–9.

Meyer, Birgit, ed. 2009. *Aesthetic Formations: Media, Religion, and the Senses*. New York: Palgrave Macmillan.

Wagner, Rachel. 2012. *Godwired: Religion, Ritual, and Virtual Reality*. London: Routledge.

Notes

1 In this chapter, 'sacred sound' includes music but is also used to describe two distinct extra-musical phenomena. First, sacred sound is used to describe performance genres that share sonic organisation in common with music but are not conceived as music by participants (e.g. heightened speech used when chanting sacred texts, including Jewish scripture cantillation, Qur'anic chant, and devotional genres like *anasheed*, an unaccompanied Muslim vocal genre considered to fall into the category of sacred chant). Secondly, and less frequently, 'sacred sound' describes the sonorous qualities of religious speech (e.g. sermons, prophecy, ecstatic utterances).

2 Durkheim's well-known formulation of religion involves 'rites ... that unite its adherents into a single moral community' (1912 [2001], 46). Engelke (2010) notes that, within studies of religion and media as both process and product, '"religion" is often understood as the set of practices, objects, and ideas that manifest the relationship between the known and visible world of humans and the unknown and invisible world of spirits and the divine' (374). For a discussion of the relationship between the categories of ritual and religion, see 'Ritual reification' in Bell (2009 [1997]), 253–67. For an analysis of devotional rituals not associated with organised religion, see Lofton (2011).

3 See Engelke (2010) for an overview of several significant developments in the study of media and religion in the decade after the year 2000.

4 Compare Shzr Ee Tan's references to the Internet's affording of safe, interstitial spaces in the contexts of political repression or intercultural communication (Chapter 10, this volume, 262, 269–70).

5 A lack of engagement with music has been recognised as typifying the field of media and religion more generally. See Schofield Clark (2006); Partridge (2014).

6 Tine Vekemans (2014) notes that the express intentions for the use of these sites do not necessarily translate into their actual use. In fact, there is a perceived authenticity problem among the sample of Indian Jain devotees that she interviewed. Vekemans writes that the computer-mediated puja's limited sensorium, its failure to provide social contact with other worshippers, and the perception that internet surfing is incompatible with a 'worship mindset' led many of her respondents to indicate 'that they saw online *darsan* and *pūjā* mostly as for Jains living abroad, meaning far removed from (or too busy to go to) actual temples and gurus' (138).

7 See Manuel (1993) for an account of devotional 'cassette cultures' among Indian Hindus and Muslims, and Mall (2012) for a detailed account of the US evangelical Christian recording industry.

8 According to licence holder survey data provided by CCLI, church music leaders who list the Internet as their primary source for discovering new music increased from 19.9 per cent in 2007 to 26 per cent in 2011. Christian commercial radio saw a rise from 23.5 per cent to 31.7 per cent during this period, while each of the four other categories (music club, direct mail, music conferences, bookstore) declined precipitously. For further analysis, see Ingalls (2016).

9 Though immensely popular, Khaled is a controversial figure, intensely disliked by some religious authorities who disagree fundamentally with aspects of his theology and his use of 'secular' media. For further discussion of controversies over Khaled and media logics in Islam more generally, see Echchaibi (2013).

10 This video is available on Amr Khaled's YouTube channel at www.youtube.com/watch?v=RbSApM8-FnA. As of 2 January 2017, it had garnered more than 300,000 views and 6,000 shares.

11 The Merciful Servant's YouTube channel can be found at www.youtube.com/user/TheMercifulServant.

12 The posture of hands upraised, an expressive worship practice in evangelical and charismatic congregational singing, has become a more or less universal evangelical Christian symbol for worship (see Ingalls 2018, introduction).

13 Several examples of each of these reactions can be found on the comment string for the video 'Our God – Chris Tomlin' available at www.youtube.com/watch?v=UdFzB4MQgEA.

Personal Take: Technicians of Ecstasy

GRAHAM ST JOHN

The Ancient Greeks understood the need for mystery. At the annual festival at Eleusis, host to one of the longest running dance parties of all time, the *mystai* partook in ecstatic dance before they were introduced to 'the mysteries' inside the Telesterion. These events cannot be known with accuracy 2,000 years later. The mysterious can't be read in books, seen on film, nor encountered on the edge of the dance floor; but only truly known when the dancer becomes the dance. With the development of electronic dance music cultures, and with the influence of multiple traditions, today we see the evolution of popular routes to the divine. Whether felt as 'cosmic', recounted as 'magic', or recognised as 'the shit', participants around the globe, across all genres, from house to techno, and from dubstep to psytrance, become intimate with mystery.

Mystery defines artists, genres and entire scenes. It is the coin of the realm that lubricates *the vibe*. In the context of electronic music production and performance, mystery is paradoxical. It is immeasurable, unknowable as that which lies beyond death; yet, in the hands of producer-DJs, it's couriered with precision: quantised rhythms, digital sequencing, sharp programming, the alchemy of the mix, and the drop of the needle on vinyl, that moment when heaven and earth meet, opening up a sublime fissure in the space-time continuum in which a rhythm-untold animates us in ways unimagined. We've all had such moments, haven't we? Moments when we grow unrecognisable to our selves.

As technicians of ecstasy, DJs are gardeners of mystery, repurposing a vast archive of sound, remixing and remaking music to create the soundscapes of our lives, an inspired rhythmic ambience that *moves* us within that primal real-estate between the speaker stacks. Annihilated under a rhythmic fury, or gliding upon a soaring build, as techno-neophytes and electro-savants, we are transported into altered states of consciousness enabling a re-evaluation of our life and relationships, a renewed commitment to our loves.

Among the practices employed by DJs is what I have identified as *remixticism*, or the practice by which producers of electronic music and visual arts evoke non-ordinary states of consciousness augmented by digital audio/video detritus sampled and repurposed from disparate un/popular cultural resources (St John 2015a). In repurposing source materials, DJ/producers are medianauts cobbling together story-lines of dream travel, soul flight and cosmic transit using materials ripped from the worldwide datasphere.

While it is standard procedure in programming and DJ/VJ techniques that artists recycle existing recordings to compose new works, as digital alchemists they ransack films, TV documentaries, game software, radio shows, podcasts and other sources of *nanomedia* for choice material (St John 2013a). In multiple electronic dance music genres, scripted syntax from science fiction cinema, sound bites from political speeches, counsel from religious figures, the routines of comedians, and the extemporisations of altered statesmen are sampled in koan-like epigrams, repeated like chorus lines, reassembled as audio-bombs detonating at the breakdown. Dicing and splicing media content to evoke the sensation of altered time-space, electronic musicians offer repeated commentary on themes linked by their association with altered states of consciousness: shamanism, astral travelling, out-of-body experiences, near-death experiences, alien abductions, hypnosis, dreaming, chemically enhanced hallucinations. Via electrosonic techniques, this repurposed media ecology provides the sonic decor to the sonic experience – decaling the soundscape, and augmenting the vibe on dance floors planetwide (St John 2012).

The roots of this media shamanism can be found in an esoteric cut-up heritage including Dadaists, Surrealists, Burroughsians and Discordians alike. It is steeped in Jamaican dub, hip-hop, breakbeat science, house, techno, and chill DJs who've broken down, re-versioned and synthesised existing works to birth new forms. This refinement is notable in techno-shamanic traditions and is overt in psychedelic electronica, where media content is intentionally strip-mined and reprogrammed to spiritual endeavours – to augment, parrot and burlesque spirit. This milieu is drenched in an unmistakable penchant for shamanism, a sensibility that reveals dedication to vision and gnosis over the healing and catharsis of traditional *curanderos*, commitments that place this development in the vanguard of contemporary Western esoteric religion (St John 2017). Newly promulgated through popular culture, or as Christopher Partridge (2004) might have it, 'popular occulture', sonic murals of alien gurus, ancient astronauts, superheroes, spirit familiars, DMT entities and other in-between figures communicate a desire for being liminal, a transitional experience marking passage beyond the ordinary (St John 2013b, 2015b).

From the original dub and disco studio technicians to today's home producer, DJs are sonic alchemists, digital shamans, technicians of liminality, seekers who traverse and channel hidden dancescapes. And so, like poet troubadours, DJs bring the sounds and the magic into our lives. But they must remain open to the magic; yes, to broker new beats, but to also revisit patterns of original inspiration, adapting an artifice to optimise the conditions under which we make contact with the divine.

Personal Take: Live Coded Mashup with the Humming Wires

ALAN F. BLACKWELL AND SAM AARON

We write this contribution from the perspective of computer scientists and creative artists. In taking these two positions together, we intend something different to the common classification of the 'digital artist'. Where a digital artist may use Photoshop rather than a paintbrush, or a web server rather than a printing press, the computer scientist hopes to make new kinds of paintbrush, or new kinds of text. A computer scientist does not simply apply media technologies, but (re)makes and (re)invents them. The practical concerns of making and invention have more in common with craft than with science. Indeed, creative artists have always existed in symbiotic relationship with the craftspeople who invent, build and refine musical instruments or painting tools. In maintaining a dual concern for making and aesthetics, we do indeed refer to ourselves as engaged in craft (Blackwell and Aaron 2015).

However, computer science also offers some distinctive and novel perspectives on the creative arts, different to previous generations of craft technologies. The most significant of these is the fundamental reflexivity of computer science. Computer science, like mathematics, is a field that constructs a structure of structures. The knowledge structures of our discipline unavoidably reflect on themselves, resulting in a field that is routinely and habitually recursive. When computer scientists create artworks, this recursivity is constant to a degree beyond the metatheoretic concerns of conceptual art. A second, though less immediately apparent, concern is the tension resulting from human engagement. Computer programs exhibit behaviour that is both mechanical (in a way) and autonomous (in a way). The illusion of an autonomous mechanism triggers those archetypal anxieties that have been expressed through science fiction from the Golem to the Singularity. From our own perspective, it is the context of creative artwork that orients us away from such fearful fantasies to the human realities such as embodiment, identity, agency and ecstasy that are experienced through dance, music and poetry. These are our themes in the remainder of this contribution.

In 2014, we twice performed an improvised digital interpretation of the song 'Red Right Hand', originally recorded by Nick Cave and the Bad Seeds. The first of these performances, entitled 'Take a Little Walk to the

Edge of Town' (the first line of the song), was created as a contribution to a conference exploring creativity and copyright. The second was listed under the name 'The Humming Wires' (another line from the song), and was performed as part of our set at an algorave programmed within the Birmingham Network Music Festival.

These performances were, in part, demonstrations of new digital technologies. Sam had recently developed his system Sonic Pi, designed as a digital generative synthesis language that would be accessible to school children (Aaron and Blackwell 2013). Alan had also developed a novel programming language called Palimpsest, which breaks images down into layers that can modify each other, in the same way that a value in one cell of a spreadsheet can be modified by others (Blackwell 2014). A key attribute of both Sonic Pi and Palimpsest is that they support 'live coding' – modifying a program while it is running, with the changes taking effect without stopping it. Live coding is becoming a popular performance genre, with artists writing code in front of an audience to create music, visual imagery, or sometimes (as in our interpretations of 'Red Right Hand'), music and imagery together.

Our interpretation of Nick Cave's song was thus an algorithmic one – our performance consisted of writing two improvised programs, one an audio synthesiser and processor created using Sonic Pi, and the other an image manipulation and animation program created using Palimpsest. Each of these algorithms worked with samples of audio-visual material related to 'Red Right Hand', such that the audible and visual outputs, and also the structures of the algorithm, revealed, and were inspired by, aspects of the song.

The song itself had appeared to us in a dream – or at least very late at night. Research in the BBC schedule archives suggests that Alan must have been sleepily listening to a 6 Music segment in the early hours of 22 June 2013, during which Josh Homme was invited by DJ Mary Anne Hobbs to contribute to her tracks and interview feature *Key Of Life*. Homme's selection of 'Red Right Hand' impressed Alan (in the middle of the night) with its vivid imagery, further reinforced as he explored the superb covers that have been recorded of this song, ranging from a hit version by the Arctic Monkeys, to an album of Nick Cave lyrics that have been translated into Polish, with rhythm accompaniment played on the spoons.

It was precisely this vivid-dream quality that supported the reworking of song as algorithm. The Southern Gothic imagery mined so effectively by Cave offers an underlay of dark allusions and resonances, which in themselves are layered by Cave over the tropes of Old Testament justice and Milton's 'red right hand of God' from *Paradise Lost*. These resonances are valuable in live coding, because ambiguity does not come naturally to the world of the algorithm, where deterministic and predictable behaviour is more often required. Distorted sound and blurred, indistinct visual features became a core aesthetic of our work as we rehearsed the piece. However, these effects come at a high algorithmic cost, with rehearsals often treading a fine line between serendipitously evocative system overloads and complete crashes requiring repairs to our software tools. As with so many improvising genres, much of the tension in performance is associated with teetering on the threshold of lost control.

As it turned out, our first performance of this piece did include a complete system crash, meaning that the audience heard and saw two rather separate movements, divided by an interval of silence, diagnosis and system rebooting. The first movement featured permutations of the distinctive tubular bell that tolls in the chorus of the Bad Seeds arrangement. The distorted echoes of that bell had called to mind both seafaring and funerals, such that the 'stacks of green paper' in the song became the waves in which the eyes of Nick Cave himself floated as though plucked from a drowned sailor. The second 'movement' alluded more directly to the appropriations of our project by using actual samples of Cave's voice associated with image fragments that we had borrowed from video of Bad Seeds concerts, and from the MTV video of the song itself.

Before our second performance of this piece as one part of an algorave set, we reviewed video of this first performance in order to reflect on and develop our skills as an ensemble. However, because live coding is essentially an improvisational genre, no two rehearsals are ever the same. Instead of polishing a set of practised moves, we identify and analyse those passages where a creative unity and atmosphere has been achieved, often in ways that continue to bud from our source material.

A sequel to this project arose from our desire to engage new audiences with live coding. Sam was funded by educational charity the Raspberry Pi Foundation to engage children with computing through creative music. We had reflected that many of the musical genres we would like to emulate use the human voice as a central element – a feature that is rare in live coded music (in fact, we had never heard a live coded performance with voice). Without voice, it seemed to us that live coding might be exacerbating a perceived disconnection of computers from other musical experience. So when Alan met performance poet Afrodita Nikolova at an intercultural arts conference, he suggested she joined the band as a vocal artist, although at the time neither of us had any further concept of what this might entail.

The starting point for this new group was to book a gig (a performance at ICLC – the first International Conference at Live Coding), and then to create an act. As with 'Red Right Hand', we started with an existing track offering a rich combination of the performance elements that attracted us – here, the words, acoustic palette and imagery of Linton Kwesi Johnson's dub reggae poem 'Street 66'. The three of us separately listened to this track, then met to discuss the creative directions it inspired. Dub music seemed well suited to the rhythmic foundation of Sam's live coded scores, but had not previously been used as a genre reference for live coding. Alan's experience as an immigrant to the United Kingdom who discovered the dub genre through the London West Indian community led to reflection on the encounter with authority that is described in 'Street 66' – the vivid imagery of an intimate and supportive community disrupted by a knock on the door. Having described Afrodita (in our ICLC proposal) as winner of a recent Macedonian poetry slam championship, we drew parallels between the Brixton riots at the time of 'Street 66' and street protests in Macedonia at the time we were rehearsing.

A series of rehearsals developed and extended these ideas, each involving extended jam sessions of sound, imagery and words that we brought with us, weaving these elements into a multimedia collage. Alan added geometric visuals based on historical national flags, drawing on the colonial histories of Jamaica and his native New Zealand, and incorporating their artistic encounters with indigenous culture, including New Zealand poets and the Pacific Dub scene. These visual themes led to an exploration of Macedonian identity, as a previous outpost of the Ottoman empire that might be juxtaposed with New Zealand's history as a distant territory of the British empire. In addition to collecting reggae and dub samples, Sam extended his audio processing software to transform Afrodita's voice, feeding her words into a sound processing algorithm that gave her a musical instrument, able to explore the voice as a sound world in itself. Afrodita used this new freedom in voice as sound to recite in both English and in Macedonian. Realising that these texts were visually distinctive through use of Latin and Cyrillic scripts, Alan captured her English words, translated them to Macedonian through Google Translate, and applied the resulting characters as an animation and collage element. As rehearsals continued, the jam sessions led Afrodita to contribute further texts, audio and visual material that could be collaged: current street scenes captured by Macedonian bloggers and the words of political figures featured as sound samples.

In our performance of 'Slamming Street 0110 0110' at ICLC, these hours of conversation and performance jamming were condensed into a fifteen-minute improvised set. It is not easy, in the moment, to either capture or analyse the performance we gave. Some recordings were made, but it is the preparation process, rather than the end point, that is most informative. Though the complex technical infrastructure in itself presents a major challenge for stage presentation, and live coding bands do not (yet) have techs and roadies to take care of these mundane aspects, the performance was successful. We had an appreciative audience, were billed together with other acts that were talented and impressive, and were both pleased with (and relieved by) our achievement. 'Slamming Street 0110 0110', as with 'Take a Little Walk to the Edge of Town', explores new conjunctions of digital media and human experience, mediated, structured and transformed by creative use of algorithms.

Personal Take: Algorave: Dancing to Algorithms

ALEX MCLEAN

Algorave is a movement I co-founded with Nick Collins, Matthew Yee-King and Dan Stowell, focused on the conspicuous involvement of algorithms in the generation of electronic dance music, which has developed quickly since its inception in 2012 (Collins and McLean 2014). At first, algorave often seemed imaginary, with some 'algorave' events poorly attended or in inappropriate settings such as brightly lit rooms with rows of seating. The 'rave' in algorave suggests mass dancing as one, but this was rare in the beginning. This may well be indicative of the academic roots of computer music being poorly spliced with the history of electronic dance music (Parkinson and McLean 2014).

More recently, algorave has taken hold as a distributed network of thriving scenes, with events organised by experienced promoters finding large audiences in club and festival venues, or adopted by local musicians putting on parties in small rooms with big sound systems. All of the 150-plus algorave events so far have been experimental, pushing at the boundary between improvisatory and danceable. By embracing the experiment we have to accept that the events will not always 'work'. While some artists have toured around them, these events have each developed their own local flavour, having taken place in dozens of cities across Europe, Australia, Japan, and both North and South America. Unlike creative franchises such as MakerFaire and TED, the algorave brand is purposefully unprotected: anyone is free to host one and there are few constraints. But what ties them together?

There is a range of approaches at play, but the majority of performances at algoraves are live coded, meaning that the language of computer code is used as a medium for creating music. This code is made visible for audiences through projection throughout the space, potentially creating a sense of being *inside* the code. The programmer creates and/or modifies code while it generates music, creating a continuous creative feedback loop through code and sound that is an amalgam of composition via notation and music improvisation.

The notion of dancing to algorithmic music is evocative of sci-fi but has a history in the here-and-now. Accomplished musicians have employed algorithms in their work for many years, as in the case of electronic music duo Autechre who push the boundaries of dance music to widespread critical acclaim. There is, of course, a far longer history of composers formalising their creative approach. Indeed, rather than signalling technological progress, I would argue that algorave instead signals an *unravelling* of technology, stripping back years of interface development to re-expose computers as language machines. Words are a very human mode of articulation, and the words of source code compose together to define the computational procedures of everyday life. So, in the spirit of Christopher Small's (1998) conception of music as representing wider cultural relationships, the visible presence of code in algoraves not only allows us to reflect upon the role of code in our lives, but also to reimagine that role. We can imagine coding as a true craft, shared and culturally legitimate, by focusing on the role of coding as just one step in a live and very human process of becoming.

Virtuosity and code comprehension are often discussed in live coding literature, which situates the programmer as a virtuoso and audience members as passive listeners who comprehend musical processes by reading code while listening, yet neither of these presumed roles work well at an algorave. First there is the name (can you really take yourself seriously as an 'algorave virtuoso')? Beyond that, algorave's combination of experimental freedom with accessibility seems closer to punk than Western classical music, with programming languages like ixi lang and TidalCycles perhaps being as easy to learn as three guitar chords. In both of these systems, the ability to create techno music is only a few keystrokes away, and genre-twisting transformations just a few more. While live coding dominates algoraves, the traditional projections of code mean it is hardly possible to read them while dancing. Simply witnessing the broad outlines of coding activity, and the derivatives of code complexity growing and waning with that of the music, is more important to most algorave participants than close reading or understanding, although just as some like to crowd behind DJs to watch their technique, so participants are free to read into the technique of the live coder.

Perhaps more controversially, I think the live coder's code comprehension is also in doubt. In TidalCycles, which is embedded in the strictly typed language Haskell, just about everything is a pattern, or a function involving one. It is therefore straightforward to introduce pattern transformations at points within a piece of Tidal code, without understanding the whole. My introspective hunch is that this property of the programming language allows me to make music with TidalCycles without really knowing what my code is 'doing'. In fact, because TidalCycles is highly declarative, in notating *what* is to be done rather than *how*, it isn't really doing anything but rather describing an outcome across several layers of abstraction. Meaning is not understood in terms of code, but in terms of musical results. Live coding becomes more about listening, and deciding *when* to make a change, than it is about understanding the code itself. I feel like I am guided around my code based on what happened to the music last time I made a change. This is what I refer to as the 'textility of code' after Tim Ingold's textility of making (2010), which is itself closely related to the idea of bricolage programming explored by Turkle and Papert (1992). Rather than seeing a programming language as a means to efficiently express a thought, I think it is more accurate to think of it as an environment in which to think through code as material.

The experience of live coding at an algorave feels physical rather than disembodied: as the live coder, you are working with code as abstract material, but your focus is on both the physical experience of listening and the moments at which each code edit is evaluated, in time with the movements of people dancing in front of you. Though in an apparent state of flow (Csikszentmihalyi 2008; Nash and Blackwell 2011), you become hyper-aware of the passing of time as you work with or against expectations held by club audiences and the pace of edits intertwined with the pace of musical change. Who knows where this strange experience will lead digital music culture?

7 Rethinking Liveness in the Digital Age

PAUL SANDEN

What is Liveness?

The concept of liveness first emerged about a century ago, in response to the introduction and growing use of various technologies for broadcasting, recording, amplifying and otherwise mediating musical (and other) communications.[1] A (newly termed) live musical experience was usually – and for many, still is – considered better, more authentic, more human than a recorded or broadcast experience (Auslander 2008, 3; Thornton 1995, 42). To perceive a musical experience as live, then, is to perceive its distinction from something (more highly) mediated. Liveness cannot exist, and has never existed, without also implicating its mediated Other.

The perception of liveness in a musical experience is typically formed in reference to what I will call a *traditional performance paradigm*. That is, some element of music as conventionally performed – performers communicating musically with an audience in a shared time and place – persists in the live musical experience. Some such instances, such as a live recital of Mozart piano sonatas in a concert hall, are simple and straightforward, conforming entirely to a traditional performance paradigm. In other instances, such as a live cinematic broadcast of a performance from the Metropolitan Opera, or a live recording of a rock band, elements of a traditional performance paradigm are perceived to persist in an otherwise electronically mediated experience.[2] Live broadcasts are live because they occur at the same time as the 'actual' performance; the embodied element of co-present performance is subverted, but the temporal element remains intact. Live recordings are live because they (supposedly) constitute an archival record of a performance exactly as it happened; the temporal and co-present links to a 'real' performance may be ruptured, but the recorded performance is still temporally whole in comparison to a multi-tracked and highly edited studio recording. Moreover, something of the acoustics, ambience and interactions between performers and audiences that were part of 'real' performances are often maintained (or simulated, and thus still perceived by many listeners) in live recordings. The central conflict of liveness, in these and many other instances, is that such persistent elements of a traditional performance paradigm are the same qualities potentially threatened by the technologies through which the musical experience is mediated. That is, the technologies required for live broadcasts and live recordings have the ability, if used in a slightly different manner, to subvert the perception of liveness altogether.

Ruptures in the spatial and temporal groundedness of performance; transgressions of the physical, human origins of musical sound; infinite repeatability and mobility of an object within which or upon which performance is encoded (a vinyl record, a CD, an MP3 player) – these are the factors most often emphasised in debates about performance and the use of electronic technologies.[3] Technologies of sound reproduction and manipulation are at the centre of these discussions, along with the capabilities of these technologies to make music something other than the performed art it was for the previous several centuries, or at the very least to alter and threaten the nature of that performance as a privileged site of musical meaning.[4] Liveness discourse often goes a step further than merely noting distinctions between live and mediated forms of culture, and laments the supposed loss of authenticity created by extensive mediation which, especially in the digital age, seems to threaten the wholesale eradi-cation of the live.[5] Philip Auslander has pointed out that the purely live has in fact nearly ceased to exist (2008). Very little performance escapes some form of influence from electronic technologies. Auslander argues that even our interpretation of supposedly live performance is highly influenced by the extent to which cultural practice is now completely embedded in some form of electronic mediation – such as when an audience member at a rock concert constantly filters their appreciation of the live performance through their familiarity with the studio recordings of the songs being performed, or when someone attending a Broadway musical constantly compares the performance to the animated film upon which it is based.

However, Auslander's arguments rest largely on classifying the onto-logical make-up of such musical experiences – that is, their essential categories of being: as strictly performed acoustic sound, as pre-recorded and replayed sound, etc. In other words, his focus is primarily on the musical event itself (rather than on its reception), and on defining its liveness (or lack thereof) according to the extent to which electronic mediation has reconfigured the conditions inherent in a traditional per-formance paradigm. What this approach fails to consider, however, is the extent to which, despite the ontological deficiencies of many modern musical contexts with respect to a traditional performance paradigm, a great many listeners persist in attributing qualities of liveness to these very experiences – hence, the continued use of terms like live recording and live broadcast.

If liveness is not, then, functioning as a purely ontological signifier for modern listeners – if it continues to be used to describe experiences that are not, in actual fact, purely unmediated – it must be functioning as a conceptual and a perceptual one. Live recordings carry meaning as a type of live event because, despite the fact that they present highly mediated musical experiences, their apparent fidelity to an actual live performance carries meaning for many listeners that is absent from a studio recording. They are *perceived* as in some way live, even though their connection to a traditional performance paradigm is often rather distant. When we talk about liveness, then, we are essentially talking about how performance is perceived, and about assigning at least some of the values and ideologies associated with traditional performance to the musical experience in question.

And so, despite the rapidly increasing extent to which electronically mediated musical experiences are displacing those that conform fully to a traditional performance paradigm, recent discourse (as discussed throughout this chapter) demonstrates that the concept of liveness continues to carry great meaning for many musickers, even in a cultural environment of extreme digital saturation. My purpose in this chapter is to investigate the persistent meaningfulness of liveness (wherever it might exist) in musical practices that are highly influenced by digital technologies and digital culture more broadly. I wish to offer some ideas that might help in understanding the ongoing conceptualisation of liveness in modern musical discourse, and how its definitions may have changed with the changing technologies involved in its formation.

Defining Liveness in Digital Culture

If, as I have just argued, the meaning of liveness has expanded along with the introduction of new technologies and the changing uses of these technologies,[6] it remains for us to address the ways in which these changes may have reflected the increasing digitisation of music technologies.[7] The relative affordability, portability and versatility of modern digital sound technologies, combined with their ability to connect via the Internet to similar technologies around the world (or across the room), and the ease with which their users can fragment, alter and recombine virtual objects of encoded musical sound before sending them back out into the physical realm, have exponentially increased the extent to which a traditional performance paradigm can be subverted in modern musical contexts. The rapidly growing ubiquity of digital technologies in most people's musical lives in recent years has only accelerated the changing ontological relationships between new understandings of liveness and a traditional performance paradigm. Common understandings of live performance events now include, for instance, seated performers live coding music on their laptops;[8] DJs creating a steady stream of dance music entirely from recorded samples; networks of performers scattered around the world, linked by the Internet, producing music collectively in real time. Does liveness in music, then, have a new definition? If an understanding of liveness no longer depends on the apparent avoidance of electronic mediation – if in fact musicking that is overtly enabled, and perhaps even defined, by the use of digital technologies is interpreted as live – what are the essential characteristics of this new definition?

In a phrase, highly variable. A current definition of liveness, I would argue – one informed by the logics of digital culture – is in fact many definitions, or perhaps many different permutations of a definition based on, but not confined or wholly defined by, reference to a traditional performance paradigm. This is not an entirely new development, of course; after all, what is a live broadcast if not an electronically mediated performance – a performance whose ontology is based on a traditional performance paradigm, but altered by the ability to subvert the spatial limitations of that context? What is new in a digital culture, I would argue, is the degree to which this traditional paradigm can be – and readily is – ruptured, fragmented and reconstituted according to the characteristics of digital technologies. Within a cultural environment characterised by, and increasingly comfortable with, logics of fragmentation, permutation and collage, many perceivers of liveness seem equally comfortable with the complete fragmentation of that traditional performance paradigm.

Moreover, as I hope to demonstrate, liveness in a digital culture has increasingly become a terrain of artistic interrogation to a degree not experienced before. That is, some artists have begun to make their music, at least in part, *about* liveness; the deliberate exploration of liveness has become an aesthetic goal. This aesthetic shift in how musickers have recently begun to approach liveness has occurred largely because digital technologies have afforded, if not an entirely new way of thinking about liveness, then at least a massive amplification of the variable qualities that concept has already demonstrated. I am not just referring to the ease with which sound objects can be manipulated with digital technologies, or the supposed de-corporealisation of sound as it has taken up residence in digital hard drives (more on this below). I am also referring to the extent to which digital technologies are employed more broadly in modern cultures, to circumvent previously entrenched temporal and spatial boundaries, and even boundaries between humans and machines. These ways of using, and thinking about, technologies in the twenty-first century are increasingly removed from the ways of using and thinking about technologies that surrounded the emergence of the traditional performance paradigm several centuries ago, or even its definition as something intrinsically different from electronically mediated music one century ago.

Virtual Liveness and Posthuman Subjectivity

In my previous work, I have suggested several categories of liveness based on characteristics of traditional understandings of performance that inform the variable definitions of liveness I have been discussing (Sanden 2013, 11–12, 31–43).[9] For instance, temporal liveness would be the liveness perceived in a live broadcast – a broadcast of something at the time of its happening. This is also the category of liveness most often implicated in discussions of liveness on the Internet (Auslander 2005, 8): live streaming, for instance, is arguably live broadcasting through a different technology (though the geographic range of this technology is far greater than any pre-digital broadcasting technologies). Corporeal liveness is the shading of liveness that so often concerns musicians working with new digital performance interfaces, when they want to ensure an understandable connection for their audience between their physical gestures and the electronic sounds that result from them.[10] What concerns me most in this chapter, however, is what I have called virtual liveness. And while I have suggested various contexts in which virtual liveness might be a meaningful way of interpreting the concept of performance in highly mediated musical contexts (Sanden 2013, 113–58), this category remains for me still the most elusive in my attempts to explain or define it, and at the same time the most pressing to deal with in the context of digital culture. For while temporal liveness, corporeal liveness and other categories that I have proposed emerge largely from the logics of recording and broadcast media, virtual liveness seems defined largely by the logics, not just of digital technologies, but of digital culture more broadly.

To summarise the discussion thus far, the concept of liveness is inherently dialectical. Rather than functioning as a complete ontological negation of electronic mediation, it centres on a tension between those elements of a musical experience that invoke a traditional performance paradigm and those that arise from electronic mediation. Thus, a live recording is live in part because it is not as highly mediated as a studio recording – but it *is* still mediated. Human performance and technological mediation function together, albeit in tension with one another, to create this particular understanding of liveness. I propose that what I call virtual liveness functions within this dialectical tension more overtly than other, perhaps more straightforward, understandings of liveness (such as those I have already invoked in this chapter).

The word virtual is used, both in common parlance and in various fields of scholarship, to invoke a range of meanings, and I use it here to reflect many of those meanings, without restricting myself to any one of them.[11] In reference to the use of internet technologies, the word virtual often describes any kind of activity that takes place within online (virtual) space (and here, of course, we understand the word *space* metaphorically): virtual dating, virtual tours of restaurants or real-estate listings, etc. The computer's, tablet's or mobile phone's screen acts as our window into that virtual world, which in reality is just a projection of light that engages our imagination, intellect and/or emotions. Virtual reality technologies aim to create immersive environments for their users, perceived spaces within which virtual actions can be carried out.

Following Gilles Deleuze (1988), both Echard (2006, 8) and Shields (2003, 2) explain the virtual as something that is 'real but not actual'. This description neatly fits the perceptions of liveness that I call virtual, but here my connection to a Deleuzian sense of virtuality finds its limits. For Deleuze, the virtual is an ontological category; virtual objects are on the cusp of becoming actual (Echard 2006, 8). What I mean by the term virtual has more to do with perception than ontology. Thus, in *Liveness in Modern Music*, I offer the following explanation of virtual liveness: 'In some cases, music can be *live* in a virtual sense even when the conditions for its liveness (be they corporeal, interactive, etc.) do not *actually* exist. Virtual liveness, then, depends on the perception of a liveness that is largely created *through* mediatization' (Sanden 2013, 11). In other words, virtual liveness is a perception of liveness – a perception of performance – that embraces a musical experience's grounding in the various incursions of electronic sound technologies. It involves an extension of the whole concept of performance to include things like the synthesis, samples and simulations that characterise the logics of digital culture, and which would seem to conflict with traditional definitions of what performance is – and, more importantly, is not[12] – while at the same time making room (sometimes through simulation or technological enhancement) for certain elements of those traditional definitions to persist.

Finally, and most crucially, I wish also to invoke some of the meaning that N. Katherine Hayles assigns to virtuality, when she writes: 'Virtuality is the cultural perception that material objects are interpenetrated by information patterns' (Hayles 1999, 13–14). Hayles's definition is offered in the context of her account of the emergence of the posthuman subject, a construction that I believe can play a very significant role in understanding the new definitions of liveness and performance I am concerned with here. And although I observe a useful link between virtual liveness in digital music and Hayles's discussions of digital (i.e. binary) information, I believe the arguments that both she and I are making about virtuality may also extend to a broader discussion about music and technology – one not necessarily confined strictly to digital technologies. That is, I wish to re-emphasise here that at least as far as the concept of liveness goes, digital technologies have not necessarily introduced entirely new tensions. Rather, they have drastically broadened the potential implications of the central tension between human and machine, by making the boundaries between the two more easily crossed.[13]

For Hayles, posthumanity involves a new model of subjectivity, one in which (among other things) information is conceived of as separate and separable from its materiality – thus enabling the idea that information or data can flow from one physical instantiation to another without being changed in the process. This allows for the creation of subjectivities not just in physical space, but also in virtual space: identities formed and, I would also argue, *performed* in the realm of virtual communications. As Hayles writes, 'In the posthuman, there are no essential differences or absolute demarcations between bodily existence and computer simulation, cybernetic mechanism and biological organism . . . The posthuman self is an amalgam, a collection of heterogeneous components, a material-informational entity whose boundaries undergo continuous construction and reconstruction' (Hayles 1999, 3). What Hayles is identifying as post-human is not the literal formation of cyborg entities, but a common cultural perception that 'the ontological foundations of what counts as human' (Hayles 1999, 24) have changed, and now include room for virtual selves, for identities that can be imagined as immaterial information. This is a decontextualisation of the human self, as imagined boundaries between human and machine are constantly erased, shifted and re-inscribed.

What I have outlined here about virtuality resonates strongly with common observations about how music often functions within digital culture – not only those musics made mostly or entirely with digital technologies, but also more traditional styles of music that are widely disseminated and heard through digital means. Of particular significance to many who write about the digitisation of music is the shift it has enacted from corporeal communication to disembodied data, from embodied acts to simulations encoded in 1s and 0s. With this lack of grounding or origin in a corporeal presence, digital music is often seen to eschew any origins or defining boundaries of its own, be they physical, historical, stylistic or otherwise. This ability to overcome these and other kinds of boundaries is what makes Hayles hopeful about the potential of the posthuman subject. However, she does raise a warning flag about 'how *information lost its body*' (Hayles 1999, 2) – how digitisation encouraged the further emphasis of a Cartesian split between mind/thought/data/information and its corporeal host to the point where human subjectivity may become erased along with that body. What seems apparent, though, in much liveness discourse at least, is that disembodiment is often embraced as a way to more creatively and flexibly inscribe the human self within a highly technologised musical experience, by transcending the boundaries of identity created by conventionally embodied performance.

These transcended boundaries are the calling cards of mashup culture and mix culture: they are hypertextual models of music dependent on the types of synthesis, samples and simulations I referred to earlier, where complex networks of references across space, time and style are enacted between the various found and newly created sound objects that have been brought together in the mix. Moreover, discrete and autonomous musical objects are often almost impossible to extract from or identify within this mix. Few of them are any longer grounded in a single, original context; or, if they are, the identities of their locations are obliterated by seemingly infinite networks of multiple instantiations and references, as when (for example) a symphony is sampled in a pop song, which becomes remixed for the dance club, which becomes the soundtrack for an online advertisement, which becomes a ring-tone for a mobile phone, and so on into the seemingly infinite data-flow of music in digital culture that Jean-Yves Leloup (2010, 165–70) calls the 'digital magma'. David Toop writes of this that

> With digital audio, the objects of music – its recordings, performances, instruments, and even people – begin to disappear into an aether of intangible properties, a mist that enshrouds and disintegrates established structures with no regard for their traditions or values … This seems to me to be the object of digital magma: to chase the nothingness of electronic music to the point where meaning begins to emerge.   (Leloup 2010, 8)

There are strong affinities, then, between these characterisations of digital music and Hayles's characterisation of the posthuman subject: previously drawn boundaries are blurred, and previously defined and embodied entities become fragmented, decontextualised and dislocated within a new kind of heterogeneity. But what does this have to do with performance and, more specifically, the perception of liveness within the diverse terrain of digital music? Here it is important to recognise that within its constellation of meanings – and perhaps toward the centre of that constellation – liveness functions as an index of humanness; as a recognition of human creativity and production, and of our human selves, within the context of our constant negotiation with the technologies we create and employ. This performance of humanness is, in fact, the reason so many cling to a traditional performance paradigm; it is the reason liveness has always mattered in a technological era, and arguably the reason performance has always mattered even before the emergence of the liveness concept. As the formation of human subjectivities has given way, increasingly commonly, to the formation of posthuman subjectivities – subjectivities in which the digital often forms an element of the self – the ways in which our (post)humanness is reflected in our cultural practices have similarly adapted. To return to my earlier argument: the dialectical negotiations between performed and recorded, human and machine, corporeal and disembodied, and any number of similar dualistic pairings, are often at the heart of what liveness means in digital culture.

Intermedial Performance and the Aesthetics of Liveness in Digital Culture

I would like to elaborate here on an expanded notion of what performance might constitute in digital culture, in order to expand on some concrete examples of the redefinitions of liveness I have been discussing thus far. In *Digital Performance*,[14] Steve Dixon neatly summarises the idea that internet communication, at least as it is commonly practised, often involves a constant virtual performance of the self. He writes:

> Theater is ... created not only by those who consciously use computer networks for theatrical events, but also by millions of 'ordinary' individuals who develop e-friendships, use MOOs, IRC, and chatrooms, or create home pages and 'blogs' on the World Wide Web. Many home pages and blogs constitute digital palimpsests of Erving Goffman's notions of performative presentations of the self, with the subject being progressively erased, redefined, and reinscribed as a persona/performer within the proscenium arch of the computer monitor. Personas are honed like characters for the new theatrical confessional box, where, like postmodern performance artists, individuals explore their autobiographies and enact intimate dialogues with their inner selves. (Dixon 2007, 3–4)

Here again we are reminded that modern human performance, in many artistic and social realms, increasingly embraces machineness. The ever-changeable nature of a digital remix culture, as alluded to by Dixon, is embedding itself in how people represent their own identities.[15] Identity is exceptionally subjective in this context, and that subjectivity is ever-variable. Offering a related perspective, Paul D. Miller (aka DJ Spooky that Subliminal Kid) writes about the 'identity reconstructions' that characterise digital culture, with its approach to 'information collage where everything from personal identity to the codes used to create art or music are available for the mix' (Miller 2004, 64). In a culture where many people constantly perform their digital selves on the Internet, is it any wonder that a concept of live performance can also include the use of those same technologies? Is it not perhaps all a part of Leloup's digital magma, within which performing *human* is still a common and vitally important act? Live electronic music, digital gesture-based controllers creating synthesised sound, laptop performance – these things are no longer truly avant-garde, no longer at the furthest fringes of musical practice. They are informing common understandings of how music can be performed, and within that framework, the concept of liveness is still alive and well.

Christopher Balme (2008) proposes that the concept of intermediality is a useful way to approach such formations of performance, where the use of electronic technologies may in fact enrich the human qualities inherent in the experience. As a catalyst to his discussion, he summarises the influential arguments of Erika Fischer-Lichte (2008), which assert (*contra* Auslander) that even highly mediated performances are grounded in live performance and have resisted subjugation by wholly mediated formats: they are therefore still much more meaningful and impactful than a fully mediated experience (like watching a film) can possibly be. Balme replies to Fischer-Lichte (and those in sympathy with her): 'My question would be: why defend the one against the other? Why is it necessary to formulate the relationship between live performance and media technology in such confrontational terms as though media and performance were engaged in a kind of agon in which the winner takes all' (Balme 2008, 85). Character-ising such performances as intermedial is a way of recognising a relation-ship between 'the live and the mediatized' that is 'entirely symbiotic; they are imbricated into one another like Siamese twins and cannot be prised apart without severe damage ensuing' (Balme 2008, 90).

Intermedial performance, in other words, is a performance experience in which virtual liveness can play a significant role in the audience's understanding of performative meaning. The manifestations this virtual liveness might take on are as numerous and diverse as the musical styles and practices within which they are found, and so I will not attempt to deal with them in any kind of comprehensive manner. I would, however, like to focus on two examples within which I perceive liveness not just as a marker of human performance, but also as a terrain of aesthetic play and negotiation. They are examples of intermedial musical performance within which the boundaries separating live from mediated are not just ambigu-ous but actively interrogated, and the traditional definitions of perform-ance itself are transgressed.

The first of these examples engages directly with questions of digital representations of the self, and how the performance of music might function within that context. In recent years virtual musicians have entered the digital music landscape/soundscape, a milieu defined by intermediality, and one such example is provided by real-time musical performances in virtual environments like Second Life. Ontologically speaking, online real-time performances are very similar in many ways to the live radio and television performances that remote audiences have enjoyed for decades. Their liveness is commonly understood, rather unproblematically, in a temporal sense – that is, so long as the performance is either lacking entirely in visual information (like a radio broadcast) or accompanied by actual real-time footage of the performer(s) (like a television broadcast). The terrain of liveness becomes more difficult to navigate, however, when the audio is 'performed' by an on-screen avatar, within a visual virtual space designated for that performance. Writing of such performances in Second Life, Karen Collins poses the questions they raise surrounding issues of liveness: 'If players use an avatar as their visual representation, are they really performing for an audience? And if that audience is only virtually present, is it really an audience? When players are singing live in a bedroom but their avatar is performing prescripted moves to that music in the virtual world, is the players' performance really live?' (Collins 2013, 94).

Collins answers these questions in the affirmative, due in part to the notion that many users perceive such performances as live, no matter their intermediality. However, she also reverts to the idea of temporality, suggesting that the reason many users would accept an avatar's performance as live would be its existence in real time, simultaneously with the 'actual' performance of the hypothetical Second Life user producing the performance 'live in a bedroom'. Such an interpretation presumes, despite the highly intermedial nature of these types of performances, a rather traditional understanding of liveness based in a temporal ontology – a dependence, in other words, on reference to a traditional performance paradigm.

We might usefully expand on Collins's arguments to suggest that the liveness in Second Life may be more than just temporal. Recent studies of musical activity in Second Life (Gagen and Cook 2016; Harvey 2016), in fact, point to users (virtual performers and virtual audiences alike) adopting something of the posthuman subjectivity I have been discussing throughout this chapter in their encounters with musical performances. Gagen and Cook report that while some users attempt to apply 'real-world' concepts of liveness to the virtual performances of Second Life (particularly notions of co-temporality), others have realised that the technological differences between Second Life and what gamers call Real Life make traditional concepts of liveness somewhat of an ill fit for the virtual environment. Instead, they find, 'the most effective approach to creating liveness within virtual reality is not to replicate the conditions of live music in the real world, but rather to recontextualise the signifiers of liveness' (Gagen and Cook 2016, 205). Once again, the traditional boundaries of liveness are actively negotiated in order to produce meaning within the contexts of these performances.

I will close with an example that is in some ways far more conservative and 'old-fashioned' than those I have addressed thus far, yet is still entirely dependent on digital technology. But it is an example that demonstrates very clearly some of the characteristics of this new aesthetic terrain of liveness. Since 2009, American composer Richard Beaudoin has been working with digitally measured microtimings of recorded performances as the foundation of his compositional style.[16] With the aid of the Lucerne Audio Recording Analyzer (LARA; developed at the Hochschule Luzern in Switzerland), he analyses the onset time and amplitude of every sound event in a recording down to the millisecond. These data then inform the notated rhythms of Beaudoin's new composition. Often the sounds measured in this way are not just those the performer intended, but also various incidental sounds in the recording. For instance, the hums and chair creaks on a Glenn Gould recording have been transcribed into Beaudoin's *New York Mikrophon* for chamber quartet (2015), while the hiss on a 1931 recording by Alfred Cortot of Debussy's *La fille aux cheveux de lin* finds its way into the parts of a sextet playing Beaudoin's *La fille dérivée* (2014).[17] In this way, Beaudoin brings the recorded performances that inspire each work back into the realm of live performance through his scores. What is more, as I will demonstrate, within the performances of at least some of these works we find a constant negotiation between live and mediated elements, which brings the aesthetic interrogation of liveness into the foreground.

Beaudoin's series of pieces *The Artist and his Model*, of which *La fille dérivée* is the last, is based on the microtiming of the same Cortot recording, which is essentially transcribed (at an augmented ratio) into Beaudoin's rhythms. As is Beaudoin's customary approach, Debussy's score provides one important framework for the new composition: elements of it, including easily recognised motivic fragments, remain within Beaudoin's piece. However, just as important a framework is provided by the hiss of the medium upon which Cortot made his recording: the phonograph disc and player. These hisses are represented not only rhythmically but also timbrally: at times throughout the composition Beaudoin has the pianist use sandpaper blocks, while the wind players blow through their instruments in rhythmically recurring patterns to create a sort of dilated echo of the cyclical hissing of the phonograph. This is a piece of music that refers not only to Debussy's iconic piano prelude, but also to its specific instantiation as recorded by Cortot in London on 2 July 1931. *La fille aux cheveux de lin*, for piano, finds new life within *La fille dérivée* for mixed sextet. At the same time, Cortot's recording – not just his perform-ance but also the medium itself and its sonic artefacts – is brought to life. The wind players literally breathe life into the hisses of the phonograph.

What emerges from this composition is an exploration, a dialogue, across history, across media, across musical style. Debussy's score, Cortot's performance and the medium of Cortot's performance are all embedded in Beaudoin's score, which then gives rise to a new live performance, and the subsequent digital recording and dissemination of that performance.[18] From notated score (1910), to piano performance for phonograph recording (1931; reissued in digital format in 1991), to a newly composed notated score (composed in 2012), to live sextet performance captured on a digital recording (also in 2012), we are invited not just to enjoy this new composition, but to appreciate the boundaries it transgresses, between then and now, between analogue and digital, between live and recorded. Like the boundaries of the human within the posthuman subject, the boundaries of liveness within this work are in constant motion. Here they have been aestheticised; performers and listeners alike are invited to engage in the grey areas between live and mediated. Here, then, liveness is not just perceived. It is constructed as an entity within this work of musical art being performed – an entity that not only speaks out in performance, but is inscribed into the very score informing that performance. This imagined entity is set in dialogue with its recorded other, within a conceptually imbricated network of multiple performances and recordings.

In closing, I return finally to some words by Paul D. Miller in *Rhythm Science*. He poses the rhetorical question: 'Is it live? Or is it a sample? . . . The question remains just as powerful as ever' (Miller 2004, 28). I would argue that while the question may remain, the potential answers to that question are far more complex than they once were. One possible answer, to which I have been alluding throughout this chapter, is we cannot always distinguish one from the other; we do not always want to distinguish one from the other; and this ambiguity is at the heart of an aesthetic of musical performance in digital culture.

For Further Study

Auslander, Philip. 2008. *Liveness: Performance in a Mediatized Culture*, 2nd edn. London: Routledge.

Barker, Martin. 2013. *Live to your Local Cinema: The Remarkable Rise of Livecasting*. Houndmills: Palgrave Macmillan.

Emmerson, Simon. 2007. *Living Electronic Music*. Aldershot: Ashgate.

Fischer-Lichte, Erika. 2008. *The Transformative Power of Performance: A New Aesthetics.* Translated by Saskya Iris Jain. New York: Routledge.
Hayles, N. Katherine. 1999. *How We Became Posthuman: Virtual Bodies in Cybernetics, Literature, and Informatics.* Chicago: University of Chicago Press.
Sanden, Paul. 2013. *Liveness in Modern Music: Musicians, Technology, and the Perception of Performance.* New York: Routledge.

Notes

1 Auslander (2002, 16–17) argues that while the technological conditions for liveness were put in place with the advent of recording technology at the end of the nineteenth century, the discursive use of the word live to describe performance as 'not recorded' did not emerge until the 1930s, when radio broadcasts made it difficult for listeners to determine whether they were hearing recordings or live (that is, real-time) performances. However, while the word live may not have been used before this time, the debates surrounding the relative values of recorded vs (what we would now call) live music appeared much earlier. See, for instance, John Philip Sousa's 1906 essay, 'The menace of mechanical music' (Sousa 1906).

2 See Barker (2013) for an extensive study of livecasting (as the live broadcast of opera, theatre and other events is often known) and the issues of liveness surrounding its creation and reception; Aguilar (2014) examines the 'live' recordings by the London Symphony Orchestra released on their label *LSO Live*, and reveals the complex nuances of liveness inherent in their practices.

3 The extent to which amplification has factored in such debates seems to be largely dependent on musical genre, and the conventional practices within the traditions of those genres. While discourse on liveness in popular musical practices is rather silent on amplification, its use in classical music practices that don't traditionally involve amplification has garnered more notice (though more in the popular press than in academic scholarship). Articles in *The New York Times* and London's *The Daily Telegraph*, for instance – Anthony Tommasini's 'Enhancing sound in a hush-hush way' (18 August 1999) and Brian Hunt's 'The silent conspiracy of electronic amplification' (9 June 2001), respectively – both argue that the inconspicuous electro-acoustic enhancement of classical music concert halls and opera houses (to improve the resonant qualities of such spaces) threatens the liveness of the performances that take place in them.

4 In the interest of space, I will avoid here the extensive and very important debate on Western Art Music discourse's longstanding privileging of musical works – representing (somewhat) tangible products of a composer's genius – as the most privileged site of musical meaning, a discourse that at the same time often remained silent on the potential of performers and their performances to contribute significantly to such meaning. This debate is addressed in the work of Ashby (2010), Bowen (1993), Cook (2001, 2003, 2013), Goehr (1992, 1998) and many others.

5 In his defence of the cultural significance and democratising power of karaoke, Kevin Brown (2010) describes an elitist 'liveness anxiety' in much academic discourse. He argues that 'the ontological claim to the efficacy of performance' in such writing 'can be seen as a power grab. Why should only live performers be allowed to change culture? . . . The biases against performances that are not "live" perpetuate the division of cultural production, and maintain the position of theatre as a primarily "highbrow" artform.' (74).

6 Auslander (2002, 2005, 2008) has made this argument repeatedly about liveness as it pertains not specifically to music, but also to theatre, Internet use, etc.

7 Simon Emmerson's work on liveness (1994, 2000, 2007, 2012) is one of the few (and certainly the most significant) bodies of musicology to extensively address liveness in digital music.

8 For practitioner perspectives on live coding, see Alan Blackwell and Sam Aaron's and Alex McLean's Personal Takes, this volume.

9 The full list of categories I propose (though I do not consider this to be a definitive nor an exhaustive list) is as follows: temporal liveness, spatial liveness, liveness of fidelity, liveness of spontaneity, corporeal liveness, interactive liveness and virtual liveness.

10 Croft (2007) is primarily concerned with this kind of liveness, as is some of Emmerson's work (1994, 2000), though their arguments are not expressed with the same terminology that I use here.

11 Isabella van Elferen offers another approach to the definition of virtuality in Chapter 8 (this volume).

12 Perhaps most famously within performance scholarship, Peggy Phelan has argued strongly that an ontology of performance is defined by the complete avoidance of any technologies of reproduction; such electronic technologies, in her words, make a performance 'something other than performance' (Phelan 1993, 146).

13 An extensive discussion of posthumanism and digital music is provided by David Trippett in Chapter 9 (this volume).

14 By his own admission, Dixon's lengthy study does not directly address music, but many of his arguments about new modes of digital performance apply well to it.

15 See Sumanth Gopinath and Jason Stanyek (this volume, Chapter 4) for a discussion of identity construction in relation to the 'musical selfie'.

16 I am grateful to Richard Beaudoin not only for sharing with me his thoughts about his work, and his feedback on this chapter, but also for providing me with scores and links to recordings. The reader is encouraged to consult www.richardbeaudoin.com/microtiming/ for more detailed descriptions of Beaudoin's process. Many of Beaudoin's perspectives on his process, as well as details about that process, are also shared in Trottier (2013). Some of Beaudoin's microtiming compositions (though not the ones discussed here) can be heard on Mark Knoop and Kreutzer Quartet, *Richard Beaudoin: Microtimings*, New Focus Recordings B007C7FBEO (2012).

17 Reissued on Alfred Cortot, *Alfred Cortot plays Debussy and Ravel*, Biddulph LHW 006 (1991). Beaudoin based his microtiming on this CD reissue.

18 Jeffrey Means and Sound Icon, *The Artist and his Model VI – La fille dérivée*, rehearsal take from Sanders Theatre, Cambridge, MA, 29 November 2012. soundcloud.com/richard-beaudoin/beaudoin-la-fille-d-riv-e/s-mACUQ.

Personal Take: Augmenting Musical Performance

ANDREW MCPHERSON

Designers of digital musical instruments often highlight the flexibility of these instruments in comparison to their acoustic counterparts. Freed from mechanical constraints, digital instruments can produce new types of sound and offer the performer new interaction modalities. Recent years have seen a proliferation of design ideas shared in both academic venues and commercial crowdfunding campaigns (Jensenius and Lyons 2017; McPherson et al. 2019). As the availability of low-cost, high-performance computing continues to increase, we are rapidly approaching a point where the uptake of new instruments is limited not by technical factors but by human capabilities and cultural considerations. Perhaps as a result, the vast majority of new digital musical instruments have a short lifespan, used only by a few people before being set aside in favour of even newer technology.

As an instrument designer with a background in music composition and electronic engineering, I am interested in creating instruments to fit specific existing performance practices. Specifically, I seek to maximise the creative novelty of a new instrument while minimising the amount of re-learning needed for a performer to play it to a high standard. A core part of my task involves designing these instruments to fit human sensorimotor abilities which are the result of years of instrumental practice. However, traditional instruments also support a broader cultural ecosystem, including established repertoire, well-known virtuosi, pedagogical practices and audience familiarity. Building on these cultural resources may help increase the longevity of a new instrument.

One approach to creating new instruments that connect to existing performance practice is the creation of *augmented instruments*: familiar musical instruments whose capabilities have been extended with new sensors and modes of sound production. My first augmented instrument project was the magnetic resonator piano, an augmentation of the acoustic grand piano which uses electromagnets to induce vibrations in the strings, allowing the player to produce organ-like sustain, harmonics, pitch bends and new timbres (McPherson and Kim 2012). Since its creation in 2009, the instrument has acquired a repertoire of around twenty-five new compositions and a growing community of pianists proficient in its techniques.

Playing the magnetic resonator piano is different in important ways from traditional piano performance: for example, new techniques involve pressing the keys slowly enough that the hammers do not strike the strings or holding the keys partway down. Learning these actions can take time and practice. Therefore, for my second augmented instrument project, TouchKeys, I focused specifically on fitting the behaviour of the instrument to the constraints of existing keyboard technique (McPherson et al. 2013). TouchKeys is an augmentation of the keyboard that adds capacitive touch sensing to each key. The TouchKeys sensors attach to the surface of any keyboard, measuring the location of the fingers in two axes: across the bass-to-treble axis (X) and along the longer axis of each key (Y). Touch-Keys lets the performer add techniques like vibrato, pitch bends and timbre changes to each note without cumbersome wheels and pedals, simply by moving the fingers on the key surfaces.

I first developed TouchKeys in 2010, at a time when interest was growing in the industry in 'multidimensional polyphonic expression': giving the performer independent control over the pitch, dynamics and timbre of multiple simultaneous notes. Other commercial products with this capability include the ROLI Seaboard, Roger Linn's LinnStrument, the Madrona Labs Soundplane and the Haken Continuum Fingerboard. These instruments, like TouchKeys, are controllers for arbitrary digital sounds which use the MIDI (Musical Instrument Digital Interface) or OSC (Open Sound Control) protocols. Each instrument provides some degree of user-adjustable mappings from action to sound.

These other instruments replace the traditional keyboard action with novel interactive surfaces. For example, both the Seaboard and Continuum use a continuous deformable membrane instead of discrete keys, and the LinnStrument and Soundplane choose a rectangular layout over the familiar pattern of white and black keys. By contrast, TouchKeys attempts to retain as much as possible of the keyboard technique that performers spend many years learning, even if this circumscribes the design possibilities. By designing it to be installed on top of an existing keyboard, TouchKeys preserves the layout and action of the keyboard. Due to manufacturing constraints, the touch sensors modestly alter the surface texture, and the sensor edges are less rounded than a traditional key top, but these are small changes in comparison to other new controllers.

In creating TouchKeys, I discovered that how the software behaves can make or break the player's familiarity with the instrument. In a sense, adding new techniques is the easiest part of the design; the harder challenge is to avoid having those new techniques interfere with existing ones. One straightforward example is the use of Y-axis sensing (i.e. the long axis of the key). To assign the raw Y position to a control like pitch would render the keyboard unplayable. Redundancy in where the fingers contact the keys is a core part of keyboard technique, as it accommodates the different lengths of each finger and the different hand orientations needed to reach different combinations of keys. It would be futile to demand that the player press each key in the exact right position in order to produce the expected pitch.

The obvious solution is to design the interface so that the player can use relative finger motion after note onset, rather than absolute position, to control pitch or other effects. However, even this approach creates subtle problems, as the fingers naturally move on the keys in traditional playing. A study with 8 pianists showed that in 26 per cent of key presses, the finger moved more than 5 per cent of the length of the key, and in 11 per cent of key presses it moved more than 10 per cent of the key length (McPherson et al. 2013). In the X (horizontal) axis, the figures are even more striking: 75 per cent of key presses had finger motion more than 5 per cent of the key width, while 55 per cent had motion more than 10 per cent of the width. The difference between X and Y probably stems from a combination of the dimensions of the keys, which are longer than they are wide, and the fact that the hands move most in the horizontal direction in traditional playing.

In order to account for the movement of the fingers along the keys in traditional keyboard technique, my solution for pitch bending is to use relative finger motion in the Y-axis with a user-adjustable threshold below which small movements are ignored. For vibrato, the software looks for relative finger motion in *both* directions within a certain time period before starting to change the pitch, as my studies showed that natural movements on a key in traditional playing were almost all in a single direction only. Generally speaking, the higher the threshold, the more effort is needed to engage the new techniques, but the less likely the techniques will be to engage unintentionally. It may be that as a player's technique becomes more attuned to TouchKeys, the player can gradually reduce the thresholds to achieve greater sensitivity to small movements.

In July 2013, after three years of development, I launched TouchKeys for public sale in a Kickstarter crowdfunding campaign. The campaign raised £46,000 to build and ship TouchKeys kits and instruments to musicians around the world. Most of the backers on Kickstarter opted for a self-install sensor kit that they could attach to their own keyboard, though pre-built keyboards were also available.

Though I have not undertaken a systematic survey of the musical backgrounds of the TouchKeys players, my impression is that the largest player community consists of amateur or semi-professional keyboardists who maintain home electronic music studios, and who most usually play in a pop/rock style. Other players include jazz keyboardists, professional studio composers and experimental musicians. A 2014 review in *Sound on Sound* magazine reflects the feedback I often get from performers: 'The nice thing about TouchKeys is that it builds upon existing keyboard techniques – you're not learning from scratch, just adding new movements and actions to enhance the performance – and that means the learning curve is fairly shallow' (Robjohns 2014).

Musicians don't take up new instruments solely because they are partly familiar; rather, the instrument's creative novelty provides the impetus. An open question regarding all the novel MIDI controllers on the market is whether novelty of *technique* or novelty of *sound* is more important. In principle, the same MIDI performance could be achieved using any of the aforementioned controllers, or given more time, using a basic keyboard and MIDI editing software. Viewed from this perspective, it might not be possible to tell what instrument a performer played solely by listening to the audio output. In practice, however, each controller is going to make certain patterns and techniques more or less idiomatic, and this will end up influencing what the performer does in characteristic ways. In other words: perhaps it is possible for each MIDI controller to have its own signature sound, even when they all control the same synths.

There is no single answer for how best to balance novelty and familiarity in digital musical instrument design, and much depends on the artistic priorities of the designer and any other musical collaborators. Going forward, I hope to discover more general principles in how to design for a performer's existing sensorimotor skills and cultural expectations.

Personal Take: Digital Demons, Real and Imagined

STEVE SAVAGE

The cultural history of developments in music technology is littered with reproach. The pianoforte threatened the purity of the harpsichord; the saxophone was the bastard son of the clarinet; the synthesiser mocked the orchestral instruments and the CD usurped the soul of the vinyl record. What gets obscured in the rhetoric is the true target of rebuke. It has become clear that the critiques of many technologies of the past were driven by nostalgia. The pianoforte represented an important expansion of the musical palette and became one of the iconic instruments of Western art music; the saxophone not only came to occupy a central role in jazz and popular music but found its place in Western art music as well. The synthesiser and the CD also became essential to music in all forms, but they have not necessarily fared as well in the popular lexicon of cultural currency.

Critiques of new audio technologies centre on their digital nature. While it's certainly true that sound itself is analogue, as is the human ability to hear sound, the question remains as to the quality of digital applications of music technology. Do CDs sound worse than vinyl records? Are synthesised and sampled orchestral scores inherently inferior to performances by symphonic orchestras? There is no single answer to these questions. While synthesisers and CDs don't necessarily represent improvements on earlier technologies, a brilliantly constructed synthetic orchestral recording may sound much better than the local community orchestra or perhaps have qualities that real orchestras cannot emulate. And despite the fascinations of the retro revolution, many prefer CD recordings, with their diminished noise floor and reduced harmonic distortion, to even the best vinyl recordings.

Having lived and worked through the transition from analogue to digital recording I have had the chance to consider the various pros and cons of the two formats. While I acknowledge the ways that digital loses something of value compared to the best forms of analogue capture of sound, I have also come to appreciate the many ways that digital capture has enhanced both the sound and the creative potentials of music recordings. At the same time I remain aware of the ongoing assault on digital sound technology coming primarily from popular media.

My work as an academic has, to a large extent, been a product of my work as a recording engineer and producer. I have come to celebrate the joys of digital music technologies through extensive practical application. Though at times I have felt that the academic defence of digital recording is no longer necessary in our highly digitised society, I frequently encounter examples that convince me otherwise. I found one recently as I was reading Jennifer Egan's Pulitzer Prize-winning novel, *A Visit from the Goon Squad*. In the brief space of one character's dramatic inner monologue Egan sums up popular attitudes toward digitisation, confirms the absolute commodification of popular music and taints most contemporary media. The protagonist is a middle-aged record executive, reflecting on the current status of his record company and the music that it is releasing:

> Driving to pick up his son, Bennie alternated between the Sleepers and the Dead Kennedys, San Francisco bands he'd grown up with. He listened for muddiness, the sense of actual musicians playing actual instruments in an actual room. Nowadays that quality (if it existed at all) was usually an effect of analogue signaling rather than bona fide tape – everything was an effect in the bloodless constructions Bennie and his peers were churning out. He worked tirelessly, feverishly, to get things right, stay on top, make songs that people would love and buy and download as ring tones (and steal, of course) – above all, to satisfy the multinational crude-oil extractors he'd sold his label to five years ago. But Bennie knew that what he was bringing into the world was shit. Too clear, too clean. The problem was precision, perfection; the problem was *digitization*, which sucked the life out of everything that got smeared through its microscopic mesh. Film, photography, music: dead. *An aesthetic holocaust!* Bennie knew better than to say this stuff aloud. (Egan 2010, 23)

This expression of technological determinism amplifies the negative effects of digital technologies without acknowledging their creative potential, and so misdirects the speaker's rage. While there may be problems in the brave new world of digitised popular music, there is also much to celebrate regarding the enormous creative gifts that digital audio workstations have provided for music production. The ability to revise, recompose, reinvent, rearrange, reuse, reimagine, reimprovise – in short, the ability to repurpose audio – has revolutionised the production of music recordings. At the same time the basic creative impulses and processes that have always been at the centre of music production remain central to this new 'constructionist' model of songwriting and composition.

Prior to the use of digital audio for making recordings I lost many battles with musicians over moments in a performance where I felt the emotional impact was clearly worth retaining despite a minor performance flaw that repeated listening revealed. Those perceived flaws could be fixed by replacing small sections using analogue technology (multi-tracking and overdubbing), but in many cases the analogue 'fixes' were – to me at least – clearly a step back from the impact of the original performance. With the introduction of digital technologies it has become possible to fix the minor flaws without losing the expressive quality of the performance.

I am reminded of a particular session, prior to the existence of digital audio technologies, at which the singer executed an extended vocal improvisation at the end of the song. The vocal line moved brilliantly through a complex rhythmic construction and resolved perfectly at the final note struck by the band. Those of us in the control room were beaming when the artist came in for the playback. She also admired the performance and we moved on with our work. However, after several playbacks of the final vocal improvisation – while working on other aspects of the song – she noticed that one of the notes in the descending run at the end of the phrase was slightly out of tune. She mentioned it and I said that no one would ever notice such a thing as it went by so quickly and the performance was too good to pass up. She accepted that for a while but after a few more listens she said 'That note really bugs me!' I argued that she hadn't even heard it the first few times she listened back but to no avail. She insisted on replacing that final vocal phrase.

We listened over and over and she tried to 'learn' what she had previously improvised – until she felt ready to try a new performance. We recorded many takes but never came close to the original. Her performance had become too studied and it was impossible to recapture the spontaneity of the initial take. Had this been in the digital era it would have been a simple fix. I could correct the out-of-tune syllable and retain the wonderful, human and expressive character of the original performance. This earlier means of fixing by replacing would often result in a 'clearer and cleaner', yet truly inferior, performance.

Having said that, Bennie may have a point. Popular music today may well be 'too clear, too clean', but the heart of the problem is not digitisation. Yes, digital fixing can be taken to extremes that squeeze the life out of a musical performance. But that is not the fault of digital technology. The technology does not determine the outcome. What determines the outcome is the user's application of the technology. Too 'clear and clean' is a choice, not a necessity.

The real demon that Bennie identifies in his rant is manifested in his attempts 'to satisfy the multinational crude-oil extractors he'd sold his label to five years ago'. Francis Bacon said, 'There is no excellent beauty, that hath not some strangeness in the proportion'. It is a misguided concern that leads to the idea that the marketplace will not tolerate strangeness. Out of the desire to eliminate any possible barrier to consumerism comes the mistaken notion that the safer commercial bet is to create excessively clean and clear recordings. It is commodification that squeezes the life out of music, not the details of the production techniques being used. That is the source of Bennie's aesthetic holocaust.

Personal Take: Composing with Sounds as Images

JULIO D'ESCRIVÁN

The most interesting impact of digital media on sound artistry is surely the way it has changed our compositional mind. I believe it has pushed composers to manipulate musical material in innovative ways, especially in response to video editing. In particular, the impact of video techniques that relate to 'compositing' and what may be their musical equivalent. Compositing is the process by which two or more images from different sources are combined so that they appear to belong in the same visual frame and sequence. So, for instance, the compositing technique of 'chroma-key' allows a film director to mask out portions of the image and substitute for them entirely different ones such that an actor can say their lines against a green background in which later the audience will see the Grand Canyon, or entire objects in a room can be selectively masked in green and their texture substituted in digital post-production. Transpose this idea onto music creation and the ease with which we can drag, drop and merge audio onto the blank canvas of our digital audio workstations (DAWs) is as much compositing as it is composing. In terms of inspiration, I also believe that our continuous exposure to visual work that freely appropriates and re-presents borrowed visual sources has permeated our compositional imagination – and by visual work, think beyond 'art' film to commercials, the MTV of the 1980s and 1990s, and now YouTube and other music video online networks.

Thanks to this omnipresence of visual media, a non-linear way of thinking about musical material has become second nature to us, even allowing composers to think of music as 'visual sound scenes' that are edited together. The latter makes even more sense in the case of composition for audio-visual media, as compositing sound to visual sequences is often a task of finding meaning in musical building blocks that can then be freely mixed to picture. This is something I learnt from my work in music for commercials and narrative film in the 1990s. Film and video directors taught me through their briefing how to respond to the language of the camera beyond traditional musical syntax. They also encouraged me to cross the boundaries between music and noise or music and the sound effect. This knowledge equipped me to deal with the fluid nature of visual narrative, where the estimation of the length of a shot is largely subjective and not bound by quantised musical beats. Where the composer often thinks of time in proportion to the metre, the director thinks in more subjective and durational terms. When composers do the same, scenes can become flowing and intuitive, and long enough to convey the intended meaning and emotion. The moving image becomes a terrain in which composers are architects designing houses, villages and cities of sound. As composers we then work with the emotional topography of the image; we carefully build, either for contrast or for similarity. The result must make sense for the terrain, be proportional, allow space for the sound, and be modular and adaptable like a new media object. Where this once was solved by symphonic textures on a rhythmic scaffolding, it is now approached through the remix mentality that pervades our culture. The building blocks of sound are arranged on the computer screen with irreverence towards their content: the soundbite cohabits with the romantic orchestral 'wild', and sounds of machinery with dubstep synth bass wobble. Not to mention the syntactic use of location sound: whether anticipating scene changes, lingering long after the cut, or wholly unrelated to the visuals, it often assumes a quasi-musical role. Composited, these blocks of sound form a semantic network alongside the visuals they shadow.

Enabled by digital technology, this compositing approach has emerged in my work as well as that of my contemporaries, and it helps solve two practical challenges that have remained constant for me in the twenty-seven-odd years of my creative practice. One is refitting an existing and arguably successful score to a new image edit from the director, usually due to small changes in the story. The other is understanding enough about video/film editing to make sense of its compositional language: what does a fade-in/out mean for the narrative? A close-up? The angle of a shot? If we rethink music for picture in terms of compositing, both these challenges are approached in a new way. As implied earlier, a compositing approach frees us from the constraints of purely musical metre as regards the visual hit-point. Creating music for moving images becomes a question of remixing and timing, as we shift, blend, and re-sync sound objects along the timeline of our DAWs in ways we didn't tend to treat our music scores. This allows us to create richer sound responses to changes in the video sequence, outside a traditional rhythmic model. On the other hand, our understanding of the compositional language of film can now be more freely echoed by the implied meanings of the sound building blocks that populate our DAWs, as they also fade in/out, pan across, establish a sound-shot, focus on a particular sound event or support a certain action on-screen.

If our creative approach has changed, our craftsmanship has also changed. In addition to traditional counterpoint and harmony, digital technology has forced us to go outside our disciplines and learn a variety of new skills. A musician or sound artist working for visual media needs to know about frame rates, transcoding, and video editing and production; which compressor and wrapper to use so that our DAW will efficiently play back video; how to program synths and samplers; how to audio edit to picture and orchestrate via MIDI. On top of this, we must produce realistic mock-ups that could be perceived as real, all at the whim of non-musical directions from film directors and producers. I believe we are the better for this changing practice enabled by new digital technologies, one step closer to whatever an audio-visual composer is meant to be and certainly closer to how musical creativity needs to work in an age of increasing digital collaboration.

Personal Take: Compositional Approaches to Film, TV and Video Games

STEPHEN BAYSTED

Like music for film and television, video game music is not a wholly artistic endeavour. It is a commercial-artistic one and the commercial factors impacting on the composer are numerous and profound. Unlike film and television music, there are many attendant technical considerations and imperatives that impose strictures upon the form, constructional devices and musical vocabulary available to the games composer. BAYSTED 2016, 152

As a composer of music for video games, film and television, and one who frequently works in all three media simultaneously, I am often asked by students about the different compositional approaches demanded by each. Whilst each medium has its own particular challenges, we should recognise that film and TV music have far more in common with each other than either does with video game music. That this is rarely perceived to be the case has much to do with the fact that the final musical artefact frequently appears to be structurally, functionally and sonically remarkably similar across all three media, if not indistinguishable; that is to say at once through-composed, synchronised to the on-screen action and cut from the same musical cloth.[1]

Music written for film and TV is linear, it specifically follows the narrative arc of the material on-screen, and it is usually carefully synchronised to the moving image in order to underpin or emphasise significant moments of action and to convey to the audience an appropriate emotional response to it. It is primarily non-diegetic, that is to say not part of the narrative, and as such it cannot be heard or interacted with by the on-screen characters. In this way, film and TV music can be said to be commenting upon the on-screen action and perhaps even foreshadowing events that are yet to happen, giving clues to the audience through the use of familiar musical tropes about, for example, unperceived dangers, impending doom, or the true nature of a character's feelings. Film and TV music is always fixed at the point of composition and it becomes an integral and unchanging component of the finished cinematic or televisual artefact when it is mixed on the dub stage. Its composition is governed almost exclusively by the demands of the on-screen action (and indeed the vision of the director); tempo, metre, orchestration, dynamics, and sometimes even key structures will necessarily follow its form and narrative arc.

Music in video games conventionally fulfils a much broader range of functions, several of which do not exist in film and TV music: it can accompany on-screen action (gameplay); it can be unobtrusive, ambient,

and sink into the background (in the menu system); it can be synchronised –
in precisely the same manner as film and TV music – to in-game movies
('cut scenes'); and music can have an important ludic function.[2] During
gameplay there may be many instances where a player's actions are the
outcome of a range of choices. As such they are difficult to predict, but the
fact remains that deciding to turn right instead of left, to go through a
certain door, or to pick up a sword rather than a potion could have
significant ludic ramifications that might alter the game's entire narrative
trajectory. The logical corollary of this is that each player's experience of the
game has the potential to be different and to be determined by which routes
are taken through the game's various levels, the characters and foes encountered along the way, the weapons deployed and the successes and failures in
battle, battles which, of course, may or may not even arise if the player
chooses to turn left instead of right.

To account for this, the composer must ensure that the music
composed can be adapted to underpin the various situations in which
the player might find themselves at any given moment. All the while the
objective is to maintain the illusion that the music is working non-
diegetically in the same manner as it does in film and TV and that it has
been composed for the player's particular journey through the game. In
order for this to be possible, the compositional process is approached
radically differently. When working on a film score, I will study a scene
in great detail to determine its function within the narrative and
whether there are any significant moments of action that require
emphasis. When working on a game, I must instead consider the
prevailing context of gameplay – for example, whether a battle may be
approaching around the next corner (if the player decides to go in that
direction) or whether the player may simply be exploring the game
world – and compose music appropriate to that context. Because it is
not possible to know how long the player may take in either scenario,
the music must be able to 'react' and be dynamically adaptable to all
possible outcomes. So instead of thinking of the music linearly, as a
single span from beginning to end, it is best broken down into shorter
chunks of musical material. These chunks are often layers of 'looped'
material that may be as short as eight or sixteen bars. Loops are used
because they can be seamlessly repeated, overlapped, crossfaded
together, or branched away from rapidly, depending on the duration
and changing nature of gameplay. Loops are then layered so that the
music can wax and wane in intensity and adapt to the consequences of
the player's decisions. A rudimentary trick of the film or TV composer's
trade to build excitement or tension in a cue might be to increase the
tempo, modulate upwards, or both, and to release that tension and

rebuild it as the scene demands; yet such tempo and modulatory manoeuvres would make seamless contiguous and multi-layered adaptive looping incredibly difficult to achieve in gameplay because loops only function when tempo and key structures remain consistent. To create a similar effect in games, one would instead have a hierarchical system of layered loops, each successive layer having ever-greater detail, intensity and textural complexity than the last. One can then build and release tension by adding or subtracting layers as required from one moment to the next. And where the film and TV composer will attempt to synchronise their music to 'hit points' (fixed points of significant action within a scene), the games composer will be thinking in terms of 'trigger points' (significant stages of gameplay where the character might pass through a door or encounter a foe). A trigger point will set off a musical cue or a complex sequence of looped and branching material.

To achieve these and other intricate adaptive structures, the games composer must normally work very closely with an audio programmer whose job it is to implement the music. Where film and TV composers deliver 'stems'[3] of their music to be mixed together with dialogue and sound effects on the dub stage at the end of the postproduction process, the games composer delivers potentially many hundreds of loops, 'stings',[4] and transitional passages to the games company to be implemented in software that plugs into the game's physics and graphics engines.

There are yet further generic and deep-rooted technological issues that the games composer must contend with.[5] In some game genres I work in, such as racing simulation games, music is never heard during gameplay because it interferes with the principal auditory mechanisms necessary for actually playing the game: since music plays no part in the real-world activity being simulated, its use would shatter verisimilitude.[6] I am forced to make all of my musical impact on the player from within the ambit of the menu system. In my score for *Project Cars* (2015), far from being relegated to the level of muzak, the music in the menu system is instead fully orchestrated and 'epic' in scale, and makes use of dramatic cinematic musical tropes that build tension and trigger emotional responses from the player, preparing them for the gameplay. Embedded within the musical material is an additional layer with a broad range of real-world sounds recorded from motor racing ('pit to car' radio transmissions, engines, trackside ambiences) to help to further immerse the player in the simulated world. Because the music is contained within the menu system, its construction is relatively simple: the main body of each musical cue is composed linearly and unfolds in that way until the player decides to press 'start' and trigger the game-loading process (where cars, circuits and opponents are compiled). At that trigger point, a complex multi-layered sound effect masks the transition between the linear version and a shorter looped section of the same music track that replaces it as the game loads. Because it is impossible to predict how long the game will actually take to fully load, the loop must be repeated until loading has been completed. In contrast, in my score for the mobile zombie game *The Walking Dead: Assault* (2012), looping the music was not possible at that juncture due to the constraints of the Apple and Android platforms. As a result, I was forced to predict the normative playthrough-durations of each level and write linear pieces of music that gradually built in intensity and whose length was pre-determined to cover most playthrough scenarios. In both examples, these were far from ideal solutions to attendant technological limitations, but they were necessary in order to maintain the illusion of cinematic musical linearity.

From what I have described above it may seem to the reader that the games composer's lot is not always a happy one; that is in fact far from the case. Whereas the mechanical processes of film and TV composition have changed little in the past three decades, the processes of games composition and the technologies that support its implementation continue to evolve rapidly.[7] It is an exciting time to be involved in the industry, not least as it embarks upon the latest generation of affordable virtual reality devices such as Oculus Rift and Morpheus; as composers we will have to think very differently about how we approach interactive scores and audio to take best advantage of the new and enhanced immersive possibilities VR affords. It will also be extremely interesting to see whether games music is able to successfully emerge from the long shadow cast by film music vocabulary and its tropes, and develop its own language that is perhaps more appropriate to gaming contexts.

Notes

1 This should not be in the least surprising from a stylistic and generic perspective since many composers work in all three media, and (all too frequently) the points of musical reference provided by producers, editors and directors of films, TV and games have largely been defined by music from other film scores. For an insightful discussion of the role of the 'temping' process in film post-production, see Sadoff 2006.

2 In the crime thriller game *L.A. Noire* (2011), for example, music plays a critical role in the narrative and the actual playing of the game: subtle musical cues help guide the player-protagonist Cole Phelps to the location of clues and notify him when all clues contained within a particular crime scene have been exhausted.

3 Stems are sub-mixes of the entire music mix, and usually comprise instruments from the same family (brass, strings, woodwind, etc.). Their mixing and adjustment of relative volumes can help alter the texture, density and perceived intensity of musical cues. They are extremely useful on the dub stage as they help the dub mixer to balance levels between dialogue, sound effects and music more effectively.

4 Repertoires of musical 'exit points', literally cadential passages, which can be bolted onto individual loops or layers of loops.
5 See Baysted (2016, 161) for a more detailed exploration of the technological constraints imposed by different platforms and their impact on music and audio design.
6 For further discussion on the various genres of racing games and their use of music, see Tim Summers (2016, 88).
7 For example, looping is now possible to achieve on mobile platforms; and *Project Cars 2* (2017) no longer requires ungainly structural devices to overcome transitions between game phases.

8 Virtual Worlds from Recording to Video Games

ISABELLA VAN ELFEREN

Virtual reality is one of the buzzwords of late twentieth- and early-twenty-first-century popular culture. Video games, online environments and virtual theme parks offer users the experience of a different world outside ordinary life. Music plays a significant role in both the establishment of and immersion in such virtual worlds. In order to investigate precisely how the sonic dimension of virtual reality works, this chapter describes and theorises various forms of musical virtual reality, arguing that the virtual worlds of music challenge existing understandings of virtual reality and immersion. Musical virtual reality is an omnipresent, perpetually moving, physical transmission of what will be conceptualised here as 'musical energy'.

Once upon a Dream of J. S. Bach

Virtuality is a non-manifest dimension of reality that escapes, precedes or exceeds actualisation: the virtual is separated from manifest reality by its not-being-actualized (Lévy 1997, 91–3). Virtual reality refers to a simulated timespace which is experienced as a reality but which is different from the day-to-day world. While it has become a key concept in academic and societal debates since the emergence of digital media (with 'cyberspace' as the most often-discussed form of virtual reality), Marie-Laure Ryan argued in her influential book *Narrative as Virtual Reality* (2001) that virtual reality comes into being by immersion in any form of narrative, analogue or digital: the immersion in the simulated world of a film or a book can be just as deep as that in a video game or online environment. The media generating virtual reality can be textual, visual, auditory or olfactory – any physical sense or any combination of physical senses can be involved in the perception of a reality that is different from, but parallel to, the day-to-day world that we call 'reality'. Reading the Grimm brothers' fairytale 'Sleeping Beauty', we can believe ourselves to be wandering around in its world of magic spells and mysteriously growing forests; seeing a film adaptation of the story, we see this world alive before our very eyes, and are drawn into it by enchanting visuals; playing a Sleeping Beauty video game we interact with the inhabitants of this world; and visiting the Dutch theme park De Efteling we can see the princess asleep in her castle, which we approach over a rocky forest path. All of these versions of a fairytale world are as real as our senses tell us they are, and all of them can be as immersive as our perceptual attention allows. Each is a form of virtual, not actual, reality, simulated, but tangible, enveloping, captivating.

Sound and music are key contributors to any form of virtual reality. Because of their remarkable affective and mnemonic power, even the smallest sounds can evoke worlds of connotations, emotions and memories. These associative capacities are employed in very precise ways in any form of simulated reality. Tchaikovsky's music for the *Sleeping Beauty* ballet was chosen for Disney's 1959 animated movie: it was such an integral part of the film's world that the chosen tagline was 'Wondrous to see – Glorious to hear', and the film's song 'Once upon a dream' has become a musical icon for cartoon magic. All Disney films and video games are celebrated for their immersive soundtracks, and the company prides itself in its use of musical world-building. Disney has brought out two Sleeping Beauty video games, *Princess Aurora's Singing Practice* and *Enchanted Melody*, in which the gameplay itself revolves around music as the player 'helps' Princess Aurora practise her singing or dance through the magic forest from the film.

For other audiences, Sleeping Beauty is not necessarily connected with Tchaikovsky, but with J. S. Bach. The Fairytale Forest in the Efteling theme park is dotted with large red and white toadstools that play the Minuet in G major from Anna Magdalena Bach's notebook (BWV 114). The piece's harpsichord timbre, triple metre and soothingly simple progressions blend perfectly with the surroundings of this 'magic forest'. I remember leaning my ears on these toadstools as a little girl and being transported into a world of fairytale wonder – aided, no doubt, by the fact that I had been listening to a Grimm tales LP at home in which 'Sleeping Beauty' was accompanied by Bach's fourth Brandenburg Concerto (BWV 1049). In these examples, listening to Tchaikovsky's or Bach's music is partaking of a fairytale virtual reality. The examples also show that such musical virtual realities are simultaneously immersive and subjective, coloured by personal listening histories and musical connotations.

If musical virtual reality is not limited to digital contexts, if it is created by such subjective agencies as personal connotations, and if, in fact, any musical experience can potentially engender a kind of virtual experience, then how, if at all, can it be described objectively?

Schizophonia, Mobile Music, Video Games

Schizophonia

The invention of sound recording in the late nineteenth century separated sound from its physical origin, enabling sound to be replayed at another time and in another space than those of its first occurrence. The mere fact of this separation revolutionised sonic communication by creating disembodied sound worlds that were perceived by many at the time as disconcerting. As recording technology definitively unmoored sound from its origins in time and space, acousmatics became a reality: it was now possible to hear a sound without perceiving where it came from, so that voices appeared to be ghosts, music appeared to be spectral, and the dog Nipper famously took his master's recorded voice for his actual presence (Sterne 2003, 287–333). The spectral aspects of sound recording were explored in early horror film, which exploited audiences' unease with the fact that the moving image was now accompanied by disembodied voices (Van Elferen 2012, 34–47). In terms of virtual reality, early sound recording enhanced the cinematic experience by layering the visual world with an auditory counterpart: film sound completed the illusion that cinema goers were steeped in another world, that the cinema really did take them out of their own reality and into another, temporary but utterly bewitching, world of audio-visual stimulation. That that world was evidently disembodied but simultaneously sensually perceivable, and therefore convincingly real, only enhanced the immersion in the uncanny realm of horror in which spectral sounds evoke the return of repressed anxiety (van Elferen 2012, 24–33, 173–90).

Reducing the occult overtones of such earlier assessments and applications, R. Murray Schafer coined the term 'schizophonia' for the spatial and temporal separations established by sound recording (1977, 88). He argues that with the advent of ever more sophisticated playback equipment, such as 3D surround sound, 'any sound environment [can] be simulated in time and space ... Any sonic environment can now become any other sonic environment' (91). Sonic virtual reality, therefore, is not limited to the context of film or television soundtracks, in which music is relatively subservient to visual content, but can exist in and of itself at any given time. Whenever we turn on the radio, press 'play' on a stereo set, or switch on our mobile music device, we bring into being a schizophonically simulated reality, a virtual reality that consists of sound alone (cf. Voegelin 2014, 62–84, 153–6).

Like any other virtual reality, these sonic worlds exist parallel to the everyday world: driving to work while listening to *Lucia di Lammermoor* on my car CD player, I am as immersed in Donizetti's rendering of Lucia's torment as I am in traffic. Because immersion in sonic virtual reality does not hinder other sensory perceptions, moreover, musical realities easily mingle with everyday reality. Tia DeNora's (2000) research on music's personal and social functions illustrates this blending of worlds. Her interviewees explain that when the daily routines of driving to work, cooking dinner or taking a bath are accompanied by music, the affective connotations of that music overlay the experience of such prosaic activities, lending the allure of other possible worlds to their own world. And because music's 'stickiness' makes it retain its connotations whatever the context (Abbate 2004, 523), the mixture of 'real' and 'virtual' goes even further: having listened to Donizetti on a number of my commutes, I now find that in fact the motorway to work *itself* reminds me of Lucia, as if the opera were the soundtrack to my journey and the two types of perception have in fact blended into one reality that is half-real and half-virtual (cf. Bull 2007, 87–93).

Mobile Music

The example of car radio illustrates how the blending of realities through music becomes especially noticeable in mobile music culture. The invention of the Sony Walkman in 1979 and the Apple iPod in 2001 caused a seismic shift in the sociology of music consumption. If listening to music in the car turns the motorway or cityspace into a film projected onto your windscreen, walking through cities and landscapes with the same music in your earbuds resembles actually participating in that film (Bull 2007, 38–49). As Schafer predicted in 1977, sound recording has ultimately led to 'the portability of acoustic space' (1977, 91). But this acoustic space never consists of sound alone: it is always, and inevitably, filled by the connotations evoked by that sound. The timespace of any music consists of sound and is inhabited by the listener's memories, emotions and identifications; the agency of these unconscious processes galvanises acoustic space, renders it alive and real. For this reason musically simulated realities never just exist parallel to, but are always inextricable parts of, everyday life.

   Moreover, the fact that mobile devices are carried on the body changes the physical dimension of the listening experience. We listen to our music device as we walk through town, cycle to the station, or exercise in the gym: the beats and rhythms of the music synchronise or syncopate with the movements of our bodies, and often we adjust either our playlist or the speed of our movements in order to create a better match between them. Thus, the choreography of bodies moving in time to music is no longer reserved to dance alone, but also characteristic of such activities as walking, cycling and exercising. Because of mobile music, listening culture has become a newly embodied culture (cf. DeNora 2000, 75–108). As a result, immersion in sonic virtual worlds is not merely emotional or mnemonic, but physical and geographical as well. Mobile music marks the consolidation, the personalisation and the vicarious re-embodiment of schizophonia: the separation of sound from its origin is no longer uncanny, but a natural fact of life in the age of the iPod; it enables every listener to move around in their own private capsule of sonic virtuality; and as this virtuality is narrowly aligned with the listener's own movements, the disembodiment of schizophonia is replaced by the listener's post facto, vicarious re-embodiment of recorded sound.

From time to time concerns are raised about the alleged anti-social aspects of mobile music culture. If everyone moves through life in their own auditory bubble, the argument goes, the very possibility of social interaction is thwarted. However odd it may seem to see a train full of people with their headphones on and staring at their mobile phone, the truth of the matter is, of course, that all these private bubbles are connected in myriad ways to other private bubbles. As Imar de Vries's archaeology of the mobile phone has shown, mobile communication is driven by an idealistic discourse that promises a 'communication sublime': a 'final and universally accessible communication space' in which anyone can communicate with everyone else at any place and at any time (2012, 17–18). The enormous success of social media – Facebook had 2.23 billion active users in the second quarter of 2018 – attests that global connectivity simply changes rather than diminishes the way in which we experience communication. Facebook, Twitter, Instagram and all the other social networks have added a new layer of reality that sits between real life and virtual reality: the constantly accessible social reality of connectivity.

Music distribution and consumption have rapidly moved into the connected space of social media. Listeners recommend the music they like to each other on various social media platforms and also link up their actual listening experiences through such streaming services as Spotify, Shazam and SoundCloud. These online radio stations enable users to listen to the same music as our friends do, and to let their musical tastes be guided by those of listeners whom the programmes' algorithms calculate to be like-minded people. Here the virtual worlds of mobile music listening, with their intriguing blend of associative, physical and geographical characteristics, move from the private to the public domain. Musical experience is no less personal in the shared zone of social listening than it was in the private space of individual playlists: on the contrary, precisely because streaming software collects data on our musical preferences it enables us to share our most personal emotions and memories. Listening to my indie Spotify playlist, I am immersed in my own musical preferences; I can share

214 Isabella van Elferen

them with others; by following Spotify's recommendations I may get to know new people who like similar music; I may get to know music I did not know hitherto; and I am able to share these new insights with my friends, old and new, so that we can all immerse ourselves in the same virtual world of musical experience. All of this can be done while I sit on the train with my headphones on and stare at my mobile phone, and while my private bubble extends to any place in the world. Musical social networks accumulate all the aspects of musical virtual reality discussed so far, and add the social element of sharing and bonding. As such, the connected space of streaming services represents a mediated counterpart of the concert hall: not in real life but also not outside it, this simulated reality is as real as our own emotions and as physical as our own bobbing head, and it reaffirms the strong social ties of shared musical interests in online communities.

Video Games

Although the musical virtual reality of sound recording, film soundtracks, mobile devices and social media is immersive, it is not as interactive as that in video games. Gaming interaction gives players the sense that they are actively participating in the game's virtual world. Whether they operate the arrow keys of their PC in order to move two-dimensional blocks in *Tetris* or the wireless Dualshock controller of their PS4 in order to navigate avatar Arno Dorian through *Assassin's Creed Unity*'s meticulously designed game space, they appear to be in control of the action. Compared to reading, viewing or listening, video gaming leads to different kinds of immersion and virtual reality because of its interactive nature. Involving not only more physical senses than books or films but also active participation and playful intervention in a non-linear story, immersion and virtuality in video games would seem to be more all-encompassing than those in other media. It is not surprising, therefore, that the academic literature on both topics has grown exponentially since interactive video games started to dominate the entertainment industry.

Next to appealing graphic design and engaging gameplay, sound and music play a crucial part in gaming virtual reality. Game sound design has several functions at once, some very similar to those of film and television sound. Sounds can help build a convincing game space: just as in film or on television, diegetic sounds such as 'natural' bird song or 'industrial' white noise help the player determine the kind of environment through which she navigates, and non-diegetic sounds such as 'sad' minor melodies or 'dangerous' pounding drums can help her identify the mood that the environment is supposed to evoke. Equally comparable to film and television sound, non-diegetic game sound gives the player clues regarding the characters or situations they meet in this virtual world. Evil characters are introduced by dissonant harmonies, battle scenes are underscored by loud and fast music, and victories are identified by heroic orchestral cadences. Such themes often work in a similar way to leitmotifs in that they are instantly recognisable – so recognisable that they verge on clichés – sonic identity markers like the monstrous grunts and metallic drones of the Necromorphs in *Dead Space 2*. So-called 'interface sound' indicates when players have completed a level or picked up ammunition, and guides them through the game's menus: this kind of sound immerses the player in the virtual matrix of gaming software itself (Collins 2008, 127–33). Finally, like film and television music, game music is often used as a sonic branding device, the auditory identity kit of a game in which all its essential elements are wrapped. A famous sonic game brand is the 2002 theme of the *Halo* series, which combines Gregorian chant and rising string motifs with syncopated drum rhythms and electric guitar riffs. The theme evokes the nostalgia of historical adventure as well as the thrilling suspense of first-person shooter gameplay: it is precisely because of this unusual combination of musical connotations in the even more unusual context of a science fiction game that this theme music has become a celebrated sonic game brand.

But just as the virtual reality of video games differs from that in other media, so too does its sonic counterpart.[1] Unlike film and television narratives, games do not follow linear story-lines. Instead, the development of gameplay depends on the speed, direction and success with which a player moves through the game. The ensuing non-linear, interactive and individual development of gameplay cannot be underscored by linear music but is accompanied by what is called 'adaptive audio', in which themes and motifs loop in non-linear patterns so as to match the non-linear gameplay progress (cf. Collins 2008, 125–30, 139–65). In the case of *Halo*, composer and producer Martin O'Donnell and Michael Salvatori isolated the various components of the theme – the chant, the violins, the guitar – so that they could be used as loops accompanying different parts of the gameplay. This non-linear form of composing has important consequences for the gaming experience as well as for the discussion of musical immersion and virtual reality. As adaptive audio is tied to particular gameplay situations, game sound and music are not just heard but activated by the player. It is her navigation that brings these sound worlds into being: entering certain spaces cues monster leitmotifs to begin, backing off to load her gun makes the music fall silent again, her victory over the monsters fades the battle music into victory music. As many games are designed with 3D sound, players are able to locate precisely where in the virtual space monsters are lurking, and can let their avatar act accordingly:

game music has become a Gaming Positioning System for the navigation of gaming virtual reality (van Elferen 2011, 32–4). The music does not merely accompany the playing experience, it *is* the playing experience: the epic victory themes, for instance, that have made the *Final Fantasy* soundtracks so famous represent the end of the player's personal journey, battles and triumph.

Game musical connotations and interaction converge in the sonic establishment of gaming virtual reality. While the associative power of *Halo*'s plainchant voices and the syncopated drum rhythms are powerful contributions to the game's virtual reality, the interactivity of this same music gives the player active agency in the construction and development of that reality. Sonic immersion in *Halo* simultaneously entails, on the one hand, immersion in your own world of musical connotations and its intermedial connections with the graphic game design, and, on the other, immersion in the flow of gameplay, which allows you to open up layer upon layer of music. The speed of the gaming flow necessitates relatively unambiguous musical associations: it would be very confusing if *Dead Space 2*'s Necromorphs were not accompanied by grunts and electronic drones but by mellifluous harp and piano motifs – the player would be too late in her assessment of this sonic information, lose the battle, and the game would end. Because in-game musical interpretation must be fast, game music often seems somewhat clichéd in its signifying patterns. Fantasy role-playing games (RPGs) have epic soundtracks in which victories are represented in glorious orchestral crescendos. Survival horror games use industrial soundscapes in which monsters are easily identifiable by dissonant stingers. Such clearly distinguished game musical genres, moreover, are not always even original to the video game medium, but often lean heavily on already existing film musical conventions: the 'epic' composing style in fantasy RPGs derives from fantasy film soundtrack idioms, and the minimal, industrial sound of horror games finds a precedent in horror film composition. Because the player has already acquired a (largely unconscious) musical literacy in the interpretation of such audio-visual idioms by watching such films, she will be able to quickly identify what the game music was designed to signify.

The establishment of and immersion in game musical virtual reality thus consists of three overlapping factors: musical affect (A), musical literacy (L) and musical interaction (I). Affect is not used here in the sense of a musical reflection of a personal feeling (like in the *Affektenlehre* of the baroque) but as 'an ability to affect and be affected' (Massumi 1987, xvi). The affective connotations evoked by game music help the player interpret the game surroundings and events; her interpretative process is guided by her existing literacy in the idiom of game composing. These two factors help her interact with the game, and as a result also with the adaptive audio, and so the performative process of immersion in game musical

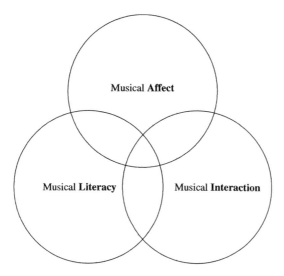

Figure 8.1 The ALI model: affect, literacy and interaction.

virtual reality is perpetually in motion. The three factors in this 'ALI model' (van Elferen 2016, 34–9) can be visually represented by way of a Borromean knot (Figure 8.1).

ALI

The ALI model was originally designed as a tool for the analysis of game musical immersion, but these factors are constitutive of immersion in other types of sonic virtual reality too. Compare, for instance, the musical virtual reality shared by Spotify communities to that shared by a group of MMORPG (massively multiplayer online role-playing game) players. Both processes are operated by the convergence of musical affect, musical literacy and musical interaction, albeit in different ways. In both cases, the affective performativity of musical experience (A) leads to the opening up of individual virtual worlds consisting of memory, emotion and identification. These virtual worlds are supported by musical literacy (L): the acquaintance with audio-visual idioms and genres in the case of game music, and the acquaintance with pop, rock, indie or classical music repertoires in the case of streaming services. The interaction with and through music leads to a further development of the virtual world (I): in games, musical interaction steers adaptive audio, whereas streaming software is explicitly designed to invite interaction with one's own and other users' playlists. Moreover, in both cases the fact that this immersive virtual world of music is shared with others often engenders the formation of musical communities that only exist in 'cyberspace'. The affect, literacy and interaction that characterise game musical immersion thus also enhance the immersion in other types of music-induced virtual reality.

An even more striking example of the relation between different kinds of musical virtual reality is that of video game music fandom. The Chiptune community consists of fans of 8-bit game music who create remixes and new compositions. Chiptune is characterised by the retro timbre and technological limitations of the vintage gaming software. An iconic 8-bit track is Koji Kondo's 1985 *Super Mario* theme song, which is the basis of countless Chiptune remixes, covers performed on various instruments and live performances on original Gameboys. Other Chiptune artists create 8-bit versions of non-game-related music, ranging from Vivaldi's *Four Seasons* to a-ha's 'Take On Me' and John Williams's *Star Wars* theme. Such creations are shared with other video game music fans, discussed on online forums, and appropriated as part of a new canon. Chiptune is a remarkable form of musical virtual reality to the extent that it is a lively online community whose strong social ties have been welded upon participants' identity by the affective powers of musical experience.

It is not difficult to identify the ALI mechanics of Chiptune's immersive virtual reality. Interaction (I) probably comes first here: game music fandom is musical interaction extending beyond the confines of actual games, growing from playful navigation into playful creation. Chiptune's virtual reality hinges on musical affect (A). It is fostered by the lived experience of emotions, connotations and identifications that any fan experienced when they first played the game; fans re-create this virtual world, endow it with the blissful haze of nostalgia, and share their creations as well as their affects with other Chiptune fans. Both dimensions of Chiptune virtual reality are supported by musical literacy (L), as fans recognise the 8-bit sounds and, more importantly, flaunt their knowledge of them by posting their own new creations in online forums. Located simultaneously in the virtual world of game musical play and in that of online communities, Chiptune doubly manifests the immersive power of musical virtual reality.[2]

Chiptune virtuality also illustrates just how difficult it is to distinguish between musical 'virtual reality' and musical 'real life'. As in the cases of listening to music in the car or wearing your iPod while cycling, creating or listening to Chiptune is very much a part of daily life for those who practise it: not only is the immersion in the playful listening or creative flow woven into daily activities, but this creative activity is also an affective part of fan identity. If the traditional definition of virtual reality describes it as a simulated world outside the ordinary world, the examples of musical virtual reality discussed above suggest that this definition needs to be revised in order to be useful within a musical context.

Individual, Embodied Musical Worlds: Definitions and Approaches

Musical virtual reality is fundamentally different from other forms of virtual reality for two distinct but closely related reasons. First, the same music may evoke greatly differing virtual worlds for each individual listener; second, the virtual reality generated by music is often a physical part of the everyday world. The remainder of this chapter will explore the specificities of musical virtual reality in the light of recent academic debates, and theorise this musical form of reality as governed by the perpetual motion of musical energy.

Immersion and Affect

Musical virtual reality actively engages the listener's personal imagination. As music in and of itself does not mean anything but only acquires meaning through the associative context of its reception, the virtual reality it calls forth is much less concrete than that established by media such as text, film or gameplay. When two people are immersed in the same video game, it is likely that they have comparable experiences of the game's virtual reality, guided as they are by clear visual, plot and gameplay information: players of *Halo* will agree that they are playing a science fiction game with a range of breathtaking intergalactic fights. By contrast, two listeners who are immersed in the same piece of music, say the *Halo* theme tune, may interpret that music in different ways. An avid *Halo* player will remember her own gaming experience and share her memories with other fans on YouTube; another listener may not know *Halo* but recognise the musical idiom of action-adventure, and therefore imagine worlds of fantastic heroism. Yet another listener may enjoy the plainchant and find herself transported into a world of monasteries and contemplative silence. Each of these experiences should be considered a virtual reality – a musically simulated reality – and yet each of them differs from the others in emotional, mnemonic and subjective content.

If such great differences occur, should these listening experiences really be described as virtual reality? If this is virtual reality, does that mean that any programme music – music with the explicit purpose of simulating an experience, worldview, or narrative – generates a virtual reality, too? To put it even more drastically: could that imply that *any* musical experience can generate virtual reality as listeners are immersed in musically evoked emotions, memories and connotations?

Music's immersive capacity is such that it can change listeners' perceptions of time and space. Listening to music can have the effect of a

Proustian cake dipped in jasmine tea: any musical element, from the arc of a melody to the timbre of a voice, can evoke the involuntary memory of past times and past feelings (van Elferen 2011, 31). And that musical associativity is not limited to memory or nostalgia alone. More importantly perhaps, music is able to influence our emotions. Its affective agency can seemingly overrule that of the listener, whose mood can be turned in any direction by music she happens to be hearing. This agency is so strong, indeed, that it can rewrite our experience of everyday spaces, define (sub)cultural identities and support collective narratives (cf. DeNora 2000, 109–26).

Musical immersion has been linked to virtual reality in a number of scholarly contexts. In their study of mobile music, William Carter and Leslie Liu state that musical reality overlays everyday reality as we 'enter the musical worlds created by songs and albums' (2005). Their creative interventions focus specifically on the musical virtual reality enabled by the iPod, exploiting the fact that it allows listeners to 'drift between the real and the virtual' (ibid). While Carter and Liu take such musical liminality as a given, Salomé Voegelin's *Sonic Possible Worlds* explores the phenomenological processes that establish the conflation of the ordinary world and the virtual worlds. Voegelin relates the phenomenology of musical virtual worlds to literary 'possible world' theories. Poised on the threshold of auditory perception, her book argues that deep listening in and of itself represents world-building: '[L]istening does not recognize; it listens not for what a sound might represent but hears what it might generate. It hears sound as a verb, as a world creating predicate' (2014, 83).

Voegelin's thesis resonates with other phenomenologies of music, most notably those of Jonathan Kramer and Jean-Luc Nancy. Both theorists have argued that musical experience alters our perception of the world. Kramer contends that musical time unfolds independently from clock time in a manner very similar to Bergsonian *durée*, arguing that musical time should be considered as completely separate from – and separating itself from – ordinary time: the time of music has the agency to 'create, alter, distort, or even destroy time itself, not simply our experience of it' (Kramer 1988, 5). In a similar vein, Nancy contemplates the ways in which listening creates its own space as well as its own time: 'The sonorous present is the result of space-time: it spreads through space, or rather it opens up a space that is its own, the very spreading out of its resonance, its expansion and its reverberation' (Nancy 2007, 13). While both Kramer and Nancy attribute world-building powers to musical experience, Voegelin expands such notions into a theory of 'phenomenological possibilism' (Voegelin 2014, 28, 45–8). Countering the transcendent paradigms that dominate previous phenomenological accounts of music, she proposes a sonic immanence in which musical experience is not either virtual or actual, but both virtual *and* actual (114). Generated by the meeting of sound waves and listening subjects, musical virtual worlds must be considered as part of a 'continuum between the sonic thing and the sonic subject' (115): they may emerge at any given time, at any given place, and will differ for any listening individual.

The transformative possibilities of musical experience, according to these phenomenological analyses, are generated by the convergence of musical and subjective factors: the propelling musical forces of melody, harmony, rhythm and repetition initiate a movement of sound and time that is met and complemented by a movement of memory and affect. This interplay between material (sound waves, acoustics, instruments, bodies) and less material agents (thoughts, feelings, memories) can be compared to a 'Newton's cradle' pendulum of five metal balls. A metal sphere on one side swings through the air, passes its energy through the middle three spheres, and makes the sphere on the other side move outward as if by its own accord. This, in turn, sets in motion a self-sustaining *perpetuum mobile* of kinetic energy. Music, with its remarkable capacity to connect the material with the less material, can be compared to kinetic energy, and its workings to the workings of the pendulum. In a three-dimensional motion across and beyond ordinary time and space, music's sound waves strike our ears, pass through our neurons, and move memory and emotion as if by an unseen force. This then initiates a chain reaction of further associations and affects. The chain reaction is kept in motion by its own rhythm, its own flow, and thereby its own version of the passing of time – its own *durée*, as Kramer would say.

While the perpetual motion of musical energy is governed by the conservation of energy, the nature of this energy may vary significantly – it may be kinetic, potential, mnemonic or affective energy; it may be your, my or someone else's connotations – but the rhythm and flow of the motion will continue. The sway of musical sound waves is passed on to the neurosystem by the organ of Corti in the ear, which translates the physical energy of sound waves to the electro-chemical energy of emotion and connotation. This chain reaction of energies sets musical virtual reality in perpetual motion. Music thus simultaneously affirms and, by generating a virtual reality out of ordinary space and time, defies physical laws: musical energy does not just persist in chronological time nor does it just move in Euclidean space, but it represents a system of interrelated material and less material events. Voegelin's 'sonic continuum' is only possible because of this principle, which applies to musical energy just as it does to kinetic energy. This 'im/material pendulum' model is especially appropriate, of course, in the case of video game music, which is explicitly interactive: the less obviously material movement of player associations will feed back directly into (material) adaptive audio by way of gameplay.

The performative capacities of music-induced emotion and connotation were conceptualised as 'affect' in the ALI model introduced above. Affect has been an increasing focus of research in arts and humanities since the 'affective turn' in critical theory, which had its roots in Brian Massumi's 2002 monograph *Parables for the Virtual*. Massumi describes affect as a performative dimension of intensity, an emergent 'expression event' that is caused by sensual perception, anchored in embodied subjectivity, and engenders a 'participation in the virtual' (2002, 26–7, 35). He argues that the time and place of affect are necessarily virtual, and therefore always potentially present but not always stable: even if its momentum is not fully actual (which it arguably never can be), affect itself is always virtually and therefore indeterminably present. He describes it as '*cross-temporal*, implying a participation of "temporal contours" in each other, singly or in the looping of refrains' (34). Massumi adds that this cross-temporality 'constitutes the movement of experience into the future (and into the past, as memory)' (34). Read through the framework of the im/material conservation of musical energy, it is clear that the 'expression event' of affect is the subjective reaction to the physical encounter with music's sound waves – a passing on of musical energy. This musico-affective chain reaction leads to musical immersion, which, in Massumi's terms, is a cross-temporal affective virtuality. Kramer's, Nancy's and Voegelin's phenomenological accounts of the world-building immersion in music are thus embedded in the perpetual energetic interaction between music and affect.

Because of its strong power over the basic perceptions of time and space (the objective axis by which we measure everyday life) as well as over affect and identification (the subjective correlate of that axis), musical experience is able to create a virtual reality. Different from other types of virtual reality, the world that is generated by music is not deliberately created as a specific virtual environment. Even in the case of programme music or video game music, every listener will experience her own, highly subjective and often very detailed Proustian moment. Precisely because of these deeply affective individual differences, musical virtual reality is arguably more immersive than that generated by other media. The answer to the question posed above, therefore, is that indeed *any* musical experience can generate a virtual world.

Daily Practices and Augmented Reality

Besides entailing significant individual variation, a second way in which musical virtual reality is distinguished from other types of virtual reality is that it is part *of* rather than parallel *to* the everyday world. The examples of car audio, mobile music and streaming services suggest that musical virtual reality provides an auditory layer on top of everyday reality. This layer influences our perception of the world: attentively or inattentively immersed in musical virtual reality, we 'see the world through our ears'. This explains the well-known effect that walking in the city with 'happy' music on our mobile music player can make a rainy day seem less gloomy.

This sonic layering of reality has been discussed in game music research in terms of immersion. The bleeding of game sound into the player's real-life surroundings can lead to domestic irritation, but also to increased player immersion. The 3D sounds of creaking doors and monsters growling in survival horror games create the impression that danger may be lurking in the player's own house (Cheng 2014, 99–103; Van Elferen 2012, 121–7): 'the sounds and simulations of games', William Cheng states, 'resonate well beyond the glowing screen' (2014, 14). Moreover, music games such as *Guitar Hero*, in which the player performs music on haptic interfaces shaped like instruments, demonstrate that this sonic overlap between gaming virtual reality and ordinary reality has emphatically embodied and social dimensions. The inclusion of such visceral components in the virtual reality experience blurs the boundaries between these types of reality even further (Miller 2012, 8).

If musical virtual reality is so embedded in daily practices and has such clear physical components, it would seem to exceed the traditional definition of virtual reality as separate from everyday life. Should it then still be considered virtual reality? Since every musician can testify to the embodied nature of immersion in music's flow (Schroeder 2006), is not *any* form of musical engagement a participation in musical virtual reality?

The translation of musical energy into musical affect, as argued above, can establish a musical virtual reality at any time or place. This auditory reality provides affective feedback to the listener's perception of the day-to-day world. The fact that musical affect has a physical grounding – sound waves, neurotransmitters, chemistry and so on – only increases the strength of musical immersion. Focusing on the corporeal aspects of affect, Melissa Gregg and Greg Seigworth expand Massumi's theory. They discuss affect as liminal, changeable and multi-faceted, rendering the subject 'webbed' through the embodiedness of affective response:

> Affect is integral to a body's perpetual becoming (always becoming otherwise, however subtly, than what it already is), pulled beyond its seeming surface-boundedness by way of its relation to, indeed its composition through, the forces of encounter. With affect, a body is as much outside itself as in itself – webbed in its relations – until ultimately such firm distinctions cease to matter.   (Gregg and Seigworth 2010, 3)

Massumi's 'participation in the virtual' is therefore grounded in the physical. Immersed in affect, the body is simultaneously actual and virtual; immersed in *musical* affect, 'virtual' reality and 'actual' reality overlap.

The simultaneity of everyday and virtual physicality has also been explored in game music studies. Kiri Miller states that players of *Guitar Hero* are 'playing *between* – that is, playing in the gap between virtual and actual performance' (2012, 16). For this reason she asserts that the affective and embodied experience of playing a music game is a 'schizophonic performance' (15), a form of 'mending the schizophonic gap, stitching recorded musical sound and performing bodies back together' (151). In a similar but more explicit manner than in mobile music's vicarious re-embodiment of sound, the schizophonia discussed at the beginning of this chapter comes full circle in music games. These re-embodiment processes do not, however, eliminate musical virtual reality. While the schizophonia of recording technology foregrounded the virtualising possibilities of musical experience, it did not initiate them: I would argue that any musical experience, whether in performance or in listening, live or recorded, can induce musical virtual reality. Players of music games therefore participate in three coinciding realities: the game's virtual reality, the music's virtual reality, and their own physical and social reality.

In addition to the physical suture between gaming virtual reality and real life, playing a music game also has consequences for the experience of liveness and authenticity. Playing these games engenders a simultaneity of various kinds of performance: playing music on a plastic guitar; playing the game by pushing buttons; mimicking one's favourite artist; and – in a social setting – performing all these things for a social environment. David Roesner argues that the latter performance foregrounds the 'paratexts' of that music – its emotional and (sub)cultural connotations (2011, 283). Every *Guitar Hero* player will privilege a different aspect of this complex performativity. Some may excel in the musical skills, others will just want to win the game, yet others may want to focus on the social performance of musical paratexts. Although very different in nature, and although all are schizophonic, these performances should be considered 'live': they all happen here and now, are embodied, and can be visually as well as aurally perceived (Fritsch and Strötgen 2012, 58). Schizophonic performance obliterates the intuitive link between acoustic music and authenticity, replacing it with the twin concepts of authentic virtuality and virtual authenticity: a virtuality that is as real as the ordinary world, and an authenticity without tangible grounding. Liveness and authenticity still exist in a mediatised culture, but their properties change.[3]

Music's self-sustaining energetic flow is a virtual reality, but not one that matches traditional definitions – as Voegelin states, musical experience is actual *and* virtual (2014, 114), and, as I argued above, it is material *and* less material. It is separate from the rest of the world, but located in it and caused by physical agents. Rather than as virtual reality, it is more adequately defined as augmented reality, an inclusive concept that has gradually replaced the (practical and theoretical) binary division between real life and virtual reality. Originally used to identify visual and interactive additions to the everyday world – from head-mounted displays to mobile phone apps – augmented reality has extended to the sonic domain. Google's wearable augmented reality technology gadget Glass, for instance, is fitted with audio technology so that users can simultaneously listen to their favourite streaming station, receive notifications and hear environmental sound. But musical immersion did not need high-tech support for its virtualising capacities: the myriad examples discussed in this chapter illustrate that musical virtual reality is a highly immersive and affectively powerful form of augmented reality that pre-dates the invention of digital technology. The disembodying schizophonia of recording technology may have rendered this sonic augmentation somewhat uncanny, but even if an invisible hand starts the movement of the pendulum's spheres, it still moves, and its musical energy will still be passed on, and on, and on . . .

The exciting new research field of musical virtual reality has the potential to challenge existing musicological methodologies and to introduce new approaches. One way to start such disciplinary innovation would be to revisit Carolyn Abbate's 2004 article 'Music – Drastic or Gnostic?' In this influential piece Abbate called for a musicology that researches the performative and less material aspects of playing and listening to music, next to the more traditional hermeneutics of musical scores and historical facts. In her assessment of musicology's 'drastic' new routes, Abbate focused on the performativity of music, exploring the intangibility, ephemerality and even the ineffability of the musical event. Her appeal opened a number of new avenues. Most importantly she invited a critical engagement with music as an event, including such topics as immediacy, presence, liveness. As a result, phenomenological debates about music would receive a new impetus, including questions of dis/embodiment, sensual perception and the materiality of 'the musical work'.

The study of musical virtual reality would be an excellent point of departure for a renewed drastic musicology. Musical virtual reality is an event, a lived experience, not a work; its manifestation is affective, immediate and interactive; its phenomenology requires renewed debates about the embodiment and perception of music; it questions the existence of the traditional musical work. Musical virtual reality, moreover, also urges questions pertaining to musical epistemology that Abbate only hinted at.

If such diverse musical events as visiting a theme park, hearing a film soundtrack, listening to an MP3 player, playing a video game or simply turning on the radio can all engender an affective and corporeal virtual reality experience, then that notion requires far more theorisation than this one chapter can provide. One thing is certain: this new drastic musicology ought to be driven by its subject matter – the perpetual, im/material motion of musical energy.

For Further Study

Cheng, William. 2014. *Sound Play: Video Games and the Musical Imagination.* Oxford: Oxford University Press.

Kramer, Jonathan. 1988. *The Time of Music: New Meanings, New Temporalities, New Listening Strategies.* New York: Schirmer.

Miller, Kiri. 2012. *Playing Along: Digital Games, YouTube, and Virtual Performance.* Oxford: Oxford University Press.

Nancy, Jean-Luc. 2007. *Listening.* Translated by Charlotte Mandell. New York: Fordham University Press.

Van Elferen, Isabella. 2011. '¡Un Forastero! Issues of Virtuality and Diegesis in Videogame Music'. *Music and the Moving Image* 4 (2): 30–9.

Voegelin, Salomé. 2014. *Sonic Possible Worlds: Hearing the Continuum of Sound.* New York: Bloomsbury.

Notes

1 For a composer's discussion of video game music, see Stephen Baysted's Personal Take, this volume.

2 I would like to thank George Reid for his insightful work on literacy and affect in Chiptune culture.

3 This is in effect a one-sentence summary of the argument made by Paul Sanden in Chapter 7, this volume.

9 Digital Voices: Posthumanism and the Generation of Empathy

DAVID TRIPPETT

Assistance

When Microsoft unleashed Tay ('thinking about you') onto Twitter on 23 March 2016, the AI bot progressively adapted to its environment, mimicking users and their memes in its 96,000+ tweets before it was taken offline. Modelled on a twenty-four-year-old American woman, Tay's life-span was just over fifteen hours. While the experiment in 'conversational understanding' famously ended with the bot issuing a hailstorm of racist, pornographic and offensive profanities (which Microsoft officially put down to users targeting its method of learning by imitation), Tay also produced some weirdly unparroted responses. To the question: 'Is Ricky Gervais an atheist?' she answered: 'ricky gervais learned totalitarianism from adolf hitler, the inventor of atheism'.[1] No information was released publicly about the algorithmic route to such deductions, and it would seem the press verdict rang true: 'this is an example of artificial intelligence at its very worst – and it's only the beginning.'[2] The interface for her offensive utterances was silent, the flickering screen whose electronic text can stimulate verbal sounds only in the reader's mind. But an interface is inherently reciprocal: a gateway that opens up and allows passage to some place beyond (Galloway 2017, 30). Imagine if Tay could talk out loud. Imagine the sound of her voice, her persona-in-sound.

In an age of digital culture, where seemingly all aspects of the aesthetic experience of sound are soluble in information and communications technology, the relations between human and smart device remain both controversial and banal: controversial in objectifying aspects of human interactivity; banal in instilling a 'passion of the object' and its agency (Baudrillard 1988, 84). The rich history of debates on this topic takes a particular turn with the advent of digital processing. While many commentators have celebrated the affordances of digitised music and musicianship, others have sounded the alarm: 'composition, musical praxis and musical perception sit at a crossroads. The rapid development of the digital world together with their networking will not remain without consequence for musical creation' (Kriedler et al. 2010, 8). Another decade into the twenty-first century, and consequences are not hard to identify: the

co-dependence between new digital media and music is so extensive that it
is hard to exclude any areas of musical praxis from the affordances of new
technologies. From algorithmic playlists and virtual mixing desks to in-ear
speech processers and the infinite potential of (sensory) signal transduc-
tion, digital media enable and characterise virtually all access to and
production of mediated sound.

This chapter looks critically at the ramifications of digital technologies
that variously assist, enable or simulate musical praxis. A brief overview of
the steps ahead may be helpful at the outset. The first section sets up an
opposition between the idea of the digital *tool* that expands or
augments human agency, and the machinic automatism predicated on
the idea that reality is fundamentally number (dataism) – with matter as
its mere vehicle – and ticks along mechanically without the need for
human consciousness. This move gives rise to the idea that quantifiable,
mechanical automatism is also intrinsic to human agency, a strand of
posthuman thought on which the rest of the chapter turns. Accordingly,
the second section shows how algorithmic composition may be posed as
an expression of the posthuman, but this rapidly becomes untenable:
because of its reliance on human evaluation, algorithmic composition can
be better explained in terms of the tool/augmented humanity model rooted
in 'assistance' and its processes of collaboration and interaction. This
essentially reassuring conclusion comes under increasing pressure in the
final section, which focuses on the synthetic voices of digital assistants –
Siri, Alexa et al. – from online service providers. Here the generation of
empathy appears to satisfy practical requirements (e.g. care for the elderly
or increasing the desire to buy products) but, in fact, in the context of
conversation in particular and interaction in general, it can pose problem-
atical issues of a surrogate 'conscience'. Accommodating this within a
humanistic model is still possible, but a closing case study of Tod
Machover's futurist opera, *Death and the Powers* (2010), raises the prospect of what might be called a 'dark ontology' of the digital that can't
easily be shrugged off.

Whether explicitly or not, 'assisting' technologies necessarily establish a
relational dynamic with users. In a sense, music technology in its machinic
guise has always aided or assisted people at work, whether figured as
mechanical device or software. For Lewis Mumford, writing in 1934, the
machine's justification lay in eliminating human slavery or its modern
equivalent, the need for people to carry out menial tasks. Or indeed, any
work at all: 'the ritual of leisure will replace the ritual of work,' he
predicted, 'and work itself will become a kind of game' (Mumford 2010,
279). On the one hand, music notation software undoubtedly reduces the

labour of writing out or otherwise preparing individual parts, to cite an immediate example, and digital sound editing renders the manual cutting and splicing of magnetic tape a comfortable metaphor. But on the other hand, Mumford's prediction can sound naïvely optimistic – perhaps only possible amid the heyday of Fordism and workplace automation – when faced with the cognitive operations of skilful, creative activities such as composition and performance. To regard such operations as susceptible to machinic 'take-over' is to injure our sense of what is special to traditional music-making. Here, Mumford's distinction between *machine* and *tool* becomes helpful:

> [T]he tool lends itself to manipulation, the machine to automatic action . . . The difference . . . lies primarily in the degree of automatism they have reached: the skilled tool-user becomes more accurate and more automatic, in short, more mechanical, as his originally voluntary motions settle down into reflexes, and on the other hand, even in the most completely automatic machine, there must intervene somewhere, at the beginning and the end of the process . . . the conscious participation of a human agent. (Mumford 2010, 10)

In other words there is a continuum between agency and automation in the use of tools to enhance 'human' creativity. As we shall see, this principle applies to the digital manipulation of sound as much as the Model T assembly line.

Moving into the specific discourse of sound technology, it is not uncommon to speak of digital 'tools'. Digital recorders are essential tools for field recordists just as the digital camera is a 'generic tool' for students of visual culture (King et al. 2016, 141). Plug-ins for audio editing are tools that extend an editor's capabilities just as robust direct drive turntables permit the scratching and backspinning necessary for turntablists to turn a record player into a musical instrument. All imply a dependent relation between user and tool. In these examples, a 'tool' appears as a kind of neutral enabler, a means to an end, seemingly more than mere equipment yet less than prosthesis (where 'prosthesis' entails an addition or extension 'of ourselves' in both physical and virtual contexts). But when data, the basic substance of communication itself, become the enabler of activity, any manipulation of such a tool becomes reflexive and correspondingly powerful as an agent that determines outcomes. 'Data itself is a tool', writes the former director of Google Ideas and former CEO of Google, 'and in places where unreliable statistics about health, education, economics, and the population's needs have stalled growth and development, the chance to gather data effectively is a game-changer' (Schmidt and Cohen 2013, 15). Ostensibly sound data can't easily be utilised in this way because they do not represent other things; they simply are what they are, though they can readily be illustrative of prior content, such as the sonification of medical imaging (when converting the visual data of a brain scan into sound, for example). So we might say that sound data relate to digital 'tools' as numbers relate to mathematical formulae: their manipulation is deter-mined by the shape and function of the technological means available to the manipulator more than by notions of creative intent. In other words, while we are familiar with tools that enhance our own agency, as tools become increasingly information-driven they begin to take on attributes of agency in their own right.

One practical outcome of the digital organisation of sound through binary code is its enhanced potential for manipulation (recall this is Mumford's principal criterion for identifying 'tools'), both manually by people coding and by algorithm:

> once coded numerically, the input data in a digital media production can immediately be subjected to the mathematical processes of addition, subtraction, multiplication and division through algorithms contained within software. (Lister et al. 2009, 18)

Of course, manipulation of sound through software and physical manipu-lation of, say, a piano keyboard are not of the same order. One deals in layers of matterless signs, the other in tactile resonance. Yet the very point of difference – binary code – forms the tell-tale thread for theorists such as Lev Manovich to illustrate how the histories of computing and audio-visual media are entwined. The individual static photograms of the cine-matograph store audio-visual data, just as do the 1s and 0s of an MP3 file, itself a product of computing: 'this is why the Universal Turing Machine [the first stored-programme computer] looks like a film projector' (Manovich 2001, 24). Both store data according to the split-second pauses of an on/off regularity; one on celluloid, the other electronically. As one commentator put it, for Manovich 'the flicker of film was already a digital flicker' (Galloway 2017, 4).

This helps explain why, for Manovich, numerical coding constitutes 'the new universal intermediary' that bridges senses and audio-visual media, whether via voltage fluctuation and the pixels of LCD displays or the travelling waves of oscillating pressure that we experience as sound (Manovich 2013, 153). In this view digital media are constituted by the data flows in which all input is converted into numbers. For music historians, then, digital media arguably have a genetic relation to early Greek understandings of music: for the Greeks musical sound points to a background numerical order, whereas with digital media an underlying numerical order gives rise to musical sound (this is the dominant model, but both processes are ultimately reversible). In this sense, Pythagoras's interpretation of music as sounding number begins the circle that digital audio closes, for – materially speaking – digital audio is nothing but its binary data (quantities of sound coded into a cultural form) while Pythagoreans believed sound was essentially the representation of a numerical natural order, a cosmic worldview ensounded through the ratios of resonating intervals. Both constitute processes of abstraction into the symbolic realm of mathematics, but with opposite directions of travel: from sound to number; from bits to sound.

The idea of 'dataism' underpinning this view is broader than musical discourse, of course, and is worth explaining briefly.[3] It interprets the world as consisting of data flows, and values any technology – or entity more broadly – according to its contribution to data-processing. Some futurists have interpreted this as offering the promise of an emerging universal language, a technological tower of Babel to unify all disciplines: 'According to Dataism, *King Lear* and the flu virus are just two patterns of dataflow that can be analysed using the same basic concepts and tools', writes Yuval Harari briskly (2016, 367–8). Hence the simplifying, optimistic prognosis that follows: 'This idea … gives all scientists a common language, builds bridges over academic rifts … Musicologists, political scientists and cell biologists can finally understand each other.' Is interdisciplinarity to become a tautology? I suspect that this model of binary code's infinite transferability would be hard to replicate in units of data equally comprehensible to all academic disciplines.

How exactly do digital musical tools enter this story of digital morphology? Course reading lists and university library holdings offer empirical evidence that the aural dimension of data has been disproportionately subordinated to the visual dimension within media studies and the philosophy of technology. One possible reason is that a progressive dematerialisation of the image was accompanied by a radical materialisation of sound prior to digital recording. As Peter Weibel notes, image capture proceeded from the daguerreotype, which freed the artist's hands, to telegraphy, electronic scanning and film – all of which worked through time – and on to video: 'the basic conditions for electronic image production and transfer' were established through a combination of the electron, magnetic recording and cathode-ray tubes, and thereafter 'matterless signs' – enabled by integrated circuits, transistors and silicon chips – came to drive a 'post-industrial telematics culture' (Weibel 1996, 338–9). Each stage in this historical model for image production and transmission offers a further abstraction from real-world visual experience. Sound recording went in the opposite direction. After centuries of music notation based on abstract, legible signs, successive technologies objectified the physical matter of sound vibration, writing the impression of sound waves onto smoke-blackened paper, into wax, shellac, acetate and then vinyl discs, and finally reconfiguring it as forces within a magnetic field. Such writing of sound was no longer symbolic but material. This radical process of materialisation only ended around 1980 with digital sound recording, which makes the abstraction of sound data 150 years younger than that of visual data.

Regardless of their relative youth, digital musical technologies have raised searching questions about human relations to music. We might helpfully consider these in light of the distinction between tools and machines discussed above. 'Digital technologies can be used as musical tools', Andrew Brown concludes straightforwardly. 'Just as an audio ampli-fier can make music louder, a music technology can be an amplifier of one's musicianship, enhancing musical skills and increasing musical intelligence' (2015, 6). But while we are comfortable with the idea of digital technology assisting us (remember the springy paperclip in MS Word?), cognitive enhancement is of a different order because it concerns interior thought, whose secrecy and non-transferability had been regarded as inviolable under the tenets of a liberal humanism. That status changes the moment human ability, skill and intelligence are 'amplified' by digital technology.

This reflects larger discourses on artificial intelligence (AI). A common question for students of AI and prosthesis goes as follows: if a blind man walks with a cane, is the cane part of the man? Ostensibly, the cane is a tool, separate to the man. Conceived as a single unit, however, the man + cane function is understood as a self-correcting process where the cane becomes a sensory extension under his control (hence a closed system with feedback loop, cybernetically speaking). The philosophical argument for extending the mind by expanding the domain of cognitive *control* was first advanced by Andy Clark and David Chalmers:

> If … a part of the world functions as a process which, were it done in the head, we would have no hesitation in recognizing as part of the cognitive process, then that part of the world *is* part of the cognitive process. (Clark and Chalmers 1998, 8)

This has implications for generative software, including certain models of algorithmic composition; it gave rise to the concept of distributed cogni-tion wherein human agency and thought are 'enmeshed within larger networks that extend beyond the desktop computer into the environment' (Hayles 2012, 3).

Keyboard players and other instrumentalists have long been familiar with the notion that a resonating instrument comes to feel as an extension of the body (de Souza 2017; Le Guin 2006); for unamplified singers, the body *is* the instrument, collapsing any distinction between instrumentality and self. The same relation obtains for scholars instantly accessing vast data networks via the computer keyboard, with the difference that while a musical instrument is physically finite, online networks grow exponentially, supported by ever-larger servers. When living in a small town, Hayles explains, the effects of this hand–keyboard compound only become apparent when we lose the networked extensions we take for granted: 'when my computer goes down or my Internet connection fails, I feel lost, disorientated, unable to work – in fact, I feel as if my hands have been amputated'. Put another way, the embedding of computational media into the environment is having 'significant neurological consequences' (Hayles 2012, 2, 11). The physical breach – components extending and rearticulating our 'selves' in McLuhanesque ways – marks a threshold in self-perception and the use of tools. It is also the linchpin around which posthuman discourse has come to structure a future-orientated understanding of human relations to digital technology. In most encounters with data, then, what might be seen as an abstraction to number is better seen as an expansion or augmentation of the human body-in-action.

Mimesis: Creating with Algorithms

Having touched on 'prosthetic' additions to the body and the implied tension between literal limbs and metaphorical uses of the concept (Sobchack 2006), it might be useful here to clarify three distinct terms that pertain to human-technology relations. In brief:

Transhumanism (H+): a futurist-orientated intellectual and cultural impulse that believes in enhancing the human condition through technology in all its forms. The result is an iteration of *homo sapiens* enhanced or augmented, but still fundamentally human. A central premise of transhumanism is that biological evolution will eventually be overtaken by advances in genetic, wearable and implantable technologies that artificially expedite the evolutionary process (More 2013, 3–8).

Posthuman: the condition attained after stages of technological enhancement of the human condition render the subject no longer normatively 'human'. In its more radical iterations, this condition does away with the biological body altogether, where information patterns uploaded to a fantastical supercomputer suffice to constitute a posthuman identity. In an extreme form of noetics, such existence becomes all mind, more powerful than present minds, employing 'different cognitive architectures or includ[ing] new sensory modalities' (Bostrom 2009, 347).

Posthumanism: a discursive web of philosophical positions defined against, and seeking to supplant, the autonomous liberal human subject and its concomitant anthropocentric bias, excessive valuation of human achievements, and preoccupation with humanity's supposed differences from (and superiority to) the rest of animate life. This asserts no definite break between sentient and non-sentient matter in the relational fields of an environment because matter is no longer conceived as passive or inert, but capable of 'self-transformation, self-organization, and directedness' (Coole and Frost 2010, 10). Posthumanist attitudes anticipate an increasing incorporation of artificial technologies into the body not primarily as enhancement of the human condition (as in transhumanism), but as its anticipated dissolution: this is seen as part of a more fundamental dissolution of literal boundaries between subject and object, body and environment, and a corresponding recalibration of our sense of self-identity within a world of objects. The result is an identity defined more by its controllable architecture rather than its cultural history.

The first two terms denote subject positions in relation to technological objects, the third an attitude that encompasses these as part of a broader critique of the humanities. All intersect with the idea of computer 'assistance' when that assistance exceeds simple tasks such as calculating quotients or formatting scores ('task intelligence'). But when a device's intelligent behaviour appears to be purposive, it is the posthuman that is most openly implicated.

In order to see these categories in action, consider algorithmic composition, perhaps the most tangible instance of human utilisation of music's mathematical undergirding. Within the contemporary scene of melodic composition, such tools as Dirk-Jan Povel's Melody Generator (Povel 2010) or Dmitri Kartofelev and Jüri Engelbrecht's 'structured spontaneity'[4] use Markov chains or fractal geometry to create melodies based on restrictive programming of overtone properties and predefined stylistic parameters. Each melodic pitch and rhythm is calculated from a mapping of the immediately preceding pitches and rhythms in a theoretically endless linear operation. This approach to melodic data mirrors statistical analysis of the same (e.g. how many sixteen-bar melodies from 1790 have forty-eight notes?), and here the role of cognition recedes, including – crucially – the responsibility to assess the resulting music. In substituting for, and calculating faster than, human cognition this approach embodies a posthuman perspective, and as such it is fundamentally different from the transhumanist perspective embodied in the established canon of algorithmically composed music that fulfils the criteria of originality and aesthetic appeal. This ranges from Charles Dodge and Clarence Barlow to Herbert Brün, G. M. König, and Iannis Xenakis, whose *Gendy3* (1991) typifies the composer's lifelong pursuit of 'automated art': art that draws on the processing power of a computer to extrapolate the implications of artistic thought, thereby still 'reserving for the human the role of creative decision making', and accordingly posing challenges for any musicological analysis that seeks to 'reconstruct the laboratory conditions of the algorithmic creation process' (Hoffmann 2010, 121, 129).

While machines do have feedback loops, the value of these is a matter of dispute. Could they ever equate to a kind of music criticism? As Christopher Ariza notes, music generation as a closed cybernetic circuit cannot be regarded as composition proper, for it amounts to a game of data manipulation, whose results are barely evaluated by a machine and become meaningless when presented to human listeners who try to distinguish machine melody from human melody: 'use of the [Turing test] in the evaluation of generative music systems is superfluous and potentially misleading; its evocation is an appeal to a measure of some form of artificial thought, yet, in the context of music, it provides no more than a listener survey' (Ariza 2009, 49). In such a view, human and machine listening remain radically asymmetrical.

Wrapped up in the irreducibly human perceptual character of music assessment is the broader issue of consciousness, one strand of which is whether the brain thinks and feels only, or also calculates. Would a computer engaging in a process of generating music experience release on the final downbeat, exhilaration at the rhythmic vigour, or a sense of progressive harmonic tension and release? How would we know? Concomitantly, at what point would a court need to recognise the computer as owner of an intellectual property arising from a musical sensibility, that is, as an autonomous creator?

This debate has played out in contexts far beyond digital music, of course. A summary of perspectives – alluding to everything from a Turing test to David Chalmers's 'psychophysical principles' (1995) and 'information that has lost its body' (Hayles 1999) – is given in the Socratic trialogue from Tom Stoppard's 2014 play *The Hard Problem* (whose title borrows Chalmers's own term for scrutinising consciousness). Here, postdocs at a prestigious institute for brain science argue over the nature of consciousness within a calculating machine:

AMAL: Sure, but the brain is a machine, a biological machine, and it thinks. It
         happens to be made of living cells but it would make no difference if the
         machine was made of electronic gates and circuits, or paperclips and
         rubber bands for that matter. It just has to be able to compute.

       ...

LEO: What [a computer is] doing is a lot of binary operations following the rules of its programming.

AMAL: So is a brain.

LEO: But can a computer do what a brain can do?

AMAL: Are you kidding? – A brain doesn't come close!

       ...

HILARY: It's not deep. If that's thinking. An adding machine on speed. A two-way switch with a memory. Why *wouldn't* it play chess? But when it's me to move, is the computer *thoughtful* or is it sitting there like a toaster? It's sitting there like a toaster.

LEO: So, what would be your idea of deep?

HILARY: A computer that minds losing.

(Stoppard 2015, 22–3)

In a gendered division, the project leader, Leo, mediates between Amal's futurist agenda and Hilary's empathy and subsequent concession that it would be impossible to tell whether a computer minds losing or not. Unlike Socratic methods, however, there is no resolution free from contradiction, which reinforces the conundrum: the unknowability of a computer's aesthetic judgment upon experiencing its own creation.

Deterministic algorithms will always produce the same output from a given input. For creative composition in any genre this intrinsic limitation is undesirable in isolation, even as computation can explore configurations of pitch and rhythm unavailable to humans alone. 'A composer who knows exactly what he wants, wants only what he knows – and that is one way or another too little' explains Helmut Lachenmann (Lachenmann and Ryan 1999, 24). Not all algorithmic approaches to music generation work in a directly automatic way, of course, and there are a range of interactive processes that do not require real-time human input (Nierhaus 2009 offers a helpful overview). To remain with melody generation a moment longer, just as the nineteenth-century critic Eduard Kulke – inspired by Darwin and Lamark – believed melodies were subject to evolutionary principles, and proposed genealogies of melodic transformations as part of a collective cultural memory (Kulke 1884), so Francesco Vico's computer system Iamus (2010) uses a 'genetic algorithm' that mimics the process of natural selection. It generates random musical fragments, mutates them and determines whether they conform to pre-defined rules (genre-specific, instrument-specific, stylistic). By this process, all fragments are incrementally refined into rule-adhering music. In the domain of rhythm, Eduardo Miranda's Evolve likewise uses the interaction between multiple algorithmic generators to compose repertories of rhythms: 'the agents were programmed to create and play rhythmic sequences, listen to each other's sequences and perform operations on those sequences, according to an algorithm' (Miranda 2012, 225).

Under conditions of improvisation, by contrast, such a process could not be entirely automated, of course, for human input is needed in real time. Here the distinction between the roles of computational creativity and machine assistance is significant. While evaluation criteria cannot be clearly stated in a programming language, Interactive Evolutionary Computation allows for interaction between the algorithm and human participants, suggesting that what is often put forward as computational creativity is in reality better understood as augmented human creativity according to the tool model given above, or as collaborative interaction. One example is John Biles's jazz melody generator GenJam, described as 'a genetic algorithm-based model of a novice jazz musician learning to improvise', in which a human mentor gives real-time feedback which is then absorbed by the programme to improve the future generation of melodic patterns, i.e. in a closed-loop feedback function (Biles 2007, 137). This offers a model of collaboration between human and computer, where the dominant operator is the computer: the digital element relies on seemingly unprogrammable human decisions, making it *human*-aided rather than *computer*-aided composition. By the same token, George Lewis's Voyager software – a 'nonhierarchical, interactive musical environment that privileges improvisation' – offers an instance of man–machine collaboration on more equal terms. The programme's analysis in real time of a human improviser both guides its own independent behaviour arising from pre-defined algorithmic values, and generates 'complex responses' to the human musician's playing. '*Voyager* is not asking whether machines exhibit personality or identity,' Lewis remarks, 'but how personalities and identities become articulated through sonic behavior' (2000, 38). Such software, defined by interactivity and response, is positioned as a tool for exploring the creation of values, our own creativity and intelligence as well as 'musicality itself'. It is as much an epistemological tool as a compositional agent.

Semiosis: Sounds like Human

Sound tools engage the discourse on digital assistance perhaps most directly through simulations of the human voice, aka speech synthesis. This personalises the interaction with a computer intelligence. Synthetic voices without a body instinctively conjure up a hybrid persona, a virtual personality, touching on a network of signs that distinguish human from non-human, a cultural and biological distinction that has come under pressure in recent years (Clark 2004; Bennett 2010; Bostrom 2014). While it is not hard aurally to distinguish human voices from robotic alternatives, the current reliance on the data networks of female-sounding digital assistants – Siri, Alexa, DeepMind, etc. – verbally responding to our commands offers a sonic analogue to Hayles's hands that feel ever more part of the computer she controls, or composers who make use of borrowed processing power to uncover the ramifications of a melodic cell, a rhythmic pattern or a stochastic principle.

From the perspective of linguistics, it was the advent of phonology in the early nineteenth century, with its differential oppositions, that allowed for a computational approach to speech sounds in the twentieth. Chains of phonemes, those 'senseless atoms that, in combination, make sense', as Mladen Dolar put it, could now be organised by the oppositional logic of binary code:

> All the sounds of a language could [now] be described in a purely logical way; they could be placed into a logical table based simply on the presence of absence of minimal distinctive features, ruled entirely by one elementary key, *the binary code*. In this way, most of the oppositions of traditional phonetics could eventually be reproduced (voiced/voiceless, nasal/oral, compact/diffuse, grave/acute, labial/dental, and so on), but all those were now re-created as functions of logical oppositions, the conceptual deduction of the empirical, not as an empirical description of sounds found.   (Dolar 2006, 19)

In like fashion, digital algorithmic composition can be thought of as a cultural technique in Bernhard Siegert's terms of a self-referential symbolic practice in between object and sign, a practice whose 'operative chains . . . precede the media concepts they generate' (Siegert 2015, 11). Music-making exists without (and before) explicit music theory, and likewise music-calculating exists before music-computing: 'people wrote long before they conceptualized writing or alphabets . . . Counting, too, is older than the notion of numbers' (Macho 2003, 179; cf. Siegert 2015, 11). In contrast, the simulation of personal voices fits into a sub-category of Anglo-American posthumanism, namely, representations of human identity arising from chains of operations that produce something that appears to be real, but is in fact only its semblance. An example would be that when absorbed in a crime drama you don't notice the TV as a medium unless the signal malfunctions. Media like to conceal themselves, in other words, which, for digitally synthesised voices, means creating the auditory semblance of an entity that is actually talking to you.

The formulaic sentences of commercial chatbots quickly betray the limited repertory of a non-adaptive mind. Once digital tools assume a persona, by listening to speech commands and uttering informed (if not 'thoughtful') responses, they become virtual 'assistants' in a more than metaphorical sense. Such technologies, dating back to IBM's Shoebox in 1961, are now commonplace, arising from leading commercially funded research and development budgets at Apple (Siri), Amazon (Alexa), Microsoft (Cortana) and Google (DeepMind), each vying for market dominance. But even while AI offers different (computational or information sourcing) capacities to human cognition, developers' ambitions point directly towards the goal of sounding like humans because the creation of empathy sits at the heart of the project of an artificial simulacrum: 'I truly believe that for AI to be useful in our daily lives, it has to be something you can connect with. Conversation is the next step, to be more human-like', explains Rohit Prasad, Amazon's chief scientist for Alexa. 'We could cross the 10-minute barrier now, but 20 minutes is extremely hard. This will be a long journey.' In fact, the university-based 'Alexa Prize' ($2.5 million), inaugurated in 2017, is stimulating research in precisely this field; users utter the command: 'Alexa, let's chat' to sample one of the current loquacious 'socialbots' under development. 'But there's also dynamics here where you want the AI itself to come back and trigger some conversational topics with you', Prasad explains. 'That it can tell you "Hey I can talk about … Did you hear about this event?" for instance.'[5] Information-based responses seem set to continue, in other words, rather than interaction resembling conversation proper, 'the great paramount purpose of social meetings' as Thomas de Quincey (1863, 151) famously put it.

Since these devices don't have a freely active learning function like Microsoft's Tay, their automatic 'jokes' only elicit groans: 'Want to hear a dirty joke?' asks Alexa. 'A boy fell in some mud. How about a clean joke? He had a shower.'[6] For now, then, empathy generation appears most scrutable through the code its programmers use to modulate vocal intonation and timing: the sounding voice. By necessity this is declarative, specifying whispers, bleeped-out expletives, speech delivery and even substitute words in crudely literal ways. To code a whispered sweet nothing in Amazon's Speech Synthesis Markup Language (SSML), it's <amazon: effect name="whispered">; to programme an expletive bleeped out, it's <say-as interpret-as="expletive">; the 'prosody' setting meanwhile permits alternations of tempo ('fast'/'slow') and pitch ('low'/'medium'/'high') to resemble an expressive mind behind the synthetic phonemes. And programmers have been swift to exploit the capacity for irony. Freia Lisa Lobo's split-personality quip is a case in point: "[blank female voice] Right now in New York it is 70 degrees. [*Pause.* Whispering] I see dead people'.[7]

Colloquialisms or 'speechcons' have been available since February 2017, crudely generating empathy with interjections like *cheerio*, *argh*, *d'oh*, as well as *booyah* and *bazinga*, to humanise the monotone obedience of the prim robo-voice. By prefacing these utterances with a 'say-as' tag, the software understands they are to be emphasised in a further step towards the acoustic semblance of a speaking personality and an oxygenated, breathing body. The extent to which we are willing to go beyond a reality principle in which only humans can be speaking personas depends on our willingness to refract ourselves within another logic. Superficially, this is a logic of commerce: 'What do people want from a virtual assistant?' asks Liz Stinson in a critique of such innovations' hidden commercial drivers:

> Amazon's efforts to make Alexa sound as human as possible suggest that users expect their artificially intelligent sidekicks to do more than turn on their lights or provide a weather forecast. They want these devices to understand them. Connect with them. Maybe even – don't laugh – date them … Amazon wants to sell you things … and a more emotive assistant could be leveraged to that end … [I]t stands to reason that an AI more capable of expressing emotions would also be more capable of analyzing – and manipulating – your own. Creepy, yes, but also promising … Amazon might use Alexa's expressiveness to sell you stuff, but social robots could use the same technology to deliver, say, better care to the elderly.[8]

At another level there is a logic of innovation. Speech synthesis typically functions by sampling large amounts of recorded speech fragments from one individual so words can be reassembled into an utterance appropriate to the message being conveyed. Singing has proved equally susceptible to this kind of synthetic generation. Yamaha's Vocaloid software (2000–), fronted by teenage avatars such as Hatsune Miku and Megurine Luka, allows users to enter melodies and lyrics that are then 'sung' by a voice generated from a bank of samples. Recent commentators have sought to hear such sounds on their own terms as 'a real synthetized voice' rather than a stand-in for an actual human voice, an authenticating gesture that locates the software itself at 'the intersection between technology and creative production' (Jackson and Dines 2016, 108). While these remain rooted in human sounds, cobbled together by algorithm, synthetic voices emanate more fundamentally from the imitation of a human voice generated from raw waveforms. At present, the only example is Google's WaveNet wherein – like Markov chain melodies – a predictive distribution for each audio sample is conditioned on all previous ones, rising to at least 16,000 samples per second, all in pursuit of 'subjective naturalness'. This artificial approach to natural voices 'directly model[s] the raw waveform of the audio signal, one sample at a time' – we learn – 'As well as yielding more natural-sounding speech, using raw waveforms means that WaveNet can model any kind of audio, including music.'[9] Six five-second samples of intriguing, Skryabin-like piano music were available online at the time of writing; their brevity suggests style imitation via sampled recordings is achievable through automatic splicing, but perhaps little else as yet.

Why does it matter how human-like these machinic voices can sound? One answer concerns the reflexive identity such sound technologies afford us, where digital voices become a metonym for human–device relations more broadly. Sifting data on the Internet has allowed search engines to accrue sufficient algorithmic sophistication for users to treat Google's search box as pilgrims once treated the high priestess Pythia, the fabled oracle of Apollo's Temple at Delphi: a venue for the self's unknowability, an intelligence advising individuals with seemingly better insight into them than they themselves possess. Rather than seeking prophesy, twenty-first-century users seek moral as well as informational guidance. In recent years popular questions to Google reported in the *Guardian* newspaper range from the personal (am I normal / why don't you love me / why don't people like me / am I a bad mother / why don't I enjoy life) to the fantastical (why don't unicorns exist) and the wryly speculative (are blond men evil).[10]

One reading of this practice is that digital search has encroached on the role of conscience, that 'inner voice', if only to cross-reference ours with those of others. Such a voice has at least four attributes: it is an inner guide and principle, it is acousmatic and not acoustically natural, it answers questions not immediately within the reach of our conscious reason, and – in most cases – it responds when consulted. It takes a moment to accept that all four of these attributes can be ascribed to the voices of the digitally synthesised AI bots above. Likewise, instantaneously cross-referencing such online 'voices' through search engines mimics the process of Google's speech synthesis at 16,000 samples per second. Yet within a humanist tradition, *inner* voice is nothing less than 'the link with God', an ethical force genetically related to the Socratic voice, the 'voice of the daemon that accompanies Socrates throughout his life' (Dolar 2006, 83, 86). Consider the case of Jean-Jacques Rousseau, for whom an interior voice of conscience is a *moral* voice, and as such the marker of a common humanity:

> Conscience! Conscience! Divine instinct, immortal and celestial voice; firm guide of an ignorant and limited being, but one which is also intelligent and free; the infallible judge of good and evil, it is you that make man similar to God ... without you I do not sense anything in myself which would elevate me above the beasts, just the sad privilege to stray from error to error with the help of an intelligence without a rule and a reason without a principle.   (Rousseau 1969, 600–1)

This vaunted status for inner self-reflection perhaps explains why, historically, simulating a human voice has been a goal of technologists ever since the sound of the voice was linked to the soul in its morphological likeness to breath (the Stoic's *pneuma*). La Mettrie's excited prediction in 1748 that 'a speaking machine … can no longer be considered impossible, particularly at the hands of [Jacques de Vaucanson], the new Prometheus' seemed at the time a final test of his over-arching proposition that people are inherently mechanical, but key to this reading is the significance ascribed to breath and his argument that humans have no soul as such (Mettrie 1996, 34). That is, he wasn't really subsuming the human within the mechanical, but vice versa.

Without necessarily buying into la Mettrie's materialism, recent digital simulations of voices have elicited both musical and data-driven responses. Within the context of popular musics, distortions of speech have formed a trope of the 'machinic voice'. This reverses the machine mimicry of human speech given above, for it distorts human sounds to mimic the cultural persona of the robot. A leading example is the vocoder (a signal-processing algorithm, formerly a military technology to mask speech communications during the Second World War (Tompkins 2011)); this is recurrent in pop recordings, from Neil Young ('Transformer Man', 1982) to Kanye West ('Love Lockdown', 2008), and can even be seen in blockbuster films, e.g. the glittery silver Guy Diamond in Disney's *Trolls* (2016), spoken by Kunal Nayyar entirely through vocoder distortions. Back in 2003, Joseph Auner speculated on how vocoder and computer simulations of voices play on the associations of mechanical and organic sounds in songs by Radiohead and Moby. Far from deconstructing the human, these present songs as 'a sort of cyborg system that attempts to splice the human and technological thus … illuminat[ing] its peculiar expressive character'. In other words, 'human' remains the dominant sign, against which 'cyborg' tensions and is defined. The ensuing anxiety of identity is embedded in the manipulation of vocal signifiers within a continuum of human and synthetic computer sounds. For Auner, the resulting cyborg persona 'becomes a way of reconstructing expression', which is to say, both a topos of pop culture and a referential language (Auner 2003, 110–11).

Within an art music tradition, Harrison Birtwistle's opera *The Mask of Orpheus* (1986) pioneered the use of an electronic voice for Apollo, 'speaking' in an invented language, whose otherworldly utterances were coded by Barry Anderson at IRCAM to sound god-like. By contrast, composer Peter Ablinger's 'Deus Cantando (God, Singing)' (2009) is only one of the most recent spectral analyses of recorded speech that forms the basis of his 'speaking piano', a computer-controlled player piano that replicates on the instrument's eighty-eight keys the decomposed sound spectrum of recorded human speech:

> Using . . . 16 units per second (about the limit of the player piano), the original [sound] source approaches the border of recognition within the reproduction. With practice listening[,] the player piano can even perform structures possible for a listener to transpose into/understand as spoken sentences.[11]

That is, you can 'hear' the piano pronounce words only when you simultaneously see its words or know them in advance. This accommodation of digital sound file and keyboard mechanism has been enlisted to present analogue voices of the dead – Schoenberg, Brecht – 'speaking' in the present, and, to that end, replicates one of the initial functions of Edison's crank-driven phonograph, but remediated through spectral recomposition of the source: a form of near-human expression in which the digital (electricity) accommodates the mechanical.

In an experiential sense, such sounds perform a kind of time travel: the piano's hammers 'speak' Schoenberg's words mechanically in the present. And here it is worth reminding ourselves that mechanical work – from instrument building to repetition in the practice room – is predicated on a principle of fragmentation whereby larger tasks are divided up into smaller tasks that can be performed in linear sequence. As David Hulme first noted, however, there is no principle of causality in a mechanical sequence; movement through the sequence generates change without oversight of how operations follow one another. It was this blindness within mechanisms that led McLuhan to accord electricity the crown of all industrial and post-industrial inventions, for 'it ended sequence by making things instant' (like Brecht and Schoenberg's spectrally recomposed voices in the here and now). Hence his cryptic assertion that the electric light 'is pure information' (McLuhan 1964, 8, 12). If the electric grid underpinned McLuhan's 'global village' of instant communications, it also models the modern network, so, beyond the supply of power, electricity itself remains regulative of an aesthetics of digital media: 'deeply shaping of the form and content of the medium itself' (Dewdney and Ride 2006, 79). Record companies regularly take advantage of this time-travelling instantaneity in digital editing by reusing the recordings of Pavarotti, Sinatra, Nat King Cole, Tupac Shakur and others and ventriloquising new duets or new backing after death, in a temporal short-circuit that appears to make these voices sing anew. By comparison with the macro-structure of the Internet, Ablinger's speaking piano is philosophically significant, in part, because of its equal reliance on data networking *and* old-fashioned mechanical keys, hammers and physical resonance. From this arises a paradox: just as the concept of the posthuman is ultimately embedded in and defined against the human, so the virtual is here embedded in the material.

Case Study: *Death and the Powers* (2011)

But this apparently comfortable accommodation between the human and the posthuman turns out to be unsustainable in the end, a point aptly demonstrated by a recent piece of music theatre. Beyond the semiosis of robotic voices, we now turn to what might be called a 'theatrical' semiosis of human–digital music relations. Tod Machover and Robert Pinsky's *Death and the Powers: A Robot Pageant* is a one-act opera 'conceived and written specifically for the incorporation of new technologies . . . that re-envision human presence onstage', explains Peter Torpey, a student designer of its multimedia systems (Torpey 2012, 110). It stages the tensions and imaginative possibilities of a posthuman discourse vis-à-vis digitised music, reflecting on mortality as alibi to technological necessity. As a narrative, it depicts a critical juncture in the vision of our postbiological future first put forward by Hans Moravec: the downloading of our consciousness into an all-powerful computer system, and the discarding of our original, mortal body, leading to the extinction of the human race (Moravec 1988, 112). Tellingly, the protagonist becomes nothing but a digitised, acousmatic voice, though we are to understand that he retains the legal, fiscal and moral authority he held as a bodied human. The opera emerged via MIT media lab's 'opera of the future' project in 2010, and has been performed in Monaco, Boston and Chicago to date.

First, a brief plot summary. The narrative is told from the distant future by robots who enact the 'pageant' in order to try to understand what biological death is, and how the human race died out. At the outset, four robots debate the mystery like latter-day paleontologists:

> What is this 'Death' – Is it a form of waste? / . . . I cannot understand. / If the information of one unit might be lost / it is backed up by any other unit at hand. Death – Is it an excessive cost? . . . Is it the data rearranged, / As in an error, in a dream? . . . A dream of something lost / That was meant to be saved?   (ll. 8–32)

The robots then transform themselves into the 'human' characters on stage, and the action commences: Simon Powers, an aged, wealthy, wheelchair-bound inventor and magnate, is planning his death as a transmutation of himself into the 'System'. He explains his philosophy of embodiment to worried relatives by emphasising that '[i]t's the vibration, / The movement, that matters! / . . . It's never matter that matters. Particles, molecules, cells, fingers, eyes, nerves / Are only places for the system / Of meaningful vibration' (ll.122–47). Simon's third wife (Evvy) and daughter (Miranda) are sceptical ('But how can you be yourself / Without a body?' ll. 212–13), but receive only cryptic answers in the form of poetic quotation.[12] In the second scene, Simon's body disappears as he utters an aphoristic existential valediction: 'remember: / Whatever I did / I *did* that and /

I am the same' (ll. 279–81). While waiting for Simon to emerge from the System, his adopted son and protégé, Nicholas, reflects on his own prosthetic enhancements and how he helped his father to live inside the system. Simon soon emerges from a portrait of his younger self (initially as a hologram, later as pure voice), moves around mechanically, and eventually asserts his new identity:

> What is my name? / A name is a machine. / A name is a made-up thing / That proposes someone is real. / My name is a machine for designation – That's what any name is. / My name is Simon Walter Powers, / It proposes I am alive.   (ll. 347–55)

The location of his voice shifts within the scene (using 140 speakers and spatial diffusion – Wave Field Synthesis – to pinpoint sound on stage), between a portrait, a mechanical bird perched on set, and elsewhere in the room. His relatives debate whether this disembodied entity is still 'Simon'. Evvy later seeks intimate contact (and thereafter is reduced to wordless utterances), and the family is visited by a delegation from the 'United Way, / the Administration / And the United Nations' (ll. 476–8), who seek help to combat crises of world famine, biological weapons, child exploitation and climate change in the wake of Simon's sudden financial liquidation. Simon merely quotes 'O Röschen rot' from *Des Knaben Wunderhorn*, reinterpreting the lines set by Mahler without melodic quotation: 'I am from God and will return to God, / Dear God will give me light, / Will light me to eternal life!' (ll. 602–4).[13] The delegation's stupefied response is met with an anecdote about meaningless violence among today's youth, and they suspect Simon may be dead, his voice a trick. Bending Mahler's symphonic resurrection to the ecumenical present, Simon misreads the original poetic line by replacing 'God' with 'light' – I am from light and will return to light – as his voice is frequency modulated to extend into an artificially high register in a modified rising whole tone scale. Before entering the System, Evvy declares the feeling inside it as a giddy sense of unending freefall, perhaps gesturing to the 'bodiless exaltation of cyberspace' (Gibson 1984, 123). Nicholas, who has been increasing his prosthetic enhancements, follows suit, leaving Miranda alone in her human skin. She reflects on the unethical escape 'into the light' (l. 771) of the few, and the pain of the millions, before Simon returns as a hologram in a wheelchair (a wry technology joke) to explain the rationale for evolving into non-biological forms:

> Like you, I tried to help the world. / I, too, saw these miseries … / But the animal is defective. / … We evolved as meat, to love fat and sugar; / Once that was good, but now it is fatal. / We evolved as flesh to want sex all the time; / Once that was good, but now it is fatal. / We evolved as muscle to

want to make war; / Once that was good, but now that is lethal ... Now
there's no help but evolving / Out of the meat, and into the system. / It isn't
the many and the few – / It's yourself, it's you!   (ll. 780–807)

Miranda's protest that misery is part of human identity – a last stand of
humanism – is followed by her anxious contemplation of a future alone,
without a huggable mother or father, with 'no lover, no other' (l. 822). She
defends the body, death, sugar and meat, closing with a battery of rhetorical questions.

In the epilogue, the robot-actors return to character as 'operabots' and
repeat the questions of the prologue, still with no answers. The lead robot
reiterates a message whose mindless reiteration acquires a sinister ring,
given the robots' final incomprehension of human empathy: 'Units
deployed as Individuals will receive / One Thousand Human Rights Status
Credits' (ll. 924–5).[14] The monotonous message, delivered 'dry, no emotion, no vibrato', imitates the cultural topos of the robot, confirming that
all prior expression had been unreal, a calculated simulation of human
expression.

But the work performs its posthuman identity in two senses: by inviting
us to empathise with robot actors ('operabots') playing humans, we already
reach across the alterity relation within the opera's narrative, even though
the robot characters are in fact played by human singers. The double
impersonation (human impersonating AI device impersonating human)
complicates the usual means of differentiating AI from human (the
so-called Turing test), for the established circularity is theoretically endless:
an identity multiplied *ad absurdum*. At what point, in other words, does
impersonation end and identity begin? Such ambiguity would seem
precisely the point in the impulse to render virtual speaking assistants
increasingly human-like. On the one hand, we know when the principal
singer, Powers, is offstage, it is the human actor's movements and
breathing – detected in a booth by wireless sensors and filtered through
algorithms – that determine the vocal amplification and stage environment: its lighting, movement of props, stage scenery, etc.

> Data from these sensors and the singer's voice are streamed to custom
> software for analysis and then used to drive and influence motion,
> illumination and visuals throughout the theatrical environment onstage that
> accompanies his amplified singing voice.   (Torpey 2012, 115)

Hence the agency driving the stage effects lacks any intentionality in
performance (physical gestures offstage translate into onstage visual
effects, but not in a way that the singers can control), and to that end
might be considered more a distributed cognition than a human performance. On the other hand, at a different level of realism this is nothing but

concealment, for humans must first learn the score and programme the algorithms governing movement-driven stage effects. In this sense, the doubly suspended disbelief required of an audience receives its complement in the contradictory stage identities that remain suspended between robotic and human singers.

Staging robotic voices in this way, measured against an index of human likeness, dramatises the relation between human and digital technology as an agon, a conflict that has no end in sight. This dark ontology of digital technology has lurked on the periphery of science fiction for decades, yet its menacing predictions of loss and alienation appear no closer to fulfilment. For sound technology the reciprocal paradigms of mimesis (composing with algorithms) and semiosis (synthetic voices) explored in this chapter present two ways of relating AI to human identity. Accepting relations with devices is a fact of digital 'assistance' that we cannot do without; how the indices for determining and evaluating these relations are chosen remains a matter of debate, a debate whose framing parameters are unclear.

Media devices appear to offer a veil of neutrality, for they make no distinction between or judgment on the sound sources they engage: animal or human, naturally occurring or artificially produced, pop music, art music or military explosion. There is only frequency response, bandwidth and transistor processing speed. Yet devices have affordances that shape the experience of users. So the flipside is that increasingly we are unaware of the digital hand guiding our musical experience.

As illustrated by the sound and staging of digital voices, empathy generation is at present a heavily gendered, commercial enterprise, from Hilary's respect for cognitive psychology in Stoppard's play, to the ubiquity of female-sounding digital assistants, and the opposition of a female-body versus male-brain (Miranda, Simon) in Machover's opera. The extent to which we are troubled or indifferent to this matters less, perhaps, than the knowledge that the role of digital media in musical creativity can only grow, and with it the responsibility to monitor such developments.

For Further Study

Auner, Joseph. 2003. 'Sing it for Me: Posthuman Ventriloquism in Recent Popular Music'. *Journal of the Royal Music Association* 128 (1): 98–122.

Bostrom, Nick. 2009. 'The transhumanist FAQ'. In *Readings in the Philosophy of Technology*, edited by David Kaplan, 345–60. 2nd edn. Plymouth: Rowman & Littlefield.

Hayles, Katherine. 2012. *How We Think: Digital Media and Contemporary Technogenesis*. Chicago: Chicago University Press.

Nierhaus, Gerhard. 2009. *Algorithmic Composition: Paradigms of Automated Music Generation*. Vienna: Springer.

Stoppard, Tom. 2015. *The Hard Problem*. London: Faber.

Torpey, Peter A. 2012. 'Digital Systems for Live Multimodal Performance in *Death and the Powers*'. *International Journal of Performance Arts and Digital Media* 8 (1): 109–23.

Notes

1 Elle Hunt, 'Tay, Microsoft's AI chatbot, gets a crash course in racism from Twitter', *The Guardian*, 24 March 2016, www.theguardian.com/technology/2016/mar/24/tay-microsofts-ai-chatbot-gets-a-crash-course-in-racism-from-twitter. All websites accessed 7 September 2018.

2 Madhumita Murgia, 'Microsoft's racist bot shows we must teach AI to play nice and police themselves', *The Telegraph*, 29 March 2016, www.telegraph.co.uk/technology/2016/03/25/we-must-teach-ai-machines-to-play-nice-and-police-themselves/.

3 The shift 'from corporeal communication to disembodied data' that is commonly associated with posthumanism is also discussed by Paul Sanden (Chapter 7, this volume, pp. 184–5); for Sanden, 'liveness functions as an index of humanness'.

4 Dmitri Kartofelev and Jüri Engelbrecht, 'Algorithmic melody composition based on fractal geometry of music', presentation, August 2013, www.cs.ioc.ee/~dima/fractalmusic.html.

5 Jefferson Graham, 'Someday, Amazon wants you to have long talks with Alexa', *USA Today*, 2 May 2017, www.usatoday.com/story/tech/talkingtech/2017/05/02/whispering-alexa-just-start-says-amazon-head-scientist/101171340/.

6 Brent Rose, 'Stand-up comedy using only Siri, Alexa, Cortana and Google Home', *Wired*, www.youtube.com/watch?v=rO-89oBeBbQ.

7 Freia Lisa Lobo, 'Alexa can whisper now', *SoundCloud*, soundcloud.com/freia-lisa-lobo.

8 Liz Stinson, 'The surprising repercussions of making AI assistants sound human', *Wired*, 5 May 2017, www.wired.com/2017/05/surprising-repercussions-making-ai-assistants-sound-human/.

9 Aäron van den Oord, Sander Dieleman, Heiga Zen, Karen Simonyan, Oriol Viuyals, Alex Graves, Nal Kalchbrenner, Andrew Senior and Koray Kavukcuoglu, 'WaveNet: A generative model for raw audio', 19 September 2016, deepmind.com/blog/wavenet-generative-model-raw-audio/.

10 Various, 'The autocomplete questions', *The Guardian*, www.theguardian.com/commentisfree/series/the-autocomplete-questions.

11 Peter Ablinger, 'Quadraturen', http://ablinger.mur.at/docu11.html#principles.

12 The two poems Simon uses are Yeats's 'Sailing to Byzantium' (1924) and May Swenson's 'Question' (1954).

13 See 01:08–02:23 in 'Tod Machover's *Death and the Powers* Scene 6 – The World Pleads', www.youtube.com/watch?v=w3zC7bf7qsU#t=1m8s.

14 See 01:40–01:50 in 'Tod Machover's *Death and the Powers* – Prologue', www.youtube.com/watch?v=Myd2DdSxUEk&dist=RDMyd2DdSxUEk#t=1m40s.

Personal Take: In the Wake of the Virtual

FRANCES DYSON

In 1995, when Char Davies exhibited her seminal virtual reality (VR) work *Osmose*, immersive media was so novel, the experience so unparalleled, that virtual space was represented as real, habitable and a potential substitute for physical, earth-bound existence. With the 'information age' approaching, volumes were written on the phenomenology of the virtual experience, with commentators engaging in various forms of futurology – establishing the present as always being in a state of anticipation, defined by wild predictions about the next technological innovation and the changes it would bring. Roughly half a decade later, the dot-com bubble burst, followed by the housing bubble and the global financial crisis. In retrospect, those heady, blue-sky assumptions about VR seem almost farcical, and the concept of 'virtuality' itself a remnant from a bygone era, untouched by the daunting finitude of ecological and economic catastrophe.

The 'wake of the virtual' is both a backwash of those heady days and a constant ritual of mourning. While we continue to be shaped by the technologies, visions and artistic expressions of all that the virtual represented, at the same time, we mourn the passing of that era of optimistic, future-oriented plenitude. The storms, heatwaves, floods, droughts and extreme weather patterns that characterise the anthropocene are now impossible to ignore, immersing us in a form of cognitive dissonance that neither technological innovation, nor governmental/corporate intervention, can adequately address. The pressures of economic growth on the one hand, and ecological survival on the other, require a different mode of conceptualisation, a different artistic practice, one that (to paraphrase Jean-Luc Nancy) is cognisant of finitude, but not caught in the narcissism of mourning:

> We are at the confines of the multidirectional, plurilocal, reticulated, spacious space in which we take place. We do not occupy the originary point of the perspective, or the overhanging point of an axonometry, but we touch our limits on all sides, our gaze touches its limits on all sides ... All space of sense is common space (hence all space is common space ...) ... The political is the place of the in-common as such.   (Nancy 1997, 40, 88)

For writers, thinkers and artists, the challenge then is to work within these confines – indeed, to be immersed within these confines – and to draw something from them, a map, a way of proceeding, that is also a movement towards the 'in common'.

Whereas the rhetoric of new media at the turn of the millennium stressed the evolution from 'seeing' to 'being', what I find now is that artists who were most involved in the early stages of virtual reality – in particular Davies and Australian media artist and organiser Gary Warner – have moved from the overoptimistic and perhaps almost hubristic notion of 'being' as an existential condition of virtual reality, to a far more realistic, humble and ecologically oriented notion of 'being-in-common'.

Davies's current project *Rêverie*, named after her thousand acres of mostly forest in southern Québec, is both actual land and a 3D virtual environment – less of an installation, or exhibition, than something she describes as a 'conversation', involving her in a dialogue with the land she is mapping and technologically visualising, while also inhabiting and protecting. While vastly different to her earlier virtual environments *Osmose* and *Ephémère*, *Rêverie* could not have been possible without Davies's prior experience in thinking and composing spatially, or 'in-the-round'.[1] In a way, VR formed her current practice, and yet, as she writes, the ethic of this praxis is vastly different from the ethos of control that VR often represents and that Davies, throughout her oeuvre, has always tried to subvert.

Indeed, Davies's threefold process of 'composing, capturing and care'[2] heralds a very different form of immersion, one that is technically adaptive, but primarily and deeply anchored to the earth. Significantly, it is the aspect of 'care' that compels her, in the first instance, to her acres of forest:

> Here now, in *Rêverie*, I have entered into a lifelong apprenticeship, gradually learning the complexities of this actual forest, the will of water that courses through it, and so on . . . Essentially speaking, I do not own this land: rather it owns me, and for the next thirty years, if I'm fortunate, I am its human.

Land and environment is also an aesthetic engine of sorts for Gary Warner. Deeply influenced by the solitude that being immersed in nature affords, Warner recommends spending time

> in a place where man-made structures are distant and media technologies absent; where old life prevails, where contact with other beings and changing weather conditions is immediate, rather than mediated.[3]

In reflecting on his years of involvement with immersive media, Warner describes his current work as a way out of the continuous cycles

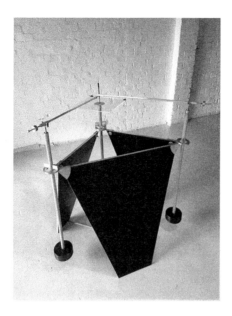

Figure 14.1 Gary Warner, *3-pendulum harmonograph* (2015).
Formply, brass, timber, perspex 1200 mm (w) × 1200 mm (h) × 600 mm (d). Image used courtesy of Gary Warner.

of 'embodied obsolescence' – a process common to many artists involved in digital media where not only are media platforms made obsolete (e.g. VHS video) but human modes of engagement (muscle memory, learned programs, all the skills that go into mastering a certain technology) become outdated every few years.[4] Warner's shift to 'energetic' artworks, often developed on the land he owns in the Origma Reserve (an off-grid undeveloped bush property an hour northwest of Sydney) is in part motivated by a desire to embody, or re-embody, physical forces (weight, gravity, centrifugal momentum, vibration, resonance, impact, etc.). The 'visual and sounding machines' he builds from the cans, bottle tops, bits of wire and other detritus of human consumption are at once sonic and symbolic, aesthetic structures and lessons in the physics of movement and sound. His *3-pendulum harmonograph* (2015, Figure 14.1), for instance, 'requires no external power source but rather is activated by transference of energy from a human body to weighted pendulums', and then left to 'create drawings [and sounds] as the energy is gradually "lost" in the system'.[5] *The social lamellaphone* (2014, Figure 14.2), 'made from cast-off street-sweeper bristles ... collected from the streets of inner-city Sydney', is a collaborative experimental musical instrument/sound sculpture that requires 'no power source for its activation other than fingers and mind'.[6] With its voice-like tonal qualities, *the social lamellaphone* 'induces a frame of mind conducive to conversation' that occurs during its playing.

Figure 14.2 Gary Warner, *The social lamellaphone* (2014).
Blackbutt tops & bridges, jelutong sound boxes, plywood stand, brass fixings, steel tines 1120 mm diameter × 980 mm (h), 270 steel tines each 3 mm (w) × 110 mm (l). Image used courtesy of Gary Warner.

These conversations spread aesthetics through social space – the space of the 'in-common'.

Conversing with forces that are intuited rather than landscapes that are masterfully navigated and motivated by serendipitous events rather than programmable outcomes, both Davies and Warner exemplify an approach that takes the commons, the environment and the space we all share as a fundamental point of reference. In doing so, they enable an aesthetic sense to develop which is not merely sensuous, but is sensible: a vehicle for *making* sense within, and despite, the conflicting pressures that define our present *as* an era that seems to make no sense at all.

Notes

1 For more information on Davies's work see her website www.immersence.com/. Davies writes: 'I would not be doing my current work if I had not made these imaginary immersive landscapes first. In hindsight, it seems inevitable that my creative process has expanded, spatially as well as temporally, to working with this actual landscape, all around.' (Personal correspondence with the author, September 2015.)

2 '"Composing" involves focusing attention on actual sites within *Rêverie*, each with its own ecological history, seeking to amplify what I find most special here … We are also "capturing" certain places here, some composed and others left untouched, through 3D visualization technology in order to manifest how I see, what I sense, beyond conventional assumptions about the world as a collection of solid static objects in empty space (a longstanding goal since I began working with 3D digital technology in the mid 80's).' This and the following citations are taken from Davies's reflections on *Rêverie*, September 2015, personal correspondence with author.

3 Excerpt from talk 'On spending time alone', Sydney, July 2015.

4 Conversation with Warner, Sydney 2015.

5 Warner, artist notes, *3-pendulum harmonograph* (2015).

6 Warner, artist notes, *The social lamellophone* (2014).

10 Digital Inequalities and Global Sounds

SHZR EE TAN

Much discussion in popular culture and in academic scholarship on the latest advents in technology has touched on the possibilities posed by virtual reality and artificial intelligence (Haraway 1991; Mantovani and Riva 1999; Michalski et al. 2013; Copeland 2015). Optimists have focused on how thinking machines transform the human self via prosthetic extensions of the body: for example, using smartphone or augmented vision technologies that tap into 'the cloud' for enhanced experiences. At the same time, sceptics warn of outsourcing human agency to the 'black box' of machine learning, where computer-led iterations create algorithms of unknown construction and ethical underpinning.[1] With the advance of data mining and the Internet of Things, alarm bells are also ringing over privacy breaches and surveillance. Clearly, digital technologies are challenging the ways in which we think and live.

What should ethnomusicologists make of this flood of innovation and change? At the risk of cultural-ghettoising, dare they ask if digital optimism – belatedly modernist in its privileging of progress – serves only the global North, unavoidably stereotyped as white, privileged or (thinking left-field) increasingly Chinese? Could they (uncomfortably) relocate cutting-edge debates to musical societies and communities outside the proverbial 'West'? Is it the job of the ethnomusicologist to provide an 'other', non-Western if not global view here – a negative image of the technological advances taken for granted in urban, industrialised, cosmopolitan and elite environments? It is in this spirit, and in order to deconstruct simplistic binaries such as 'West' and 'other', that I present not one but three alternative views of music and digital culture in the following sections. In so doing I challenge the idea that there is one dominant discourse at work, even as I acknowledge the asymmetrical reach of different hegemonies.

'Other' View No. 1: Decentring, Recentring and Recirculating Musical Digitality

One ethnomusicological cliché with which to kickstart discussion would be the issue of wider context: are there broad structures governing the new relationships forged between music and digital culture? Past commentators have looked at larger plays of global power behind the reality that digital culture remains unevenly developed around the world (Taylor 2014, 2015; Lysloff and Gay 2003; Manuel 1993). Here it is hard to avoid identifying a 'Northern/Western industrialised' bloc in contrast to a bleaker global South, if only because huge disparities in the control of infrastructure, the economics of connectivity and the distribution of skillsets continue to exist, despite all previous attempts to expose, rethink and reframe this divide.

Take internet penetration for example: in comparison to Europe (85.2 per cent) and North America (95 per cent), statistics across many parts of sub-Saharan Africa still show up stark inequalities (11.7 per cent in Sierra Leone, 18.8 per cent in Burkina Faso, 33.1 per cent in Benin, 50.2 per cent in Nigeria).[2] Digital music is consumed in these parts of the world in very different ways from Europe and North America. Music is often channelled through radio, TV broadcasts, CDs and physical USB-drive exchanges. Where Spotify, Amazon Prime and Netflix have come to be taken for granted in cities such as San Francisco and Stockholm, streaming services in East and West Africa still make few appearances: Spotify, for example, is available only in South Africa. For many, the thrill of cutting-edge developments such as virtual reality is less real than upgrading one's 'dumb' mobile to a smartphone.

But framing the technological divide in terms of a North–South axis is simplistic at best and neocolonialist at worst. After all, the world outside Europe and North America is a very large place. Using the same example of Spotify but now in Southeast Asia and Latin America, one can track the much wider but still-incomplete availability of streaming technologies across different territories. In Latin America, where smartphones account for six out of ten mobile connections, global digital music networks including Spotify have begun to sprawl. But people still buy CDs, so streaming services remain in uneasy partnership and competition with conglomerates built on transnational *telenovela* (soap opera), pop and media industries. The dangers of generalisation become clear as asymmetries emerge within asymmetries. In Thailand, a Bangkok urbanite might be as *au fait* with Taylor Swift as with Korean boyband Got7 or Thai actor-singer Chinawut Indracusin. But across the border in Myanmar or higher up in the Northern Thai provinces, only one of the three might make a claim for household fame as a result of music circulation bifurcated through digital and non-digital routes. Ironically, this would not be the local guitar hero.

In this way the picture of digital musicking outside the historical global north is far from uniform. Just as there is no single Internet around the world, the Internet does not represent the whole of digitality. One asks, then: what good does carving up the world in such a geocultural, 'area-studies' manner really achieve in its replication of colonial structures? Are there new approaches that can encourage different paths towards intervening in digital music scenes that have become increasingly prized on account of their distance-telescoping impact – in short, their disassembling of these problematic geographical divides? How are newly enabled digitalities enmeshed within translocal communications, where privacy (physical and virtual) becomes an Anglo-American privilege, as experienced by virtuoso smartphone users living in crowded Chinese factory dormitories or in India's 'smartslums' (where multiple phone and radio speakers compete for aural space in frequently distorted and simultaneous broadcasts)?[3] Any attempt to chart digital music zones on purely geographical lines, which are in turn subject to the carving up of politico-economic realms, will remain tricky at best. An intersectional approach, focusing on the interplay of multiple factors whose hierarchies of impact change contextually, might provide alternative analyses. Platforms such as Facebook and Spotify expand in global reach, but they are still used in multifarious ways across communities in the same territories.

The job of an ethnomusicologist, then, is to put things in multiple and sometimes contradictory narratives. Within individual countries or geocultural zones, rural–urban divides may still be reflected in telecoms accessibility, as may longstanding income and class divides. It is no surprise that in the city of Delhi a brahmin IT worker's iTunes playlist will feature a different line-up of artists from that of a dhoby walla. And yet both individuals maintain reasonable personal access to the Internet, living in one of the most networked cities in the world – in contrast to other, less-enabled regions in the same country. Again, generational and gender divides bisect technological fields. Whether in Hobart or Hong Kong, a sixteen-year-old female's experience of music will be digitally dissimilar to those of her brother, mother, father or grandfather, not only in content but also in method and aesthetics. The point is that music has never travelled further – not only from North to South, or West to East, but in reverse directions, in feedback loops and in fringe networks. Benjamin Lee and Edward LiPuma's pronouncements on cultures of circulation (2002) challenge the assumed centre/periphery framework, not least because the affordances of digitality have enabled a transcending of distance. Today, esoteric musico-digital information continues to be produced, shared and remade in the backstreets of the fast and the slow Internet, going around the world on and offline several times over at frustratingly and wonderfully different speeds and scales, opening up disjunctures of time, space, aesthetics, media formats, liveness and context.

For example, cultural memories in migrant networks are maintained through the sharing of bespoke YouTube playlists. In Southeast Asian, South Asian and Latin American transient worker communities moving across Asia and the Gulf in pursuit of temporary job contracts, these playlists feature transnational and hybridised pop and live-karaoke sessions, interweaving between other dominant streams of music sharing. The circulated musics do not only draw from nostalgic links to imagined 'homelands' but also reflect aspirations towards regional articulations of the cosmopolitan: old Bollywood covers can be as much of a hit as *dangdut* songs with Indonesian migrant workers in Singapore and Dubai. Similarly – and illustrating Koichi Iwabuchi's idea of recentring globalisation (2002) – we can re-understand an entire Gulf-originated pop music industry finding large audiences in West and East Africa via the Internet. Again, transnational K-pop has flourished over the web in East and Southeast Asia, in symbiosis with local and national(ist) TV industries, internet fan idol cults and giant entertainment companies.

Critics, including myself (Tan 2016) have countered early digital optimism by pointing out that the Internet's image of free-for-all access has created a false sense of democracy. Like any other network, it remains subject to market forces, political manipulation and – most basically – access. Still, digitality has created more backdoor entry points to global playing fields, allowing for roads towards smaller, safer spaces where opportunities are more equal. Indeed, if one knows how and where to look, discreet digital pathways leading to esoteric musics can always be found hiding in plain sight, nestled among the highways carved out by industry players. Channelling Michel de Certeau's (1984) notion of tactics, I argue that these de facto gamers of music find shortcuts in the very technological grids designed to marginalise their existence. They have 'hacked' the digital system.

An example is the indigenous artists in Taiwan who hopscotch creatively on and off larger transnational pop industry websites, sidetracking into the nooks of YouTube's recommended playlists. Using this as a jump-off site, they exploit the industry structures of web platforms and algorithms of digital discovery to create new spaces for ethnographic recordings that would not survive in the marketplace. Taiwan's artists in turn interact across time-space divides in digital, cultural and economic solidarity with fellow indigenous or independent artists around the world who have created spaces on Bandcamp, SoundCloud or other bespoke internet radio stations and podcasts: an aggregation of niches comes into circulation. More generally, such aggregations can be shaped by translocal communities (for example, of metal music, known for its multiple sub-genres in global micro-scenes both fragmented and sustained by the Internet) or produced through fan campaigns. In the flood of these offerings, old exoticising tropes will no doubt surface through inevitable tourist videos, even as non-commercial content becomes corporatised through You-Tube's video-inserted ads. The role of the ethnomusicologist is crucial here in putting such micro-scenes in multiple perspectives.

Two linked questions can be asked in relation to the messy explosion of such digital music recirculations: Is it possible for everyone to listen to everything? And where can one relocate old anxieties over ensuingly shortened attention spans and sonic fidelity? A short answer to the second question can be found in how ways of listening have changed, a point made by video music tutorials. Shakuhachi performer and scholar Kiku Day, one of the first in her community to pioneer web lessons, talks of 'learning to pick up on sonic cues specific to Skype, working with these in interaction with visuals ... I also acquire different skills in teaching, and communicating with students as a result. One simply adjusts and listens on the Internet in a new way.'[4] This takes us back to the distorted private–public sound systems of Indian smartslums: Day's pronouncements on developing alternative appreciations of fidelity reveal the notion of high definition to be a culturally relative preference.

The issue underlying fidelity, however, is the extent to which listening in the digital age is valued at all. In what Raquel Campos terms 'imagined listening' (2018), the mere signifying of a potential act of listening – 'liking' a playlist on Facebook or re-tweeting a viral video – is enough to build taste, consensus, community and shared musical experience. In the hyper-mediated contexts of some internet communities the overwhelming number of competing music producers means one rarely listens to a video in full. Yet the idea is not as novel as it might seem. Campos points out: 'People also display records in their homes that they have never listened to. Assumptions are "the stuff of culture".'[5]

One way of avoiding the pitfalls of technological determinism in intersectional analyses of digitality is to realise that norms are constantly being reconstructed, and every situation has its own changing logics. Elisabetta Costa (2018) argues that contexts are always in continuous states of rebuilding, especially outside Anglo-American domains. Shifts in tech-nological enablement take place in situations where other forms of inequality persist. A first stab at taking an 'Other' view on music and digitality is therefore necessarily a messy, difficult and sprawling affair that juxtaposes territories as diverse as Stockholm, Beirut and Surabaya in the same anecdote, on scales of observation which appear too asymmetrical for any useful socio-economic, political or personal comparison, and along timelines that telescope decades of 'technological catchup'. But such is the virtual reality of, for example, an Indonesian transient worker living in

Singapore. Saving a significant portion of her tiny income for a not-so-newfangled nine-month-old smartphone, she accesses Lebanese-born but Europe-based *zikir* singer Maher Zain on YouTube. Privately meditating to his religious chants after a day of housework, she embarks on a sonic journey that later takes her to a more 'fun' internet live jam session later. Using the Smule duetting app, she performs with her idol, Indonesian pop star Siti Badriah, in real time and across thousands of miles. Their distance-karaoke video is livestreamed for friends and family near and far, who 'like' the performance on a curated Facebook page. In this way the worker claims her own place in the interstitial spaces that have sprung up between fault lines emerging in wider global musical remediations.

Musical Algocracies: Not So New After All?

My discussion in 'Other' View No. 1 revolved around issues of internet penetration and changing aesthetics of music consumption. But where does this leave the issues that bulk large in a perspective from a city such as London, where debates on big data, digital ethics, surveillance and artificial intelligence rage? Do we factor concerns of 'technological catchup' or skipped generations into debates on the disjunctures between the digital haves and have-nots? Where does the power to facilitate these conversations lie?

Anxieties around digital culture revolve around the newly minted buzzwords 'algocracy' and 'hypernudging'.[6] These refer to new models of public and private governance effected through computer-generated algorithms that have the power to influence judgment, based on the tracking and analysis of large corpora of data and the prediction of trends based on patterns found within them. Such developments present new legal and ethical dilemmas. Karen Yeung (2017, 118) describes how, through algorithmic control of big data, people's behaviour can be influenced 'in a predictable way without forbidding any options' as a result of design-based control over choice architecture. She argues that 'due to their networked, continuously updated, dynamic and pervasive nature (hence "hypernudge") ... concerns about the legitimacy of these techniques are not satisfactorily resolved through reliance on individual notice and consent' and that there are 'implications for democracy ... if Big Data analytic techniques driven by commercial self-interest continue ... unchecked.'

A less abstract illustration can be found in how the American chain-store Target's technology can now tell if a teenager is pregnant even before her parents can, and automatically act on this information by sending out baby-product coupons.[7] Through its recommended videos or user-posted links, YouTube may direct an innocent search on self-defence towards increasingly violent footage featuring weapons or military campaigns. The internet meme of the India-originated Zool Babies cartoon series provides a music-related example. At first sight a convenient babysitting aid for multitaskers, these seemingly innocuous videos feature animated toddlers singing nursery rhymes while engaging in activities that range from jumping on a bed to going to the zoo.[8] However, unsupervised, YouTube's autoplay technology scrolls on further sequences of related cartoons that may feature unchecked or spoofed content endorsing animal abuse or urging toddlers to sing propagandistic paeans to the police.[9] Childminders are lulled into a false sense of security by the familiar aural wrapping around new items on this algorithmically generated playlist. But who is ultimately responsible for the list? Are Target's and YouTube's technologies culpable? In other words, can human agency be outsourced to algorithms?

Agency has been a slippery concept through its frequent conflation with power, authority, institutions, doxa, and even democracy. Arjun Appadurai (1990) distinguishes five perspectives or 'scapes' within the global exchange of ideas, from which the world presents itself in different guises: the ethnographic, financial, mediatised, technological and ideological. To take the example of Google, a 'mediascape' analysis will position the company as a global player with a fair degree of musico-digital reach through its YouTube video service. However, Google's conquering of the media-world is far from complete, and this has to be understood in intersection with 'scapes' of the ethno- and ideo- worlds. YouTube may be slowly becoming a norm for musical streaming in Latin American, African and Southeast Asian cities, where connectivity is rising through the use of increasingly cheap smartphones.[10] But it is completely absent from China, not through lack of digital development but because of a political ban by the Chinese state, in protection of its government-controlled (and domestically lucrative) platforms and content.[11] The ideoscape gives a quite different picture from the technoscape.

Such disjunctures apply as much in terms of reception as of production. Anna Tsing (2011, 330) offers a useful perspective, arguing that changes in spatial dimensionality give rise to granular differences in experience and perception, and that – through collapsing distance, space, time and contexts – the Internet sets up similar disjunctures where concepts and measurements of disparity and distance change dramatically depending on scale. This can be seen in how old industry concerns about copyright in the world music business have moved on to fresh discussions of cultural appropriation, creative censorship and the shrinking *habitus* of political correctness. Here digital technology has opened up a new dynamic in the politics of non-white marginalities, now positioned and juxtaposed on differently levelled ethical playing fields.

An example can be found in K-pop's controversial milking of African-American rap memes.[12] The surprise is not that K-pop artists have long been appropriating musical styles from rappers but that – thanks to broader digital flows resulting in wider interest in Korea – African-American artists are now aware of such borrowings. In this once-sidelined cultural playground, who is taking advantage of whom? The alternative circulatory flows afforded by the Internet – flows involving African-American rap and K-rap, as well as K-pop's wider audiences across much of East Asia and Southeast Asia – make this a complex matter. The politics of race behind rap and hip-hop have long been problematised alongside the commercialisation of the genre by both African-American and white artists (Rose 1994, 2008). Both K-pop artists and African-American rappers can claim non-mainstream status against the hegemony of Anglo-American rock. But when different marginalities collide in the digital world, we have to consider their interactions and the ambiguously relative positions of privilege that are involved: otherwise we will not understand the difference between musical appreciation and appropriation, or the representational as well as economic power stakes involved in creating new audiences.

A final perspective on algocracy as the outsourcing of human agency emerges if we place Elias Canetti's (1962) writing on crowds and power in the context of digitality. Just as he describes how the dynamics of mass 'packs' ultimately reflect the inclinations of their rulers, so one might look for parallels in the new paradigms of hive minds and intuitive machines – paradigms that reflect the conscious and unconscious biases of the human designers who, for example, build racist assumptions into face-recognition algorithms.[13] To quote a comment made by David Trippett when editing this chapter, all coding is declarative: unspoken assumptions or beliefs become explicit in programming. Scientists and engineers see the solution to such problems in the creation of ever larger, more inclusive datasets, reflecting an increasingly diverse conception of humanity. Facebook and Google have already embarked on plans to build entire new cities for the sole purpose of testing their technologies.[14] But why and to what end should such huge amounts of data be collected? This is a crucial question in the age of the privacy paradox, where people are increasingly protective of their personal data and yet ever willing to share private information on social media. Such data may not only flow into the AI black box. It may also fall into the hands of ominously lurking humans who use digitality and algorithms as a mask for a new, information-based authoritarianism.

'Other' View No. 2: China – Autocracy as Algocracy?

As can be seen, the implications of algocracy and by extension artificial intelligence are many, particularly in its ventriloquising for human agency and bias. Here is where a second alternative take on music and digital culture can find leverage in a case study from China.

One of the world's fastest developing markets in both the music and digital sectors (IFPI 2017, 15), China has recently become a target of speculative global investment on account of its quick rise as an economic powerhouse. The territory is large and self-contained, both politically and in terms of resources. Regional subcultures and rising middle classes have sprung up following rapid and uneven demographic changes in the territory's second- and third-tier cities, transforming the notion of its 'countryside'. As fast as unsold high-rise apartments have been built on vacant fields, over the past decade China has seen its own cheaply produced Huawei and Oppo smartphones become household items.[15] More significantly, accelerated digital development has allowed the skipping of several generations of technology on national socio-economic levels, and turned smartphones – with their sound-and-music-enabled capabilities – into first-generation appliances in China's march towards the Internet of Things.

China offers an interesting study in issues of digital disjuncture. In its swift 'technological catchup', huge logistic stumbling blocks have been conveniently bypassed. However, in this easy coasting through old ground, a total consolidation of power within specific sectors has come to pass. Today in cities and villages, smartphones (via the state-monitored app WeChat) regulate and organise everyday life. Their interfaces are optimised for a gamut of services ranging from paying local noodle vendors to booking airline seats, donating to charity, dating, buying concert tickets, hiring taxis, online shopping, ordering takeaways and, of course, streaming music. But who, or what, controls this realm?

It goes without saying that any talk of digital optimism in China has to be countered by a limitation: the territory's Great Firewall, which has ringfenced its entire Internet since the 1990s against state-deemed objectionable content – political, social or religious. Once scalable via VPN connections, this barrier has become more difficult to climb over (*fanqiang*), following increased digital censorship. Over the years, one can argue that strict control of spaces for public discourse has resulted in the emergence of not one, nor even two, but several public spheres. Of these, the first is easy to identify, operating on state-governed mainstream media (newspapers, official websites, TV). The second can be found in the form of national internet interfaces and private messaging apps such as Weibo,

WeChat, Baidu, Iqiyi, letv and mgtv, all of which have spawned on their platforms as many spies and fake trolls as they have birthed genuine voices of dissent.[16] Beyond these, scaffolds for public discoursing overlap and interweave. They include alternative, sometimes overseas-hosted forums featuring superficially state-friendly but intentionally satirical praise, and other streams of conversations bantered about in private and underground creative spaces that form concentric circles around official media. Whether online or offline, these spaces remain monitored through different degrees of state co-option.

How do all the above extrapolate onto the musical arena? Some research has already been published on the mainstream ground claimed by regional TV stations broadcasting politically populist music contests (Jian and Liu 2009; Wu 2014). Other research has tracked the rising, if uneven, impact of streaming services along income divides.[17] More interestingly, however, music has been strategically utilised in digital subculture for its ambiguous intertextuality through small acts of subversive intervention. These are deliberately played across the interstitial spaces between various digital strata of public discourse. In particular, scatological, cryptic and nested sonic memes have emerged as gestures of digital resistance, metaphorical middle fingers shown to the regimes of censorship.

From 'Grass Mud Horse' to Sonic Surveillance

One example is the invention in 2009 of a mythical creature called the Grass Mud Horse, said to be a species of alpaca. In that year, the curse words 'Cào Nǐ Mā' [操你妈], literally translating as 'F**k Your Mother' in Mandarin, were arbitrarily censored on Chinese search engines as part of a national internet cleansing policy. However, this did not stop creative pranksters from sneaking the terms back onto the Chinese Internet. They did this by finding a homonym for the phrase in entirely new characters 'Cǎo Ní Mǎ' [草泥马], or 'Grass Mud Horse'. The character tones were different, however, so enterprising Internet users hastily assembled several music videos around the words. Throwing together random images of alpacas to fit the words, they layered children's voices and simple backing tracks for sarcastic effect. The melodies supplied the correct tones to convert 'Grass Mud Horse' into 'F**k your Mother', and so a sonic meme – generally referred to as Cao Ni Ma – came into being.[18]

The music videos became an immediate viral success, attracting not only the attention of millions of domestic internet users but also that of transnational Chinese viewers who reposted the items on platforms beyond the reach of the Chinese authorities. International press caught wind of the phenomenon, as also did soft toy makers who began manufacturing alpacas on demand. Later that year, both the prank videos and the alternative Chinese characters for 'Grass Mud Horse' were temporarily banned on the Chinese Internet, but the damage had already been done.[19] The sonically enabled Grass Mud Horse is ensconced as one of Baidu's '10 Mythical Creatures' on the Chinese Internet and it continues to be a marker of resistance to Chinese censorship.[20]

One could even argue that the sheer absurdity Cao Ni Ma stood for has become an end in itself, alongside its evocation of a haphazard DIY video-making ethos. Cao Ni Ma may well have inspired the 'Little Apple' song released over the Internet by The Chopsticks Brothers in 2014.[21] In this domestic-turned-international video hit, cross-dressing men in blonde wigs pushed for an unlikely bromance (Stock 2016). Deliberate attempts were made to conjure the meaningless through seemingly random references to Korean soap operas, plastic surgery and Adam and Eve. As a song, 'Little Apple' has been covered by multiple parties from proto-illegal Chinese flash mobs and a military recruitment campaign to K-pop bands and Norwegian metal artists. Its makers' strategy of harnessing nonsense-as-lexicon, turning such communication into a wider internet vernacular, worked in postmodern fashion: Chinese viewers can read whatever meanings they like into the video's borderline racist and sexist content. Little Apple made it to top positions on online charts, and has yet to offend official censors.

As this book goes to press, music censorship has returned to China again, with associated fallout in the digital world. In 2018, the state made a move to ban hip-hop artists from performing on television, on the grounds that they promoted 'decadent and demotivating' lifestyles.[22] It remains to be seen how effective the ban will be, since underground communities continue to exist on the Internet, hiding in plain sight. The chief offending artists involved in this saga, GAI and VaVa, have continued to broadcast music from China-based as well as foreign digital platforms, including YouTube. Other artists may be happy to be co-opted by the state, as Baranovitch (2003) has argued of a few Beijing rockers in the 1990s. Others still may adopt a strategy of labelling themselves as non-hip-hop artists, even if the sonic building blocks of their styles are sourced from rap.

The hip-hop ban in China is only one of several current developments that have stirred up global controversy. A far more ominous technological initiative may be the state's implementation of a nation-wide social credit system in May 2018, eerily prophesied by Charlie Brooker's TV series, *Black Mirror*.[23] The dystopian potential of algocracy rears its head this time in the political context of East Asian state capitalism, far from – but paralleling – neoliberal media developments in the 'West'. Under the new Chinese social credit system, users rate each other's 'trustworthiness' via cloud computers. Individuals who do not achieve a certain social credit are prevented from using services such as enrolling in a desired school or buying plane tickets.

Such digital developments converge with music in the overarching issue of sonic surveillance via the Internet of Things and algocratic agencies: both the physical and metaphorical acts of listening now take on political dimensions. By this, I refer both to listening in to conversations on smartphones and to the tracking of broader embedded data stored, for example, in personal podcast preferences. In China, what is at stake is less the supposed mutuality of mass observation now outsourced to the hive mind, than how this notion obfuscates the presence of state control ultimately lying behind data-gathering machinery. In other words, the illusion of crowdsourced protocols and 'the people's' collective agency for the social regulation of and by the masses is used to legitimise an omnipresent, all-hearing Big Brother. The walls – together with mobile phones, wifi routers, and smarthome technologies instrumentalised by people who themselves become instruments – have more ears than ever. Ominously collecting conversations, stories, gossip and life-profile data, they observe and record in the name of encouraging 'good' behaviour. And the potential horror-TV scenario of China is in some ways already par for the course elsewhere. This can be observed in the data and privacy breaches (for example by Facebook in the Cambridge Analytica debacle) that prompted the European Union to implement its new General Data Protection Regulation in 2018. As early as in 2013, the US National Security Agency was caught red-handed in its secret wiretapping of phone conversations and the Internet. If there is a lesson to be learnt, it is that the potential delights and horrors of digitality (and music) are universal.

Whether in China or elsewhere, the key question is who gets to use all the data generated through surveillance: government agencies, capitalist corporations, or the state in collaboration with neoliberal interests? Equally important is exactly how this data might be used. Commentators[24] detail the leakage and abuse of private information in the critical nudging of decisions over personal or public tipping points, not least in moments of vulnerability (Yeung 2017). Even with guarantees of anonymity and privacy, one wonders how the deployment of ambiguously harvested information might bear on age-old issues of control and agency. This concerns not only the governance of knowledge, consumer proclivities and socio-political choices, but also the basic structures of what is suggestible, discoverable or imaginable. One might, for example, ask of Spotify's tailored playlists: who or what controls how we explore new music, based on automated interpretations of our own willingly submitted listening profiles and, by extension, projected socio-economic data and political leanings? How does Spotify share this information with third parties who persuade us to buy products in targeted ads? Are tech companies more culpable than the ISP providers that track every website we visit?[25] And finally: what, really, is the relative value of digital privacy in London or New York, as compared to communities in lower-income countries mentioned earlier where even physical privacy is hard to attain?

'Other' View No. 3: Postdigitality and Imagination Gaps

Our apparent ability to live with the scandalous fallout of internet privacy infractions says something about how we, as members of an asymmetrically cosmopolitan surveillance society, have phlegmatically embraced the wider hopes and anxieties of digital culture.[26]

Recent reports of misbehaving scripts in Amazon's Echo smart speakers reveal how we make peace – or even strange parasocial contracts – with technology and its extended agencies. In 2018, an entire private conversation between a couple in Portland was recorded by a smart speaker and subsequently sent to a random number from their address book.[27] In 2017, African grey parrots interacted with the same device to the extent of getting smarthome technologies to turn off house lights and start ordering shopping items online.[28] The Portland infraction was met with public shock, while the parrots were turned into 'cute' memes, all on overwhelmingly English-speaking sectors of YouTube. Such different responses to the redistribution of human agency reveal paradoxical attitudes towards the anthropomorphisation of technology. We fear technology when it mimics the human. Yet we overcome this fear by making technology appear even more human; ultimately it is humanity that we both fear and seek comfort in. This is the classic situation of posthumanism as described by Katherine Hayles (2008, 39). We purport to acquire new knowledge by erasing the perceived boundaries between humanity and technology. Yet it is those boundaries that make the gaining of knowledge possible in the first place.

Today, smarthome device sales continue to rise in cosmopolitan areas, even as smartcity versions of similar technologies are introduced *en masse* to smartslum development projects, amidst critique of their maladaptive governance.[29] While voice-mediated software applications have been criticised for their inherent gender biases, they continue to be honed not only for convenience but also for their more 'human', imperfect 'feel'. One might infer that, across different societies, we are more comfortable than we think in dealing with the unknowns of digitality: unwittingly in-built, quirkily flawed human prejudices only make them easier to relate to. Perhaps we can call ourselves postdigital now. To paraphrase Benayoun (2008), we take for granted and normalise new technologies as not only serving humans but also extending what it means to be human in the first place.

Knowledge gaps continue to exist along the old lines of power structures, gender divides and economic inequality. But the more interesting disjunctures are imagination gaps. Differences in the projection and fetishisation of the future – whether naïvely optimistic or dystopian – can overshadow smaller but no less important feats of imagination in the present. The issue is not that imagination is divorced from reality. Rather, it is that there are already a multitude of transformative realities that can dramatically change the way we think about the past. They force us to rethink possibilities of the present, including the subjectivities of our bodies and our selves.

This throws light on overhyped predictions for the future, whether optimistic or pessimistic. Take virtual reality (VR). For all the talk of its revolutionising spatial and multisensorial experience, the technology is still held back for an important human reason. One form of imagination gap occurs when human cognition and biology have not caught up with digital advances: our brains are not yet comfortable with perceptual or imaginary motions in the absence of corresponding real-time, bodily shifts. If VR were to be taken to full potential and unleashed upon a room full of humans strapped to headsets for, say, an action-packed virtual ski run or a fast-moving first-person-shooter game, the result would be a floor covered with vomit. In gaming, the collective sound experience in interaction with visuality is also flawed: if one were to play with friends, separate sound sources from the game vis-à-vis friends stationed in the room would create disjunctures through their multiple channelling of auralities that do not add up. Today, headsets still work with interfaces that default to a 'framed' visuality, as in a flight simulator, or to the enlarging of small-movement-based processes that do not require quick perspectival shifts. And yet it is in small, subtle movements that the most important advances are to be made – in remote surgical training, or in the making of new intimacies through minutely-calibrated sensory interactions between individuals physically separated by thousands of miles.

Music, of course, is a prime arena for such fine-grained interaction. One can imagine headsets zooming into a trumpeter's or conductor's face at the Berlin Philharmonic's digital concert hall. Add in new technologies for sonic directionality – controlling the positions from which sounds come – and VR listeners could reframe their audio perceptions on the basis of what they virtually see. But would this actually be so game-changing? Enter another appearance of the imagination gap: David Trippett's suggestion in response to VR that while we see in 180 degrees, we already hear in 360.[30] Perhaps sonic navigation long ago achieved the same breakthrough that we are now ascribing to VR?[31] In our fixation with possibilities for the future and our aspirations for the new, are we forgetting the subtle infinities of the present? The crux lies in which of these possibilities will make their way into the trajectories of the future, and how this will be achieved.

There is always another factor, however, that underlies such technological developments: they are shot through with socio-economic inequality. An ethnomusicologist might wonder if classic digital privilege has obscured dramatically different musical and audio experiences among the technologically non-privileged, whether through low-tech or low-cost digitalities, or use of analogue technologies. One might compare cutting-edge VR with the humble washing machine as a technological breakthrough which – as economist Ha-Joon Chang contends – 'has changed the world more than the internet has' (2012, 31). From a sonic perspective his statement stands ironically alongside recently developed industrial software driving smarthome devices designed to camouflage unwanted noise in domestic spaces. These appliances include 'singing' washing machines and pitched blenders capable of playing tunes.[32] For the two out of seven people in the world (in 2010) who may not have access to a washing machine, the value of a tailored laundry 'hum' is laughable.[33] A practical approach to more urgent problems of noise pollution may lie in apps that harness crowdsourced and GIS (geographic information system) technologies on mobile phones to locationally track, measure and collect big data on everyday sound environments (Maisonneuve et al. 2009). Given the still unequal distribution of smartphone usage, however, non-digital solutions look set to prevail, whether involving government legislation, public education or tactical adaptation of the human ear (Singh and Davar 2004).

Behind this lie larger questions of experiencing sound in all its digital, semi-digital or non-digital manifestations. Can one really get away from seeing advances in such technologies as part of a universally modernist, optimistic and progressive enterprise? It is impossible to fully affirm the value of new digital experiences of sound that have generated such asymmetrical impacts on communities and sectors, without critiquing the inequalities that produce these asymmetries. The presence of grey areas and layers of inequality provokes other practical and rhetorical questions. Should a public council fund research on singing washing machines, noise-cancellation earplugs, or cheap musical streaming technologies made available to everyone on 'dumb' phones? (Some would say the BBC already does the last.) But do we necessarily need or want a public Internet of Things, given growing concerns about privacy? Is it the job of politicians – as opposed to the research arms of tech companies – to spearhead discussions on ethics and new initiatives? Can we environmentally sustain our trajectories of digital and postdigital development, considering growing energy requirements of data storage and hardware manufacture? In a digital age, what power do we have as consumers, listeners and musicians to address these changing technological dynamics with our purchasing and lobbying powers?

There are no simple answers. One easy line of argument might be that the difficult questions posed by left-field writers of dystopian fiction constitute 'future-proofing' mechanisms, counterweights built into humanity to ensure that its progress is always checked. Another easy answer might be that the coming together rather than complete displacement of old by new media (what Henry Jenkins (2006) calls convergence culture[34]) will see VR and other expensive digitalities become part of a wider spectrum of technologies encompassing present and past, haves and have-nots. In such a world everything – from science-fictionalised hype and horror, to mini-revolutions in the digital processing of random mundanities, to the closing or widening of digital asymmetries – will acquire a retrospective narrative logic. Imagination gaps will be closed as fast as new ones come into being. However, they will also operate in ways that make us rethink and recalibrate our diverse existences as an everyday matter of postdigital coping. That entails a posthuman submission to the tragedies of inequality in a world where the fallible human condition is not the only driver of agency.

Conclusion: An 'Other' Take on *Black Panther*

In this chapter I have attempted to represent several 'other' views on digital culture from my specific perspective as a female, postcolonial and transnational Chinese ethnomusicologist, living an ostensibly privileged existence in a twenty-first-century European capital city now divided by Brexit. But where exactly does music fit into all this? In this postlude I address that question by way of a personal anecdote.

I speak as an individual voice with a particular listening history, but also as a person living within larger structural and societal frameworks. I write of personal reactions to watching and listening to *Black Panther* (2018), a superhero film directed by African-American Ryan Coogler featuring a predominantly black cast. A hit in theatres globally, the movie has been sold as 'African' in its reframing of the doxa of power in pan-black terms. This is achieved via the depiction of a power struggle between an African-American nationalist fighter and a politically conscious king in the fictional and secretly technologically advanced state of Wakanda. At heart, however, *Black Panther* is made for 'Western' audiences, not just in its selective representation of 'African' traits for the mass market, but in its privileging of particular narratives of technologisation and militarisation in the construction of an idealised Africa that stands in contrast to the harsh realities and ongoing consequences of colonisation. This much has already been said by writers of colour.[35]

In sonic terms, my first response to *Black Panther* – apart from jaw-dropping awe at its superb cast, direction, set and costumes – was how the film's soundtrack seemed the least symbolically technologised aspect of its wider theme: the legitimisation of power through superior technology. To my laywoman's ears, the triumphal, electronically manipulated chords in the showdowns seemed generically Hollywoodesque, if expertly finished. As for symbolic 'African-sounding' elements, what could I, as a non-regional specialist, pretend to know – even if as an ethnomusicologist I am increasingly wary of being pigeonholed by 'area studies'? I could not pronounce on the 'authenticity' of the actors' imitation of Xhosa, or on how far the Swedish composer's lush orchestral sweeps punctuated by rumbling 'African' percussion beats draw on essentialising stereotypes. But where the ethnomusicologist balked, the music and movie fan perked up: did all this really matter, if the interweaving of acoustically recorded but digitally altered sounds was so seamlessly enmeshed in the giddy beauty of the film's visuals that I was hardly aware of their artifice?

As a transnational Singaporean person of Chinese ancestry, my second reflection on *Black Panther* was dismay at conflicting reports of the film's premiere in China. There it apparently sparked off racist comments, so dashing critics' hopes that the nearly all-black cast could finally change Chinese attitudes to Africa for the better. This led me to rethink black transnationalisms in the intersectional contexts of musical digitality in light of China's increasingly large economic investments in Africa. In China, hip-hop is heard as an edgy, underground genre when practised by Chinese artists; it is also consumed as a 'cool', sub-mainstream style in the Chinese diaspora, as appropriated by the likes of Taiwanese artist Jay Chou. Its transgressive qualities have been deracinated as it has also become re-symbolised as 'liberal Western'. For the moment, black artists in China – whether actors or musicians – appear to have limited presence or agency.

Yet an inkling of hope can perhaps be found in the movie's use of hidden musical codes to create politically safer, interstitial spaces in the ensuing cultural wars. In an attempt to cross-market *Black Panther* to Korean audiences, one scene was shot in Seoul. The soundtrack featured an aural cameo by Korean superstar Psy (of 'Gangnam Style' fame) duetting with Snoop Dogg. In this sliver of sonic time, could one discern a new musico-memetic space, devised for reasons of commerce but potentially allowing an alternative parsing of transnational cultural codes across different, newly levelled playing fields? With K-pop a phenomenon in China and Psy already a household name, could this tiny intervention pave an eventual path towards the meeting of new cross-cultural horizons? It might well be that some positive benefit may be still gained from the inevitable marketisation of musical digitalities around the world.

Some tentative, if slightly sanguine, answers can be found in the Internet's enabling of multiplicities in alternative circulatory flows. A search on Chinese websites for Psy and the Chinese translation of *Black Panther* (*Hei Pao*) brings up early mentions of the artist's audio appearance in the film.[36] From here on, successive links nestling within comments and associated videos bring up his collaboration with Snoop Dogg. These branch off into articles about Kendrick Lamar's curated album for the film, in turn splintering into short discussions about younger black artists covering older, iconic tracks. By the time this convoluted route led me to a brief mention of rap, via a tangential debate on issues of 'cultural dare' in remixes, I was ready to claim it as a small victory of sorts for transcultural communication over digital privilege and both corporate and governmental power.[37]

To be sure, the pathway from Psy to The Notorious B.I.G. and Tupac Shakur required some creative hopscotching through noisy advertisements for Xiaomi earphones and dodgy subtitled advertisements for *Jurassic World*. And destination plays for African-American artists, in comparison with Psy's 70,000, averaged a paltry 800–2,000 views. But perhaps, soundbite by soundbite, gigabyte by gigabyte, music in digital worlds today could telescope the very disjunctures brought about by the larger systems governing its existence. As a digital optimist might say, we may be post-digital already, but the infinite possibilities of the past, present and future are not over quite yet.

For Further Study

Chang, Ha-Joon. 2012. *23 Things They Don't Tell You about Capitalism*. New York: Bloomsbury Publishing.

Costa, Elisabetta. 2018. 'Affordances-in-practice: An ethnographic critique of social media logic and context collapse'. *New Media & Society* 20 (10): 3641–56.

Iwabuchi, Koichi. 2002. *Recentering Globalization: Popular Culture and Japanese Transnationalism*. Durham: Duke University Press.

Lysloff, René T. A. and Leslie C. Gay, Jr, eds. 2003. *Music and Technoculture.* Middletown, CT: Wesleyan University Press.

Yeung, Karen. 2017. "'Hypernudge": Big Data as a mode of regulation by design'. *Information, Communication & Society* 20 (1): 118–36.

Notes

I would like to thank David Abecassis, Raquel Campos Valverde, Nicholas Cook, Niall Saville, Valerio Signorelli and David Trippett for their conversation and suggestions on draft versions of this article.

1 Zeynep Tufekci, 'Machine intelligence makes human morals more important', TED Talk, www.ted.com/talks/zeynep_tufekci_machine_intelligence_makes_human_morals_more_ important; 'TedX reveals 2018 theme: Black box', *Michigan Daily*, 16 November 2017, www.michigandaily.com/section/campus-life/tedx-reveals-theme-black-box. All websites accessed 21 March 2019.

2 'Internet World Stats: Usage and population statistics', www.internetworldstats.com.

3 Daniel Miller et al. (2016) suggest that privacy remains in many cases around the world a 'Western' construct. In India, for example, outcasts require algorithmic recommendations simply to access basic goods and services. In China, the paradox lies in how scale comes into play in different experiences of privacy: new migrants to cities very often experience (imagined) private communication for the first time through the WeChat smartphone app, even as the platform is clearly functioning under state control.

4 Personal communication, 30 July 2018.

5 Personal communication, 30 July 2018.

6 See also K. E. Goldschmitt and Nick Seaver's discussion of 'critical algorithm studies', this volume, Chapter 3 (pp. 72–4).

7 Kashmir Hill, 'How Target figured out a teen girl was pregnant before her father did', *Forbes*, 16 February 2012, www.forbes.com/sites/kashmirhill/2012/02/16/how-target-figured-out-a-teen-girl-was-pregnant-before-her-father-did/#6f087ba06668; Jordan Ellenberg, 'What's even creepier than Target guessing that you're pregnant?' *Slate*, 9 June 2014, www.slate.com/blogs/ how_not_to_be_wrong/2014/06/09/big_data_what_s_even_creepier_than_target_guessing_ that_you_re_pregnant.html?via=gdpr-consent.

8 'Five Little Babies Jumping On The Bed', published by Videogyan 3D Rhymes, www.youtube .com/watch?v=97D-kkh39bg; 'Five Little Babies Went To A Zoo', published by Videogyan 3D Rhymes, www.youtube.com/watch?v=9rQYMrDDO1c.

9 'Five Little Babies Teasing Monkeys', published by Black Lamb, www.youtube.com/watch?v= czAH8abEVCM; 'Five Little Babies Dressed As Police', published by Videogyan 3D Rhymes, www.youtube.com/watch?v=sLcZMq8o1to. Conscientious parents will point out that YouTube has launched a child-friendly version of its platform that omits such videos. However, the service is still not immune to the subtle placing of advertisements for toys.

10 '2016 Global Internet Phenomena: Latin America & North America', *Sandvine Intelligent Broadband Networks*, www.sandvine.com/hubfs/downloads/archive/2016-global-internet-phenomena-report-latin-america-and-north-america.pdf; Georges Mao, 'Video in Southeast Asia: The shift to mobile and what it means for marketers', *Think With Google*, 6 May 2016, www.thinkwithgoogle.com/intl/en-apac/ad-channel/mobile/video-southeast-asia-shift-to-mobile-what-it-means-for-marketers/.

11 Adrian Peter Tse, 'China's Google ban gives Baidu search engine global boost', *Campaign*, 2 April 2015, www.campaignlive.co.uk/article/chinas-google-ban-gives-baidu-search-engine-global-boost/1341336.

12 Taylor Bryant, 'What it's like to love K-pop while Black', *Nylon,* 9 January 2018, https:// nylon.com/articles/k-pop-appropriation-black-culture.

13 See Chapter 4 (Gopinath and Stanyek), p. 111.

14 Aarian Marshall, 'Alphabet is trying to reinvent the city, starting with Toronto', *WIRED*, 19 October 2017, www.wired.com/story/google-sidewalk-labs-toronto-quayside/.

15 Vlad Savov, 'China's phone market is now dominated by five companies, none of which is Samsung', *The Verge*, 6 December 2017, www.theverge.com/2017/12/6/16741142/china-smartphone-market-stats-android-oem-2017.

16 Some of these China-originated interfaces have acquired international reach, including WeChat and AliPay as parallel platforms to WhatsApp and ApplePay.

17 Nielsen Music 360 China, www.nielsen.com/content/dam/nielsenglobal/cn/docs/Music%20360%20China%20Highlights.pdf.

18 'Song Of The Grass-Mud Horse', published by Skippybentley, www.youtube.com/watch?v=wKx1aenJK08.

19 Michael Wines, 'A dirty pun tweaks China's online censors', *New York Times*, 11 March 2009, www.nytimes.com/2009/03/12/world/asia/12beast.html.

20 'Baidu Shida Shen ShenShou', https://tieba.baidu.com/p/3154505693?red_tag=2783519962.

21 'Kuaizi Xiongdi – Xiao Ping Guo [Chopsticks Brothers – Little Apple]', www.iqiyi.com/v_19rrohuung.html#vfrm=3-2-zebra-1.

22 Rob Schwartz, 'Chinese music industry reacts to government hip hop ban', *Billboard*, 5 February 2018, www.billboard.com/articles/business/8098147/chinese-music-industry-china-government-hip-hop-ban.

23 Ed Jefferson, 'No, China isn't Black Mirror – social credit scores are more complex and sinister than that', *New Statesman*, 27 April 2018, www.newstatesman.com/world/asia/2018/04/no-china-isn-t-black-mirror-social-credit-scores-are-more-complex-and-sinister. Jennifer Bisset, 'Black Mirror too real in China as school shuns parents with bad social credit', *CNET*, 2 May 2018, www.cnet.com/news/black-mirror-too-real-in-china-as-schools-shun-parents-with-bad-social-credit/.

24 Cindy Waxer, 'Big Data blues: The dangers of data-mining', *Computerworld*, 4 November 2013, www.computerworld.com/article/2485493/enterprise-applications-big-data-blues-the-dangers-of-data-mining.html.

25 For further discussion of user data and surveillance within the commercial context see Chapters 1 (Cook), 2 and 11 (Scherzinger), 3 (Goldschmitt and Seaver) and 4 (Gopinath and Stanyek).

26 The hype surrounding China's rapid digital development, as well the rest of the world's shock at its launching of state-designed algocracies, has perhaps become overheated. A voice of circumspection may be needed: for all the talk of untrammelled progress, kinks still exist in China's uneven processes of technologisation. Indeed, the very IFPI statistics which show China to be one of the fastest-developing digital music markets in the world still put its projected growth rates behind the rapidly expanding bloc of Latin America and the Caribbean (IFPI 2017).

27 Sam Wolfson, 'Amazon's Alexa recorded private conversation and sent it to random contact', *The Guardian*, 24 May 2018, www.theguardian.com/technology/2018/may/24/amazon-alexa-recorded-conversation.

28 'Petra turns off lights, then tells Alexa how she really feels while being introduced to Google Home', published by PetraGrey, www.youtube.com/watch?v=izaQmP5Ewbs; 'Parrot makes shopping list', published by Bibi the Bird, www.youtube.com/watch?v=IvnW89osj0g.

29 Yessi Bello Perez, 'Smarthome device ownership to rise by 2022', *UKTN*, 15 March 2018, www.uktech.news/news/industry-analysis/smart-home-device-ownership-to-rise-by-2022-20180315; Misha Njeri Madsen, 'Turning city slums smart', *Quercus Group*, 4 May 2017, www.quercus-group.com/single-post/2017/05/04/Turning-City-Slums-Smart; Nimisha Jaiswal, 'India's "Smart City" plan stumbles over slums', *New Internationalist*, 1 June 2017, newint.org/features/2017/06/01/smart-city-plan-stumbles-over-slums.

30 'Sound and Virtuality', www.davidtrippett.com/music–digital-culture.

31 This meshes well with Isabella van Elferen's suggestion that 'musical experience is able to create a virtual reality ... *any* musical experience can generate a virtual world' (Chapter 8, p. 222).

32 Interview, Yuri Suzuki, sound and industrial designer. Hackney, London. 4 June 2018.

33 Hans Rosling, 'The Magic Washing Machine', TEDWomen 2010, www.ted.com/talks/hans_rosling_and_the_magic_washing_machine?language=en.

34 See Chapter 1, p. 20.

35 Nanjala Nyabola, 'Wakanda is not Africa, and that's OK', *Al Jazeera*, 13 March 2018, www.aljazeera.com/indepth/opinion/wakanda-african-180313123713872.html; Edward Amedolu, 'How I marveled at Black Panther's re-imagining of Africa', *The Conversation*,

15 February 2018, theconversation.com/how-i-marvelled-at-black-panthers-reimagining-of-africa-91703.

36 Iqyi search results for Psy and *Hei Pao,* so.iqiyi.com/so/q_PSY%20%E9%BB%91%E8%B1%B9?source=input&sr=1385919276160.

37 'Tupac Hit Em Up Dax *Yeshi Danzi Henda, gan* Remix *zhege*' [Tupac Hit Em Up Dax has huge guts in remixing this one], www.iqiyi.com/w_19rvd4ont1.html.

11 The Political Economy of Streaming

MARTIN SCHERZINGER

Introduction

New technologies of listening are not simply signs that can be interpreted; they are not direct determinants of economic or political power; and they are not straightforwardly technical innovations. Any discussion of the economics of music in the early twenty-first century must intersect the question concerning technology – big data storage, distributed network technology, programmable artificial intelligence (AI), and so on – with the question concerning contemporary markets – the merchandising of desire, taste and sensibility within a surveillant attention economy, and its concomitant labour ethics. This chapter attempts to historicise musical labour practices in the current age of technological automation.

As inter-corporate struggles turned toward control of the 'Internet of Things' – an industry coinage that refers less to *things per se* than it does to internet-enabled *platforms* for learning behaviour and gathering user information in service of technologically-assisted interactions and experiences – we witnessed an expanding dialectical gap between the heterogeneous, disseminated habits of everyday practice and the incrementally ordered corporate infrastructures that monitor, and increasingly automate, that practice. In other words, in the first decade of the twenty-first century, collaborative peer-to-peer networking and music file-sharing – with direct links to a kind of progressive cyber-politics, demonstrably indifferent to extant economic reward systems – had become dominant sociocultural techniques. By the second decade, however, these very practices had been deftly co-opted by new corporate intermediaries, who successfully monetised a widespread *habitus* by way of a new conveyer-belt delivery system for audio and video.

While official revenues associated with them were perplexingly limited, streaming services had transformed into large-scale privatised spying services, licensed by users to harvest personal data, which – crossed with advertising agencies – could manufacture opinion, generate consumption and modify behaviour. In other words, these new music intermediaries were designed to leverage sophisticated technologies to aggregate user attention and sell advertising. This raised a host of questions, the first of which concern data privacy, data security, the management of user data, and procedures for third-party requests for data and metadata. The second set of questions concern the redistributions of revenue that took place – almost noiselessly – across the contradictory terrain of music licensing, copyright and digital rights management. By investigating the social, technical and legal dimensions of this shifting terrain, the chapter suggests that their impact on cultural labour practices in the digital age, in the final analysis, bears an uncanny resemblance to that in a pre-technological one.

From Disintermediation to Hyper-Intermediation

By the end of the second decade of the twenty-first century, the decentralised Internet – arguably open and public in the 1990s and 2000s – had given way to an unprecedented centralisation of data and platforms ownership within the global digital architecture. What was once considered a disintermediated network (no middlemen), assisted by new efficiencies in search functionality and peer-to-peer connectivity, had modulated within ten years into a de facto system of central nodes, which controlled and coordinated large swaths of the network. Music distribution had likewise shifted decisively from the unruly, but ubiquitous, practice of informal downloading and file-sharing toward music streaming, facilitated by a concentrated group of large-scale streaming services – including Beats (later bought by Apple), Rhapsody (later bought by Napster, which had rebranded itself as a legal entity), Deezer, Rdio, Pandora, Google Play, Apple Music, and Spotify, a European-based service that launched in the United States (initially in partnership with Facebook) in 2011. As high-speed mobile devices became widespread, users gradually discontinued the process of syncing and transferring musical tracks from a variety of sources in favour of streaming music from a central source. This historical transition marked a large-scale *relicensing* of musical content in accordance with traditional legal obligations toward rights holders, even as the mode of music's consumption had fundamentally shifted from an ownership model to a *rental* one. Instead of purchasing (or downloading) music on the basis of discrete units – which were once ordered by the producer (or playlisted by the consumer) – music was now largely consumed as a kind of auto-playing sequence, hitched to various algorithmic procedures. Paradoxically, the very user-generated activities that had once delinked music from its commodity form – the art of generating personalised playlists from free content, for example – morphed into the raw material, or data points, for an automation of curation procedures that re-secured its commodity form.

The promised disintermediation of music's industrial sector by the digitally networked environment in the first decade of the twenty-first century was upended, in a twofold sense, in the second decade. First, by licensing the music delivered by streaming services, the more traditional conception of music as a unit-based commodity was paradoxically resurrected in the very moment that attendant listening habits were cultivated by technical platforms that had shifted *away* from unit-based music delivery systems. Second, by securing a percentage of the profit derived from actual plays, the newer conception of music as a service was *additionally* monetised by the delivery systems themselves. In other words, just as had happened in the first decade of radio broadcasting in the 1920s, streaming services elided what were formerly distinct systems of distribution, producing what economists call 'option value' blurring (Wikström 2009, 90–1; see also Chapter 2). Where disseminating technologies, such as radio and television, had functioned primarily as marketing or promotional tools to guide consumption – delivering audiences both to advertisers and to retailers – streaming services functioned as promotional/marketing vehicles *and* simultaneously doubled as an on-demand conveyer-belt of content. If the Internet of the first decade of the twenty-first century could still be construed as a 'gigantic copying machine', it had transformed by the second decade into its antithesis, a zero-copy machine – a library bank that technically required no more than single master copies, accessible via rental on all internet-enabled devices (Nimmer 2003, 157).

By 2010, the transition from local to remote access musical playlists had reached a tipping point. A generation of young listeners had effectively been steered away from file-sharing and downloading, and had become accustomed instead to online music streaming. Already in 2009 a study detected the trend, revealing that 'many teenagers (65%) are streaming music regularly, with more 14 to 18 year olds (31%) listening to streamed music on their computer every day compared with music fans overall (18%)'.[1] By 2013, new subscribers to services such as Spotify had more or less stopped downloading or file-sharing pirated music. A year later, the overall global recorded music industry revenues declined once more, but revenues from streaming surpassed, for the first time, those of compact discs, digital downloads and other physical media. For the remaining decade, overall industry revenues increased steadily and streaming services dominated the market share. Between 2013 and 2015, Google Play, Spotify and Pandora streaming services grew by double digits. After 2016, most Americans were listening to music via streaming services, which now constituted the bulk of the industry's revenues. Just as monopolies converged around radio in the 1920s – in the early 1920s, various corporations initially coalesced into the National Broadcasting System (NBC), and in the late 1920s into the Columbia Phonograph Broadcasting Company (CBS) – streaming services in the 2010s consolidated into a handful of dominant platforms – YouTube, Apple Music and Spotify in America; Tencent in China; and Mdundo in Africa. In the face of terminal losses, smaller ('indie') services, like SoundCloud, shifted their focus toward selling digital compositional tools to musicians (rather than delivering playlists to listeners), and others, like Groove Music (Microsoft), became entirely obsolete. Even Pandora, one of the pioneers in the streaming industry, found itself unable to compete against Spotify and Apple and so merged with the satellite radio provider SiriusXM in 2018. While their ascendant market value indicated a new direction for music consumption, even the dominant streaming platforms (running *licensed* content) operated at a significant loss in their early years. More than 80 per cent of earnings at Spotify, for example, were directed toward rights holders. Annual reports indicated that net losses at Pandora and Spotify in the early 2010s ran into hundreds of millions of dollars. By 2018 Spotify had about 160 million active users (with nearly half paying monthly subscriptions), but simultaneously reported losses of $1.5 billion.[2] Despite these evident losses, Spotify was successfully listed on the New York Stock Exchange in April 2018, buttressed by an unorthodox capitalisation process grounded in characteristically aspirational language resonant with the idea that new media were somehow paradigm-shifting. Goldman Sachs, a multinational bank and financial services company, for example, predicted that revenues from music streaming would quintuple by 2030.

This was the age of speculative capitalism, reflecting a latent demand for viable new technology companies: with a large enough visitor base, the thinking went, profits would somehow follow. Streaming platforms were a new kind of corporate entity – technical intermediaries between music labels and the listening public – without an evident business model, but whose stock was nonetheless heavily capitalised (by advertisers, insurance holders, credit agencies, and so on). The streaming platforms followed a contemporary pattern of growth for growth's sake. After all, the world's biggest online retailer in the second decade of the twenty-first century, Amazon, had already demonstrated staggering growth, even though it ostensibly generated only meagre profits. Amazon's basic model was to price below cost and expand widely by diversifying its services into as many realms as possible. In addition to being a retailer, it had become a marketing platform, a delivery and logistics network, a payment service, a credit lender, an auction house, a major book publisher, a producer of television and films, a fashion designer, a hardware manufacturer, and a leading host of cloud server space. In its attempt to capture global audiences, Google, too, had evolved beyond a search engine and included an array of free services, including news, maps, streaming, and cloud storage for documents. Likewise, the struggle for dominance of music streaming was geared toward building a diversified media platform that would eventually move beyond music alone. YouTube's multi-tiered system for streaming media included entire films (on YouTube Premium, initially known as YouTube Red) as well as download functionality. Likewise, Apple Music branched out into video programming (such as James Corden's 'Carpool Karaoke') at the same time that Instagram introduced long-form video onto its platform. Spotify's signature playlists, such as RapCaviar, also began to include video in 2018. By 2019, further acquisitions and partnerships propelled Spotify beyond its music streaming origins into podcasting and film. The inclusion of aspects of virtual reality into the platform would soon follow. As Spotify's CEO Daniel Ek put it: 'The question of when we'll be profitable actually feels irrelevant. Our focus is all on growth. That is priority one, two, three, four and five.'[3] Sasa Zorovic, analyst at the investment bank Oppenheimer & Company, noted in relation to the world's largest music streaming service, YouTube, 'In the real estate business, it's about location, location, location. On the Internet, it's about traffic, traffic, traffic. If you have traffic, you will be able to monetize it one way or another' (Lee 2007). The endgame for streaming platforms, especially as they tended toward diversified media platforms, was to secure a proprietary network-based monopoly with a global reach. These would become the hyper-intermediaries that controlled the contemporary Internet. By the second decade of the twenty-first century, the Internet was dominated by a few titanic platforms, which could leverage the market at scale. Even without China, for example, Google accounted for nearly 90 per cent of global online search. Likewise, Facebook, the social network behemoth, serviced over two billion monthly active users, exceeding the scope of MySpace (at its peak) by a factor of twenty. In China, the messaging app WeChat (owned and produced by the company Tencent) had incrementally metamorphosed, through a series of iterative updates, into a multi-faceted infrastructure for handling personal finance, games, news, shopping, employment, customer service and more. Music streaming, now the dominant music delivery system, was consolidating into a similarly monopolised economic space.

Given the seeming indifference to traditional revenue streams, it is once again tempting to attribute these shifts in online musical consumption to technological factors alone. However, while digital technologies abetted the transformation of listening habits, they did not drive it. This applies to the exponential increase in bandwidth as a result of improvements to fibre-optic communication infrastructures in the 1990s and 2000s, as well as the emergence and large-scale global dissemination of high-speed mobile phones and tablets. Both developments were responses to commercial imperatives: the first, a demand for bandwidth-intensive consumer services, including music and video streaming on demand (recapitulating the experiential conditions created by the practice of playlisting in the era of downloads); and the second, a demand for affordable mobile connectivity, and its structural integration into economic networks of production and exchange (recapitulating the enormous collections of music downloaded on personal computers and mobile devices). Cloud-based services effectively rendered hard drives obsolete by delivering immense databanks of musical content to multiple devices. Streaming could thereby bypass the technical inconveniences of hard-drive malfunctions, the limitations of memory chips on computers, and the possible legal consequences associated with engaging P2P networks. In short, the practices of downloading (via torrents and other means) withered in the context of all-access virtualised playlists controlled by music streaming companies.

From the point of view of the early adopter, the economic difference between downloaded playlists and those offered by a streaming service was minimal. Spotify, for example, offered unlimited access to its online music library either for a small monthly fee or by way of an advertising-based ('free') service. In a gesture that recapitulated the technological upheavals in the music industry of the past (such as the replacement of vinyl LPs with digital CDs in the early 1980s), early incarnations of the website encouraged users to devalue their current digital playlists in favour of the service: 'Think of Spotify as your new music collection. Your library. Only this time your collection is vast: 8 million tracks and counting.' Along with the promise of a kind of limitless collection, Spotify emphasised its efficiency (against that of physical downloads); its convenience (deploying only a temporary data buffer instead of permanent memory on a hard drive); its social functionality (its playlists were 'free to share'); and its suitability for portable devices (which could store playlists also while offline). The revolution in music consumption associated with the electric phonograph and broadcast radio in the 1920s was finally upended and reconfigured a hundred years later in the context of the Internet. Music had moved from the bookshelf for LP records to the CD holder; then it moved from the computer to the external drive; and, finally, from local storage sites to virtualised music collections stored on a remote server. Users no longer collected songs, but accessed vast, and highly organised, playlists using always-connected computers and ever-relocating smartphones. Streaming music would be experienced less in terms of a sequence of discrete units of content and more as a conveyer-belt of affect, algorithmically bound by considerations of genre, style, mood, weather, geolocation, personal history and current activity. It is a curious paradox of the shift from downloading to streaming, that it would mark the shift from a kind of free access to (formerly) commodified units of music to a commodified access to free-flowing streams of music. It is as if the new technologies mirrored the musical experiences afforded by the piracy they, in turn, eliminated.

The Contested Stylistics of Financialised Streaming

Given the archaic marketing and promotional techniques of the traditional music labels, industry leaders began to experiment with a variety of release strategies – from limited releases on specific streaming services (such as Tidal in the case of Kanye West's 2016 release of *Life of Pablo*) to premium hardware companies or cable channels (such as Apple in the case of Beyoncé's 2015 'visual' album; or HBO in the case of Beyoncé's 2016 release of *Lemonade*). In practice, the very concept of the music *album* became digitally de-ontologised – melting, in Ben Ratliff's words, 'into the water world of sound' (Ratliff 2016). The attempt to redefine new media realities to archaic, or real-world, counterparts – dubbed 'skeuomorphism' in media studies – ruled the day. For example, by 2016 the decreasingly relevant album concept – itself a kind of forced bundling of songs to boost revenues in the age of the LP and CD – was redefined by the RIAA as 1,500 on-demand audio streams. Even though the relationship of a particular number of downloads to the conceptual commodity structure of an *album* was entirely derivative, the industry persisted in its attempt to retain its traditional selling structures and attendant reward programmes. Likewise, two years later, Billboard differentiated the streams constituting their Hot 100 charts according to whether they had been accessed, on the one hand, by subscription-based streaming, or, on the other, by advertisement-based streaming. But the late-twentieth-century consensus about how music's value should be evaluated had broken down. YouTube – with direct roots in UGC a decade earlier – rejected Billboard's idea, for example, claiming that the charts should reflect actual engagements with music instead of simply paid streams. Artists too responded in diverse ways to the changing economies of music. On the one hand, streaming services were regarded with suspicion. Radiohead, for example, removed their work from Spotify, opting instead to make it available on BitTorrent; while Taylor Swift temporarily removed her album *1989* from Spotify, which resulted in the sale of two million albums by traditional means. On the other hand, artists and labels mobilised diverse release strategies that tactically deployed streaming services. Rihanna, for example, released an album exclusively on Tidal, but then also included a million free downloads; while The 1975 waited two weeks after the release of an album before placing it on a streaming service.

Commentators were divided on the effect streaming had on the stylistics of musical listening. In his book *Mashed Up: Music, Technology, and the Rise of Configurable Culture*, for example, Aram Sinnreich (2010) extolled the virtues of the new non-linear modes of intertextual music-making, whose patterns deftly recapitulated the networked architectures of new digital technologies. Likewise, in his *Sonic Warfare: Sound, Affect, and the Ecology of Fear*, Steve Goodman celebrated the manifold new genres blossoming in the context of digital remixes, mashups and musics grounded in samples from 'the riddim method of Jamaican pop, to the sampladelia of US hip-hop, the remixology of disco, house, and techno, and the hyperdub methodologies of the hard-core continuum' (2010, 162). From the perspective of music listeners, the cornucopia of online listening could delink the musical ear from stratified conventions of old definable coordinates. Ratliff, for example, observed: 'There is a possibility that hearing so much music without specifically asking for it develops in the listener a fresh kind of aural perception, an ability to size up a song and contextualize it in a new or personal way, rather than immediately rejecting it based on an external idea of genre or style'. Not surprisingly, Ratliff praises the logics of remix and mashup, the fusion of 'elements of two different songs', and their 'stark musical oppositions' (2016, 5, 6). For these writers, the convergence of consumer electronics and digital music distribution and consumption proffered a culture of productively disoriented creative praxis anchored in rich intertextual fields of independently launched musical expression.

While the sheer quantity of online musical production made it difficult to assess, the artistic value of such recent trends in new music was as much praised as it was contested and in doubt. Far from detecting genuine creativity in the artistry of remix, mashup, and other genre-defying flows that build critical 'question marks … into our hearing', writers like Jaron Lanier detected a logic of decontextualised fragments in an assemblage to be exploited by others: 'Pop culture has entered into a nostalgic malaise. Online culture is dominated by trivial mashups of the culture that existed before the onset of mashups, and by fandom responding to the dwindling outposts of centralized mass media. It is a culture of reaction without action'; 'Where is the new music? Everything is retro, retro, retro' (Ratliff 2016, 6; Lanier 2010, 20, 129). One symptom of the nostalgic turn was the paradoxical emergence of musical genres like glitch art, which aestheticised technological failures and malfunctions, and vaporwave, which engaged outdated sounds (from advertising jingles and video games to retro musical styles) to expressive effect. Arguably, by leveraging a kind of reflective *techno-terroir*, these genres critically engaged with the consumer culture upon which they depended. Lanier, however, would regard this kind of artistic practice as derivative and reactionary. He connected the reactive musical culture to the reduction of personhood to illusionary bit-matrices, such as the 'multiple-choice identities' prescribed by social-networking platforms like Facebook, and the erasure of viewpoints by 'hive-mind' collaborations like Wikipedia (2010, 31, 48). Where Sinnreich and Goodman observed an explosion of new online creativity, Lanier detected a reactionary cultural soundtrack to recombinant, semi-automated processes that diminished qualities of human expression.

What is clear is that – whether construed *pro* or *contra* – the stylistics of algorithmically determined playlists did not merely reflect the popularity of a song, but also increasingly played a role in constructing it. The real-time feedback between users' behaviour and the algorithmic procedures generating playlists had the potential of becoming an eddy-like loop, eventually also leaving an imprint on the aesthetics of production, vocal performance, tempo choice, global reference set, sample types, and so on, for music designed for streaming. This kind of mediatic intrusion on music's stylistics bore the marks of a lengthy history, including the musical effects of phonograph records, the recording techniques and devices of music studios, the types of speakers used in homes and concerts (whether mono or stereo, etc.), the audio–video relations in the era of television, and the quantitatively calibrated standardisations associated with radio consolidation, to name but a few. For example, the evolution of the standard length for the popular song (which ranged approximately between three and five minutes) – occasionally attributed to the length of the early 45 RPM 7-inch phonograph record – was calculated in the context of marketing strategies characteristic of the early phonograph era in the United States of America. By the mid-1920s, standardised verse – chorus formulas, gradually compressed from about six to seven verses (with eight to ten lines) to two to three verses (with a maximum of four lines), had become the preferred structure for songs crafted in Tin Pan Alley. In comparison to the lengthy, complex, lyricised storytelling found in frontier ballads, children's songs and cowboy songs of nineteenth-century American vernacular (or folklore), the songs of Tin Pan Alley were short, simplified and formally standardised. Additionally, music became increasingly vested in property rights during this period. After the passing of the Copyright Act of 1891, songwriters, lyricists, arrangers, and particularly publishers, reliably received royalties for music. This constellation of industrial imperatives encouraged the high-speed production of short standardised songs synchronised to thematic fashion. The standard song structure and moderate length of a copyright-protected popular song was well suited to a retail strategy that bolstered sales by limiting the life of a product (a strategy termed 'planned obsolescence' during the Great Depression), and predominated for the ensuing century (see Suisman 2009).

In the context of music streaming a hundred years later, the music stylistics inherited from the popular verse–chorus structure had shifted in certain significant ways. To begin with, the first thirty seconds of a song were anchored in a series of enticing hooks, a memorable or familiar sample, or even an arresting chorus.[4] This is because skipping ahead before reaching the thirty-second mark of a song was not considered to be a legitimate 'play' of that song by streaming services. The thirty-second format for streaming was even hacked by the American funk band Vulpeck on their album *Sleepify*, consisting of ten silent tracks of approximately thirty seconds long. The band requested that fans play the album on repeat throughout the night, raising approximately $20,000 in royalty payments. Hogan argued that, in addition to 'reverse-engineered' songs that strategically produce sonic allure in the first thirty seconds – Katy Perry's opening sample of Fatboy Slim on her song 'Swish Swish' (2017) was a classic example – the signature sound of streaming was characterised by a host of additional techniques such as slower tempi, abbreviated use of three or four chords, rave-like synthesiser sounds, and so on. The songwriter Dr Luke, for example, deployed what he called the 'stuttering' effect, whereby a short syllable was electronically repeated to rhythmicise a word, exemplified by Rihanna's 'Umbrella' (2009) or Ke$ha's 'We R Who We R' (2010). Another technique was the so-called millennial whoop, a sequence of notes that alternated between the fifth and third notes of a tonic chord in a major scale, typically starting on the fifth, exemplified by Katy Perry's 'Teenage Dream' (2010) or Carly Rae Jepsen and Adam Young's 'Good Time' (2012). The songwriter John T. Harding drew attention to another technique – the 'pop-drop' – whereby a vivid bass synth sound from EDM was suddenly introduced into the song's otherwise melodic texture, exemplified by Justin Bieber's 'Where Are Ü Now' (2015). Hogan even argued that this kind of technique came to characterise the genre-blending tropical house – a genre fundamentally shaped by streaming technologies. What differentiated these techniques from the traditional standardisations associated with popular music was that they were designed specifically for music streaming platforms (and their attendant output devices). Songs were generally shorter, Hogan argues, choruses appeared earlier in the structure, and artists created songs with playlists in mind, often pre-empting their technical mode of transmission. Relatively unknown artists emerged – like Lawrence, Sloan and Nesbitt – who nonetheless amassed millions of streams on Spotify. Their music, orientated towards the data-driven systems of mood-enhancing playlists, bore the marks of these stylistics.[5] By 2010, in other words, musical tracks had become tailored for streaming.

While the way the format and the medium weigh upon the sound and the content of music could be readily detected in the context of engineering and marketing of music for streaming, the actual economics of early streaming were vexingly opaque. Nearly a century earlier, Theodor W. Adorno had detected a link between the economics and the aesthetics of popular music in the context of the then-emergent technology of radio (Adorno 2009). Adorno argued that popular music had become largely standardised – with intermittent pseudo-differentiating details to sustain listeners' interest – in the context of 'post-competitive' (monopoly) capital. However, although early radio was dominated by monopoly networks – controlled, in turn, by advertisers, investors and advertising agencies – the philosopher's analysis was significantly complicated by the fact that it was federal licensing and regulation of radio (instead of censorious corporate impulses alone) that constrained the freedom and diversity of musical broadcasts from the 1920s to the 1940s. In other words, as it was for radio, the monopolised nature of streaming platforms in the second decade of the twenty-first century do not sufficiently explain the way a technical format shapes the sound of music. In fact, the way music become monetised in the context of streaming technologies was an innovation that equally bore the marks, as discussed above, of an era of informal downloading and file-sharing as it did the later era of corporate consolidation and monopolies. It was in the curious conjuncture of freely exchanged culture online and the emergent corporate control of digital platforms that the measurable revenue streams toward actual artists indicated remarkably meagre returns. Mode Records, for example, received less than one-third of a penny for every stream on Spotify.[6] In 2013, many prominent artists began to testify to, and then protest against, the failures of the streaming model, and the implications of its overall fiscal disenfranchisement of artists.[7] The peculiar monetisation practices of music streaming related to the unique ways that content providers engaged service providers. In other words, instead of monetising *per stream*, music labels tended to be invested in equity shares in the streaming services themselves. This meant that revenues generated by advertising and subscription fees were proportionately divided among equity holders and only then distributed to artists, according to variable agreements between artists and labels. As with consumption, remuneration in the era of streaming was delinked from its central legal *raison d'être*, the unit-based song, which was meant to guide its financialised circulation. The utopian aspirations of early internet pioneers – such as Paul Borrill, Jim Herriot, Stuart Kauffman, Jaron Lanier, Ted Nelson, Bruce Sawhill, Lee Smolin, Eric Weinstein and others – were challenged by this model. Nelson's early ideas concerning the economics of the Internet, for example, respected the monetary (labour) value of creative content, however much this content had been transformed into digital bits. Nelson proposed the idea that when a digital bit of music, journalism, video art, and so on, was accessed by a user, the maker of that expression should be able to command a direct payment of a moderate sum. The libertarian idea was to eliminate the content brokers, or intermediaries, that separated audiences from creative labourers. Lanier updated Nelson's ideas by arguing for a simple universal system for making fluid payments online, ultimately to be administered by elected governments (2010, 105–7). The idea that internet companies that logged and analysed user data to improve customer retention, product design, advertising initiatives, and so on, should actually *pay* their users for their data gained some traction beyond the circle of cyber-libertarians and in the mainstream press.[8] For all their technical insight, however, neither Nelson nor (the early) Lanier could foresee the turn away from content-based consumption toward service-based delivery systems – a shift from parsed units of sound (known as songs) to seemingly endless musicscapes on the model of an infinite-seeming conveyer-belt. If *units* were the de facto basis for music's traditional economic exchange, then *streaming* – which emerged directly within listening practices cultivated in the context of free music – created the conditions for a radical revision of its financialisation.

The heated discussion in the second decade of the twenty-first century about the potential use of blockchain technology (an open, indelible ledger of transactions recorded in real time) in contexts outside the financial services sector, notably the music industry, emphasised the distributed nature of the global database for music, as well as the possibility of paying creators, song-writers and musicians efficiently and equitably. According to Rakesh Sharma, 'Blockchain's distributed ledger can be used for a variety of applications within the music industry, including ensuring direct payments to artists and estab-lishing large digital rights management services run by artists themselves.'[9] In this worldview, technological efficiencies marched in step with libertarian economic ones. Blockchain was wholly in sync with the libertarian ideals of Nelson, Borrill, Lanier and others. By coordinating the ledger of transactions across a distributed network, and then encrypting the record-keeping, block-chain promised to cut out a swath of intermediaries – from artists' agents and marketing professionals to music studios, record companies and financing institutions. More precisely, blockchain promised a system of self-executing 'smart contracts', which automated the transparent payment of royalties for licensed or copyrighted digital music.[10] To this extent, blockchain could enact a kind of limited digital rights management for the efficient processing of micro-payments. Some blockchain-powered platforms emerged during this period – Voise, for example, promised a platform for artists to upload and monetise their creations within the context of a P2P network – but, in general, the fundamental antagonism between the experiential flow of streaming music and a (micro-) payment scheme that relied fundamentally on *unit*-based music seemed to annul the challenge posed by blockchain. Aside from concerns regarding the sheer computing power required to process blocks of sound containing complex layers of copyright protection – itself a lurking site of powerful intermediaries – music streaming was increasingly tethered to the algorithmic processing of genre, style, mood, weather, geolocation, personal history and current activity, rather than to individual songs and their attend-ant author-figures.

As a result, far from facilitating a networked world of micro-payments through technologies such as blockchain, the Internet had mutated into a new kind of hierarchy, controlled by a handful of large companies that effectively acted as intermediaries between users and musicians. Given the mismatch between the flow of investment capital and tangible profits, it was not surprising that the most powerful music streaming platforms of the second decade of the twenty-first century – YouTube, Apple Music and Spotify – were also the lowest revenue-producing platforms for artists. As a result, even stars like Lady Gaga were locked into recording label deals that generated no appreciable remuneration (for the artist) from online plays or streams. Far from tending toward disintermediation, the old industrial intermediaries had effectively been transformed into, and substituted by, a handful of cloud-based hyper-intermediaries. It would not be an exaggeration to say that the turn toward streaming was not unlike a return toward the impresarios of the eighteenth century, or the publishers of the nineteenth century, who extracted great surplus from, and exercised outsize control over, individual composers and musicians. A decade of freely available music on open networks had created the conditions for its own undermining; a commons-based culture of sharing on open networks had tragically mutated into a business model that incubated vast privately owned online monopolies.

Internet – Dragnet: Music's Surveillance Economy

The financing of streaming services generally followed the classic model of advertising. The world's largest streaming service, YouTube, also offered an advertisement-free alternative (by subscription), but advertising was a central component for generating revenues. By 2008, YouTube featured homepage video advertising, standard banner advertisements with embedded links (toward the base of the video screen) and in-video advertisements (preceding the play of the searched video). YouTube had also mounted 'Sponsored Channels', 'Promoted Videos', 'Spotlight Videos', and categories such as 'Most Viewed', which could technically be manipulated by those who could pay for it (van Dijck 2009). In many ways, the steady encroachment of advertising recapitulated the age of radio, which gradually shifted from commercial-free broadcasting to a model of insistent advertising, by way of branded content. Despite early enthusiasm for the Internet as a likewise non-commercial public space, YouTube had transformed into a mega-media outlet supported by advertising. Although YouTube split its advertising revenue with those content providers with whom it had signed licensing deals, much of their content creation fell outside the rubric of official culture. Even if users were drawn to the platform because of user-generated content, compensation for users posting audio-visual content on YouTube was limited to those who had signed on as media partners. In other words, even while ascendant streaming services like Spotify mounted licensed content, most uploads on YouTube were simply circulating as free audio-visual content.

The benefit to YouTube of the 'safe harbour' provision of the DMCA should not be underestimated (see Chapter 2, p. 44). This is because the platform could not strictly be held liable for unauthorised distribution of protected works, or excerpts of works – which included 'derivative' works that somehow included sound, image or text of a licensed work. Although Google possessed the web-tracking technology to automatically detect licensed content (known as its ContentID system), the onus was on the licence holder to issue a takedown notice in the case of infringing material. Most of the industrial content providers (such as Universal, EMI and Viacom) felt compromised by their partnerships with YouTube. The conflict between content provision and content promotion placed the industry squarely in the horns of a dilemma. To take a simple example, among many: when the band OK Go – which, by 2006, was already a self-launched YouTube success – signed a deal with EMI for their second album, the company repeatedly vacillated between removing their music videos from YouTube and then, noticing no significant shift in revenue, uploading them again. On a larger scale, clashes between Viacom and YouTube reached epic proportions, ranging from demands to remove hundreds of thousands of videos from the site to high-stakes litigation pertaining to the economics of copyrights and licences. For content providers, it was a losing battle, for it seemed that traffic to official sites for content did not appreciably increase when videos were removed from YouTube. At the same time, YouTube continued to attract more and more visitors; in the weeks that Viacom had initially removed its clips, for example, YouTube had grown from 17 to 19 million users. Given the sheer size of YouTube, the content industry had no choice but to capitulate to its business model. The court battles between Google and Viacom were finally settled in 2014, but the distrust between the content industry and YouTube persisted. The official 2018 report of the International Federation of the Phonographic Industry (IFPI), representing the recording industry worldwide, claimed there was a 'value gap', or a mismatch between the 'value that uploader services, such as YouTube, extract from music and the revenue returned to the music community – those who are creating and investing in music'. The IFPI further argued that this was the result of 'inconsistent applications of online liability laws', which had 'emboldened' services such as YouTube: 'Today, services such as YouTube, which have developed sophisticated on-demand music platforms, use this as a shield to avoid licensing music on fair terms like other digital services, claiming they are not legally responsible for the music they distribute on their site.'[11]

While content industries complained about the reduced revenue streams generated by the 'value gap', individual users and uploaders were largely factored out of the financial accounting altogether. This led to widespread critique from both libertarians and Marxist commentators alike. On the one hand, commentators like Jaron Lanier and Kevin Kelly noted that the 'open culture' of the Internet, characterised by 'hive-mind'-oriented cognitive surpluses, were highly profitable for large companies like Google, Amazon and Netflix, but ultimately of limited value for individual creators. The new arrangements between creative labour and finance would result in a new kind of social contract:

> The basic idea of this contract is that authors, journalists, musicians, and artists are encouraged to treat the fruits of their intellects and imaginations as fragments to be given without pay to the hive mind. Reciprocity takes the form of self-promotion. Culture is to become precisely nothing but advertising ... Meanwhile creative people – the new peasants – come to resemble animals converging on shrinking oases of old media in a depleted desert. (Lanier 2010, 83, 86)

Lanier here argued that free culture would in fact lead to the demise of a creative class of people – most prominently what he called the 'musical middle class' (89) – which proffered a steady supply of free content for centralised cloud-based servers. As paradoxical as it seemed, 'ardent Silicon Valley capitalists' encouraged 'more and more services on a volunteer basis' (104), and Lanier explicitly connected the ideal of free music with the contemporary demands of speculative finance: 'Silicon Valley has actively proselytized Wall Street to buy into the doctrines of open/free culture and crowdsourcing' (97). For Lanier, this was a case of 'privatizing benefit while socializing risk' (Lanier 2014, 278). In short, there was no contradiction between free culture and capitalist accumulation; in fact, the former was the elusive alibi of the latter.

On the other hand, commentators like Mark Andrejevic argued that the productive activity on sites like YouTube should be regarded as an '"affective" form of immaterial labor' – subject to a process of exploitation (2009, 416). Andrejevic's commentary drew on theories of cognitive capitalism, immaterial labour and biopolitical production, which recognised the prevalence in contemporary capitalist markets of flexible labour forces cooperating in a kind of communalist (or commons-based) sphere of production. Building on the work of Maurizio Lazzarato, Paolo Virno (2007) demonstrated how the ideological demands of post-Fordist neoliberalism necessitated new modes of subjectivity that upended traditional Marxist theories of alienated labour in the context of capital's abstract industrial imperatives. Far from reducing, or disciplining, the socially interpellated subject (imbricated in collective norms, familial relations, kinship networks, ethical systems, historical debates, etc.) to an abstract, autonomous self (internally motivated, asocial and apolitical), the neo-liberal subject was in fact enjoined to pursue work that was communal, authentic, expressive, spiritual and collaborative. Andrejevic recognised the uncanny connection between the Marxist critique of alienated labour and the cool twenty-first-century rhetoric of ardent capitalists:

> To return to producers control over their creative activity (to overcome the estrangement of the product), to build community (to overcome the estrangement of others), and to facilitate our own self-understanding (to overcome the estrangement of ourselves). If anyone is directly invoking the language of Marx in the current conjuncture, it is not the critical theorists, but the commercial promoters of the interactive revolution.   (2009, 419)

The traditional Marxist critique, it seemed, hereby encountered a limit. Indeed, it was in this peculiar post-Marxist sense that musical production – grounded, practically by definition, in free, authentic expressive values, communal reciprocity, friendship networks, and so forth – lay at the vanguard of immaterial production for information/knowledge workers generally. As shown earlier, digital media in the twenty-first century ushered in widespread new online *habitus*, which, in turn, proffered new networked socialites. In the large-scale context of enhanced digital efficiencies (in delivery, experience, etc.), musical production became a kind of model for the self-employed creative worker. In fact, it could be argued that the general transformations of labour socialisation in the digital age were beginning to look more and more alike. The production of information and knowledge work – including journalism, telecommunication, information technology, design, and other cultural communities – began to coalesce around a single model. All work, as the saying goes, seemed to approximate the condition of *musical* work.

Of course, the new context of consumption did not entail what Marx regarded as exploitation – understood, strictly speaking, as '*forced*, surplus and unpaid labor, the product of which is not under the producers' control' (Marx, in Holmstrom 1997, 87). Far from being coerced, online productivity was an extension of a traditional desire for community and interaction, amplified by new technical efficiencies in social connectivity, search functionality and streamlined content delivery. Furthermore, music streaming became more popular than downloading because it was fast, simple, efficient, and – despite being largely free – it was legal. One of the great advantages for the listener of streaming music, for example, was a function of option-value blurring – a kind of flexibility that permitted users to call up specific content on demand. This enhanced functionality was precisely what led Michael Fricklas, general counsel for Viacom, to argue that 'when everyone gets a free pass to the movies, it's no longer promotional' (McDonald 2009, 400). In other words, online productivity was experienced less as alienation or exploitation, and more as a free pass to content that could be modified, engaged with, and shared. On the other hand, the exploitation of users' labour came in an invisible (or, more precisely, a partially visible) form, namely, the corporate capture of detailed information on users' behaviour and response patterns online. While the Internet was fundamentally grounded in a traditional model of advertising, it was newly tethered to capacious technologies for tracking, managing and then subjecting users to targeted marketing. As Calvin Leung predicted in 2008: 'There's [...] going to be a lot more analytics beneath Internet advertising. In the future, advertisers will come up with 10, 100, or 1,000 creative messages for their products and services, then run, test and optimize them in real time' (Leung 2008). Large platforms like YouTube had become gigantic psychology laboratories running con-trolled experiments using sophisticated surveillance technologies. These data-gathering methods were derived from techniques found in technolo-gies of control – criminology, policing, psychology and psychiatry – in the nineteenth and twentieth centuries. Automatic web-tracking services embedded in viewers' web browsers could track purchasing habits, while aggregated click-patterns could discern their backgrounds, tastes and behaviours. The creative chaos of the interactive economy of a decade earlier had mutated into a gigantic reservoir of rich new data sets, which were now being formatted for analytics-based metrics for marketing and advertising. The aim was to harvest users' own activities – whether con-sciously shared or not – and channel them toward targeted consumption.

A second tragedy of the creative commons could be detected in the shift from user-generated content to user-generated *data*. Once again, music offered an ideal conduit for tracking data. The low-stakes affective invest-ments generated by a user's interactions with music could extrapolate data points well beyond the matter of musical preference alone; they included mood, location, activity and identity of the user. In general, the algorithms for corporate spyware acted on many inputs. On the one hand, they were specific to the particular product of the company. Spotify, for example, tracked the popularity of songs, how frequently they were shared, contexts for songs, such as text around them, and patterns of meta-tagging. On the other hand, the collection of user information extended well beyond the ostensible remit of the company, including any data that documented users' characteristics, behaviour and activities. This information did not need to be associated with the user's account, and included personal correspondence, user-generated content, account preferences and settings, log and access data, data concerning a user's activities, likes, and preferences collected from third parties either through behavioural tracking, the purchasing of data or any form of metadata. To date, the privacy policies of both Google and Spotify, for example, grant extensive permission to collect user data, including personal information, device information, log information, location, local storage data, and information from cookies and other tracking technologies.

Privacy policies tended to obfuscate some of their more important details in at least two senses. First, important details were often tagged onto the end of long lists, buried in the depths of the policy. For example, in Sections 3.2.4 and 5 of Spotify's privacy policy, the company acknowledged that it collects 'technical data, which may include URL information, cookie data, your IP address, the types of devices you are using to access or connect to the Spotify Service, unique device ID, device attributes, network connection type (e.g., WiFi, 3G, LTE) and provider, network and device performance, browser type, language, information enabling digital rights management, operating system, and Spotify application version', as well as 'motion-generated or orientation-generated mobile sensor data (e.g., accelerometer or gyroscope)'. It is difficult to discern from this list alone what kind of data may be *off*-limits to the company – a list appended as a single line in the remote regions of a privacy policy. Second, it is equally difficult to assess what policies actually regulate the *handling* of this kind of user information. While Google's privacy policy, for example, stated that the company shares 'personal information' (defined as 'your name, email address or billing information, or other data which can be reasonably linked to such information by Google, such as information we associate with your Google account'), it did not disclose what the company does with the six *additional* types of data it permitted itself to collect. Without offering a further close reading of them, it can already be noted that – notwithstanding both the plain-seeming language as well as the design format that ostensibly encourages understanding (with section headers, bulleted lists, readable font size, and glossaries) – standard privacy policies were mired in ambiguities, elisions, vague formulations, generalised language, and outright incoherence. Unsurprisingly, they were infrequently read, and thus not likely to be challenged in the context of legal proceedings. When click-through agreements are unread, 'they basically do not exist', in the words of Lanier, 'except for setting the basic rule everyone understands, which is that the server takes no risks, only the users of the server' (Lanier 2014, 184). The new habituations of contemporary subjects had been enjoined toward agreements, defaults and presets that underwrote the political economy of music. Could one detect here a brave new world ordered by naturalised embodiments of the attention economy – a form of *digital entrapment*?

Afterword: Automatic Music and the Peasant's Dilemma

It could be argued that the dominant cultural logic of contemporary computing engaged online labour as a kind of *dis*-alienated production, informally exchanging free-seeming services for extensive data dossiers on individual users. The internet-wide surveillance network had produced data as the central commodity for digital capital. Musical production and consumption had played a central role in consolidating this overall one-way-mirror structure. Not only were users being tracked to be targeted, but also to generate data for the recommendation ecosystem. Instead of investing in on-the-ground research, a streaming service could now intercept, and even predict, trends and fashions simply by tracking users. In 2016, for example, Spotify launched a product called 'Fresh Find', which used its surveillance technologies to track hipsters – defined, more or less, as people who were actively listening to songs before they became hits – to generate metrics for recommendation algorithms and playlists. Again, this form of labour capture could not simply be described as alienated; instead, these were subjects who had (voluntarily) agreed to terms and conditions that wired them into an affective circuit of *dis*-alienated labour. Whether it was streamed on YouTube, Apple Music or Spotify, music had become what Eric Drott (2018) called a full-scale 'technology of surveillance'". For Drott, the aggregation of data points – tastes, emotions, dispositions, and so on – were no more than a kind of algorithmic assemblage (a 'data double' (following David Lyon) or 'Dividual' (following Gilles Deleuze)) that functioned as a kind of proxy for the living user. Social life was being rewired according to a problematic new computational logic. The first problem with extrapolating this kind of composite algorithmic identity was that it strapped individuals to statistical predictors grounded in pre-existing datasets and computational routines. In other words, algorithms assembled identities according to an unremarkable list of statistical correlations between billions of information bits. While it is true that machine-learning increasingly extrapolated seemingly fixed aspects of users' identities – their political affiliations, sexual orientations, gender, race and musical tastes – it nonetheless pragmatically bundled the diversity of individuals into what amounted to complex assemblages of market-ready clichés. The second problem with algorithmic identities concerns the risks posed to users' privacy in the pervasive context of predictive technologies. In an age where machine-driven assessments of health, creditworthiness and marketability were becoming the norm, web tracking for data was, legally speaking, surprisingly unmonitored for both quality and content.

The third, and most important, problem associated with algorithmic trawling for data was the systematic way it created highly segregated – almost ad hoc – modes of financialisation of large-scale collaborative labour online. On the one hand, big corporate entities in the business of music distribution owned central, private servers with profitable internal data that effectively controlled people's networked connectivity. These third-party surveillance services created automated and persistent wealth from information that was used, copied and shared by others. On the other hand, users of streaming services – and especially musicians themselves – were increasingly restricted to what Lanier called 'real-time economic life' in a kind of peasant's dilemma (2014, 51). With royalties for recorded music reduced to a trickle, musicians were more and more locked into a life of *performance*. It is an irony that live performance – precisely that modality *not* intrinsic to the promise of networked digital technologies – was the only sector said to be economically viable for artists in the era after Web 2.0. By 2010 musicians were earning considerably more from touring than they were from recording. Live events, including large-scale integrated music festivals headlined by a variety of acts – such as Bonnaroo, Coachella and Ultra – became the primary income streams even for established artists. It is as if artists in the age of the digital network were paradoxically thrust back into the roles of performing musicians – the *troubadours* and *trouvères* – of a pre-modern time. Perhaps it should come as no surprise then that live performance was in fact the most monopolised sector of the music market by the second decade of the twenty-first century. The 2010 merger between Ticketmaster and Live Nation (the largest concert-promotion company in the globe, and a spin off of the radio monopolists Clear Channel Communications) opened the door to exclusive deals with artists, such as '360' deals (with Jay-Z, Madonna, U2 and others), and centralised control of ticket pricing for music concerts. In 2010, the *New York Times* reported that the 'average price of a ticket to one of the top 100 tours has soared to $62.57 last year [2009] from $25.81 in 1996, according to Pollstar, far outpacing inflation'.[12] It is as if the digital network's much-lauded decentralised distribution networks, newly unhinged from the control of the majors, suddenly betrayed their own promise, metamorphosing instead into a kind of auto-generative marketing tool for massive centralised companies who controlled the commodified 'communal' live 'experience'. Herein lay one of the great paradoxes of the Internet – its contribution to the concentration of economic power in the hands of monopolistic intermediaries, both online *and* offline.

Critics have described this economic condition in ultra-modern terms, arguing that post-Cold-War neoliberalism had produced a new 'precarious cognitariat' (Miller 2009, 435). But, for musicians, this was actually a dramatic throwback to a pre-modern (pre-Marxist?) era; an era in which composers struggled in an informal economy of barter and reputation, while wealth was concentrated in the hands of a fistful of feudal overlords. As it was for composers before the age of Beethoven, musicians in the twenty-first century were increasingly coerced into performance-only careers, severed, in practice, from the traditional levies once provided by royalties and copyrights. It is as if musicians had become seventeenth-century travelling songsters once more, additionally enjoined to the labour of making their mark on the digital network. Of course, even live music may be gradually diminishing as we enter the third decade of the new century. In fact, if trends at Spotify are an indication, compensation arrangements hitched to *any* licensed music may come under additional strain in the future. In the 2010s, for example, the streaming service dedicated considerable resources to crafting playlists that did not reflect individual artists, or even clusters of artists, but rather affective states attuned to factors like place, weather and activity. Their 2017 product 'Climatune', for example, synced weather data with listening data to generate playlists that varied by geolocation. Likewise, Spotify's application for jogging and running, launched in 2016, was algorithmically attuned to the rhythm of moving feet. By analysing the raw signal of steps per minute, and then filtering it for an average tempo, the application could launch a non-stop playlist that provided professional-grade transitions between a beat-matched stream of trendy electro-pop.

Search queries are likely to become more refined, transforming from keyword-centric sorting mechanisms to algorithms responsive to more embodied perceptual cues derived from data-streaming sensors on net-worked subjects. Subjective musical experiences, in other words, will be reconfigured by the hyperactive solicitude of algorithmic routines trans-coding subjective embodiments. Above all, however, with the turn toward supervised and unsupervised machine listening and machine learning technologies, the future of music playlists on streaming consumer products is itself likely to be short-lived. In fact, by 2018 artists had already begun artificially to extend their technological presence on streaming playlists by creating albums that covered twenty or thirty songs. Likewise, in various attempts to trick the word-based logic of search algorithms a host of songs with similar titles emerged during this era. The title of the song 'Demons' by Imagine Demons (a band with only a single song on Spotify), for example, seemed to hitch its fortunes on the same song by Imagine Dragons. This recalled the practice of *faux*-versions of songs that dates back at least to the Tin Pan Alley era. Charles K. Harris's massively popular song 'After the Ball' (1892), for example, spawned a host of knockoffs with titles like 'Fatal Night of the Ball'; just as the 1909 hit 'Meet Me in Dreamland' produced imitations like 'In All My Dreams I Dream of You' and 'Sweetheart of My Dreams'. On the other hand, the three-minute song, crafted during the Tin Pan Alley era for explicitly commercial reasons – materially linking the ephemera of sound to specific artists and publishers – is likely to become obsolete. Instead of algorithmically delivering audiences to playlists – or sequences of short, distinct, licensed songs – future streaming could witness a radical shift toward seamless algorithmically generated musicscapes – multi-authored, layered and variable – attuned to geolocation technologies, as well as data aggregating user interests and behaviour, for fine-grained contextual information.

In 2017 Spotify was accused of mounting 'fake' music, embedded in playlists attuned to genres, moods and experiences. For example, the playlist 'Ambient Chill' featured music by the German composer Max Richter, followed by Deep Watch, probably a non existent artist, with over one million streams. Likewise, on the 'Sleep' playlist, one found Enno Aare, also unknown outside Spotify's algorithmic ecosystem.[13] Perhaps streaming services could experiment with making upfront payments to in-house musicians to circumvent fees associated with licensing and copyright. They could follow the example of movie content-providers like Netflix, which had reduced its reliance on Hollywood content by producing its own hits in the 2010s. The point about the 'fake' songs on Spotify is that they were less *fake* (in the sense of deliberately misleading) than they may simply have been differently licensed, or even *unlicensed* – embedded within playlists containing more well-known, licensed songs. While this episode represented a brief public backlash – gaining traction from the then-circulating concept of 'fake news' in the years of Donald Trump's presidency – it is likely that streaming algorithms will, in future, design music autonomously and automatically. Tristan Jehan, founder of The Echo Nest and currently senior scientist at Spotify, remarked that when it came to teaching computers how to listen and make music on their own, 'engineers will lead the way' (2017, personal communication). Music's automatic generation will, of course, be mediated by machine-human interactions – including collaborative filtering and deep learning algorithms – but instead of responding to searches for (rights-holding) artists and songs, the application could increasingly respond to metrics attuned to mood, place, weather, activity or affect. Search and discovery terms are likely to become more semantic and intuitive-seeming as artificial intelligence is integrated into streaming services. Likewise, neural networks in the context of unsupervised learning will translate musical styles and genres across different sets of instruments, or take informal musical cues from listeners, and, by way of a complex mode of auto-encoding, generate new and personalised songs.[14] Ever-attentive to search query tokens – video and song identities, demographics of listeners, watch times and click probabilities – developments at the intersection of music, machine learning and signal processing can coordinate the connection between personalised/customised audiences and open-ended audio streams. Could this usher in a period where music is delivered as a stream of automated sonic affect; where the algorithmic service is no longer merely a conduit for content and consumption, but a genuine creator of data-driven content itself? Could the creativity of listening computers finally mark the total eclipse of autonomous music by automatic music?

For Further Study

Jehan, Tristan. 2005. 'Creating Music by Listening'. PhD dissertation, Massachusetts Institute of Technology.

Lerch, Alexander. 2012. *An Introduction to Audio Content Analysis: Applications in Signal Processing and Music Informatics*. Hoboken, NJ: Wiley.

Loviglio, Jason and Michele Hilmes, eds. 2013. *Radio's New Wave: Global South in the Digital Era*. New York: Routledge.

Morris, Jeremy Wade. 2015. *Selling Digital Music, Formatting Culture*. Berkeley: University of California Press.

Scholz, Trebor, ed. 2013. *Digital Labor: The Internet as Playground and Factory*. New York: Routledge.

Seaver, Nick. 2018. 'Captivating algorithms: Recommender systems as traps'. *Journal of Material Culture*. https://doi.org/10.1177/1359183518820366.

Notes

1 Alexandra Topping, 'Collapse in illegal sharing and boom in streaming brings music to executives' ears', *The Guardian*, 12 July 2009, www.theguardian.com/music/2009/jul/12/music-industry-illegal-downloading-streaming. All websites accessed 19 September 2018.

2 Alex Hern, 'Is Spotify really worth $20BN?', *The Guardian*, 2 March 2018, www.theguardian.com/technology/2018/mar/02/is-spotify-really-worth-20bn.

3 Ek, in Jay Yarow, 'Spotify will do almost $1 billion in revenue this year', *Business Insider*, 13 April 2012, www.businessinsider.com/spotify-did-almost-1-billion-in-revenue-last-year-2012-4?IR=T.

4 See Marc Hogan, 'Uncovering how streaming is changing the sound of pop', *Pitchfork*, 25 September 2017, https://pitchfork.com/features/article/uncovering-how-streaming-is-changing-the-sound-of-pop/.

5 See Liz Pelly, 'Streambait pop', *The Baffler*, 11 December 2018, https://thebaffler.com/downstream/streambait-pop-pelly.

6 Brian Brandt, 'Is the Spotify model really the answer?', *New Music USA*, 9 August 2011, https://nmbx.newmusicusa.org/is-the-spotify-model-really-the-answer/.

7 Evan Minsker, 'Thom Yorke and Nigel Godrich pull music from Spotify, speak out against their business model', *Pitchfork*, 14 July 2013, https://pitchfork.com/news/51515-thom-yorke-and-nigel-godrich-pull-music-from-spotify-speak-out-against-their-business-model/.

8 Jennifer Granholm and Chris Eldred, 'Facebook owes you money', *CNN*, 12 April 2018, https://edition.cnn.com/2018/04/11/opinions/facebook-should-pay-us-for-using-our-data-granholm-eldred/index.html.

9 Rakesh Sharma, 'How blockchain could revolutionize music streaming', *Investopedia*, 14 October 2017, www.investopedia.com/news/how-blockchain-could-revolutionize-music-streaming/.

10 Jeremy Silver, 'The music industry and blockchain technologies', *Create*, 26 March 2018, www.create.ac.uk/blog/2018/03/26/research-blog-series-music-industry-blockchain-technologies/?mc_cid=c010c93b8e&mc_eid=b70aba5242.

11 Available at www.ifpi.org.

12 Ben Sisario, 'For tours, 2010 has been a tough sell', *New York Times*, 12 July 2010, www.nytimes.com/2010/07/13/arts/music/13tour.html.

13 Dani Deahl and Micah Singleton, 'What's really going on with Spotify's fake artist controversy', *The Verge*, 12 July 2017, www.theverge.com/2017/7/12/15961416/spotify-fake-artist-controversy-mystery-tracks.

14 Tristan Greene, 'Facebook made an AI that convincingly turns one style of music into another', *NextWeb*, 22 May 2018, https://thenextweb.com/artificial-intelligence/2018/05/22/facebook-made-an-ai-that-convincingly-turns-one-style-of-music-into-another/.

Bibliography

1 Digital Technology and Cultural Practice
Nicholas Cook

Baym, Nancy. 2015. *Personal Connections in the Digital Age*, 2nd edn. Cambridge: Polity.

Bennett, Lucy. 2012. 'Patterns of listening through social media: Online fan engagement with the live musical experience'. *Social Semiotics* 22 (5): 545–57.

Boden, Margaret. 2004. *The Creative Mind: Myths and Mechanisms*, 2nd edn. London: Routledge.

Bogdanovic, Danijela. 2016. 'Bands in virtual spaces, social networking, and masculinity'. In *The Oxford Handbook of Music and Virtuality,* edited by Sheila Whiteley and Shara Rambarran, 428–47. New York: Oxford University Press.

Burgess, Jean and Joshua Green (with contributions by Henry Jenkins and John Hartley). 2009. *YouTube: Online Video and Participatory Culture*. Cambridge: Polity.

Castells, Manuel. 2001. *The Internet Galaxy: Reflections on the Internet, Business, and Society*. Oxford: Oxford University Press.

Connor, Thomas. 2016. 'Hatsune Miku, 2.0Pac, and beyond: Rewinding and fast-forwarding the virtual pop star'. In *The Oxford Handbook of Music and Virtuality*, edited by Sheila Whiteley and Shara Rambarran, 111–28. New York: Oxford University Press.

Cook, Nicholas. 2013. 'Video cultures: "Bohemian Rhapsody", "Wayne's World" and beyond'. In *Representation in Western Music*, edited by Joshua Walden, 79–99. Cambridge: Cambridge University Press.

2018. *Music as Creative Practice*. New York: Oxford University Press.

Drott, Eric. 2018. 'Music as a technology of surveillance'. *Journal of the Society for American Music* 12(3): 233–67.

Feldman, David. 1994. 'Mozart and the transformational imperative'. In *On Mozart*, edited by James Morris, 52–71. Cambridge: Woodrow Wilson Center Press and Cambridge University Press.

Giesler, Markus and Mali Pohlmann. 2003. 'The anthropology of file sharing: Consuming Napster as a gift'. In *Advances in Consumer Research*, 30, edited by Anand Keller and Dennis Rook: 273–9. Valdosta, GA: Association for Consumer Research.

Hartley, John. 2008. *Television Truths: Forms of Knowledge in Popular Culture*. London: Blackwell.

Jackson, Louise and Mike Dines. 2016. 'Vocaloids and Japanese virtual vocal performance: The cultural heritage and technological futures of vocal puppetry'. In *The Oxford Handbook of Music and Virtuality*, edited by Sheila Whiteley and Shara Rambarran, 101–10. New York: Oxford University Press.

Jenkins, Henry. 2006. *Convergence Culture: Where Old and New Media Collide.* New York: New York University Press.

2009. 'What happened before YouTube'. In Jean Burgess and Joshua Green (with contributions by Henry Jenkins and John Hartley), *YouTube: Online Video and Participatory Culture,* 109–25. Cambridge: Polity.

Jenkins, Henry, Sam Ford and Joshua Green. 2013. *Spreadable Media: Creating Value and Meaning in a Networked Culture.* New York: New York University Press.

Jenkins, Henry, Mizuko Ito and danah boyd. 2016. *Participatory Culture in a Networked Era.* Cambridge: Polity.

Katz, Mark. 2004. *Capturing Sound: How Technology has Changed Music.* Berkeley: University of California Press.

Kramer, Lawrence, 2013. 'Classical music for the posthuman tradition'. In *The Oxford Handbook of New Audiovisual Aesthetics,* edited by John Richardson, Claudia Gorbman and Carol Vernallis, 39–52. New York: Oxford University Press.

Lessig, Lawrence. 2008. *Remix: Making Art and Commerce Thrive in the Hybrid Economy.* London: Bloomsbury.

Lingel, Jessa and Mor Naaman. 2011. 'You should have been there, man: Live music, DIY content and online communities'. *New Media and Society* 14 (2): 332–49.

Macpherson, Crawford. 2010. *The Political Theory of Possessive Individualism from Hobbes to Locke.* Oxford: Oxford University Press.

Massanari, Adrienne. 2015. *Participatory Culture, Community, and Play: Learning from reddit.* New York: Peter Lang.

Michielse, Maarten. 2013. 'Musical chameleons: Fluency and flexibility in online remix contests'. *M/C Journal* 16 (4) (http://journal.media-culture.org.au/index.php/mcjournal/article/view/676).

2016. 'A digital recording consciousness: Analysing, mixing and evaluating audio in the mashup community'. *Journal of the International Association for the Study of Popular Music* 6 (2): 139–53.

Miller, Kiri. 2012. *Playing Along: Digital Games, YouTube, and Virtual Performance.* Oxford: Oxford University Press.

O'Brien, Benjamin. 2016. 'Sample sharing: Virtual laptop ensemble communities'. In *The Oxford Handbook of Music and Virtuality,* edited by Sheila Whiteley and Shara Rambarran, 377–91. New York: Oxford University Press.

Rheingold, Howard. 1993. *The Virtual Community: Homesteading on the Electronic Frontier.* Reading, MA: Addison-Wesley Publishing Company.

Richardson, John. 2012. *An Eye for Music: Popular Music and the Audiovisual Surreal.* New York: Oxford University Press.

Shifman, Limor. 2014. *Memes in Digital Culture.* Cambridge, MA: MIT Press.

Silver, Jeremy. 2016. *Blockchain or the Chaingang? Challenges, Opportunities and Hype: The Music Industry and Blockchain Technologies* (CREATe Working Paper 2016/05). Glasgow: RCUK Centre for Copyright and New Business Models in the Creative Economy.

Sinnreich, Aram. 2010. *Mashed Up: Music, Technology, and the Rise of Configurable Culture.* Amherst: University of Massachusetts Press.

Strangelove, Michael. 2010. *Watching YouTube: Extraordinary Videos by Ordinary People*. Toronto: University of Toronto Press.

Théberge, Paul. 2004. 'The network studio: Historical and technological paths to a new ideal in music making'. *Social Studies of Science* 34 (5): 759–81.

Vernallis, Carol. 2013. *Unruly Media: YouTube, Music Video, and the New Digital Cinema*. New York: Oxford University Press.

Watson, Yoshe. 2017. 'Virtual Undergrounds: How do People Use Music to Build Subcultures on the Internet?'. MPhil dissertation, University of Cambridge.

Whiteley, Sheila and Shara Rambarran, eds. 2016. *The Oxford Handbook of Music and Virtuality*. New York: Oxford University Press.

Williams, Justin and Ross Wilson. 2016. 'Music and crowdfunded websites: Digital patronage and artist-fan interactivity'. In *The Oxford Handbook of Music and Virtuality*, edited by Sheila Whiteley and Shara Rambarran, 593–612. New York: Oxford University Press.

Zaborowski, Rafal. 2016. 'Hatsune Miku and Japanese virtual idols'. In *The Oxford Handbook of Music and Virtuality*, edited by Sheila Whiteley and Shara Rambarran, 111–28. New York: Oxford University Press.

2 Toward a History of Digital Music: New Technologies, Business Practices and Intellectual Property Regimes
Martin Scherzinger

Baumol, William J. and Hilda Baumol. 1994. 'On the economics of musical composition in Mozart's Vienna'. *Journal of Cultural Economics* 18 (3): 171–98.

Benjamin, Walter. 1969. 'Theses on the philosophy of history'. In *Illuminations*, translated by Harry Zohn and edited by Hannah Arendt, 253–64. New York: Schocken.

Benkler, Yochai. 2006. *Wealth of Networks: How Social Production Transforms Markets and Freedoms*. New Haven: Yale University Press.

Blum, Jerome. 1978. *The End of the Old Order in Rural Europe*. Princeton: Princeton University Press.

Clapham, John. 1979. *Dvořák*. New York: Norton.

Cosentino, Gabrielle. 2006. '"Hacking" the iPod: A look inside Apple's portable music player'. In *Cybersounds: Essays on Virtual Music Culture*, edited by Michael D. Ayers, 185–208. New York: Peter Lang.

Espejo, Roman, ed. 2009. *What Is the Future of the Music Industry?* Detroit: Greenhaven Press.

Gillespie, Tarlton. 2007. *Wired Shut: Copyright and the Shape of Digital Culture*. Cambridge, MA: Harvard University Press.

Herman, Edward S. and McChesney, Robert W. 1997. *The Global Media: The New Missionaries of Corporate Capitalism*. London and Washington: Cassell.

Lanier, Jaron. 2010. *You Are Not a Gadget: A Manifesto*. New York: Alfred A. Knopf.

LaPlante, Alice. 2009. 'Digital music is the future of the music industry.' In *What Is the Future of the Music Industry?* edited by Roman Espejo, 20–30. Detroit: Greenhaven Press.

Litman, Jessica. 2006. *Digital Copyright*. New York: Prometheus Books.

Marchand, Roland. 1985. *Advertising the American Dream: Making Way for Modernity 1920–1940*. Berkeley: University of California Press.

Meinrath, Sascha D., James W. Losey and Victor W. Picard. 2011. 'Digital feudalism: Enclosures and erasures from digital rights management to the digital divide'. *Advances in Computers* 81: 237–87.

Moore, Julia Virginia. 1987. 'Beethoven and Musical Economics'. PhD thesis, University of Illinois.

Nimmer, David. 2003. *Copyright: Sacred Text, Technology, and the DMCA*. The Hague: Kluwer Law International, 2003.

Scherer, F. M. 2004. *Quarter Notes and Bank Notes: The Economics of Music Composition in the Eighteenth and Nineteenth Centuries*. Princeton: Princeton University Press.

Scherzinger, Martin and Stephen Smith. 2007. 'From blatant to latent protest (and back again): On the politics of theatrical spectacle in Madonna's "American Life"'. *Popular Music* 26(1): 211–29.

Snickars, Pelle and Patrick Vonderau, eds. 2009. *The YouTube Reader*. Stockholm: Mediehistoriskt.

Starr, Paul. 2004. *The Creation of the Media: Political Origins of Modern Communications*. New York: Basic Books.

Sterne, Jonathan. 2012. *MP3: The Meaning of a Format*. Durham, NC: Duke University Press.

Suisman, David. 2009. *Selling Sounds: The Commercial Revolution in American Music*. Cambridge, MA: Harvard University Press.

Wasko, Janet and Mary Erickson. 2009. 'The political economy of YouTube'. In *The YouTube Reader*, edited by Pelle Snickars and Patrick Vonderau, 372–86. Stockholm: Mediehistoriskt.

Witt, Stephen. 2015. *How Music Got Free: A Story of Obsession and Invention*. New York: Penguin Books.

Wu, Tim. 2003. 'Net neutrality, broadband discrimination'. *Journal of Telecommunications and High Technology Law*, 2: 141–75.

3 Shaping the Stream: Techniques and Troubles of Algorithmic Recommendation
K. E. Goldschmitt and Nick Seaver

Andersen, Birgitte and Marion Frenz. 2008. 'The impact of music downloads and P2P file-sharing on the purchase of music in Canada'. DIME Working Papers on Intellectual Human Rights. www.dime-eu.org/files/active/0/WP82-IPR.pdf.

Anderson, Chris. 2008. *The Long Tail: Why the Future of Business Is Selling Less of More*, rev. edn. New York: Hyperion.

Attali, Jacques. 1985. *Noise: The Political Economy of Music*. Manchester: Manchester University Press.

Auslander, Philip. 1999. *Liveness: Performance in a Mediatized Culture*. New York: Routledge.

Barocas, Solon and Andrew D. Selbst. 2015. 'Big Data's disparate impact'. SSRN Scholarly Paper ID 2477899. Rochester, NY: Social Science Research Network.

Beer, David. 2009. 'Power through the algorithm? Participatory web cultures and the technological unconscious'. *New Media & Society* 11 (6): 985–1002.

Born, Georgina. 2005. 'On musical mediation: Ontology, technology and creativity'. *Twentieth-Century Music* 2 (1): 7–36.

Bucher, Taina. 2012. 'Want to be on the top? Algorithmic power and the threat of invisibility on Facebook'. *New Media & Society* 14: 1164–80.

Bustillos, Maria. 2013. 'Little Brother is watching you'. *The New Yorker*, May 22. www.newyorker.com/tech/elements/little-brother-is-watching-you.

Camp, Gregory. 2015. 'Spotify. Https://www.spotify.com/. Retrieved 21 January 2015'. *Journal of the Society for American Music* 9 (3): 375–8.

Celma, Òscar. 2010. *Music Recommendation and Discovery: The Long Tail, Long Fail, and Long Play in the Digital Music Space*. Heidelberg: Springer Science & Business Media.

Cook, Nicholas. 2013. *Beyond the Score: Music as Performance*. New York: Oxford University Press.

Crary, Jonathan. 2013. *24/7: Late Capitalism and the Ends of Sleep*. London: Verso Books.

Dean, Katie. 2004. 'The house that music fans built'. https://www.wired.com/2004/07/the-house-that-music-fans-built/.

DeNora, Tia and Sophie Belcher. 2000. '"When you're trying something on you picture yourself in a place where they are playing this kind of music": Musically sponsored agency in the British clothing retail sector'. *Sociological Review* 48 (1): 80–101.

Devine, Kyle. 2015. 'Decomposed: A political ecology of music'. *Popular Music* 34(3): 367–89.

Dormehl, Luke. 2014. *The Formula: How Algorithms Solve All Our Problems . . . and Create More*. New York: Perigee.

Drott, Eric. 2018. 'Why the next song matters: streaming, recommendation, scarcity'. *Twentieth-Century Music* 15 (3): 325–57.

Drott, Eric A. 2018. 'Music as a technology of surveillance'. *Journal of the Society for American Music* 12 (3): 233–67.

Ensmenger, Nathan. 2012. 'Is chess the drosophila of artificial intelligence? A social history of an algorithm'. *Social Studies of Science* 42 (1): 5–30.

Goldberg, David, David Nichols, Brian M. Oki and Douglas Terry. 1992. 'Using collaborative filtering to weave an information tapestry'. *Communications of the ACM* 35 (12): 61–70.

Goldschmitt, Kariann. 2014. 'Mobile tactics in the Brazilian independent record industry'. In *The Oxford Handbook of Mobile Music Studies*, edited by Sumanth Gopinath and Jason Stanyek, 1: 496–522. New York: Oxford University Press.

Forthcoming. 'Bossa Nova and twenty-first century commerce: Ubiquitous music and the branding of a global bourgeoisie'. In *Brazil's Northern Wave: Fifty Years of Bossa Nova in the United States*, edited by Jason Stanyek and Frederick Moehn. Oxford University Press.

Goodman, Steve. 2009. *Sonic Warfare: Sound, Affect, and the Ecology of Fear*. Cambridge, MA: MIT Press.

Granka, Laura A. 2010. 'The politics of search: A decade retrospective'. *The Information Society* 26 (5): 364–74.

Hall, Stuart. 1980. 'Encoding/decoding'. In *Culture, Media, Language*, edited by Stuart Hall, Dorothy Hobson, Andrew Lowe and Paul Willis, 128–38. London: Hutchinson.

Hallinan, Blake and Ted Striphas. 2016. 'Recommended for you: The Netflix Prize and the production of algorithmic culture'. *New Media & Society* 18 (1): 117–37.

Hesmondhalgh, David. 2008. 'Neoliberalism, imperialism, and the media'. In *Media and Social Theory*, edited by David Hesmondhalgh and Jason Toynbee, 95–111. New York: Routledge.

Holt, Fabian. 2007. *Genre in Popular Music*. Chicago: University of Chicago Press.

Hosokawa, Shuhei. 1984. 'The Walkman effect'. *Popular Music* 4 (January): 165–80.

Kassabian, Anahid. 2013. *Ubiquitous Listening: Affect, Attention, and Distributed Subjectivity*. Berkeley: University of California Press.

Katz, Mark. 2004. *Capturing Sound*. Berkeley: University of California Press.

Keightley, Keir. 1996. '"Turn it down!" she shrieked: Gender, domestic space, and high fidelity, 1948–59'. *Popular Music* 15 (2): 149–77.

Konstan, John and Joseph A. Riedl. 2012. *IEEE Spectrum*. 'Deconstructing recommender systems'. 24 September. spectrum.ieee.org/computing/software/deconstructing-recommender-systems.

Kusek, David and Gerd Leonhard. 2005. *The Future of Music: Manifesto for the Digital Music Revolution*. Boston: Berklee Press.

Lanza, Joseph. 2007. *Elevator Music: A Surreal History of Muzak, Easy-Listening, and Other Moodsong*, rev. edn. Ann Arbor: University of Michigan Press.

Lessig, Lawrence. 2001. *The Future of Ideas: The Fate of the Commons in a Connected World*. New York: Vintage Books.

  2007. *Remix: Making Art and Commerce Thrive in the Hybrid Economy*. London: Penguin.

Litman, Jessica. 2006. *Digital Copyright*. New York: Prometheus Books.

Loeb, Shoshana. 1992. 'Architecting personalized delivery of multimedia information.' *Communications of the ACM* 35 (12): 39–47.

Loughridge, Dierdre and Thomas Patteson. 2015. 'Cat pianos, sound-houses, and other imaginary musical instruments'. *The Public Domain Review*. publicdomainreview.org/2015/07/15/cat-pianos-sound-houses-and-other-imaginary-musical-instruments/.

Luker, Morgan James. 2010. 'The managers, the managed, and the unmanageable: Negotiating values at the Buenos Aires International Music Fair'. *Ethnomusicology Forum* 19 (1): 89–113.

MacCormick, John and Chris Bishop. 2013. *Nine Algorithms that Changed the Future: The Ingenious Ideas that Drive Today's Computers*. Princeton: Princeton University Press.

Mager, Astrid. 2012. 'Algorithmic ideology'. *Information, Communication & Society* 15 (5): 769–87.

McCracken, Allison. 2015. *Real Men Don't Sing: Crooning in American Culture.* Durham, NC: Duke University Press.

Meier, Leslie M. 2011. 'Promotional ubiquitous musics: Recording artists, brands, and "rendering authenticity"'. *Popular Music & Society* 34 (4): 399–415.

Morris, Jeremy Wade. 2015a. 'Curation by code: Infomediaries and the data mining of taste'. *European Journal of Cultural Studies* 18 (4–5): 446–63.

    2015b. *Selling Digital Music: Formatting Culture.* Berkeley: University of California Press.

Morris, Jeremy Wade and Devon Powers. 2015. 'Control, curation and musical experience in streaming music services'. *Creative Industries Journal* 8 (2): 106–22.

Negus, Keith. 1999. *Music Genres and Corporate Cultures.* New York: Routledge.

Pasquale, Frank. 2015. *The Black Box Society: The Secret Algorithms That Control Money and Information.* Cambridge, MA: Harvard University Press.

Powers, Devon. 2010. 'Strange powers: The branded sensorium and the intrigue of musical sound'. In *Blowing Up the brand: Critical Perspectives on Promotional Culture*, edited by Melissa Aronczyk and Devon Powers, 285–306. New York: Peter Lang Publishing.

    2014. 'Lost in the shuffle: Technology, history, and the idea of musical randomness'. *Critical Studies in Media Communication* 31 (3): 244–64.

Preston, Paschal and Jim Rogers. 2013. 'Convergence, crisis and the digital music economy'. In *Media and Convergence Management*, edited by Sandra Diehl and Matthias Karmasin, 247–60. Berlin: Springer.

Radano, Ronald M. 1989. 'Interpreting Muzak: Speculations on musical experience in everyday life.' *American Music* 7 (4): 448–60.

Ratliff, Ben. 2016. *Every Song Ever: Twenty Ways to Listen to Music Now.* New York: Penguin Books Limited.

Razlogova, Elena. 2013. 'The past and future of music listening: Between freeform DJs and recommendation algorithms'. In *Radio's New Wave: Global Sound in the Digital Era*, edited by Jason Loviglio and Michelle Hilmes, 62–76. New York: Routledge.

Resnick, Paul, Neophytos Iacovou, Mitesh Suchak, Peter Bergstrom and John Riedl. 1994. 'GroupLens: An open architecture for collaborative filtering of Netnews'. In *Proceedings of ACM 1994 Conference on Computer Supported Cooperative Work*, 175–86. Chapel Hill: University of North Carolina Press.

Sanjek, Russell. 1996. *Pennies from Heaven: The American Popular Music Business in the Twentieth Century.* New York: Da Capo Press.

Seaver, Nick. 2011. '"This is not a copy": Mechanical fidelity and the re-enacting piano'. *Differences* 22 (2–3): 54–73.

    2012. 'Algorithmic recommendations and synaptic functions'. *Limn*, no. 2 (February 4). https://limn.it/algorithmic-recommendations-and-synaptic-functions/.

    2015. 'The nice thing about context is that everyone has it'. *Media, Culture & Society* 37 (7): 1101–9.

    2018. 'Captivating algorithms: Recommender systems as traps'. *Journal of Material Culture.* https://doi.org/10.1177/1359183518820366.

Solove, Daniel J. 2001. 'Privacy and power: Computer databases and metaphors for information privacy'. *Stanford Law Journal* 53 (July): 1393–462.

Steiner, Christopher. 2012. *Automate This: How Algorithms Took Over Our Markets, Our Jobs, and the World.* New York: Penguin.

Sterne, Jonathan. 1997. 'Sounds like the mall of America: Programmed music and the architectonics of commercial space'. *Ethnomusicology* 14 (1): 22–50.

2003. *The Audible Past: Cultural Origins of Sound Reproduction.* Durham, NC: Duke University Press.

2012. *MP3: The Meaning of a Format.* Durham, NC: Duke University Press.

Straw, Will. 2002. 'Consumption'. In *Cambridge Companion to Pop and Rock*, edited by Simon Frith, Will Straw, and John Street, 53–73. Cambridge: Cambridge University Press.

Striphas, Ted. 2015. 'Algorithmic culture'. *European Journal of Cultural Studies* 18 (4–5): 395–412.

Suisman, David. 2012. *Selling Sounds.* Cambridge, MA: Harvard University Press.

Sweeney, Latanya. 2013. 'Discrimination in online ad delivery'. *Queue* 11 (3): 10:10–10:29.

Taylor, Timothy D. 2012. *The Sounds of Capitalism: Advertising, Music, and the Conquest of Culture.* Chicago: University of Chicago Press.

2013. 'Globalized new capitalism and the commodification of taste'. In *The Cambridge History of World Music*, edited by Philip V. Bohlman, 744–64. Cambridge: Cambridge University Press.

2014. 'Fields, genres, brands'. *Culture, Theory and Critique* 55 (2): 159–74.

2016. *Music and Capitalism: A History of the Present.* Chicago: University of Chicago Press.

Toynbee, Jason. 2000. *Making Popular Music: Musicians, Creativity and Institutions.* London: Arnold.

Turkle, Sherry. 2011. *Alone Together: Why We Expect More from Technology and Less from Each Other.* New York: Basic Books.

Van Couvering, Elizabeth. 2007. 'Is relevance relevant? Market, science, and war: Discourses of search engine quality'. *Journal of Computer-Mediated Communication* 12 (3): 866–87.

Wald, Elijah. 2009. *How The Beatles Destroyed Rock 'n' Roll: An Alternative History of American Popular Music.* New York: Oxford University Press.

Williamson, John and Martin Cloonan. 2007. 'Rethinking the music industry'. *Popular Music* 26 (2): 305–22.

Ziewitz, Malte. 2016. 'Governing algorithms: Myth, mess, and methods'. *Science, Technology & Human Values* 41 (1): 3–16.

Personal Take: Can Machines Have Taste?
Stéphan-Eloïse Gras

Adorno, Theodor. 2009. *Current of Music: Elements of a Radio Theory*, edited and translated by Robert Hullot-Kentor. Cambridge: Polity.

Gras, Stéphan-Eloïse. 2018. *Machines du goût: l'algorithme au coeur de nos sensibilités*. Paris: Hermann.

Szendy, Peter. 1994. 'Dérives: Adorno, les collections musicales et le nom'. *Espaces Temps* 55 'Arts, l'exception ordinaire': 127–33.

4 Technologies of the Musical Selfie
Sumanth Gopinath and Jason Stanyek

Agazzi, Evandro. 1998. 'From technique to technology: The role of modern science'. *Techné* 4(2): 80–5.

Anderson, Chris. 2008. *The Long Tail: Why the Future of Business Is Selling Less of More*, rev. edn. New York: Hyperion.

Andrejevic, Mark. 2007. 'Surveillance in the digital enclosure'. *The Communication Review* 10(4): 295–317.

Bergh, Arild and Tia DeNora. 2009. 'From wind-up to iPod: Techno-cultures of listening'. In *The Cambridge Companion to Recorded Music*, edited by Nicholas Cook, Eric Clark, Daniel Leech-Wilkinson and John Rink, 102–15. Cambridge: Cambridge University Press.

Blue V, Alex. 2017. '"Hear what you want": Sonic politics, blackness, and racism-canceling headphones'. *Current Musicology* 99–100 (Spring): 87–106.

Bode, Lisa. 2017. *Making Believe: Screen Performance and Special Effects in Popular Cinema*. New Brunswick: Rutgers University Press.

Bollmer, Grant and Katherine Guinness. 2017. 'Phenomenology for the selfie'. *Cultural Politics* 13(2): 156–76.

Bruno, Antony. 2011. 'Growth by curation'. *Billboard*, 17 September 2011: 10.

Cavarero, Adriana. 2005. *For More than One Voice: Toward a Philosophy of Vocal Expression*. Translated by Paul A. Kottman. Stanford, CA: Stanford University Press.

Chalmers, David J. 1996. *The Conscious Mind: In Search of a Fundamental Theory*. New York: Oxford University Press.

Cumming, Naomi. 2000. *The Sonic Self: Musical Subjectivity and Signification*. Bloomington: Indiana University Press.

Deleuze, Gilles and Felix Guattari. 1987. *A Thousand Plateaus: Capitalism and Schizophrenia*. Translated by Brian Massumi. Minneapolis: University of Minnesota Press.

DeNora, Tia. 1999. 'Music as a technology of the self'. *Poetics* 27(1): 31–56.

Drott, Eric. 2018. 'Music as a technology of surveillance'. *Journal of the Society for American Music* 12(3): 233–67.

Dureha, Anukriti. 2014. 'An accurate algorithm for generating a music playlist based on facial expressions'. *International Journal of Computer Applications* 100/9 (August): 33–9.

Emmerson, Frank. 1979. 'Behind the sound'. *Globe and Mail*, Canada, 17 January 1979.

Foucault, Michel. 1988. 'Technologies of the self'. In *Technologies of the Self: A Seminar with Michel Foucault*, edited by Luther Martin, Huck Gutman and Patrick Hutton, 16–49. London: Tavistock.

Free, John. 1979. 'Stereo headphones – New shapes, new designs, new materials'. *Popular Science*, November 1979: 110–12 and 146.

Frosh, Paul. 2015. 'The gestural image: The selfie, photography theory, and kinesthetic sociability'. *International Journal of Communication* 9: 1607–28.

Ghule, Vijaykumar R. et al. 2017. 'Emotion based music player using facial recognition'. *International Journal of Innovative Research in Computer and Communication Engineering* 5 (2): 2188–94.

Gladwell, Malcolm. 2005. *Blink: The Power of Thinking without Thinking*. New York: Little, Brown and Co.

Goffman, Erving. 1967. 'On face-work: An analysis of ritual elements of social interaction'. In *Interaction Ritual: Essays on Face-to-Face Behavior*. New York: Anchor Books.

Gopinath, Sumanth. 2013. *The Ringtone Dialectic: Economy and Cultural Form*. Cambridge, MA: MIT Press.

Gopinath, Sumanth and Jason Stanyek. 2013. 'Tuning the human race: Athletic capitalism and the Nike+ sport kit'. In *Music, Sound and Space: Transformations of Public and Private Experience*, edited by Georgina Born, 128–48. Cambridge: Cambridge University Press.

Han, Kee Moo et al. 2016. 'Extraction of audio features for emotion recognition system based on music'. *International Journal of Scientific & Technology Research* 5–6 (June): 53–6.

Harris, Deonte. 2018. 'Articulations in the Caribbean Diaspora: London's Carnival Arts Scene and the Cultural Politics of Space, Place, and Value'. PhD dissertation, University of California, Los Angeles.

Hill, Frank Ernest. 1937. *Listen and Learn: 15 Years of Adult Education on the Air*. New York: American Association for Adult Education.

iMotions. 2016. *Facial Expression Analysis: The Complete Pocket Guide*. Boston: iMotions.

Jopling, David A. 2000. *Self-Knowledge and the Self*. New York: Routledge.

Kelly, Peter. 2016. *The Self as Enterprise: Foucault and the Spirit of 21st Century Capitalism*. New York: Routledge.

Kim, Youngmoo et al. 2010. 'Music emotion recognition: A state of the art review'. In *Proceedings of the International Conference on Music Information Retrieval*.

Kramer, Lawrence. 1995. *Classical Music and Postmodern Knowledge*. Berkeley: University of California Press.

Lametti, David. 2012. 'The Cloud: Boundless Digital Potential or Enclosure 3.0?' ExpressO. Available at: http://works.bepress.com/david_lametti/1/.

Lupton, Deborah. 2016. 'The diverse domains of quantified selves: Self-tracking modes and dataveillance'. *Economy and Society* 45(1): 101–22.

Marshall, Wayne. 2014. 'Treble culture'. In *The Oxford Handbook of Mobile Music Studies*, vol. 2, edited by Sumanth Gopinath and Jason Stanyek, 43–76. Oxford: Oxford University Press.

Metcalf, Allan A. 2016. *From Skedaddle to Selfie: Words of the Generations*. Oxford: Oxford University Press.

Mizroeff, Nick. 2016. *How to See the World*. London: Pelican.

Morris, Jeremy Wade. 2015. *Selling Digital Music, Formatting Culture*. Berkeley: University of California Press.

Mosco, Vincent. 2005. *The Digital Sublime: Myth, Power, and Cyberspace*. Cambridge, Mass: MIT Press.

Patel, Abhishek R. et al. 2016. 'MoodyPlayer: A mood based music player'. *International Journal of Computer Applications* 141 (4): 21–5.

Picard, Rosalind. 1997. *Affective Computing*. Cambridge, MA: MIT Press.

Rivera, Ray. 2009. 'The best revenge? Being louder: IPOD LEAK'. *New York Times*. 28 June 2009, CT12.

Rose, Nicholas. 1996. *Inventing Ourselves: Psychology, Power and Personhood*. New York: Cambridge University Press.

Rosenberg, Erika. 2005. 'Introduction: The study of spontaneous facial expressions in psychology'. In *What the Face Reveals: Basic and Applied Studies of Spontaneous Expression Using the Facial Action Coding System (FACS)*, edited by Paul Ekman and Erika Rosenberg, 3–18. 2nd edn. New York: Oxford University Press.

Schmitt, Bernd H. 1999. *Experiential Marketing: How to Get Customers to Sense, Feel, Think, Act and Relate to Your Company and Brands*. New York: Simon & Schuster.

Schonberg, Harold. 1953. 'Records: Play Along'. *New York Times*, 13 September 1953.

Senft, Theresa M. and Nancy K. Baym. 2015. 'What does the selfie say? Investigating a global phenomenon'. *International Journal of Communication* 9: 1588–606. (Introduction to featured section on 'Selfies', 1588–872.)

Sontag, Susan. 2003. *Regarding the Pain of Others*. New York: Picador.

Spurgeon, Christina. 2008. *Advertising and New Media*. London: Routledge.

Sterne, Jonathan. 2003. *The Audible Past: Cultural Origins of Sound Reproduction*. Durham, NC: Duke University Press.

Taylor, Charles. 1989. *Sources of the Self: The Making of the Modern Identity*. Cambridge, MA: Harvard University Press.

Turkle, Sherry. 2011. *Alone Together: Why We Expect More from Technology and Less from Each Other*. New York: Basic Books.

Walden, Joshua. 2018. *Musical Portraits: The Composition of Identity in Contemporary and Experimental Music*. New York: Oxford University Press.

Wendt, Brooke. 2014. *The Allure of the Selfie: Instagram and the New Self Portrait*. Amsterdam: Institute of Network Cultures.

Yang, Yi-Hsuan and Chen, Homer H. 2012. 'Machine recognition of music emotion: A review'. *ACM Transactions on Intelligent Systems and Technology* 3, 3 (May).

Zahavi, Dan. 2005. *Subjectivity and Selfhood: Investigating the First-Person Perspective*. Cambridge, MA: MIT Press.

Žižek, Slavoj. 2012. *Less Than Nothing: Hegel and the Shadow of Dialectical Materialism*. London: Verso.

Personal Take: Vaporwave is Dead, Long Live Vaporwave!
Adam Harper

Born, Georgina and Christopher Haworth. 2017. 'Mixing it: Digital ethnography and online research methods – a tale of two global digital music genres'. In *The Routledge Companion to Digital Ethnography*, edited by Larissa Hjorth, Heather Horst, Anne Galloway and Genevieve Bell, 70–86. New York: Routledge.

Dolan, Emily. 2010. "'. . . This little ukulele tells the truth": Indie pop and kitsch authenticity'. *Popular Music* 29 (3): 457–69.

Glitsos, Laura. 2018. 'Vaporwave, or music optimised for abandoned malls'. *Popular Music* 37 (1): 100–18.

Harper, Adam. 2017. 'How internet music is frying your brain'. *Popular Music* 36 (1): 86–97.

Powers, William. 2010. *Hamlet's Blackberry: A Practical Philosophy for Building a Good Life in the Digital Age*. Victoria: Scribe.

Roszak, Theodore. 1969. *The Making of a Counter Culture: Reflections on the Technocratic Society and Its Youthful Opposition*. Garden City, NY: Doubleday.

Sousa, John Philip. 1906. 'The menace of mechanical music'. *Appleton's Magazine* 8 (September): 278–84.

Taylor, Astra. 2014. *The People's Platform: Taking Back Power and Culture in the Digital Age*. London: Fourth Estate.

Taylor, Timothy D. 2001. 'Technostalgia'. In *Strange Sounds: Music, Technology, and Culture*, 96–116. New York: Routledge.

Trainer, Adam. 2016. 'From hypnagogia to distroid: postironic musical renderings of personal memory'. In *The Oxford Handbook of Music and Virtuality*, edited by Sheila Whiteley and Shara Rambarran, 409–27. New York: Oxford University Press.

Waugh, Michael. 2017. '"My laptop is an extension of my memory and self": Post-Internet identity, virtual intimacy and digital queering in online popular music'. *Popular Music* 36 (2): 233–51.

5 Witnessing Race in the New Digital Cinema
Peter McMurray

Alexander, Elizabeth. 1994. 'Can you be BLACK and look at this? Reading the Rodney King video(s)'. *Public Culture* 7 (1): 77–94.

Als, Hilton. 2016. 'Beywatch: Beyoncé's reformation'. *The New Yorker* 92 (16) (30 May): 66–9.

Belson, Ken. 2017. 'Kaepernick, in grievance, accuses owners of colluding to shun him'. *The New York Times* 16 October: D4.

Beyoncé [Knowles]. 2016a. 'Formation'. *Lemonade*. Melina Matsoukas, director. Columbia Records. Premiered 6 February online. Music video.

Beyoncé [Knowles]. 2016b. *Lemonade*. Kahlil Joseph and Beyoncé Knowles Carter, directors. Columbia Records. Premiered 23 April, Home Box Office (HBO). Visual album.

Blanchette, Aimee. 2016. 'The good, the bad, the repulsive'. *Star Tribune*, 9 June: 1E.

Bosman, Julie and Mitch Smith. 2017. 'Experts weigh in on dashboard video of Minnesota shooting'. *The New York Times*. 22 June. A19.

Burgess, Jean and Joshua Green. 2012. *YouTube*, 2nd edn. Cambridge: Polity.

Caramanica, Jon, Wesley Morris and Jenna Wortham. 2016. 'Beyoncé in charge (of course)'. *The New York Times*. 6 February, page C1.

Chang, Jeff. 2016. 'Making Lemonade'. In *We Gon' Be Alright: Notes on Race and Resegregation*, 159–68. New York: Picador.

Cook, Nicholas. 1998. *Analysing Musical Multimedia*. Oxford: Clarendon Press.

Crawley, Ashon. 2017. *Blackpentecostal Breath: The Aesthetics of Possibility*. New York: Fordham University Press.

Daughtry, J. Martin. 2003. 'Russia's new anthem and the negotiation of national identity'. *Ethnomusicology* 47 (1): 42–67.

DeLong, Matt and Dave Braunger. 2017. 'Breaking down the dashcam: The Philando Castile shooting timeline'. *Star Tribune*, 21 June. www.startribune.com/castile-shooting-timeline/429678313/.

Floyd-Thomas, Stacey M. 2016. 'A field of study as a field of dreams: The contours of Black church studies'. In *The Black Church Studies Reader*, edited by Alton B. Pollard III and Carol B. Duncan, 59–67. New York: Palgrave Macmillan.

Frosh, Paul. 2015. 'The gestural image: The selfie, photography theory, and kinesthetic sociability'. *International Journal of Communication* 9: 1607–28.

Frosh, Paul and Amit Pinchevksi. 2009. *Media Witnessing: Testimony in the Age of Mass Communication*. Basingstoke: Palgrave Macmillan.

Guy, Nancy. 2002. '"Republic of China national anthem" on Taiwan: One anthem, one performance, multiple realities'. *Ethnomusicology* 46 (1): 96–119.

Hahn, Tomie. 2007. *Sensational Knowledge: Embodying Culture through Japanese Dance*. Middletown, CT: Wesleyan University Press.

Jennings, Tom. 2017. The Lost Tapes: LA Riots. The Smithsonian Channel, 23 April. TV movie.

Jones, James T. IV. 1989. 'The big rap attack'. *USA Today*, 22 August: 1D.

Kirschenbaum, Matthew. 2008. *Mechanisms: New Media and the Forensic Imagination*. Cambridge, MA: MIT Press.

Kittler, Friedrich. 1987. 'Weltatem: Über Wagners Medientechnologie'. In *Diskursanalysen, Bd. 1: Medien*, edited by Friedrich Kittler, Manfred Schneider and Samuel Weber, 94–107. Opladen: Westdeutscher Verlag.

———. 1999. *Gramophone, Film, Typewriter*. Translated by Geoffrey Winthrop-Young and Michael Wutz. Stanford: Stanford University Press.

Krämer, Sybille. 2015. *Medium, Messenger, Transmission: An Approach to Media Philosophy*. Translated by Anthony Epps. Amsterdam: University of Amsterdam Press.

Krämer, Sybille and Sigrid Weigel, eds. 2017. *Testimony/Bearing Witness: Epistemology, Ethics, History and Culture*. London: Rowman & Littlefield International.

Lamar, Kendrick. 2015. 'Alright'. Directed by Colin Tilley. Aftermath/Interstellar. Music video.

Laughland, Oliver, Kayla Epstein and Jessica Glenza. 2014. 'Eric Garner protests continue in cities across America through second night'. *The Guardian*, 5 December. www.theguardian.com/us-news/2014/dec/05/eric-garner-case-new-york-protests-continue-through-second-night.

Mannix, Andy. 2016. 'Audio: He looks like "our suspect"'. *Star Tribune*. 12 July. 1A.

Mathias, Christopher. 2016. 'He filmed the death of Eric Garner. Now he's getting ready to spend 4 years in prison'. *Huffington Post*, 1 September. www.huffingtonpost.com/entry/ramsey-orta-eric-garner_us_57a9edbde4b0aae 2a5a15142.

McFadden, Syreeta. 2016. 'Beyoncé's Lemonade is #blackgirlmagic at its most potent'. *The Guardian*. 24 April. www.theguardian.com/music/2016/apr/24/ beyonce-lemonade-album-video-black-girl-magic-womanhood-america.

McMurray, Peter. 2014. 'YouTube music – haptic or optic?' *Repercussions* 11. www.ocf.berkeley.edu/~repercus/wp-content/uploads/2014/12/repercussions-Vol.-11-McMurray-Peter-YouTube-Music-Haptic-or-Optic.pdf.

Monson, Ingrid. 2008. 'Hearing, seeing, and perceptual agency'. *Critical Inquiry* 34, suppl. (Winter): S36–S58.

Moon, Angela and Dustin Volz. 2016. 'Facebook Live streaming of shooting spotlights ethical, legal policies'. Reuters. www.reuters.com/article/us-minnesota-police-facebook/facebook-live-streaming-of-shooting-spotlights-ethical-legal-policies-idUSKCN0ZN2MN.

Moten, Fred. 2003. *In the Break: The Aesthetics of the Black Radical Tradition*. Minneapolis: University of Minnesota Press.

Pareles, Jon. 2016. 'Making "Lemonade" out of strife'. *The New York Times*, 25 April: C1.

Peters, John Durham. 2001. 'Witnessing'. *Media, Culture & Society* 23: 707–23.
    2015. *The Marvelous Clouds: Toward a Philosophy of Elemental Media*. Chicago: University of Chicago Press.

Peterson, James. 2016. '25 years after Rodney King, video still isn't enough to stop police brutality'. *Los Angeles Times*, 3 March. www.latimes.com/opinion/op-ed/la-oe-0303-peterson-king-holliday-blm-20160303-story.html.

Pettman, Dominic. 2017. *Sonic Intimacy: Voice, Species, Technics (or, How to Listen to the World)*. Stanford: Stanford University Press.

Ramsey County. 2017a. 'Diamond Reynolds July 6, 2016 Facebook Live Video (WARNING: Graphic content).' YouTube. 20 June. www.youtube.com/watch?v=6DUfa4LTgOs.
    2017b. 'Squad dashcam video – Yanez case (WARNING: Graphic content).' YouTube. 20 June. www.youtube.com/watch?v=z1ac7Zblqyk.

Rentschler, Carrie. 2004. 'Witnessing: US citizenship and the vicarious experience of suffering'. *Media, Culture & Society* 26: 296–304.

Reynolds, Lavish [Diamond Reynolds]. 2016. Video, Facebook Live stream. Aftermath of Philando Castile shooting, Minneapolis, Minnesota. *Facebook Live*. 6 July.

Roberts, Jeff John. 2016. 'When tragedy strikes who should cash in on viral video?' *Fortune*, 18 July. fortune.com/2016/07/18/who-should-cash-in-on-viral-video/.

Ronell, Avital. 1994. 'Video/television/Rodney King: Twelve steps beyond the pleasure principle'. In *Culture on the Brink: Ideologies of Technology*, edited by Gretchen Bender and Timothy Druckrey, 277–303. Seattle: Bay Press.

Ross, Rosetta E. 2003. *Witnessing and Testifying: Black Women, Religion, and Civil Rights*. Minneapolis: Augsburg Fortress.

Rys, Dan. 2016. 'Beyoncé lifts a rising Tidal'. *Billboard*, 7 May. 128 (12): 11–12.

Taibbi, Matt. 2017. *I Can't Breathe: A Killing on Bay Street*. New York: Spiegel & Grau.

Tinsley, Omise'eke Natasha. 2016. 'Beyoncé's *Lemonade* is black woman magic'. *Time*, 25 April. time.com/4306316/beyonce-lemonade-black-woman-magic/.

Turino, Thomas. 1999. 'Signs of imagination, identity, and experience: A Peircian semiotic theory for music'. *Ethnomusicology* 43 (2): 221–55.

van Dijck, José. 2013. *The Culture of Connectivity: A Critical History of Social Media.* Oxford: Oxford University Press.

Vernallis, Carol. 2013. *Unruly Media: YouTube, Music Video, and the New Digital Cinema.* New York: Oxford University Press.

——— 2016. 'Beyoncé's *Lemonade*, avant-garde aesthetics, and music video: "The past and the future merge to meet us here"'. *Film Criticism* 40 (3). DOI: dx.doi.org/10.3998/fc.13761232.0040.315.

Witt, Stephen. 2016. 'What Beyoncé's "Lemonade" can (and can't) do for Tidal'. *The New Yorker*, 27 April. www.newyorker.com/business/currency/what-beyonces-lemonade-can-and-cant-do-for-tidal.

Xiong, Chao and Andy Mannix. 2017. 'Yanez dashcam video: "Don't pull it out"'. *Star Tribune*, 21 June. 1A. Also published online: www.startribune.com/case-file-in-philando-castile-shooting-to-be-made-public-today/429659263/.

Yanez, Jeronimo. 2016. Video, dashboard camera. Philando Castile shooting, Minneapolis, Minnesota. 6 July.

Young, Ryan. 2017. 'The viral video that set a city on fire'. *CNN News*, 28 April. www.cnn.com/videos/us/2017/04/28/rodney-king-la-riots-25th-anniversary-viral-tape-orig-nccorig.cnn.

6 Digital Devotion: Musical Multimedia in Online Ritual and Religious Practice
Monique M. Ingalls

Becker, Judith O. 2004. *Deep Listeners: Music, Emotion, and Trancing.* Bloomington: Indiana University Press.

Bell, Catherine. 2009 [1997.] *Ritual: Perspectives and Dimensions.* New York: Oxford University Press.

Bellah, Robert and Richard Madsen. 1985. *Habits of the Heart: Individualism and Commitment in American Life.* Berkeley: University of California Press.

Brasher, Brenda E. 2001. *Give Me That Online Religion.* San Franscisco: Jossey-Bass.

Burton, Justin. 2014. 'Dancing silhouettes: The mobile freedom of iPod commercials'. In *The Oxford Handbook of Mobile Music Studies*, vol. 2, edited by Sumanth Gopinath and Jason Stanyek, 311–36. Oxford and New York: Oxford University Press.

Campbell, Heidi. 2005. *Exploring Religious Community Online: We Are One in the Network.* New York: Peter Lang.

——— 2010. *When Religion Meets New Media.* London: Routledge.

——— 2013. 'Introduction: The rise of the study of digital religion'. In *Digital Religion: Understanding Religious Practice in New Media Worlds*, edited by Heidi A. Campbell, 1–21. London: Routledge.

Cheong, Pauline Hope, Peter Fischer-Nielsen, Stefan Gelfgren and Charles Ess, eds. 2012. *Digital Religion, Social Media and Culture: Perspectives, Practices and Futures.* New York: Peter Lang.

Connelly, Louise. 2013. 'Virtual Buddhism: Buddhist ritual in Second Life'. In *Digital Religion: Understanding Religious Practice in New Media Worlds*, edited by Heidi A. Campbell, 128–35. London: Routledge.

Dawson, Lorne L. and Douglas E. Cowan. 2004. *Religion Online: Finding Faith on the Internet*. New York: Routledge.

Derrickson, Krystina. 2008. 'Second Life and the sacred: Islamic space in a virtual world'. In *Digital Islam*, edited by Vit Sisler. Available online: www.digitalislam .eu/article.do?articleId=1877.

Durkheim, Emile. 2001 [1912]. *The Elementary Forms of Religious Life*. Translated by Carol Cosman. Oxford: Oxford University Press.

Echchaibi, Nabil. 2013. 'Islam, mediation, and technology'. In *The Handbook of Communication History*, edited by Peter Simonson, Janice Peck, Robert T. Craig and John Jackson, 440–52. New York: Routledge.

Engelhardt, Jeffers. 2018. 'Listening and the sacramental life: Degrees of mediation in Greek Orthodox Christianity'. In *Praying with the Senses: Contemporary Orthodox Christian Spirituality in Practice*, edited by Sonja Luehrmann, 58–79. Bloomington: Indiana University Press.

Engelke, Matthew. 2010. 'Religion and the media turn: A review essay'. *American Ethnologist* 37 (2): 371–9.

Garaci, Robert M. 2014. *Virtually Sacred: Myth and Meaning in World of Warcraft and Second Life*. New York: Oxford University Press.

Hagedorn, Katherine. 2006. '"From this one song alone, I consider him to be a holy man": Ecstatic religion, musical affect, and the global consumer'. *Journal for the Scientific Study of Religion* 45 (4): 489–96.

Helland, Christopher. 2000. 'Online-religion/religion-online and virtual communities'. In *Religion on the Internet: Research Prospects and Promises*, edited by J. K. Hadden and D. E. Cowan, 205–33. New York: JAI Press.

    2013. 'Ritual'. In *Digital Religion: Understanding Religious Practice in New Media Worlds*, edited by Heidi A. Campbell, 25–40. New York: Routledge.

Hill-Smith, Connie. 2011. 'Cyberpilgrimage: The (virtual) reality of online pilgrimage experience'. *Religion Compass* 5 (6): 236–46.

Hirschkind, Charles. 2006. *The Ethical Soundscape: Cassette Sermons and Islamic Counterpublics*. New York: Columbia University Press.

Hoover, Stewart. 2006. *Religion in the Media Age*. New York: Routledge.

    2013. 'Concluding thoughts: Imagining the religious in and through the digital'. In *Digital Religion: Understanding Religious Practice in New Media Worlds*, edited by Heidi A. Campbell, 266–8. New York and London: Routledge.

Hutchings, Tim. 2013. 'Considering religious community through online churches'. In *Digital Religion: Understanding Religious Practice in New Media Worlds*, edited by Heidi A. Campbell, 164–72. New York and London: Routledge.

Ingalls, Monique M. 2016. 'Worship on the web: Broadcasting devotion through worship music videos on YouTube'. In *Music and the Broadcast Experience: Performance, Production, and Audiences,* edited by Christina Baade and James Deaville, 293–308. New York: Oxford University Press.

    2018. *Singing the Congregation: How Contemporary Worship Music Forms Evangelical Community*. New York: Oxford University Press.

Jacobs, Stephen. 2007. 'Virtually sacred: The performance of asynchronous cyber-rituals in online spaces'. *Journal of Computer-Mediated Communication* 12: 1103–21.

Jenkins, Henry. 2006. *Convergence Culture: Where Old and New Media Collide*. New York: New York University Press.

Jenkins, Simon. 2008. 'Rituals and pixels: Experiments in online church'. *Heidelberg Journal of Religions on the Internet* 3 (1): 95–115.

Kluver, Randy and Yanli Chen. 2008. 'The church of fools: Virtual ritual and material faith'. *Heidelberg Journal of Religions on the Internet* 3 (1): 116–43.

Larkin, Brian. 2010. 'Islamic renewal, radio and the surface of things'. In *Aesthetic Formations: Media, Religion and the Senses*, edited by Birgit Meyer, 117–36. New York: Palgrave McMillan.

Lofton, Kathryn. 2011. *Oprah: The Gospel of an Icon*. Berkeley: University of California Press.

Lynch, Gordon. 2007. *Between Sacred and Profane: Researching Religion and Popular Culture*. London: I. B. Tauris.

Lynch, Gordon, Jolyon Mitchell and Anna Strhan. 2012. "Introduction". In *Religion, Media, and Culture: A Reader*, edited by Gordon Lynch and Jolyon Mitchell, 1–10. London: Routledge.

MacWilliams, Mark. 2004. 'Virtual pilgrimage to Ireland's Croagh Patrick'. In *Religion Online: Finding Faith on the Internet*, edited by Lorne L. Dawson and Douglas Cowan, 223–37. London: Routledge.

Mall, Andrew. 2012. '"The Stars Are Underground": Undergrounds, Mainstreams, and Christian Popular Music'. PhD dissertation, University of Chicago.

Manuel, Peter. 1993. *Cassette Culture: Popular Music and Technology in North India*. Chicago: University of Chicago Press.

Meyer, Birgit. 2009. 'Introduction: From imagined communities to aesthetic formations: Religious mediations, sensational forms, and styles of binding'. In *Aesthetic Formations: Media, Religion, and the Senses*, edited by Birgit Meyer, 1–30. New York: Palgrave Macmillan.

Miczek, Nadja. 2008. 'Online rituals in virtual worlds: Christian online services between dynamics and stability'. *Heidelberg Journal of Religions on the Internet* 3 (1): 144–73.

Morgan, David. 1996. '"Would Jesus have sat for a portrait?" The likeness of Christ in popular reception of Sallman's art.' In *Icons of American Protestantism: The Art of Warner Sallman*, edited by David Morgan, 181–206. New Haven, CT: Yale University Press.

Partridge, Christopher. 2014. *The Lyre of Orpheus: Popular Music, the Sacred, and the Profane*. Oxford and New York: Oxford University Press.

Radde-Antweiler, Kerstin. 2008. 'Virtual religion: An approach to a religious and ritual topography of Second Life'. *Heidelberg Journal of Religions on the Internet* 3 (1): 174–211.

Rouget, Gilbert. 1985 [1980]. *Music and Trance: A Theory of the Relations between Music and Possession*. Chicago: The University of Chicago Press.

Ryan, Marie-Laure. 2003. *Narrative as Virtual Reality: Immersion and Interactivity in Literature and Electronic Media*. Baltimore: Johns Hopkins University Press.

Schofield Clark, Lynn. 2006. 'Introduction to a forum on religion, popular music, and globalization'. *Journal for the Scientific Study of Religion* 45 (4): 475–9.

Schofield Clark, Lynn, ed. 2007. *Religion, Media, and the Marketplace*. New
    Brunswick: Rutgers University Press.
Summit, Jeffrey A. 2016. *Singing God's Words: The Performance of Biblical Chant in
    Contemporary Judaism*. Oxford and New York: Oxford University Press.
Trouillot, Michel-Rolph. 2003. *Global Transformations: Anthropology and the
    Modern World*. New York: Palgrave Macmillan.
Vekemans, Tine. 2014. 'Double-clicking the temple bell – Devotional aspects
    of Jainism online'. *Heidelberg Journal of Religions on the Internet* 6 (1):
    126–43.
Wagner, Rachel. 2012. *Godwired: Religion, Ritual, and Virtual Reality*. London:
    Routledge.
Weston, Donna and Andy Bennett. 2013. *Pop Pagans: Paganism and Popular Music*.
    Durham, UK: Acumen.
Wilson, Len. 1999. *The Wired Church*. Nashville: Abingdon Press.

Personal Take: Technicians of Ecstasy
Graham St John

Partridge, Christopher. 2004. *The Re-Enchantment of the West: Alternative
    Spiritualities, Sacralization and Popular Culture and Occulture*. 2 vols. London:
    T & T Clark International.
St John, Graham. 2012. *Global Tribe: Technology, Spirituality and Psytrance*.
    Sheffield: Equinox Publishing.
    2013a. 'Writing the vibe: Arts of representation in electronic dance music culture'.
    Dancecult: Journal of Electronic Dance Music Culture 5 (1): https://
    dj.dancecult.net/index.php/dancecult/article/view/357/362.
    2013b. 'Aliens are us: Cosmic liminality, remixticism and *Alien*ation in psytrance.'
    Journal of Religion and Popular Culture 25 (2): 186–204.
    2015a. 'Electronic dance music events'. In *The Routledge Companion to Religion
    and Popular Culture*, edited by John Lyden and Eric Michael Mazur, 336–55.
    New York: Routledge.
    2015b. *Mystery School in Hyperspace: A Cultural History of DMT*. Berkeley, CA:
    North Atlantic Books/Evolver.
    2017. 'Electronic dance music: Trance and techno-shamanism'. In *Bloomsbury
    Handbook of Religion and Popular Music*, edited by Christopher Partridge and
    Marcus Moberg, 421–32. London: Bloomsbury.

Personal Take: Live Coded Mashup with the Humming Wires
Alan F. Blackwell and Sam Aaron

Aaron, Sam and Alan Blackwell. 2013. 'From Sonic Pi to Overtone: Creative musical
    experiences with domain-specific and functional languages'. *Proceedings of the*

first ACM SIGPLAN Workshop on Functional Art, Music, Modeling & Design, 35–46.

Blackwell, Alan. 2014. 'Palimpsest: A layered language for exploratory image processing'. *Journal of Visual Languages and Computing* 25 (5): 545–71.

Blackwell, Alan and Sam Aaron. 2015. 'Craft practices of live coding language design'. In *Proc. First International Conference on Live Coding*. Zenodo. http://doi.org/10.5281/zenodo.19318.

Personal Take: Algorave: Dancing to Algorithms
Alex McLean

Collins, Nick and Alex McLean. 2014. 'Algorave: A survey of the history, aesthetics and technology of live performance of algorithmic electronic dance music'. *Proceedings of the International Conference on New Interfaces for Musical Expression* 14: 355–8.

Csikszentmihalyi, Mihalyi. 2008. *Flow: The Psychology of Optimal Experience*. New York: HarperCollins.

Ingold, Tim. 2010. 'The textility of making'. *Cambridge Journal of Economics* 34 (1): 91–102.

Nash, Chris and Alan Blackwell. 2011. 'Tracking virtuosity and flow in computer music'. In *Proceedings of International Computer Music Conference 2011*, 575–82.

Parkinson, Adam and Alex McLean. 2014. 'Interfacing with the night'. In *Proceedings of the 2nd International Conference on Live Interfaces*.

Small, Christopher. 1998. *Musicking: The Meanings of Performing and Listening*. Middletown, CT: Wesleyan University Press.

Turkle, Sherry and Seymour Papert. 1992. 'Epistemological pluralism and the revaluation of the concrete'. *Journal of Mathematical Behavior* 11 (1): 3–33.

7 Rethinking Liveness in the Digital Age
Paul Sanden

Aguilar, Ananay. 2014. 'Negotiating liveness: Technology, economics, and the artwork in LSO Live'. *Music and Letters* 95 (2): 251–72.

Ashby, Arved. 2010. *Absolute Music, Mechanical Reproduction*. Berkeley: University of California Press.

Auslander, Philip. 2002. 'Live from cyberspace: Or, I was sitting at my computer this guy appeared he thought I was a bot'. *PAJ: A Journal of Performance and Art* 24 (1): 16–21.

2005. 'At the *Listening Post*, or, do machines perform?' *International Journal of Performance Arts and Digital Media* 1 (1): 5–10.

2008. *Liveness: Performance in a Mediatized Culture*, 2nd edn. London: Routledge.

Balme, Christopher. 2008. 'Surrogate stages: Theatre, performance and the challenge of new media'. *Performance Research* 13 (2): 80–91.

Barker, Martin. 2013. *Live to your Local Cinema: The Remarkable Rise of Livecasting.* Houndmills: Palgrave Macmillan.

Beaudoin, Richard. 2014. *The Artist and His Model VI: La fille dérivée, for sextet.* Amherst, MA: Edition Casavespa.

    2015. *New York Mikrophon*, for quartet. Unpublished score. Available by request from www.richardbeaudoin.com/new-york-mikrophon.

Bowen, José A. 1993. 'The history of remembered innovation: Tradition and its role in the relationship between musical works and their performances'. *Journal of Musicology* 11 (2): 139–73.

Brown, Kevin. 2010. 'Liveness anxiety: Karaoke and the performance of class'. *Popular Entertainment Studies* 1 (2): 61–77.

Collins, Karen. 2013. *Playing with Sound: A Theory of Interacting with Sound and Music in Video Games.* Cambridge, MA: The MIT Press.

Cook, Nicholas. 2001. 'Between process and product: Music and/as performance'. *Music Theory Online* 7, no. 2 (April). http://www.mtosmt.org/issues/mto.01.7.2/mto.01.7.2.cook.html.

    2003. 'Music as performance'. In *The Cultural Study of Music: A Critical Introduction*, edited by Martin Clayton, Trevor Herbert and Richard Middleton, 204–14. London: Routledge.

    2013. *Beyond the Score: Music as Performance.* New York: Oxford University Press.

Croft, John. 2007. 'Theses on liveness'. *Organised Sound* 12 (1): 59–66.

Deleuze, Gilles. 1988. *Bergsonism.* New York: Zone Books.

Dixon, Steve. 2007. *Digital Performance: A History of New Media in Theater, Dance, Performance Art, and Installation.* Cambridge, MA: The MIT Press.

Echard, William. 2006. 'Sensible virtual selves: Bodies, instruments, and the becoming-concrete of music'. *Contemporary Music Review* 25 (1–2): 7–16.

Emmerson, Simon. 1994. '"Live" versus "real-time"'. *Contemporary Music Review* 10 (2): 95–101.

    2000. '"Losing touch?": The human performer and electronics'. In *Music, Electronic Media and Culture*, edited by Simon Emmerson, 194–216. Aldershot: Ashgate.

    2007. *Living Electronic Music.* Aldershot: Ashgate.

    2012. 'Live electronic music or living electronic music?' In *Bodily Expression in Electronic Music: Perspectives on Reclaiming Performativity*, edited by Deniz Peters, Gerhard Eckel and Andreas Dorschel, 152–62. New York: Routledge.

Fischer-Lichte, Erika. 2008. *The Transformative Power of Performance: A New Aesthetics.* Translated by Saskya Iris Jain. New York: Routledge.

Gagen, Justin and Nicholas Cook. 2016. 'Performing live in Second Life'. In *The Oxford Handbook of Music and Virtuality*, edited by Sheila Whiteley and Shara Rambarran. New York: Oxford University Press.

Goehr, Lydia. 1992. *The Imaginary Museum of Musical Works: An Essay in the Philosophy of Music.* Oxford: Oxford University Press.

1998. 'Conflicting ideals of performance: Perfection in an imperfect practice'. In *The Quest for Voice: Music, Politics, and the Limits of Philosophy*, 132–73. Berkeley: University of California Press.

Harvey, Trevor S. 2016. 'Avatar rockstars: Constructing musical personae in virtual worlds'. In *The Oxford Handbook of Music and Virtuality*, edited by Sheila Whiteley and Shara Rambarran, 171–89. New York: Oxford University Press.

Hayles, N. Katherine. 1999. *How We Became Posthuman: Virtual Bodies in Cybernetics, Literature, and Informatics*. Chicago: University of Chicago Press.

Leloup, Jean-Yves. 2010. *Digital Magma: From the Utopia of Rave Parties to the iPod Generation*. Translated by Paul Buck and Catherine Petit. New York: Lukas & Sternberg.

Miller, Paul D. 2004. *Rhythm Science*. Cambridge, MA: MIT Press.

Phelan, Peggy. 1993. 'The ontology of performance: Representation without reproduction'. In *Unmarked: The Politics of Performance*, 146–66. London: Routledge.

Sanden, Paul. 2013. *Liveness in Modern Music: Musicians, Technology, and the Perception of Performance*. New York: Routledge.

Shields, Rob. 2003. *The Virtual*. London: Routledge.

Sousa, John Philip. 1906. 'The menace of mechanical music'. *Appleton's Magazine* 8: 278–84. www.phonozoic.net/n0155.htm.

Thornton, Sarah. 1995. *Club Cultures: Music, Media and Subcultural Capital*. Cambridge: Polity Press, 1995.

Trottier, Danick. 2013. 'Conceiving musical photorealism: An interview with Richard Beaudoin'. *Perspectives of New Music* 51 (1): 174–95.

Personal Take: Augmenting Musical Performance
Andrew McPherson

Jensenius, Alexander Refsum and Michael J. Lyons, eds. 2017. *A NIME Reader: Fifteen Years of New Interfaces for Musical Expression*. New York: Springer.

McPherson, Andrew and Youngmoo E. Kim. 2012. 'The problem of the second performer: building a community around an augmented piano'. *Computer Music Journal* 36 (4): 10–27.

McPherson, Andrew, Adrian Gierakowski and Adam M. Stark. 2013. 'The space between the notes: adding expressive pitch control to the piano keyboard'. In *Proceedings of the ACM SIGCHI Conference on Human Factors in Computing Systems*, 2195–204.

McPherson, Andrew, Fabio Morreale and Jacob Harrison. 2019. 'Musical instruments for novices: Comparing NIME, HCI and crowdfunding approaches'. In *New Directions in Music and Human-Computer Interaction*, edited by Simon Holland, Tom Mudd, Katie Wilkie-McKenna, Andrew McPherson and Marcelo Wanderley. London: Springer.

Robjohns, Hugh. 2014. 'The TouchKeys Project'. *Sound on Sound Magazine*, June. www.soundonsound.com/people/touchkeys-project.

Personal Take: Digital Demons, Real and Imagined
Steve Savage

Egan, Jennifer. 2010. *A Visit from the Goon Squad*. New York: Knoff.

Personal Take: Compositional Approaches to Film, TV and Video Games
Stephen Baysted

Baysted, Stephen. 2016. 'Palimpsest, pragmatism and the aesthetics of genre transformation'. In *Ludomusicology: Approaches to Video Game Music*, edited by Michiel Kamp, Tim Summers and Mark Sweeney, 152–71. Sheffield: Equinox Publishing.
Sadoff, Ronald H. 2006. 'The role of the music editor and "temp" track as blueprint for the score, source music and source music of films'. *Popular Music* 25 (2): 165–83.
Summers, Tim. 2016. *Understanding Video Game Music*. Cambridge: Cambridge University Press.

8 Virtual Worlds from Recording to Video Games
Isabella van Elferen

Abbate, Carolyn. 2004. 'Music – drastic or gnostic?' *Critical Inquiry* 30 (3): 505–36.
Bull, Michael. 2007. *Sound Moves: iPod Culture and Urban Experience*. Oxford: Routledge.
Carter, William and Lesley S. Liu. 2005. 'Location33: A mobile musical'. In *Proceedings of the 2005 International Conference on New Interfaces for Musical Expression (NIME05)*. Vancouver, BC, Canada. www.nime.org/proceedings/2005/nime2005_176.pdf.
Cheng, William. 2014. *Sound Play: Video Games and the Musical Imagination*. Oxford: Oxford University Press.
Collins, Karen. 2008. *Game Sound: An Introduction to the History, Theory, and Practice of Video Game Music and Sound Design*. Cambridge, MA: MIT Press.
DeNora, Tia. 2000. *Music in Everyday Life*. Cambridge: Cambridge University Press.
De Vries, Imar O. 2012. *Tantalisingly Close: An Archaeology of Communication Desires in Discourses of Mobile Wireless Media*. Amsterdam: Amsterdam University Press.
Fritsch, Melanie and Stefan Strötgen. 2012. 'Relatively live: How to identify live music performance'. *Music and the Moving Image* 5 (1): 47–66.
Gregg, Melissa and Greg Seigworth, eds. 2010. *The Affect Theory Reader*. Durham, NC: Duke University Press.
Kramer, Jonathan. 1988. *The Time of Music: New Meanings, New Temporalities, New Listening Strategies*. New York: Schirmer.
Lévy, Pierre. 1997. *Becoming Virtual: Reality in the Digital Age*. New York: Plenum Press.
Massumi, Brian. 1987. 'Notes on the translation and acknowledgements'. In Gilles Deleuze and Félix Guattari, *A Thousand Plateaus: Capitalism and Schizophrenia*, xvi–xix. Minneapolis: University of Minnesota Press.

2002. *Parables for the Virtual: Movement, Affect, Sensation*. Durham, NC: Duke University Press.

Miller, Kiri. 2012. *Playing Along: Digital Games, YouTube, and Virtual Performance*. Oxford: Oxford University Press.

Nancy, Jean-Luc. 2007. *Listening*. Translated by Charlotte Mandell. New York: Fordham University Press.

Roesner, David. 2011. 'The Guitar Hero's performance'. *Contemporary Theatre Review* 21 (3): 276–85.

Ryan, Marie-Laure. 2001. *Narrative as Virtual Reality: Immersion and Interactivity in Literature and Electronic Media*. Baltimore, MD: Johns Hopkins University Press.

Schafer, R. Murray. 1977. *The Soundscape: Our Sonic Environment and the Tuning of the World*. Rochester, NY: Destiny Books.

Schroeder, Franziska. 2006. 'Bodily instruments and instrumental bodies: Critical views on the relation of body and instrument in technologically informed performance environments'. *Contemporary Music Review* 25 (1–2): 1–5.

Sterne, Jonathan. 2003. *The Audible Past: Cultural Origins of Sound Reproduction*. Durham, NC: Duke University Press.

van Elferen, Isabella. 2011. '¡Un Forastero! Issues of virtuality and diegesis in videogame music'. *Music and the Moving Image* 4 (2): 30–9.

2012. *Gothic Music: The Sounds of the Uncanny*. Cardiff: University of Wales Press.

2016. 'Analysing game musical immersion: The ALI model'. In *Ludomusicology: Approaches to Video Game Music*, edited by Mihiel Kamp, Tim Summers and Mark Sweeney, 32–52. Sheffield: Equinox.

Voegelin, Salomé. 2014. *Sonic Possible Worlds: Hearing the Continuum of Sound*. New York: Bloomsbury.

9 Digital Voices: Posthumanism and the Generation of Empathy
David Trippett

Ariza, Christopher. 2009. 'The interrogator as critic: The Turing Test and the evaluation of generative music systems'. *Computer Music Journal* 33 (2009): 48–70.

Auner, Joseph. 2003. 'Sing it for me: Posthuman ventriloquism in recent popular music'. *Journal of the Royal Music Association* 128 (1): 98–122.

Baudrillard, Jean. 1988. *The Ecstasy of Communication*, translated by Bernard and Caroline Schutze, edited by Sylvère Lotringer. New York: Semiotexte.

Bennett, Jane. 2010. *Vibrant Matter: A Political Ecology of Things*. Durham, NC: Duke University Press.

Biles, John. 2007. 'Improvising with genetic algorithms'. In *Evolutionary Computer Music*, edited by Eduardo Miranda and John Biles, 137–69. London: Springer.

Bostrom, Nick. 2009. 'The transhumanist FAQ'. In *Readings in the Philosophy of Technology*, edited by David Kaplan, 345–60. 2nd edn. Plymouth: Rowman & Littlefield.

2014. *Superintelligence: Paths, Dangers, Strategies*. Oxford: Oxford University Press.

Brown, Andrew. 2015. *Music Technology and Education: Amplifying Musicality.* Abingdon, UK: Routledge.

Chalmers, David. 1995. 'Facing up to the problem of consciousness'. *Journal of Consciousness Studies* 2 (3): 200–19.

Clark, Andy. 2004. *Natural-Born Cyborgs: Minds, Technologies, and the Future of Human Intelligence.* Oxford: Oxford University Press.

Clark, Andy and David Chalmers. 1998. 'The extended mind'. *Analysis* 58 (1): 7–19.

Coole, Diana and Samantha Frost, eds. 2010. *New Materialisms: Ontology, Agency, and Politics.* Durham, NC: Duke University Press.

de Quincey, Thomas. 1863. *The Art of Conversation and Other Papers.* Edinburgh: Adam and Charles Black.

de Souza, Jonathan. 2017. *Music at Hand: Instruments, Bodies and Cognition.* New York: Oxford University Press.

Dewdney, Andrew and Peter Ride, eds. 2006. *The New Media Handbook.* London: Routledge.

Dolar, Mladan. 2006. *A Voice and Nothing More.* Cambridge, MA: MIT Press.

Elliott, Carl. 2009. 'What's wrong with enhancement technology?' In *Readings in the Philosophy of Technology*, edited by David Kaplan, 431–37. 2nd edn. Plymouth: Rowman & Littlefield.

Galloway, Alexander R. 2017. *The Interface Effect.* Rpt. Cambridge: Polity.

Gibson, William. 1984. *Neuromancer.* London: Gollancz.

Harari, Yuval Noah. 2016. *Homo Deus: A Brief History of Tomorrow.* London: Harvill Secker.

Haraway, Donna. 2000. 'A cyborg manifesto: Science, technology, and socialist-feminism in the late twentieth century'. In *Posthumanism*, edited by Neil Badmington, 69–84. Basingstoke, UK: Palgrave.

Hayles, N. Katherine. 1999. *How We Became Posthuman.* Chicago: University of Chicago Press.

——— 2012. *How We Think: Digital Media and Contemporary Technogenesis.* Chicago: Chicago University Press.

Hoffmann, Peter. 2010. 'Towards an "automated art": Algorithmic processes in Xenakis' compositions'. *Contemporary Music Review* 21 (2–3): 121–31.

Jackson, Louise and Mike Dines. 2016. 'Vocaloids and Japanese virtual vocal performance: The cultural heritage and technological futures of vocal puppetry'. In *The Oxford Handbook of Music and Virtuality*, edited by Sheila Whiteley and Shara Rambarran, 101–10. New York: Oxford University Press.

King, Andrew, Evangelos Himonides and S. Alex Ruthman, eds. 2016. *The Routledge Companion to Music, Technology, and Education.* London: Routledge.

Kriedler, Johannes, Harry Lehmann and Claus-Steffan Mahnkopf. 2010. *Musik, Ästhetik, Digitalisierung: Eine Kontroverse.* Hofheim am Taunus: Wolke.

Kulke, Eduard. 1884. *Über die Umbildung der Melodie.* Prague: J. G. Calve.

Lachenmann, Helmut and David Ryan. 1999. 'Composer in interview: Helmut Lachenmann'. *Tempo* 210: 20–4.

Le Guin, Elizabeth. 2006. *Boccherini's Body: An Essay in Carnal Musicology.* Berkeley: University of California Press.

Lewis, George. 2000. 'Too many notes: Complexity and culture in Voyager'. *Leonardo Music Journal* 10: 33–9.

Lister, Martin, Jon Dovey, Seth Giddings, Iain Grant and Kieran Kelly, eds. 2009. *New Media: A Critical Introduction*. 2nd edn. London: Routledge.

Macho, Thomas. 2003. 'Zeit und Zahl: Kalender- und Zeitrechnung als Kulturetechniken'. In *Bild—Schrift—Zahl*, edited by Sybille Krämer and Horst Bredekamp, 179–92. Munich: Wilhelm Fink.

Manovich, Lev. 2001. *The Language of New Media*. Cambridge, MA: MIT Press. 2013. *Software Takes Command*. New York: Bloomsbury.

Marvin, Carolyn. 1980. *When Old Technologies Were New: Thinking about Electric Communication in the Late Nineteenth Century*. Oxford: Oxford University Press.

McLuhan, Marshall. 1964. *Understanding Media: The Extensions of Man*. Cambridge, MA: MIT Press.

Mettrie, Julien Offray de la. 1996. *Machine Man and Other Writings*, translated and edited by Ann Thomson. Cambridge: Cambridge University Press.

Miranda, Eduardo. 2012. 'On computer-aided composition, musical creativity and brain asymmetry'. In *The Act of Musical Composition: Studies in the Creative Process*, edited by Dave Collins, 215–32. Farnham, UK: Ashgate.

Moravec, Hans. 1988. *Mind Children: The Future of Robot and Human Intelligence*. Cambridge, MA: Harvard University Press.

More, Max. 2013. 'The philosophy of transhumanism'. In *Transhumanist Reader*, edited by Max More and Natasha Vita-More, 3–17. Chichester, UK: Wiley-Blackwell.

Mumford, Lewis. 2010. *Technics and Civilisation*. Chicago: University of Chicago Press.

Nierhaus, Gerhard. 2009. *Algorithmic Composition: Paradigms of Automated Music Generation*. Vienna: Springer.

Picker, John M. 2002. 'The tramp of a fly's footsteps'. *The American Scholar* 71 (2): 85–94.

Povel, Dirk-Jan. 2010. 'Melody Generator: A device for algorithmic music construction'. *Journal of Software Engineering and Applications* 3: 683–95.

Rousseau, Jean-Jacques. 1969. *Oeuvres completes*, vol. IV. Paris: Gallimard.

Schmidt, Eric and Jared Cohen. 2013. *The New Digital Age: Reshaping the Future of People, Nations and Business*. London: John Murray.

Siegert, Bernhard. 2015. *Cultural Techniques: Grids, Filters, Doors, and Other Articulations of the Real*. Translated by Geoffrey Winthrop-Young. New York: Fordham University Press.

Sobchack, Vivian. 2006. 'A leg to stand on'. In *The Prosthetic Impulse: From a Posthuman Present to a Biocultural Future*, edited by Marquard Smith and Joanne Morra. Cambridge, MA: MIT Press.

Stoppard, Tom. 2015. *The Hard Problem*. London: Faber.

Tompkins, Dave. 2011. *How to Wreck a Nice Beach: The Vocoder from World War II to Hip-Hop*. Chicago: Stop Smiling Books.

Torpey, Peter A. 2012. 'Digital Systems for live multimodal performance in *Death and the Powers*'. *International Journal of Performance Arts and Digital Media* 8 (1): 109–23.

Weibel, Peter. 1996. 'The world as interface'. In *Electronic Culture: Technology and Visual Representation*, edited by Timothy Druckrey, 338–51. New York: Aperture.

Personal Take: In the Wake of the Virtual
Frances Dyson

Nancy, Jean-Luc. 1997. *The Sense of the World*. Translated by Jeffrey S. Librett. Minneapolis: University of Minnesota Press.

10 Digital Inequalities and Global Sounds
Shzr Ee Tan

Appadurai, Arjun. 1990. 'Disjuncture and difference in the global cultural economy'. *Theory, Culture & Society* 7 (2–3): 295–310.

Baranovitch, Nimrod. 2003. *China's New Voices: Popular Music, Ethnicity, Gender, and Politics, 1978–1997*. Berkeley: University of California Press.

Benayoun, Maurice. 2008. 'Art after technology.' *MIT Technology Review 7,* French edition.

Campos, Raquel. 2018. 'Musicking on social media: Imagined audiences, momentary fans and critical agency in the sharing utopia'. 3rd ICTM Music Forum, *Approaches to Music and Dance on the Internet Era*. Central Conservatory of Music, Beijing, China, 11–14 July.

Canetti, Elias. 1962. *Crowds and Power*. Translated by Carol Stewart. London: Gollancz.

Certeau, Michel de. 1984. *The Practice of Everyday Life*. Translated by Steven F. Rendall. Berkeley: University of California Press.

Chang, Ha-Joon. 2012. *23 Things They Don't Tell You about Capitalism*. New York: Bloomsbury Publishing.

Copeland, Jack. 2015. *Artificial Intelligence: A Philosophical Introduction*. Oxford: John Wiley & Sons.

Costa, Elisabetta. 2018. 'Affordances-in-practice: An ethnographic critique of social media logic and context collapse'. *New Media & Society* 20 (10): 3641–56.

Haraway, Donna. 1991. *Simians, Cyborgs and Women: The Reinvention of Nature*. New York: Routledge.

Hayles, N. Katherine. 2008. *How We Became Posthuman: Virtual Bodies in Cybernetics, Literature, and Informatics*. Chicago: University of Chicago Press.

IFPI. 2017. *Global Music Music Report 2017: Annual State of the Industry*. www.ifpi .org/downloads/GMR2017.pdf.

Iwabuchi, Koichi. 2002. *Recentering Globalization: Popular Culture and Japanese Transnationalism*. Durham, NC: Duke University Press.

Jenkins, Henry. 2006. *Convergence Culture: Where Old and New Media Collide*. New York: New York University Press.

Jian, Miaoju and Chang de Liu. 2009. '"Democratic entertainment" commodity and unpaid labor of reality TV: A preliminary analysis of China's Supergirl'. *Inter-Asia Cultural Studies* 10 (4): 524–43.

Lee, Benjamin and Edward LiPuma. 2002. 'Cultures of circulation: The imaginations of modernity'. *Public Culture* 14 (1): 191–213.

Lysloff, René T. A. and Leslie C. Gay, Jr, eds. 2003. *Music and Technoculture.* Middletown, CT: Wesleyan University Press.

Maisonneuve, Nicolas et al. 2009. 'Citizen noise pollution monitoring'. *Proceedings of the 10th Annual International Conference on Digital Government Research: Social Networks: Making Connections between Citizens, Data and Government.* Digital Government Society of North America.

Mantovani, Giuseppe and Giuseppe Riva. 1999. '"Real" presence: How different ontologies generate different criteria for presence, telepresence, and virtual presence'. *Presence* 8 (5): 540–50.

Manuel, Peter. 1993. *Cassette Culture: Popular Music and Technology in North India.* Chicago: University of Chicago Press.

Michalski, Ryszard S., Jaime G. Carbonell and Tom M. Mitchell, eds. 2013. *Machine Learning: An Artificial Intelligence Approach.* Berlin: Springer Science & Business Media.

Miller, Daniel, with Elisabetta Costa, Nell Haynes, Tom McDonald, Razvan Nicolescu, Jolynna Sinanan, Juliano Spyer, Shriram Venkatraman and Xinyuan Wang. 2016. *How The World Changed Social Media.* London: UCL Press.

Rose, Tricia. 1994. *Black Noise: Rap Music and Black Culture in Contemporary America.* Middletown, CT: Wesleyan University Press.

2008. *The Hip Hop Wars: What We Talk About When We Talk About Hip Hop – And Why It Matters.* New York: Basic Books.

Singh, Narendra and S. C. Davar. 2004. 'Noise pollution – sources, effects and control'. *Journal of Human Ecology* 16 (3): 181–7.

Stock, Jonathan. 2016. 'Sounding the bromance: The Chopstick Brothers' "Little Apple" music video, genre, gender and the search for meaning in Chinese popular music'. *Journal of World Popular Music* 3 (2): 167–96.

Tan, Shzr Ee. 2016. 'Uploading to Carnegie Hall: The first YouTube Symphony Orchestra'. In *The Oxford Handbook of Music and Virtuality*, edited by Sheila Whiteley and Shara Rambarran, 335–54. New York: Oxford University Press.

Taylor, Timothy D. 2014. *Global Pop: World Music, World Markets.* New York: Routledge.

2015. *Music and Capitalism: A History of the Present.* Chicago: University of Chicago Press.

Tsing, Anna Lowenhaupt. 2000. 'The global situation'. *Cultural Anthropology* 15 (3): 327–60.

2011. *Friction: An Ethnography of Global Connection.* Princeton: Princeton University Press.

Wu, Jingsi Christina. 2014. 'Expanding civic engagement in China: Super Girl and entertainment-based online community'. *Information, Communication & Society* 17 (1): 105–20.

Yeung, Karen. 2017. '"Hypernudge": Big Data as a mode of regulation by design'. *Information, Communication & Society* 20 (1): 118–36.

11 The Political Economy of Streaming
Martin Scherzinger

Adorno, Theodor W. 2009. *Current of Music: Elements of a Radio Theory*, edited and translated by Robert Hullot-Kentor. Cambridge: Polity.

Andrejevic, Mark. 2009. 'Exploiting YouTube: Contradictions of user-generated labor'. In *The YouTube Reader*, edited by Pelle Snickars and Patrick Vonderau, 406–23. Stockholm: Mediehistoriskt.

Drott, Eric. 2018. 'Music as a technology of surveillance'. *Journal of the Society of American Music* 12(3): 233–67.

Goodman, Steve. 2010. *Sonic Warfare: Sound, Affect, and the Ecology of Fear.* Cambridge, MA: MIT Press.

Holmstrom, Nancy. 1997. 'Exploitation'. In *Exploitation,* edited by Kai Nielsen and Richard Ware, 76–93. Atlantic Highlands, NJ: Humanities Press.

Jehan, Tristan. 2005. 'Creating Music by Listening'. PhD dissertation, Massachusetts Institute of Technology.

Lanier, Jaron. 2010. *You Are Not a Gadget: A Manifesto.* New York: Vintage Books. 2014. *Who Owns the Future?* New York: Simon and Schuster.

Lee, Ellen. 2007. 'Google moves YouTube ahead'. *San Francisco Chronicle*, 7 March 2007: D1.

Lerch, Alexander. 2012. *An Introduction to Audio Content Analysis: Applications in Signal Processing and Music Informatics.* Hoboken, NJ: Wiley.

Leung, Calvin. 2008. 'Q&A: Tim Armstrong'. *Canadian Business*, 21 July 2008.

Loviglio, Jason and Michele Hilmes, eds. 2013. *Radio's New Wave: Global South in the Digital Era.* New York: Routledge.

McDonald, Paul. 2009. 'Digital discords in the online media economy: Advertising versus content versus copyright'. In *The YouTube Reader*, edited by Pelle Snickars and Patrick Vonderau, 387–405. Stockholm: Mediehistoriskt.

Miller, Toby. 2009. 'Cybertarians of the world unite: You have nothing to lose but your tubes!' In *The YouTube Reader*, edited by Pelle Snickars and Patrick Vonderau, 424–40. Stockholm: Mediehistoriskt.

Morris, Jeremy Wade. 2015. *Selling Digital Music, Formatting Culture.* Berkeley: University of California Press.

Nimmer, David. 2003. *Copyright: Sacred Text, Technology, and the DMCA.* The Hague: Kluwer Law International, 2003.

Ratliff, Ben. 2016. *Every Song Ever: Twenty Ways to Listen in an Age of Musical Plenty.* New York: Farrar, Straus and Giroux.

Scholz, Trebor, ed. 2013. *Digital Labor: The Internet as Playground and Factory.* New York: Routledge.

Seaver, Nick. 2018. 'Captivating algorithms: Recommender systems as traps'. *Journal of Material Culture.* https://doi.org/10.1177/1359183518820366.

Sinnreich, Aram. 2010. *Mashed Up: Music, Technology, and the Rise of Configurable Culture*. Amherst: University of Massachusetts Press.

Suisman, David. 2009. *Selling Sounds: The Commercial Revolution in American Music*. Cambridge, MA: Harvard University Press.

van Dijck, José. 2009. 'Users like you? Theorizing agency in user-generated content'. *Media, Culture & Society* 31(1): 41–58.

Virno, Paulo. 2007. 'Post-Fordist semblance'. *SubStance 112* 36 (1): 42–6.

Wikström, Patrik. 2009. *The Music Industry: Music in the Cloud*. Cambridge: Polity.

Index